Making Java Groovy

KENNETH A. KOUSEN

MANNING
SHELTER ISLAND

For online information and ordering of this and other Manning books, please visit www.manning.com. The publisher offers discounts on this book when ordered in quantity. For more information, please contact

Special Sales Department
Manning Publications Co.
20 Baldwin Road
PO Box 261
Shelter Island, NY 11964
Email: orders@manning.com

Photographs in this book were created by Martin Evans and Jordan Hochenbaum, unless otherwise noted. Illustrations were created by Martin Evans, Joshua Noble, and Jordan Hochenbaum. Fritzing (fritzing.org) was used to create some of the circuit diagrams.

♾ Recognizing the importance of preserving what has been written, it is Manning's policy to have the books we publish printed on acid-free paper, and we exert our best efforts to that end. Recognizing also our responsibility to conserve the resources of our planet, Manning books are printed on paper that is at least 15 percent recycled and processed without the use of elemental chlorine.

Manning Publications Co.
20 Baldwin Road
PO Box 261
Shelter Island, NY 11964

Development editor: Cynthia Kane
Copyeditor: Melinda Rankin
Proofreader: Melody Dolab
Typesetter: Dennis Dalinnik
Cover designer: Marija Tudor

ISBN: 9781935182948
Printed in the United States of America
1 2 3 4 5 6 7 8 9 10 – MAL – 19 18 17 16 15 14 13

To my father, Morton Kousen, MD,
who taught me everything I know about dedication,
persistence, and facing the future with a positive and
upbeat attitude, despite whatever pain and difficulties lay ahead.
He will always be my best example of what a man should be.

brief contents

contents

foreword

When we designed the Groovy language almost 10 years ago, our main goal was to create a language that is a complement to Java, a close companion, that Java developers would be familiar with and could learn easily. The idea was to empower users to be more productive by removing the boilerplate of Java, and to simplify their programming lives by giving them compelling and straightforward APIs to work with. I'm proud to say that the Groovy team attained that goal, making Groovy the most popular alternative language for the Java platform.

Along the way, and by virtue of its nature, Groovy was adopted by Java developers in a number of ways. For example, it was introduced in Java projects for testing purposes, because the Groovy syntax is light and readable but still resembles that of Java. For interacting with XML payloads, web services, or databases, Groovy provides handy and elegant wrappers around the Java Development Kit that make those tasks a breeze. And for writing business rules in Java applications, Groovy shines, thanks to its metaprogramming capabilities and its concise and expressive grammar.

I had the pleasure and honor of meeting Ken a few years ago at a Groovy conference, and our paths have crossed several times since then. Among other topics, we talked about how Groovy is a great fit for various assignments that Java developers have to accomplish every day but that are painful with the heavier-weight Java. So when Ken told me that he envisioned writing a book on this same topic, I was excited about the idea!

What makes this book stand out of the pack of Groovy books is its focus on the tasks that Java developers must tackle every day. How can I more easily parse or emit

XML or JSON documents? How can I test my Java code with a more expressive syntax? How can I talk to my database without the error-prone JDBC API? How can I build and test Java applications more efficiently? In this book, Ken answers all of these questions and shows you a Groovy solution for each of those chores.

GUILLAUME LAFORGE
GROOVY PROJECT MANAGER

preface

A few months ago I enjoyed a pleasant dinner with Marjan Bace, Grand Poobah[1] at Manning Publications, the company that printed the book you now hold in your hands.[2] Eventually the conversation turned to Joseph Campbell's *Hero's Journey* as it might apply to nonfiction, technical books. The basic concept is that a Hero is called to Action, encounters various Forces arrayed against Him (or Her); Defeats them; wards off Temptation; is Transformed by the journey; and eventually returns Home Triumphant.[3] Some publishing companies strongly recommend that their books follow that model, with the reader as hero.

Marjan's idea, however, was that sometimes it isn't the reader who is the hero; it's the technology covered by the book. In the case of *Making Java Groovy*, I interpret that to mean that Groovy is the hero. Where does that put Java? Not as antagonist, surely; the whole point of this book is that Java is already your ally, and that adding Groovy makes it better. Groovy and Java are like Frodo and Samwise Gamgee, headed into the black depths of Mordor, battling privation and despair, desperately trying to defeat the horrible programming challenges that await them, as well as any orcs, Nazgûl, or clueless managers they might encounter along the way.

1 His actual title is Publisher.

2 In print form, on a tablet, or whatever.

3 In case you don't want to read the original Campbell, the Wikipedia page at http://en.wikipedia.org/wiki/Monomyth summarizes all 17 (!) stages.

That's a little dark. Plus, I have no idea what the Ring of Power is in this analogy, or why you'd want to destroy it.[4] Instead, I'll simply say that Groovy and Java work really, really well together, and I'll spend the rest of the book demonstrating how, when, and why.

For those of you shifting nervously from side to side, worried that the attempts at "humor" in this preface will be sprayed liberally throughout the book (thus distracting from the actual content), let me assure you that other than in this preface, I promise to confine any attempts at humor to footnotes that can be safely skipped.[5]

When I'm teaching my technical training classes,[6] I realize that humor is a high-risk/high-reward tool. Nobody wants to hear a joke when they're confused. On the other hand, programming can be a dry[7] subject, and some humor can break up the monotony. Hopefully I've found the right balance in this book. If not, or if you have any other questions, comments, or heard any good jokes lately, feel free to contact me through the book forum at Manning, or directly through my blog on my website at http://www.kousenit.com.

The source code for the book is available in my GitHub repository.[8] If you examine it, you'll find more examples than the ones covered in the book. Books have length limits, but source code repositories don't, and extra examples can't hurt. I decided to use the book's repository as a home for any examples I felt were interesting or relevant, even if I couldn't justify the extra pages necessary to discuss them.

Again, keeping to the principle that the chapters should be as independent as possible, each project has its own Gradle build file.[9] All the examples have tests as well. The short snippets of code include Groovy `assert` statements, and test cases are used to execute the scripts during a build. The rest of the examples have a mix of JUnit tests, in Java or Groovy, and Spock tests. In practice I freely intermix both, so it seemed natural to do so here, too.

Enjoy the hero's journey[10] that is *Making Java Groovy*!

---

4 I do hope that if you're holding a print copy of the book (that is, dead-treeware), no Ents were involved.

5 Like this one: How many developers does it take to change a light bulb? The classic answer is, "None; that's a hardware problem." My answer is, "The developer is the person by the light switch saying, 'Maybe this time the light will go on. Or maybe this time. Reboot *again*.'"

6 Seriously, Best Training Anywhere. Contact me for a quote, which will inevitably rise once this book is published.

7 I was going to make a DRY—Don't Repeat Yourself—joke here but eventually decided against it.

8 Check it out at https://github.com/kousen/Making-Java-Groovy.

9 Except in the build chapter (chapter 5), where they have Ant or Maven build files, as appropriate.

10 So are you the hero, or is Groovy? Let me be blunt. Did you pay for this book? Then you're my hero. Duh.

acknowledgments

To paraphrase the great American poet Jerry Garcia, what a long, strange trip this has been! *Making Java Groovy* has consumed several years of my life, a fact that leaves me both horrified and endlessly amused. What I do know for sure, is that even though I'm the sole author, I never could have done it alone.

In late 2006, I attended a user group presentation[11] by Jason Rudolph on Grails that changed my life. He started me on my way into the wonderful world of Groovy. The fact that Dierk König et al. had written the fantastic *Groovy in Action* (Manning, 2007) sealed the deal.

I owe a great debt of gratitude to Dierk König, Guillaume Laforge,[12] Paul King,[13] and the other members of the Groovy core team for teaching me how much fun it can be to code in Groovy, through their writings, examples, and, at times, direct assistance. I want to express my heart-felt appreciation to Guillaume for contributing the foreword to my book.

Many members of the Grails team have been just as kind and helpful, and I want to specifically mention Graeme Rocher, Jeff Brown, Peter Ledbrook, and Burt Beckwith. This is a common theme in the Groovy world: I've never met so many incredibly

[11] I think it was the Spring User Group in Philadelphia. Seriously, support your local Java/Groovy/Grails user groups. They're a great source of knowledge, networking, and experience.

[12] Note the lowercase *f*. He's not Geordi, although I do occasionally call him Bill.

[13] Because he and I have PhDs and work with Groovy, we're groovydocs together. Russel Winder is one, too.

humble, brilliant[14] people in my life. Andres Almiray also fits into that category, and I feel privileged to know him and his wife Ixchel Ruiz.

I've been very happy to learn from other developers involved in Groovy projects in one form or another, including Dean Iverson, Cédric Champeau, Dave Klein (and the rest of the Klein group), Hans Dockter, Peter Niederwieser, Marco Vermeulen, Hamlet D'Arcy, Luke Daley, Bobby Warner, Colin Harrington, Jim Shingler, Danno Ferrin, Scott Davis, Glen Smith, Adam Murdoch, Chris Judd, Tim Yates, Marc Palmer, Rob Fletcher, Andrew Eisenberg, Russel Winder, and the indefatigable Hubert A. Klein Ikkink.

Over the past few years, I've become an active participant on the No Fluff Just Stuff Conference Tour[15] and will always be grateful to Jay Zimmerman for giving me that opportunity. My list of NFJS colleagues and friends has to start with Nate Schutta for a variety of technical and non-technical reasons, but I'm always happy to learn from (and just hang out with) Venkat Subramaniam, Ken Sipe, Matt Stine, Brian Sletten, Mark Richards, Pratik Patel, Matthew McCullough, Tim Berglund, Neal Ford, Peter Bell, Craig Walls, Brian Sam-Bodden, Andy Painter, Paul Rayner, Daniel Hinojosa, Doug Hawkins, Jim Harmon, Stuart Halloway, Raju Gandhi, Jeremy Deane, and David Bock.

As friends and allies, I want to mention Mike Kimsal (editor of GroovyMag), Shawn Hartsock, Steve Heckler, Nat Dunn, Will Provost, and especially Chris Stone, who has been a friend and accomplice for much longer that than either of us care to admit. I also need to single out Sandra Hartdagen for special attention. She contributed both perspective and wisdom on a regular basis.

I want to thank the people at Manning for all their assistance as well. Cynthia Kane is everything I ever wanted in an editor. She continually came up with insightful suggestions that fix problems in ways that never would have occurred to me. I also want to mention Dan Robb, who has been a good friend longer than he has been at Manning. My copyeditor, Melinda Rankin, was not only efficient and effective; she even got my science fiction references. Thanks also to everyone at Manning who worked on my book behind the scenes.

Thanks to the following reviewers who read the manuscript at different stages of its development for their helpful insights and comments: Al Scherer, Benjamin Muschko, Bill Fly, Brandon Harper, Dan Alford, Dan Sline, Dave Klein, Domingo Torres, George Jempty, Gorden Dickens, Greg Helton, Hien Luu, Joshua White, Marina Chernyavska, Martin Senne, Michael Smolyak, Oleksandr Alesinskyy, Sean Reilly, Stephen Harrison, Tariq Ahmed, Tim Vold, and Tom Fulton.

I need to make a special reference to Valentin Crettaz, who did a full technical proofread shortly before the book went into production. His review gave me a "Michael Corleone in *The Godfather: Part III*" moment,[16] and his feedback and sug-

---

14 Given my academic background, trust me, I know what brilliant looks like.
15 That's http://nofluffjuststuff.com, coming soon to a city near you.
16 "Just when I thought I was out, they pull me back in!"

gestions made the book so much better I almost don't recognize it. He is simply the best there is.

I am most grateful to my wife Ginger for her unending support and endurance throughout the entire grueling writing process.[17] My son Xander tolerated my absences and lame geek humor with only a moderate number of eye rolls. Honestly, if I could have been the rock star every kid dreams of being, he's the model I would have followed. I love you both with all my heart.

---

[17] For example, one day I was reading my email and noticed there was a monthly list of recommended books from Amazon.com. I wondered idly out loud how I could get my book on that list, when from the kitchen I suddenly heard a rather exasperated, "Write it!" burst forth. Sigh.

about this book

Who are you?

I assume you are a developer and are at least comfortable with Java.[18] You don't have to be an expert, but any discussions of the basics of object-oriented programming are beyond the scope of this book.

I do *not*, however, assume that you have experience with Groovy. The Groovy concepts are covered where they are used, and because I wanted the chapters to be as independent as possible, that means some redundancy is involved. The question of how to teach Groovy bothered me for some time, because I knew that some people prefer the traditional, feature-by-feature tutorial, whereas others much prefer small but nontrivial examples. In the end, I solved the problem by doing both. Chapter 2 is entitled "Groovy by example," and appendix B is called "Groovy by feature." Hopefully one or the other or both will provide you with what you need.[19]

---

[18] That unfortunate burst of blatant honesty just cut my potential audience by far too many. If you're buying the book just to have it look cool on your bookshelf, or to build a book fort, or to prop open your office door, or to hold down stacks of new cover sheets for your T.P.S. reports, or for any other reason that doesn't involve actually reading it, please feel free to do so. By the way, you can get your own T.P.S. report cover sheets at http://www.chrisglass.com/journal/downloads/TPSreport.pdf, among other places.

[19] The definitive reference for Groovy is still *Groovy in Action*, 2nd edition, by Dierk König et al., http://manning.com/koenig2/, my all-time favorite technical book.

Roadmap

The book is divided into three parts. The first part is about the Groovy language and how to combine Groovy and Java in the same project. The second part covers testing and build processes with which Groovy can help. The third part is a survey of the typical problems Java developers encounter and how you can use Groovy to make them easier to solve.

Note that the chapters are as independent as possible. By that I mean that each chapter contains projects that combine build files, tests, persistence layers, and so on. The chapter titles represent which topic is covered in depth in that chapter, but you don't need to read them in any particular order.

The chapters in part 1, "Up to speed with Groovy," are as follows:

1. *Why add Groovy to Java?*—Here I try to identify the issues that make Java awkward or verbose, as well as the inconsistencies that have accumulated over the years, and how Groovy can help you manage them. This is the "elevator pitch" chapter, with the arguments you can use on your manager to justify adding Groovy to a Java project.
2. *Groovy by example*—This chapter contains a handful of examples that highlight features of the language that I'll use throughout the book. As noted earlier, appendix B ("Groovy by feature") provides an alternative way to help you learn any Groovy you need.
3. *Code-level integration*—How can Groovy and Java be mixed at the language level? This chapter also explores how to work with Groovy scripts from Java, including how to test them.
4. *Using Groovy features in Java*—What features does the Groovy language provide that can be used anywhere, regardless of problem? This chapter covers POGOs, operator overloading, AST transformations, and the Groovy JDK.

Part 2, "Groovy tools," discusses testing and build processes and how Groovy can make them easier:

5. *Build processes*—Managing automated builds is a pain point in many organizations. In this chapter, I look at both Ant and Maven from the Java world and how Groovy works with each, and then I discuss one of the breakout projects from the Groovy ecosystem: Gradle.
6. *Testing Groovy and Java projects*—Groovy is a dynamic language, making testing even more important than usual. This chapter discusses testing tools like JUnit and how Groovy works with them, along with the great mocking capabilities built into the language. It finishes with a serious discussion of the Spock testing framework.[20]

---

[20] The Spock discussion includes far too many *Star Trek* references, but they were no tribble at all. (Sorry.)

Part 3, "Groovy in the real world," examines various topics that Java developers encounter on a regular basis:

7. *The Spring framework*—Spring is one of the most successful and pervasive open source projects in the Java world, and it works well with Groovy in a variety of ways. This chapter uses Groovy classes as regular Spring beans and aspects and then discusses refreshable beans, inline scripted beans, and the `BeanBuilder` from Grails.
8. *Database access*—Every Java developer eventually works with persistent storage. This chapter talks about using the `groovy.sql.Sql` class to handle raw SQL and uses an example from MongoDB as a representative NoSQL database. It also contains a discussion of GORM, the Grails Object Relational Mapping API from Grails, that uses Groovy domain-specific languages to combine and configure Spring and Hibernate.
9. *RESTful web services*—The REST approach for designing web services that can be combined in scalable, efficient ways is examined, using the JAX-RS 2.0 specification as a foundation. In addition to the typical URL-driven database, though, I show how Groovy can be used to implement hypermedia as transitional links, as structural links, or through custom providers.[21]
10. *Building and testing web applications*—Groovy uses metaprogramming to make web development easier. It also includes groovlets, which make developing simple applications easy. Finally, this chapter includes a basic discussion of the Grails framework, arguably the Groovy killer app.

Each chapter in parts 2 and 3 discusses a particular aspect of Java programming. I try to follow this structure:

- Review the current Java approach to the problem.
- Present any hybrid Java/Groovy solutions.
- Introduce pure Groovy alternatives.

For example, in chapter 6 on testing, I start with JUnit, then show the `GroovyTestCase` subclass of JUnit's `TestCase`, and later talk about the Spock testing framework. Because not all the chapter topics break down cleanly that way, the beginning of each chapter includes a figure that summarizes the technologies covered and how they relate to each other. Also, at the end of each major section is a "Lessons Learned" block to summarize the main points.[22]

Three appendixes cover additional topics:

A. *Installing Groovy*—This appendix explains how to install Groovy using the downloads, the Windows installer, and the latest cool tool: GVM, the Groovy Environment Manager.

B. *Groovy by feature*—Here I provide a topic-by-topic review of Groovy, meant to complement chapter 2, "Groovy by example."

---

[21] This really is good stuff you won't find anywhere else.

[22] Think of those as the tl;dr ("too long; didn't read" in internet parlance) sections.

- **C** *SOAP-based web services*—(Available as a bonus download from www.manning.com/MakingJavaGroovy.) Most companies have moved on from the Service Oriented Architecture (SOA) approach to integration that dominated the early 2000s, but Groovy works easily with the existing Java tools for SOAP and WSDL. In case you're working with legacy applications, this appendix shows how to use Groovy in those situations.

Code conventions and downloads

All source code in the book is in a `fixed-width font like this`, which sets it off from the surrounding text. Code examples appear throughout the book. Longer listings appear under clear listing headers, while shorter listings appear between lines of text. In many listings, the code is annotated to point out the key concepts.

Source code for all the working examples is available from the publisher's website at www.manning.com/MakingJavaGroovy and from the GitHub repository at https://github.com/kousen/Making-Java-Groovy. You will find many extra examples here, beyond those covered in the book.

Author Online

Purchase of *Making Java Groovy* includes free access to a private web forum run by Manning Publications where you can make comments about the book, ask technical questions, and receive help from the author and from other users. To access the forum and subscribe to it, point your web browser to www.manning.com/MakingJavaGroovy. This page provides information on how to get on the forum once you're registered, what kind of help is available, and the rules of conduct on the forum.

Manning's commitment to our readers is to provide a venue where a meaningful dialog between individual readers and between readers and the author can take place. It's not a commitment to any specific amount of participation on the part of the author, whose contribution to the AO remains voluntary (and unpaid). We suggest you try asking the author some challenging questions lest his interest stray!

The Author Online forum and the archives of previous discussions will be accessible from the publisher's website as long as the book is in print.

About the author

Ken Kousen is an independent consultant and technical trainer specializing in all areas related to Java, especially involving open source projects like Spring, Hibernate, Android, Groovy, and Grails. He has over 20 years of experience in the field and numerous technical certifications. His academic background includes BS degrees in both Mathematics and Mechanical Engineering from M.I.T., an MS and PhD in Aerospace Engineering from Princeton, and an MS in Computer Science from Rensselaer Polytechnic Institute.

about the cover illustration

The figure on the cover of *Making Java Groovy* is captioned "The Orchestra Conductor." The illustration is taken from a nineteenth-century edition of Sylvain Maréchal's four-volume compendium of regional dress customs published in France. Each illustration is finely drawn and colored by hand. The rich variety of Maréchal's collection reminds us vividly of how culturally apart the world's towns and regions were just 200 years ago. Isolated from each other, people spoke different dialects and languages. Whether on city streets, in small towns, or in the countryside, it was easy to identify where they lived and what their trade or station in life was just by their dress.

Dress codes have changed since then, and the diversity by region and class, so rich at the time, has faded away. It is now hard to tell apart the inhabitants of different continents, let alone different towns or regions. Perhaps we have traded cultural diversity for a more varied personal life—certainly for a more varied and fast-paced technological life.

At a time when it is hard to tell one computer book from another, Manning celebrates the inventiveness and initiative of the computer business with book covers based on the rich diversity of regional life of two centuries ago, brought back to life by Maréchal's pictures.

Part 1

Up to speed with Groovy

Welcome to part 1: "Up to speed with Groovy." This section is made up of four chapters, covering topics that are independent of any particular application. In the first chapter I try to help you make the business and technical case for Groovy. The second chapter is a tutorial by example in how to use Groovy to solve small but interesting problems. Combined with appendix B it should give you the Groovy background you need to understand the rest of the book.

The third chapter reviews how closely Groovy and Java work together. It covers running Groovy scripts programmatically from Java, as well as other ways the two languages can be mixed. The easiest way to integrate the two languages is just to make classes in each, instantiate them, and invoke their methods. This chapter provides examples of doing exactly that.

The final chapter in this part reviews idiomatic Groovy features that can be particularly helpful when working with Java problems. From POGOs to AST transformations to the Groovy JDK, this chapter shows many ways that Groovy can simplify Java development.

1 Why add Groovy to Java?

This chapter covers

- Issues with Java
- Groovy features that help Java
- Common use cases for Java and how Groovy makes them simpler

For all of its flaws (and we'll be reviewing them shortly), Java is still the dominant object-oriented programming language in the industry today. It's everywhere, especially on the server side, where it's used to implement everything from web applications to messaging systems to the basic infrastructure of servers. It's therefore not surprising that there are more Java developers and more Java development jobs available than for any other programming language. As a language, Java is an unmitigated success story.

If Java is so ubiquitous and so helpful, why switch to anything else? Why not continue using Java everywhere a Java Virtual Machine (JVM) is available?

In this book, the answer to that question is, go right ahead. Where Java works for you and gets the job done, by all means continue to use it. I expect that you already have a Java background and don't want to lose all that hard-earned experience. Still, there are problems that Java solves easily, and problems that Java makes difficult. For those difficult issues, consider an alternative.

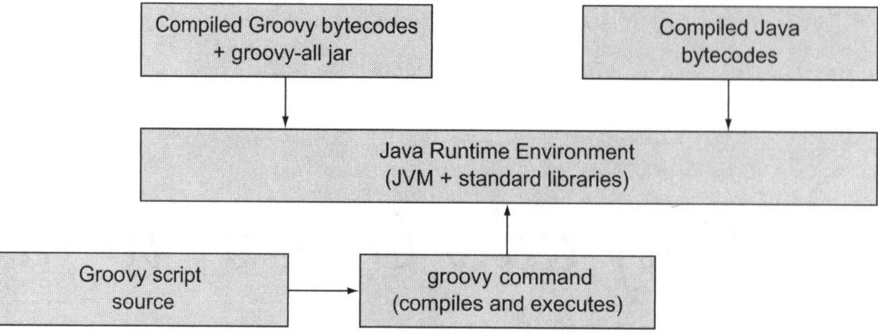

Figure 1.1 Groovy generates bytecodes for the Java Virtual Machine. Either compile them ahead of time or let the `groovy` command generate them from source.

That alternative is Groovy. In this chapter I'll review some of the issues with Java that lead to problems for developers and discuss how Groovy can help alleviate them. I'll also show a range of tools, provided as part of the Groovy ecosystem, that can make pure Java development easier. In the long run, I suggest a blended approach: let Java do what it does well, and let Groovy help where Java has difficulties.

Throughout, this will be the mantra:

> **GUIDING PRINCIPLE** Java is great for tools, libraries, and infrastructure. Groovy is great for everything else.

Use Java where Java works well, and use Groovy where it makes your life easier. Nobody is ever going to rewrite, say, the Spring Framework, in Groovy. There's no need. Groovy works beautifully with Spring, as I'll discuss in detail in chapter 7. Likewise, the JVM is everywhere. That's a good thing, because wherever Java can run, so can Groovy, as shown in figure 1.1.

I'll discuss the practical details in the next chapter, but at its base Groovy *is* Java. Groovy scripts and classes compile to bytecodes that can be freely intermixed with compiled Java classes. From a runtime point of view, running compiled Groovy means just adding a single JAR file to your environment.

One of the goals of this book is to identify opportunities where Groovy can significantly help Java developers. To do that, let me first review where Java might have some issues that need help.

1.1 Issues with Java

A perfect storm swept through the development world in the mid- to late-1990s, which ultimately resulted in moving the primary development language from C++ to Java. Java is effectively the next-generation language in the C++ family. Its syntax shares much in common with C and C++. Language constructs that caused intermediate-level developers problems, like memory management and pointer arithmetic, were handled automatically or removed from programmer control altogether. The language was small (as hard as that might be to imagine now), easy to write, and, above all, free. Just download a JDK, access the library docs (making available clean, up-to-date, hyperlinked library documentation was quite the innovation at the time), and start coding. The leading browser of the day, Netscape, even had a JVM built right into it. Combined with the whole Write Once, Run Anywhere mantra, Java carried the day.

A lot of time has passed since then. Java has grown considerably, and decisions made early in its development now complicate development rather than simplify it. What sorts of decisions were those? Here's a short, though hardly exhaustive, list:

- Java is statically typed.
- All methods in Java must be contained within a class.
- Java forbids operator overloading.
- The default access for attributes and methods is "package private."
- Java treats primitives differently from classes.

Over time Java also accumulated inconsistencies. For example, arrays have a `length` property, strings have a `length` method, collections have a `size` method, and node lists (in XML) have a `getLength` method. Groovy provides a `size` method for all of them.

Java also lacks metaprogramming capabilities.[1] That's not a flaw, but it limits Java's ability to create domain-specific languages (DSLs).

There are other issues as well, but this list will give us a good start. Let's look at a few of these items individually.

1.1.1 Is static typing a bug or a feature?

When Java was created, the thinking in the industry was that static typing—the fact that you must declare the type of every variable—was a benefit. The combination of static typing and dynamic binding meant that developers had enough structure to let the compiler catch problems right away, but still had enough freedom to implement and use polymorphism. Polymorphism lets developers override methods from superclasses and change their behavior in subclasses, making reuse by inheritance practical. Even better, Java is dynamically bound by default, so you can override anything you want unless the keyword `final` is applied to a method.

Static typing makes Integrated Development Environments useful too, because they can use the types to prompt developers for the correct fields and methods. IDEs like Eclipse and NetBeans, both powerful and free, became pervasive in the industry partly as a result of this convenience.

So what's wrong with static typing? If you want an earful ask any Smalltalk developer. More practically, under Java's dynamic binding restrictions (that you can't override anything unless two classes are related by inheritance), static typing is overly restrictive. Dynamically typed languages have much more freedom to let one object stand in for another.

---

1 That's for a variety of good reasons, many of which relate to performance. Metaprogramming depends on dynamic capabilities like reflection, which was very slow when Java was first released. Groovy in 1998 on Java 1.2 would have been a daunting prospect at best.

As a simple example, consider arrays and strings. Both are data structures that collect information: arrays collect objects, and strings collect characters. Both have the concept of appending a new element to the existing structure. Say we have a class that includes an array and we want to test the class's methods. We're not interested in testing the behavior of arrays. We know they work. But our class has a dependency on the array.

What we need is some kind of mock object to represent the array during testing. If we have a language with dynamic typing, and all we are invoking is the `append` method on it using character arguments, we can supply a string wherever we have an array and everything will still work.

In Java one object can only stand in for another if the two classes are related by inheritance or if both implement the same interface. A static reference can only be assigned to an object of that type or one of its subclasses, or a class that implements that interface if the reference is of interface type. In a dynamically typed language, however, we can have any classes stand in for another, as long as they implement the methods we need. In the dynamic world this is known as *duck typing*: if it walks like a duck and it quacks like a duck, it's a duck. See figure 1.2.

We don't care that a string is not an array as long as it has the `append` method we need. This example also shows another feature of Groovy that was left out of Java: operator overloading. In Groovy all operators are represented by methods that can be overridden. For example, the + operator uses a `plus()` method and * uses `multiply()`. In the previous figure the << operator represents the `leftShift()` method, which is implemented as `append` for both arrays and strings.

> **GROOVY FEATURE** Groovy features like optional typing and operator overloading give developers greater flexibility in far less code.

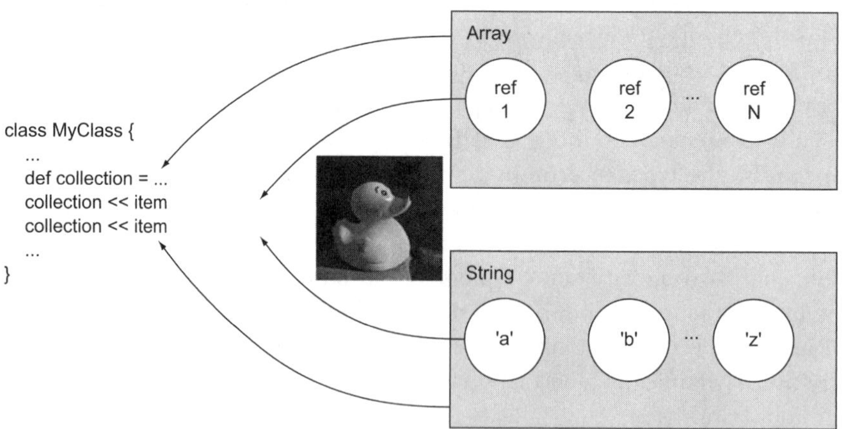

Figure 1.2 Arrays and strings from a duck-typing point of view. Each is a collection with an `append` method. If that's all we care about, they're the same.

Regarding optional typing, Groovy gives you the best of both worlds. If you know the type of a variable, feel free to specify it. If you don't know or you don't care, feel free to use the `def` keyword.

1.1.2 Methods must be in a class, even if you don't need or want one

Some time ago, Steve Yegge wrote a very influential blog post called "Execution in the Kingdom of the Nouns."[2] In it he described a world where nouns rule and verbs are second-class citizens. It's an entertaining post and I recommend reading it.

Java is firmly rooted in that world. In Java all methods (verbs) must reside inside classes (nouns). You can't have a method by itself. It has to be in a class somewhere. Most of the time that's not a big issue, but consider, for example, sorting strings.

Unlike Groovy, Java does not have native support for collections. Although collections have been a part of Java from the beginning in the form of arrays and the original `java.util.Vector` and `java.util.Hashtable` classes, a formal collections framework was added to the Java 2 Standard Edition, version 1.2. In addition to giving Java a small but useful set of fundamental data structures, such as lists, sets, and maps, the framework also introduced iterators that separated the way you moved through a collection from its underlying implementation. Finally, the framework introduced a set of polymorphic algorithms that work on the collections.

With all that in place we can assemble a collection of strings and sort them as shown in the following listing. First a collection of strings must be instantiated, then populated, and finally sorted.

Listing 1.1 Sorting strings using the `Collections.sort` method

```
import java.util.ArrayList;
import java.util.Collections;
import java.util.List;

public class SortStrings {
    public static void main(String[] args) {
        List<String> strings = new ArrayList<String>();     // Instantiating a list
        strings.add("this"); strings.add("is");            // Populate the list
        strings.add("a");    strings.add("list");
        strings.add("of");   strings.add("strings");

        Collections.sort(strings);                          // A destructive sort
        System.out.println(strings);
    }
}
```

The collections framework supplies interfaces, like `List`, and implementation classes, like `ArrayList`. The `add` method is used to populate the list. Then the `java.util.Collections` utility class includes static methods for, among other things, sorting and searching lists. Here I'm using the single-argument `sort` method, which sorts its

[2] Read the post from March 30, 2006 at Steve Yegge's blog: http://mng.bz/E4MB.

argument according to its natural sort. The assumption is that the elements of the list are from a class that implements the `java.util.Comparable` interface. That interface includes the `compareTo` method, which returns a negative number if its argument is greater than the current object, a positive number if the argument is less than the current object, and zero otherwise. The `String` class implements `Comparable` as a lexicographical sort, which is alphabetical, but sorts capital letters ahead of lowercase letters.

We'll look at a Groovy equivalent to this in a moment, but let's consider another issue first. What if you want to sort the strings by length rather than alphabetically? The `String` class is a library class, so I can't edit it to change the implementation of the `compareTo` method. It's also marked final, so I can't just extend it and override the `compareTo` implementation. For cases like this, however, the `Collections.sort` method is overloaded to take a second argument, of type `java.util.Comparator`.

The next listing shows a second sort of our list of strings, this time using the comparator, implemented as an anonymous inner class. Instead of using a `main` method as in the previous example, here's a `StringSorter` class that sorts strings either using the default sort or by length.

Listing 1.2 A Java class to sort strings

```
import java.util.Collections;
import java.util.Comparator;
import java.util.List;

public class StringSorter {
    public List<String> sortLexicographically(List<String> strings) {
        Collections.sort(strings);                                      <-- Default sort
        return strings;
    }

    public List<String> sortByDecreasingLength(List<String> strings) {
        Collections.sort(strings, new Comparator<String>() {         <-- Anonymous inner class
            public int compare(String s1, String s2) {
                return s2.length() - s1.length();
            }
        });
        return strings;
    }
}
```

Here we see a consequence of the triumph of the nouns over the verbs. The `Comparator` interface has a `compare` method, and all we want to do is to supply our own implementation of that method to `Collections.sort`. We can't implement a method, however, without including it in a class. In this case, we supply our own implementation (sort by length in decreasing order) via the awkward Java construct known as an anonymous inner class. To do so, we type the word `new` followed by the name of the interface we're implementing (in this case, `Comparator`), open a brace, and stuff in our implementation, all as the second argument to the `sort` method. It's an ugly, awkward syntax, whose only redeeming feature is that you do eventually get used to it.

Here's the Groovy equivalent in script form:

```
def strings = ['this','is','a','list','of','strings']
Collections.sort(strings, {s1,s2 -> s2.size() - s1.size()} as Comparator)
assert strings*.size() == [7, 4, 4, 2, 2, 1]
```

First of all, I'm taking advantage of Groovy's native support for collections by simply defining and populating a list as though it's an array. The `strings` variable is in fact a reference to an instance of `java.util.ArrayList`.

Next, I sort the strings using the two-argument version of `Collections.sort`. The interesting part is that the second argument to the `sort` method is a closure (between the braces), which is then "coerced" to implement `Comparable` using the `as` operator.[3]

The closure is intended to be the implementation of the `compare(String,String)` method analogous to that shown in the previous Java listing. Here I show the two dummy arguments, `s1` and `s2`, to the left of the arrow, and then use them on the right side. I provide the closure as the implementation of the `Comparator` interface. If the interface had several methods and I wanted to supply different implementations for each method, I would provide a map with the names of the methods as the keys and the corresponding closures as the values.

Finally, I use the so-called spread-dot operator to invoke the `size` method on each element of the sorted collection, which returns a list of results. In this case I'm asking for the length of each string in the collection and comparing the results to the expected values.

By the way, the Groovy script didn't require any imports, either. Java automatically imports the `java.lang` package. Groovy also automatically brings in `java.util`, `java.net`, `java.io`, `groovy.lang`, `groovy.util`, `java.math.BigInteger`, and `java.math.BigDecimal`. It's a small thing, but convenient.

> **GROOVY FEATURE** Native syntax for collections and additional automatic imports reduces both the amount of required code and its complexity.

If you've used Groovy before you probably know that there's actually an even simpler way to do the sort. I don't need to use the `Collections` class at all. Instead, Groovy has added a `sort` method to `java.util.Collection` itself. The default version does a natural sort, and a one-argument version takes a closure to do the sorting. In other words, the entire sort can be reduced to a single line:

```
strings.sort { -it?.size() }
```

The closure tells the `sort` method to use the result of the `size()` method on each element to do the sorting, with the minus sign implying that here I'm asking for descending order.

> **GROOVY FEATURE** Groovy's additions to the JDK simplify its use, and Groovy closures eliminate artificial wrappers like anonymous inner classes.

[3] Closure coercion like this is discussed further in chapter 4.

There were two major productivity improvements in this section. First, there are all the methods Groovy added to the Java libraries, known as the Groovy JDK. I'll return to those methods frequently. Second, I take advantage of Groovy's ability to treat methods as objects themselves, called closures. I'll have a lot to say about closures in the upcoming chapters, but the last example illustrated one advantage of them: you almost never need anonymous inner classes.

Incidentally, in the closure I used an additional Groovy feature to protect myself. The question mark after the word `it` is the safe de-reference operator. If the reference is null it invokes the `size` method here. If not it returns `null` and avoids the `NullPointerException`. That tiny bit of syntax wins over more Java developers to Groovy than I ever would have believed.[4]

1.1.3 Java is overly verbose

The following listing shows a simple POJO. In this case I have a class called `Task`, perhaps part of a project management system. It has attributes to represent the name, priority, and start and end dates of the task.

Listing 1.3 A Java class representing a task

```
import java.util.Date;

public class Task {
    private String name;
    private int priority;
    private Date startDate;
    private Date endDate;

    public Task() {}

    public Task(String name, int priority, Date startDate, Date endDate) {
        this.name = name;
        this.priority = priority;
        this.startDate = startDate;
        this.endDate = endDate;
    }

    public String getName() { return name; }
    public void setName(String name) { this.name = name; }
    public int getPriority() { return priority; }
    public void setPriority(int priority) { this.priority = priority; }
    public Date getStartDate() { return startDate; }
    public void setStartDate(Date startDate) { this.startDate = startDate;}
    public Date getEndDate() { return endDate; }
    public void setEndDate(Date endDate) { this.endDate = endDate; }

    @Override
    public String toString() {
        return "Task [name=" + name + ", priority=" + priority +
```

Annotations: **Data we care about** (the private fields); **Public getters and setters for the data**; **Typical override of toString**

[4] Sometimes they get tears in their eyes. "Really?" they say. "I don't have to put in all those null checks?" It's touching how happy they are.

```
            ", startDate=" + startDate + ", endDate=" + endDate + "]";
    }
}
```

We have private fields and public getter and setter methods, along with whatever constructors we need. We also add a typical override of the `toString` method. I could probably use an override of `equals` and `hashCode` as well, but I left those out for simplicity.

Most of this code can be generated by an IDE, but it still makes for a long listing, and I haven't added the necessary `equals` and `hashCode` overrides yet. That's a lot of code for what's essentially a dumb data structure.

The analogous Plain Old Groovy Object (POGO) is shown here:

```
@EqualsAndHashCode
class Task {
    String name
    int priority
    Date startDate
    Date endDate

    String toString() { "($name,$priority,$startDate,$endDate)" }
}
```

Seriously, that's the whole class, and it does include overrides of the `equals` and `hashCode` methods. Groovy classes are public by default, as are Groovy methods. Attributes are private by default. Access to an attribute is done through dynamically generated getter and setter methods, so even though it looks like we're dealing with individual fields we're actually going through getter and setter methods. Also, Groovy automatically provides a map-based constructor that eliminates the need for lots of overloaded constructors. The `@EqualsAndHashCode` annotation represents an Abstract Syntax Tree (AST) transformation that generates the associated methods. Finally, I use a Groovy string with its parameter substitution capabilities to convert a task into a string.

> **GROOVY FEATURE** Groovy's dynamic generation capabilities drastically reduce the amount of code required in a class, letting you focus on the essence rather than the ceremony.

Java also includes checked exceptions, which are a mixed blessing at best. The philosophy is to catch (no pun intended) problems early in the development cycle, which is also supposed to be an advantage to static typing.

1.1.4 Groovy makes testing Java much easier

Just because a class compiles doesn't mean it's implemented correctly. Just because you've prepared for various exceptions doesn't mean the code works properly. You've still got to test it, or you don't really know.[5]

---

[5] My favorite example of this comes from a friend who used to teach C++ back when that language was shiny and new. He looked at a student's code, and it was a mess. Then he noticed the first line was /* and the last line was */. He said, "You commented out your entire program." The student shrugged and said, "That's the only way I could get it to compile!"

One of the most important productivity improvements of the past decade or so has been the rise of automated testing tools. Java has tools like JUnit and its descendants, which make both writing and running tests automated and easy.

Testing is another area where Groovy shines. First, the base Groovy libraries include `GroovyTestCase`, which extends JUnit's `TestCase` class and adds a range of helpful methods, such as `testArrayEquals`, `testToString`, and even `shouldFail`. Next, Groovy's metaprogramming capabilities have given rise to simple DSLs for testing.

One particularly nice example is the Spock framework, which I'll discuss in chapter 6 on testing. Spock is lean and expressive, with blocks like `given`, `expect`, and `when/then`.

As an example, consider sorting strings, as implemented in Java and discussed earlier. In listing 1.3 I presented a Java class that sorted strings both lexicographically and by decreasing length. Now I'd like to test that, and to do so I'm going to use the Spock testing framework from Groovy.

A Spock test that checks both sorting methods is shown in the following listing.

Listing 1.4 A Spock test that checks each Java sorting method

```
import spock.lang.Specification;

class StringSorterTest extends Specification {
    StringSorter sorter = new StringSorter()                    // Testing a Java class
    def strings = ['this','is','a','list','of','strings']

    def "lexicographical sort returns alphabetical"() {         // Test the lexicographical sort
        when:
        sorter.sortLexicographically strings

        then:
        strings == ['a','is','list','of','strings','this']
    }

    def "reverse sort by length should be decreasing size"() {  // Test the reverse length sort
        when:
        sorter.sortByDecreasingLength strings

        then:
        strings*.size() == [7, 4, 4, 2, 2, 1]
    }
}
```

In the Spock test the Java class under test is instantiated as an attribute. I populate the data using the native collection in Groovy, even though the class under test is written in Java and the methods take Java lists as arguments.[6] I have two tests, and in each case, even without knowing anything about Spock, it should be clear what the tests are doing. I'm taking advantage of Groovy capabilities like optional parentheses and the

[6] Applying Groovy tests to Java code is discussed in chapter 6.

spread-dot operator, which applies to a list and returns a list with the specified properties only.

The test passes, and I can use the same test with the Groovy implementation. The point, though, is that I can add a Groovy test to a Java system without any problems.

1.1.5 Groovy tools simplify your build

Another area where Groovy helps Java is in the build process. I'll have a lot to say about Groovy build mechanisms in chapter 5, but here I'll just mention a couple of ways they help Java. If you're accustomed to using Apache Ant for building systems, Groovy adds execution and compilation tasks to Ant. Another option is to use `AntBuilder`, which allows you to write Ant tasks using Groovy syntax.

That's actually a common theme in Groovy, which I should emphasize:

> **GROOVY FEATURE** Groovy augments and enhances existing Java tools, rather than replacing them.

If your company has moved from Ant to Maven you're using a tool that works at a higher level of abstraction and manages dependencies for you. In chapter 5 two ways are provided to add Groovy to a Maven build. The Groovy ecosystem, however, provides another alternative.

In chapter 5 I discuss the latest Groovy killer app, Gradle. Gradle does dependency management based on Maven repositories (though it uses Ivy under the hood) and defines build tasks in a manner similar to Ant, but it's easy to set up and run. Maven is very powerful, but it has a lot of trouble with projects that weren't designed from the beginning with it in mind. Maven is a very opinionated framework, and customization is done through plugins. Ultimately, in Maven the build file is written in XML. Gradle is all about customization, and because the build file is written in Groovy you have the entire power of the Groovy language available to you.

That fact that Gradle build files are written in Groovy doesn't limit it to Groovy projects, though. If your Java project is in fact written in Maven form and has no external dependencies, here's your entire Gradle build file:

```
apply plugin:'java'
```

Applying the Java plugin defines a whole set of tasks, from compile to test to JAR. If that one line of code is in a file called build.gradle, then just type `gradle build` at the command line and a whole host of activities ensue. If you're (hopefully) going to do some testing, you'll need to add a dependency on JUnit, or even Spock. The resulting build file is shown here:

```
apply plugin:'java'

repositories {
    mavenCentral()          <-- Standard Maven repository
}
```

```
dependencies {
    testCompile 'junit:junit:4.10'
    testCompile "org.spockframework:spock-core:0.7-groovy-2.0"
}
```

Dependencies in Maven form

Now running `gradle build` results in a series of stages:

```
:compileJava
:processResources
:classes
:jar
:assemble
:compileTestJava
:processTestResources
:testClasses
:test
:check
:build
```

The result is a nice, hyperlinked set of documentation of all the test cases, plus a JAR file for deployment.

Of course, if there's a plugin called `java`, there's a plugin called `groovy`. Better yet, the Groovy plugin includes the Java plugin and, as usual, augments and improves it. If your project is similar to the ones discussed in this book, in that it combines Groovy and Java classes and uses each where most helpful, then all you need is the Groovy plugin and you're ready to go. There are many other plugins available, including `eclipse` and `web`. I'll talk about them in chapter 5 on build processes.

In this section I reviewed several of the features built into Java and how they can lead to code that's more verbose and complicated than necessary. I demonstrated how Groovy can streamline implementations and even augment existing Java tools to make them easier to use and more powerful. I'll show more details throughout the book. First I want to list some of the additional capabilities Groovy brings to Java in the next section.

1.2 Groovy features that help Java

I've actually been discussing these all along, but let me make a few specific points here. First, the Groovy version of a Java class is almost always simpler and cleaner. Groovy is far less verbose and generally easier to read.

As true as that statement is, though, it's a bit misleading. I'm not advocating rewriting all your Java code in Groovy. Quite the contrary; if your existing Java code works, that's great, although you might want to consider adding test cases in Groovy if you don't already have them. In this book, I'm more interested in helping Java than replacing it.

What does Groovy offer Java? Here's a short list of topics that are discussed in much more detail in the rest of the book:

1 *Groovy adds new capabilities to existing Java classes.*
  Groovy includes a Groovy JDK, which documents the methods added by Groovy to the Java libraries. The various `sort` methods added to the `Collection` interface

that I used for strings was a simple example. You can also use Java classes with Groovy and add features like operator overloading to Java. These and related topics will be discussed in chapter 4.

2. ***Groovy uses Java libraries.***
   Practically every Groovy class relies on the Java libraries, with or without Groovy additions. That means virtually every Groovy class is already an integration story, mixing Groovy and Java together. One nice use case for Groovy is to experiment with Java libraries you haven't used before.
3. ***Groovy makes working with XML and JSON easy.***
   Here's an area where Groovy shines. Groovy includes classes called `Markup-Builder`, which makes it easy to generate XML, and `JsonBuilder`, which produces JSON objects. It also has classes called `XmlParser` and `XmlSlurper`, which convert XML data structures into DOM structures in memory, and `JsonSlurper`, to parse JSON data. These will be used throughout the book, especially in chapter 9 on RESTful web services.
4. ***Groovy includes simplified data source manipulation.***
   The `groovy.sql.Sql` class provides a very simple way to work with relational databases. I'll talk about this in chapter 8 on databases, chapter 7 on working with the Spring framework, and chapter 9 on RESTful web services.
5. ***Groovy's metaprogramming streamlines development.***
   The builder classes are an example of Groovy metaprogramming. I'll show examples of DSLs in several chapters.
6. ***Groovy tests work for Java code.***
   The Spock testing tool, demonstrated in this chapter and extensively discussed in chapter 6 on testing, is a great way to test Java systems.
7. ***Groovy build tools work on Java (and mixed) projects.***
   In chapter 5 on enhancing build processes, I'll talk about `AntBuilder`, how to add Groovy to Maven builds, and Gradle.
8. ***Groovy projects like Grails and Griffon make developing web and desktop applications easier.***
   The Grails project is a complete-stack, end-to-end framework for building web applications, based on Spring and Hibernate. Griffon brings the same convention-over-configuration ideas to desktop development. Grails is discussed in chapter 8 on databases and chapter 10 on web applications.

When looking at the sorts of problems Java developers typically encounter, this list will be a source of ideas for making implementations simpler, easier to read and understand, and faster to implement.

1.3 Java use cases and how Groovy helps

The examples I've discussed so far are all code-level simplifications. They're very helpful, but I can do more than that. Groovy developers work on the same sorts of problems that Java developers do, so many higher-level abstractions have been created to make addressing those problems easier.

In this book I'm also going to survey the various types of problems that Java developers face on a regular basis, from accessing and implementing web services to using object-relational mapping tools to improving your build process. In each case I'll examine how adding Groovy can make your life easier as a developer.

Here's a list of some of the areas I'll discuss as we go along, and I'll give you a brief idea of how Groovy will help. This will also provide a lightweight survey of the upcoming chapters.

1.3.1 Spring framework support for Groovy

One of the most successful open source projects in the Java industry today is the Spring framework. It's the Swiss Army chainsaw of projects; it's pervasive throughout the Java world and has tools for practically every purpose.

No one is ever going to suggest rewriting Spring in Groovy. It works fine in Java as it is. Nor is there any need to "port" it to Groovy. As far as Spring is concerned, compiled Groovy classes are just another set of bytecodes. Groovy can use Spring as though it's just another library.

The developers of Spring, however, are well aware of Groovy and built in special capabilities for working with it. Spring bean files can contain *inline scripted* Groovy beans. Spring also allows you to deploy Groovy source code, rather than compiled versions, as so-called *refreshable* beans. Spring periodically checks the source code of refreshable beans for changes and, if it finds any, rebuilds them and uses the updated versions. This is a very powerful capability, as chapter 7 on working with Spring will show.

Finally, the developers of the Grails project also created a class called `BeanBuilder`, which is used to script Spring beans in Groovy. That brings Groovy capabilities to Spring bean files much the way Gradle enhances XML build files.

1.3.2 Simplified database access

Virtually all Java developers work with databases. Groovy has a special set of classes to make database integration easy, and I'll review them in chapter 8 on databases. I also show an example of working with a MongoDB database through a Groovy library that wraps the corresponding Java API.

I'll also borrow from the Grails world and discuss GORM, the Grails Object-Relational Mapping tool, a DSL for configuring Hibernate. In fact, GORM has been refactored to work with a variety of persistence mechanisms, including NoSQL databases like MongoDB, Neo4J, Redis, and more.

1.3.3 Building and accessing web services

Another area of active development today is in web services. Java developers work with both SOAP-based and RESTful services, the former involving auto-generated proxies and the latter using HTTP as much as possible. REST is covered in chapter 9, and

SOAP-based web services are discussed in appendix C, available as a free download. In both cases, if a little care is applied, the existing Java tools work just fine with Groovy implementations.

1.3.4 Web application enhancements

Groovy includes a "groovlet" class, which acts like a Groovy-based servlet. It receives HTTP requests and returns HTTP responses, and it includes pre-built objects for requests, responses, sessions, and more. One of the most successful instances of Groovy and Java integration, and arguably the killer app for Groovy, is the Grails framework, which brings extraordinary productivity to web applications. Both are covered in chapter 10 on web development.

In each of these use cases, Groovy can work with existing Java tools, libraries, and infrastructure. In some situations, Groovy will simplify the required code. In other cases, the integration is more deeply embedded and will provide capabilities far beyond what Java alone includes. In all of them, the productivity gains will hopefully be both obvious and dramatic.

1.4 Summary

Java is a large, powerful language, but it's showing its age. Decisions made early in its development are not necessarily appropriate now, and over time it has accumulated problems and inconsistencies. Still, Java is everywhere, and its tools, libraries, and infrastructure are both useful and convenient.

In this chapter I reviewed some of the issues that are part of the Java development world, from its verbosity to anonymous inner classes to static typing. Most Java developers are so accustomed to these "problems" that they see them as features as much as bugs. Add a little bit of Groovy, however, and the productivity gains can be considerable. I demonstrated that simply using Groovy native collections and the methods Groovy adds to the standard Java libraries reduced huge sections of code down to a few lines. I also listed the Groovy capabilities that will be a rich source of ideas for simplifying Java development.

As powerful as Groovy is (and as fun as it is to use), I still don't recommend replacing your existing Java with Groovy. In this book I advocate a blended approach. The philosophy is to use Java wherever it is appropriate, which mostly means using its tools and libraries and deploying to its infrastructure. I add Groovy to Java wherever it helps the most. In the next chapter I'll begin that journey by examining class-level integration of Java and Groovy.

2 Groovy by example

This chapter covers

- Basic Groovy syntax
- Collections and closures
- Using the Groovy JDK

As the previous chapter stated, this book isn't intended to be an exhaustive reference for Groovy, but a certain minimum level of Groovy proficiency is necessary. While some people learn best through short, simple code examples illustrating each concept, others prefer to see basic concepts combined to solve actual problems. For those who prefer snippets of code for each feature I've provided appendix B, a Groovy tutorial arranged by feature.

In this chapter, I'll instead walk through a few small but non-trivial Groovy examples. Hopefully this will help communicate not only the syntax of the language, but some of the standard Groovy idioms as well. Some of the examples will be used again in other chapters in the book, but are used here as illustrations of basic Groovy practices.

2.1 Hello, Groovy

Because every programming language book is required by law to include a "Hello, World!" program, here's Groovy's version:

```
println 'Hello, World!'
```

In Java you compile with `javac` and execute the resulting bytecodes with `java`. In Groovy you can compile with `groovyc` and execute with `groovy`, but you don't actually have to compile first. The `groovy` command can run with a source code argument, and it will compile first and then execute. Groovy is a compiled language, but you don't have to separate the steps, though most people do. When you use an IDE, for example, every time you save a Groovy script or class, it is compiled.

The single line shown earlier is a complete program. Unlike with Java, you don't need to put all Groovy code into a class. Groovy supports running scripts. Everything is still Java bytecodes under the hood, so what happens is that Groovy scripts eventually become the body of the `main` method in a class that extends `groovy.lang.Script`.

Note two additional differences in syntax between Groovy and Java:

- *Semicolons are optional.* You can add them, and it's appropriate to use them if you have more than one statement on a line, but they're not normally necessary.
- *Parentheses are often optional.* The `println` command is actually a method call, and the `String` is the argument to the method. Because there's no ambiguity, you can leave out the parentheses. It's not wrong to include them, though, if you want.

OPTIONAL PARENTHESES Parentheses are optional until they aren't. Simple method calls normally omit them, but if there's any uncertainty, add them. Groovy is all about simplicity and understandability.

Now that the "Hello, World!" example is out of the way, I can move on to something a bit more interesting. One helpful use case for Groovy is that it makes a nice client for RESTful web services like Google Chart.

2.2 Accessing Google Chart Tools

One of the APIs that Google makes available is a RESTful web service known as the Chart API, or, more formally, Google Chart Tools Image API.[1] The documentation is located at https://developers.google.com/chart/image/. The chart tools provide a rich API for JavaScript users, but the inputs are ultimately URLs with query parameters.

A developer sends a request to the base URL https://chart.apis.google.com/chart and appends query parameters to specify the type of chart, its size, the data, and any

[1] Google officially deprecated the image charts portion of Google Chart Tools on April 20, 2012. As of summer, 2013, the API still works. It is used here both as a nice, self-contained example and as a simple application that illustrates many Groovy features. Other examples of accessing publicly available services are given throughout the book.

labels. Because that API also needs a "Hello, World" example, here's the URL for a three-dimensional pie chart:

```
https://chart.apis.google.com/chart?
        cht=p3&
        chs=250x100&
        chd=t:60,40&
        chl=Hello|World
```

This URL would be all on one line but is written out here (and in the documentation) for illustration purposes. After the base URL, the parameters list the chart type (`cht`) as a 3D pie chart, the chart size (`chs`) as 250 by 100 pixels, the chart data (`chd`) as 60 and 40 in simple text format, and the chart labels (`chl`) "Hello" and "World." Type that URL into a browser and the resulting image is returned, as shown in figure 2.1.

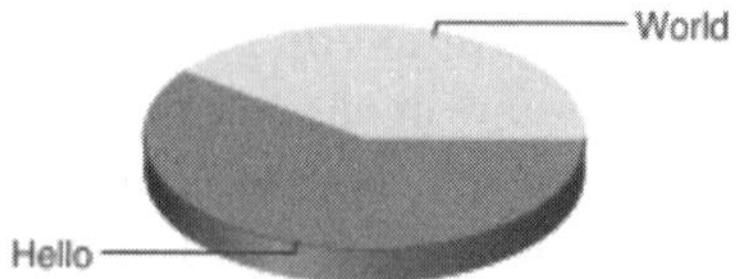

Figure 2.1 The Google Chart API "Hello, World" example

The URL shown is hard-wired to produce the chart in figure 2.1. To make this more general, I'll show how to produce the URL from strings, lists, maps, closures, and builders.

> **GOAL** Write a Groovy script to generate the "Hello, World" 3D pie chart as a desktop application.

In the process, I'll discuss

- String manipulation
- Lists and maps
- Processing data using closures
- Groovy builder classes

In this case I'll implement the steps in a simple script; later, it could be converted to a class for integration purposes.

2.2.1 Assembling the URL with query string

To start, I need a variable to represent the base URL. In a Groovy script you don't actually have to declare any types at all. If you declare a type the variable becomes local to the script. If not, it becomes part of the "binding," which is discussed in the next chapter. Here, because I know the URL will be contained in a string before I convert it, I'll declare the variable to be of type `java.lang.String`:

```
String base = 'http://chart.apis.google.com/chart?'
```

Groovy is optionally typed. This means you can specify a type if you want to, or you can use the keyword `def` if you don't know or care. There's some debate among developers about when to use `def` and when to specify a type. Dierk Koenig, lead author on the superb *Groovy in Action* (Manning, 2007), says it this way:

USING DEF If you think of a type, type it (from Dierk Koenig). In other words, if you know a variable will be a `String`, or a `Date`, or an `Employee`, use that type of variable.

In my own experience, I used to use `def` a lot, but as time goes by I use it less and less. I agree with Dierk, with the addition that when I'm tempted to use `def` I often pause a moment and try to think of an actual type before using it. Other developers have other styles, though. That's the beauty of an optionally typed language: there's room for everybody.

I now need to append the query parameters to this URL. Rather than write the query string directly I'm going to use a typical idiom for this type of application, which is to build a map and then generate the query string from the map parameters. With that in mind, here's the map of parameters:

```
def params = [cht:'p3',chs:'250x100',
              chd:'t:60,40',chl:'Hello|World']
```

In Groovy you create a map with square brackets, and each entry consists of keys and values separated by a colon. The keys are assumed to be strings by default. The values can be anything. By default, the `params` variable is an instance of `java.util.LinkedHashMap`.

COLLECTIONS Groovy has native syntax for lists and maps. Map keys are assumed to be strings.

Each corresponding value is surrounded by single quotes. In Groovy, single-quoted strings are instances of `java.lang.String`. Double-quoted strings are "interpolated" strings, known (unfortunately) as `GStrings`. I'll show an example of string interpolation later in this program.

To transform the map into a query string I first need to convert each of the map entries into strings of the form "key=value," and then I need to concatenate them all together using ampersands as separators.[2] The first step is accomplished by using a special method added to all Groovy collections, known as `collect`. The `collect` method takes a closure as an argument, applies the closure to each element of the collection, and returns a new collection containing the results.

Closures are introduced in the next sidebar and discussed extensively throughout the book, but for the moment think of them as blocks of code representing the body of a function, which may take dummy arguments. In the case of `collect`, when applied to a map, the closure can take either one or two arguments. If the closure takes one argument, the argument represents a `Map.Entry`; with two arguments, the first is the key and the second is the value for each entry.

---

[2] I also need to URL-encode the map entries, but in this case they're already fine. In other examples of RESTful web services I'll demonstrate the encoding process.

To transform the map into a list of key=value pairs, the following two-argument closure works in the collect method:

```
params.collect { k,v -> "$k=$v" }
```

In Groovy, if the last argument to any method is a closure you can put the closure outside the parentheses. In this case the only argument to collect is a closure, so even the optional parentheses are omitted.

> **What is a closure?**
> A closure is a block of code, delimited by curly braces, which can be treated as an object. The arrow notation is used to specify dummy arguments. In the closure applied to the map in the current example, the two dummy arguments are k and v, which represent the key and value of each entry. The expression on the right side of the arrow says to substitute each key and value into a GString separated by an equals sign. This collect method takes each entry in the map and converts it into a string with the key assigned to the value, and produces a list of results.

The result of the operation is shown here:

```
["cht=p3", "chs=250x100", "chd=t:60,40", "chl=Hello|World"]
```

This process is illustrated in figure 2.2.

To create the query string, use another method added by Groovy to collections, called join. The join method takes a single argument that's used as the separator when assembling the elements into a string. To create a query string, invoke join with an ampersand as an argument:

```
["cht=p3", "chs=250x100", "chd=t:60,40", "chl=Hello|World"].join('&')
```

The result is the needed query string, as shown here:

```
"cht=p3&chs=250x100&chd=t:60,40&chl=Hello|World"
```

Here's the entire process so far, taking the base URL and the parameter map, and building the Google Chart URL:

```
String base = 'http://chart.apis.google.com/chart?'
def params = [cht:'p3',chs:'250x100',
              chd:'t:60,40',chl:'Hello|World']
String qs = params.collect { k,v -> "$k=$v" }.join('&')
```

[cht:'p3', chs:'250x100',
chd:'t:60,40', chl:'Hello|World']
collect { k,v -> "$k=$v" }
["cht=p3", "chs=250x100", "chd=t:60,40", "chl=Hello|World"]

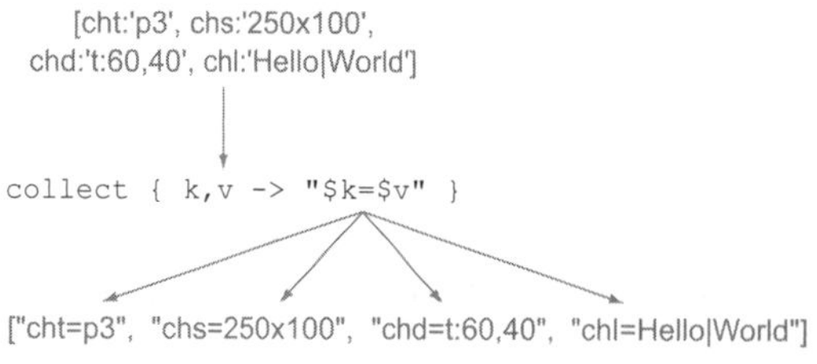

Figure 2.2 Apply collect to a map to convert it into a list, where each entry is transformed into a string.

The result of all this manipulation is actually a string, not a URL. Before converting it to a URL, let me first verify that the process worked. Normally this would require a test, as discussed extensively in chapter 6 on testing. Here, however, I'll just use the Groovy `assert` keyword, which takes a boolean expression as an argument. If the expression is true, nothing is returned, but if not, you get the error printed to the console. In this case I'll use the `contains` method from the `Map` interface to check that each of the entries from the `params` map appears in the query string in the proper format:

```
params.each { k,v ->
    assert qs.contains("$k=$v")
}
```

> **THE ASSERT KEYWORD** Groovy asserts are an easy way to verify correctness. An assert returns nothing if the expression is true, and prints a detailed error message if it's not.

One of the advantages of the `join` method is that you don't have to worry about accidentally adding an ampersand at the beginning or end of the string. It only adds the separator internally.

Note also that this is a case where the parentheses (on the `join` method) are needed. In Groovy, if you leave off the parentheses when calling a method with no arguments the compiler assumes you are asking for the corresponding getter or setter method. Because I want the `join()` method (and not `getJoin()`, which doesn't exist), I need the parentheses.

2.2.2 *Transmitting the URL*

The Groovy JDK adds the `toURL()` method to the `String` class. As you might imagine, this method converts an instance of `java.lang.String` into an instance of `java.net.URL`.

> **The Groovy JDK**
>
> Groovy adds many helpful methods to existing Java library classes. Many, many times I've found methods added to, say, `String`, `Date`, or `Collection` that I always wished were in Java all along. The set of methods added by Groovy is known as the Groovy JDK and has its own set of JavaDocs. The Groovy JDK documentation is available via a link from the Groovy home page.
>
> The Groovy JDK is discussed in more detail in chapter 3.

To send an HTTP GET request to a URL and retrieve the results, convert the string to a URL and invoke another Groovy JDK method, the `getText()` method, added to `java.net.URL`. In other words, the data on a web page can be retrieved from this code:

```
url.toURL().text
```

Here I'm deliberately using the `text` property of the URL class, knowing that the effect will be to invoke the `getText()` method. There's nothing wrong with actually calling `getText`, but this is more idiomatic Groovy.

Normally this would be exactly the code I want, and I use this technique in some of the examples in the chapters on web services, but in this particular case the result isn't text. Google Chart takes the URL generated here and returns a binary image, so converting it to text isn't very helpful.

> **GROOVY PROPERTIES** Accessing properties in Groovy automatically invokes the associated getter or setter method.

Next I'll build a Swing user interface that includes the image in a `javax.swing.ImageIcon`. This will give me a chance to illustrate a builder, which is a great illustration of Groovy metaprogramming.

2.2.3 Creating a UI with SwingBuilder

In Groovy every class has a metaclass. A metaclass is another class that manages the actual invocation process. If you invoke a method on a class that doesn't exist, the call is ultimately intercepted by a method in the metaclass called `methodMissing`. Likewise, accessing a property that doesn't exist eventually calls `propertyMissing` in the metaclass. Customizing the behavior of `methodMissing` and `propertyMissing` is the heart of Groovy runtime metaprogramming.

Groovy metaprogramming is a large subject, but here I'll demonstrate one of its helpful results: the creation of builder classes. In a builder, the call to `methodMissing` does something specific for that type of builder.

Here I'll illustrate a Swing builder. This is a class that intercepts names of components and constructs a Swing user interface out of the results. This is actually easier to demonstrate than to explain. I'll start, however, by adding some imports to the Google Chart script I've been constructing so far:

```
import java.awt.BorderLayout as BL
import javax.swing.WindowConstants as WC
import groovy.swing.SwingBuilder
import javax.swing.ImageIcon
```

> **Automatic imports**
>
> You may have noticed that I haven't yet needed any import statements at all. Java automatically imports the `java.lang` package. Groovy imports `java.lang`, as well as `java.util`, `java.io`, `java.net`, `groovy.lang`, `groovy.util`, `java.math.BigInteger`, and `java.math.BigDecimal`.[3]

---

[3] That's another one of the "Duh! Why didn't we do that all along?" type of revelations that Java developers get all the time when they first learn Groovy. Why is it we only import `java.lang` in Java programs? Why not import lots of typical packages? Wouldn't that make coding easier? Groovy says yes.

In this script I'm importing three classes from the Java standard library. The first two imports use the as operator to build an alias for the respective classes. That way the code that uses BorderLayout and WindowConstants can just write BL or WC instead. I'm also adding in the ImageIcon class, which will hold the image returned by Google Chart. The import from the Groovy library is SwingBuilder, which will be used to construct the Swing UI.

THE AS KEYWORD The as keyword has several uses, one of which is to provide an alias for imported classes. The as keyword corresponds to the asType method, which was added to java.lang.Object as part of the Groovy JDK.

In the case of SwingBuilder you invoke methods that don't exist on the builder but that are translated to the corresponding Swing API. For example, by calling the frame method you're actually instantiating the JFrame class. Giving it a map-like argument of visible:true corresponds to calling the setVisible method with a true argument.

Here's the code that uses the builder. Each method not in SwingBuilder is translated to the proper method call on the Swing library class:

```
SwingBuilder.edt {
    frame(title:'Hello, World!', visible:true, pack: true,
        defaultCloseOperation:WC.EXIT_ON_CLOSE) {
            label(icon:new ImageIcon("$base$qs".toURL()),
                constraints:BL.CENTER)
    }
}
```

The edt method on SwingBuilder builds a GUI using the event dispatch thread. It takes a closure as an argument, and this is where the fun starts. The first statement inside the closure is a call to the frame method, but the fact is, there's no frame method in SwingBuilder. The builder's metaclass intercepts that call (via methodMissing) and interprets it as a request to instantiate the javax.swing.JFrame class. The frame method here lists a series of map entries, which are intended to supply values for the title, visibility, and close operation on the JFrame. The builder interprets them as calls to setTitle, setVisible, and setDefaultCloseOperation on the JFrame instance.

After the parentheses there's another closure. That's interpreted to mean I'm about to supply components that will be added to the JFrame instance. The next call is to the label method, which of course doesn't exist. The Swing builder knows to generate a JLabel instance as a result, call its setIcon method with a new ImageIcon holding the image returned by Google Chart, and place the JLabel in the center of a BorderLayout.

Finally, after the frame closure I invoke the pack method on JFrame to make the resulting GUI just big enough to hold the image. The next listing contains the complete script (without the asserts, just to keep the listing short).

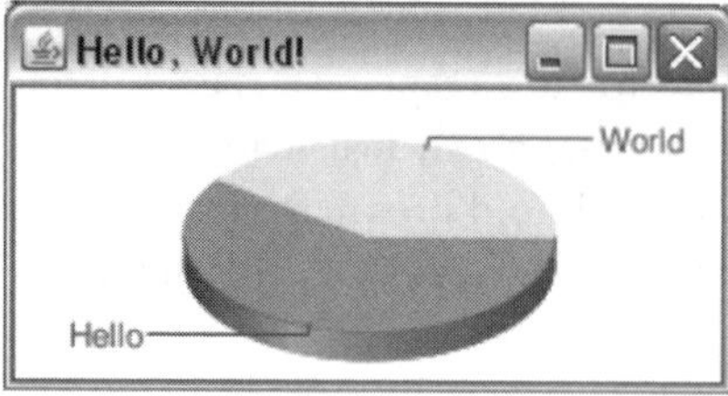

Figure 2.3 The "Hello, World" Swing user interface, holding the image returned by Google Chart

Listing 2.1 Building a Swing UI 3D pie chart using Google Chart

```
import java.awt.BorderLayout as BL
import javax.swing.WindowConstants as WC
import groovy.swing.SwingBuilder
import javax.swing.ImageIcon

def base = 'http://chart.apis.google.com/chart?'

def params = [cht:'p3',chs:'250x100',
              chd:'t:60,40',chl:'Hello|World']

String qs = params.collect { k,v -> "$k=$v" }.join('&')

SwingBuilder.edt {
    frame(title:'Hello, Chart!', pack: true,
        visible:true, defaultCloseOperation:WC.EXIT_ON_CLOSE) {
            label(icon:new ImageIcon("$base$qs".toURL()),
                constraints:BL.CENTER)
    }
}
```

The resulting image is shown in figure 2.3.

Lessons Learned (Google Chart)

1. Groovy variables can have types, or you can use the `def` keyword if you don't know or don't care. The keyword `def` can also be used as a method return type or argument.
2. Groovy has native syntax for lists and maps. This example used a Groovy map; lists are used in many other examples throughout the book.
3. Closures are like anonymous function bodies with parameters.
4. The `collect` method transforms a collection by applying a closure to each element and returning the resulting list.
5. The Groovy JDK adds many methods to the standard Java API.
6. Groovy parsers and builders simplify working with many APIs.

The next example demonstrates Groovy's XML parsing and generation capabilities, database manipulation, regular expressions, groovlets, and more.

2.3 Groovy Baseball

Figure 2.4 shows a web application I call Groovy Baseball. For a given date during baseball season the page creates a Google Map that displays the results of all Major

Groovy Baseball

Select a date to see all games that day

Game data from MLB, from the beginning of the 2005 season to the present.

Games for Fri Jun 17 2011

Los Angeles Angels 4, New York Mets, 3
Baltimore Orioles 4, Washington Nationals, 8
Chicago White Sox 1, Arizona Diamondbacks, 4
Detroit Tigers 6, Colorado Rockies, 13
Florida Marlins 1, Tampa Bay Rays, 5
Houston Astros 7, Los Angeles Dodgers, 3
Kansas City Royals 5, St. Louis Cardinals, 4
Milwaukee Brewers 4, Boston Red Sox, 10

Date 2011-6-17

June 2011

« ‹ Today › »

S	M	T	W	T	F	S
29	30	31	1	2	3	4
5	6	7	8	9	10	11
12	13	14	15	16	17	18
19	20	21	22	23	24	25
26	27	28	29	30	1	2

Figure 2.4 Groovy Baseball is a web application that shows the results of MLB games on a given date.

League Baseball games on that day, using info markers centered on the stadium of the home team. Game results are also listed in a small table. A calendar widget is provided so the user can select an alternative date, which updates the page via an Ajax call.

Some of the functionality is provided by JavaScript via the Google Maps API, which creates the map and adds the markers. Also, the set of game results for a given day is acquired via an Ajax call using the prototype JavaScript library. I'll show the code for that later. In the meantime I want to highlight the Groovy parts of this application.

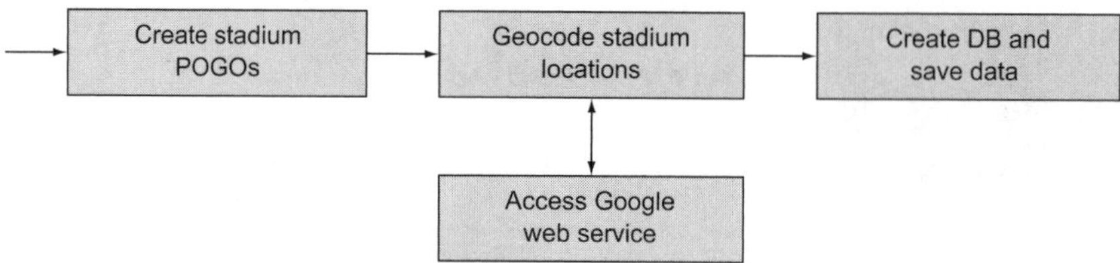

Figure 2.5 Building Groovy Baseball, part 1—geocoding stadium data and saving in DB

The application is simple but it has a fair number of moving parts, so I'll build it in stages. The first task is to collect the geographic information for the individual MLB stadiums and save it in a database, as illustrated in figure 2.5.

In this part of the process, I'll cover

- Plain Old Groovy Objects
- Accessing a RESTful web service
- The `groovy.sql.Sql` class

The next step is to access the online box scores and parse the resulting XML files, illustrated in figure 2.6.

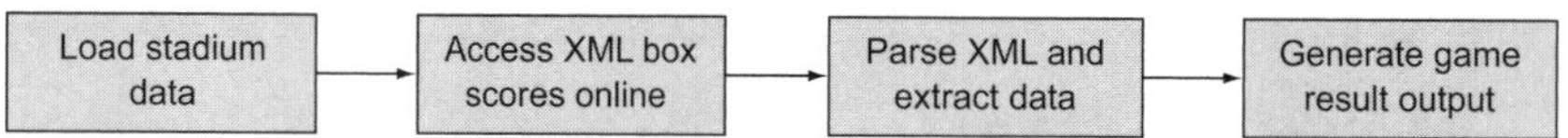

Figure 2.6 Building Groovy Baseball, part 2—extracting box score data and creating output POGOs

During this stage, I'll discuss

- Reading from a database
- Downloading information over the internet
- Parsing XML

Finally, I need to send the resulting data to the view layer in a form it can understand, as shown in figure 2.7.

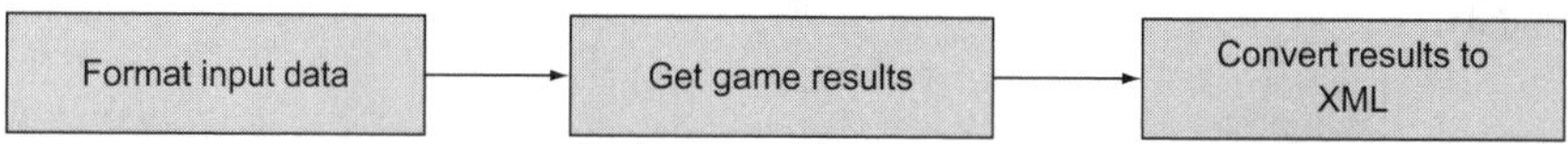

Figure 2.7 Building Groovy Baseball, part 3—drive system and generate XML

During this stage, I'll cover

- Using a groovlet
- Generating XML

I'll begin the process with part 1, creating POGOs and saving data in a database.

2.3.1 Database data and Plain Old Groovy Objects

The game results on the web page are centered on the home stadiums of each game. Google Maps places markers based on the latitude and longitude of a given location. Because stadiums don't tend to move much, it's worth it to compute those locations ahead of time and save them in some kind of persistence structure. In this case I used a MySQL database, but any database would do.

I'll build a script here to collect the necessary info for each MLB stadium, compute its latitude and longitude, and store them in a database table. I'll start with a class to represent a stadium.

THE STADIUM POGO

In Java we would call this class a Plain Old Java Object, or POJO. In Groovy I'll use a Plain Old Groovy Object, or POGO, instead. The following listing shows the `Stadium` class.

Listing 2.2 `Stadium.groovy`: a POGO to hold stadium information

```
package beans

class Stadium {
    int id
    String name
    String city
    String state
    String team
    double latitude
    double longitude

    String toString() { "($team,$name,$latitude,$longitude)" }
}
```

If you're used to Java, what's conspicuous here is what's absent. The lack of semicolons is probably not surprising at this point. What may be a surprise is that there are no public or private access modifiers anywhere. In Groovy, if you don't specify an access modifier, attributes are assumed to be private, and methods are assumed to be public.[4]

You might also note that there are no constructors in the `Stadium` class. In Java, if you don't add a constructor, the compiler gives you a default constructor for free. In Groovy, however, you get not only the default, but also a map-based constructor that allows you to set any combination of attribute values by supplying them as key-value pairs.

With this in mind, here's the first part of the script to populate a database table with the `Stadium` locations:

[4] That's another "duh" moment. The default access in Java is "package private," which means the member is accessible from any other class in the same subdirectory. In roughly 15 years of Java coding I've used this access deliberately maybe twice, and both times there were reasonable alternatives. I can understand trying to create some sort of friend access, but why make it the default? Once again, Groovy does what makes sense.

```
def stadiums = []
stadiums <<
    new Stadium(name:'Angel Stadium',city:'Anaheim',state:'CA',team:'ana')
stadiums <<
    new Stadium(name:'Chase Field',city:'Phoenix',state:'AZ',team:'ari')
...
stadiums <<
    new Stadium(name:'Rogers Centre',city:'Toronto',state:'ON',team:'tor')
stadiums <<
    new Stadium(name:'Nationals Park',
    city:'Washington',state:'DC',team:'was')
```

The `stadiums` variable is initialized to an empty `java.util.ArrayList`. The left-shift operator has been implemented in `Collection` to be an append method, so the rest of the listing instantiates each of the MLB stadiums and appends it to the list.

Each constructor sets the `name` of the stadium, as well as its `city`, `state`, and the three-letter `team` abbreviation. What are missing are the `latitude` and `longitude` values. To supply those I use the Google geocoder, which is another RESTful web service provided by Google, similar to the Google Chart API discussed in the previous section.

> **POGO** Plain Old Groovy Objects are like POJOs, but with auto-generated getters, setters, and map-based constructors.

GEOCODING

The Google Geocoding API is documented at https://developers.google.com/maps/documentation/geocoding/. A geocoder transforms an address into a latitude and longitude. To use the Google geocoder you need to assemble a URL that includes the address information. According to the documentation, the URL has the form

```
http://maps.googleapis.com/maps/api/geocode/output?parameters
```

Here the value of `output` is either `xml` or `json`, depending on which type of data you want back.[5] The `parameters` property contains the address, as well as a `sensor` value. Here's the sample from the documentation, which (naturally enough) uses the address of Google's headquarters in Mountain View, CA:

```
http://maps.googleapis.com/maps/api/geocode/
     xml?address=1600+Amphitheatre+Parkway,+Mountain+View,+CA&sensor=true_or_
     false
```

If you intend to access the geocoder using JavaScript, I would say to use `json` (JavaScript Object Notation) for the output value. Because I'm working with Groovy, and Groovy works well with XML, I'll use the `xml` value. The query string contains two parameters. The first is the address, which holds URL-encoded values of the street, city, and state (separated by `","`). The other parameter is called `sensor`, whose value is true if the request is coming from a GPS-enabled device and false otherwise.

---

[5] True REST advocates prefer that content negotiation be done in an `Accept` header on the HTTP request. Here Google does it through separate URIs.

I'll start the geocoding process by setting a variable to the base URL:

```
def base = 'http://maps.googleapis.com/maps/api/geocode/xml?'
```

To assemble the query string, consider a list containing the stadium name, city, and state:

```
[stadium.name, stadium.city, stadium.state]
```

Each of these values could potentially include spaces, apostrophes, or other symbols that wouldn't be legal in a URL. I therefore need to URL-encode each of the values. As I showed in the last section, applying the `collect` method to a list returns a new list containing the transformed values. In this case, the transformation I want is to use the `encode` method in the `java.net.URLEncoder`, as shown:

```
[stadium.name, stadium.city, stadium.state].collect {
    URLEncoder.encode(it,'UTF-8')
}.join(',')
```

If you use a closure without specifying a dummy parameter, as here, each element of the list is assigned to a variable called `it`. The body of the closure executes the static `encode` method on the name, city, and state, using the UTF-8 encoding scheme. The result is a list containing the encoded values. Finally, the values of the list are joined into a string using "`,`" as a separator.

That takes care of assembling the address. Forming a complete query string is done using the same closure used in the Google Chart listing. The complete process so far is shown here:

```
def url = base + [sensor:false,
    address: [stadium.name, stadium.city, stadium.state].collect {
        URLEncoder.encode(it,'UTF-8')
    }.join(',')
].collect {k,v -> "$k=$v"}.join('&')
```

> **Building a query string**
> The combination of parameter map, `collect` closure, and `join` method is a convenient way to build a query string. A developer can store the parameters in any order, or accept them from the user (as in a Grails application), and turn them into a query string with a minimum of effort.

The result of all this string manipulation is to create a full URL, similar to the one shown in the previous example, which can be transmitted to the Google geocoder.

Now comes the fun part. The geocoder returns a fairly extensive block of XML (not shown here, but available online in the Google geocoder documentation at https://developers.google.com/maps/documentation/geocoding/#XML). Processing the XML using Java would be quite verbose. Fortunately, XML is nothing to Groovy.

The entire process of transmitting the URL to the Google geocoder and parsing the result into a DOM tree takes one line:

```
def response = new XmlSlurper().parse(url)
```

Groovy has two classes for parsing XML. One is called `XmlParser`, and the other is `XmlSlurper`. Both convert XML into a DOM tree. The underlying structure and process are somewhat different, but from a practical point of view the slurper is more efficient and takes less memory, so that's what I'll use here. Extracting the results I need is a simple matter of walking the tree. I could paste in a copy of the XML output to show you the structure, but it's easy enough to understand if you see the Groovy parsing code:

```
stadium.latitude = response.result[0].geometry.location.lat.toDouble()
stadium.longitude = response.result[0].geometry.location.lng.toDouble()
```
[6]

In other words, the slurper returns the root of the DOM tree, which is assigned to a variable called `response`. The root has a child element called `result`, which has a child called `geometry`, which has a child called `location`, which then has two children, one called `lat` and the other called `lng`. Sometimes the geocoder returns multiple results, so I used the array index 0 on `result` to use only the first one. Because everything in XML is a `String` and I want to assign the results to double values in `Stadium`, I finally use the `toDouble` method added to `String` to do the conversion.

> **PARSING XML** Whether you use an `XmlParser` or an `XmlSlurper`, extracting data from XML means just walking the tree.[7]

The following listing shows the complete `Geocoder` class, with its method `fillInLatLng` that takes a `Stadium` as an argument and fills in the latitude and longitude values.

Listing 2.3 `Geocoder.groovy`, which uses the Google geocoder to compute lat and lng

```
class Geocoder {
    def base = 'http://maps.googleapis.com/maps/api/geocode/xml?'

    def fillInLatLng(Stadium stadium) {
        def url = base + [sensor:false,
            address: [stadium.name, stadium.city, stadium.state].collect {
                URLEncoder.encode(it,'UTF-8')
            }.join(',')
        ].collect {k,v -> "$k=$v"}.join('&')
        def response = new XmlSlurper().parse(url)
        stadium.latitude =
            response.result[0].geometry.location.lat.toDouble()
        stadium.longitude =
            response.result[0].geometry.location.lng.toDouble()
        return stadium
    }
}
```

[6] Try *that* in Java. Nothing sells Groovy to Java developers like working with XML.

[7] Parsing (actually, slurping) JSON is just as easy. The book source code for chapter 2 includes another example that accesses and parses JSON data.

THE GROOVY.SQL.SQL CLASS

Returning to the original problem, I want to store the stadium information in a database. I'm now going to take advantage of a very useful class in the Groovy library, `groovy.sql.Sql`. This class connects to a database and allows you to execute SQL against it. To begin the process, here's how the `Sql` class is instantiated:

```
Sql db = Sql.newInstance(
    'jdbc:mysql://localhost:3306/baseball',
    '...username...',
    '...password...',
    'com.mysql.jdbc.Driver'
)
```

The `Sql` class has a static `newInstance` method, whose arguments are the JDBC URL, the username and password, and the driver class. The result is a connection to the database. Next, I drop the stadium table if it already exists:

```
db.execute "drop table if exists stadium;"
```

The `execute` method takes a SQL string and runs it against the database. Here again, I'm taking advantage of the optional parentheses.

The next step is to create the table to hold the stadium information:

```
db.execute '''
    create table stadium(
        id int not null auto_increment,
        name varchar(200) not null,
        city varchar(200) not null,
        state char(2) not null,
        team char(3) not null,
        latitude double,
        longitude double,
        primary key(id)
    );
'''
```

The three single quotes represent a multiline string in Groovy. Three double quotes would be a multiline `GString`, which I could use for parameter substitution, but they're not needed in this particular case.

Now that the table has been constructed it's time to populate the table with stadium data:

```
Geocoder geo = new Geocoder()
stadiums.each { s ->
    geo.fillInLatLng s
    db.execute """
        insert into stadium(name, city, state, team, latitude, longitude)
        values(${s.name},${s.city},${s.state},
               ${s.team},${s.latitude},${s.longitude});
    """
}
```

After instantiating the geocoder I walk through each stadium in the collection, assigning each to the dummy variable `s`. For each one, after computing the latitude and longitude, I execute an insert statement contained within three double quotes, where I substitute the values I need from the stadium using the standard `${…}` notation.

All that remains is to do some kind of sanity check to make sure that the values received are reasonable. Here are some assert statements to do just that:

```
assert db.rows('select * from stadium').size() == stadiums.size()
db.eachRow('select latitude, longitude from stadium') { row ->
    assert row.latitude > 25 && row.latitude < 48
    assert row.longitude > -123 && row.longitude < -71
}
```

The first assert statement checks that the total number of rows in the table matches the number of stadiums in the collection. The next statement invokes the eachRow method on the connection, selecting just the latitude and longitude, and assigning the dummy variable row to each of the rows in the result set. The two contained assert statements verify that the latitudes are between 25 and 48 and that the longitudes are between -123 and -71.

THE SQL CLASS The groovy.sql.Sql class removes almost all the ceremony surrounding raw JDBC and adds convenience methods as well.

The complete script is shown in the next listing.

Listing 2.4 populate_stadium_data.groovy

```
package service

import groovy.sql.Sql

def stadiums = []                                  <-- Populate a list with Stadium instances
stadiums <<
    new Stadium(name:'Angel Stadium',city:'Anaheim',state:'CA',team:'ana')
...
stadiums <<
    new Stadium(name:'Nationals Park',city:'Washington',
    state:'DC',team:'was')

Sql db = Sql.newInstance(                          <-- Access database
    'jdbc:mysql://localhost:3306/baseball',
    '...username...',
    '...password...',
    'com.mysql.jdbc.Driver'
)

db.execute "drop table if exists stadium;"
db.execute '''                                     <-- Multiline string
    create table stadium(
        id int not null auto_increment,
        name varchar(200) not null,
        city varchar(200) not null,
        state char(2) not null,
        team char(3) not null,
        latitude double,
```

```
        longitude double,
        primary key(id)
    );
'''

Geocoder geo = new Geocoder()                    Insert results
stadiums.each { s ->                          <-- into DB
    geo.fillInLatLng s
    db.execute """
        insert into stadium(name,city,state,team,latitude,longitude)

     values(${s.name},${s.city},${s.state},${s.team},${s.latitude},${s.longit
     ude});
    """
}

assert db.rows('select * from stadium').size() == stadiums.size()   <-- Check
db.eachRow('select latitude,longitude from stadium') { row ->           results
    assert row.latitude > 25 && row.latitude < 48
    assert row.longitude > -123 && row.longitude < -71
}
```

This script collects all the latitude and longitude values for each MLB stadium, creates a database table to hold them, and populates the table. It only has to be run once, and the application can then use the table. In the process of reviewing the code I used a `Stadium` POGO, a list, a couple of `collect` methods with closures, an example that used the `URLEncoder` class from Java in a Groovy script, and database manipulation through the `groovy.sql.Sql` class.

The next step is to collect box score data from a site maintained by Major League Baseball, and generate XML information that can be sent to a view page.

2.3.2 Parsing XML

Major League Baseball continuously updates the results of baseball games online. The information is kept in XML format in links descending from http://gd2.mlb.com/components/game/mlb/.

On the site the games are arranged by date. Drilling down from the base URL requires links of the form `"year_${year}/month_${month}/day_${day}/"`, where the year is four digits, and the month and day are two digits each. The games for that date are listed as individual links. For example, figure 2.8 shows links for each game played on May 5, 2007.[8]

The link for each individual game has the form

```
gid_${year}_${month}_${day}_${away}mlb_${home}mlb_${num}
```

The `year`, `month`, and `day` values are as expected. The values for `away` and `home` are three-letter lowercase abbreviations for each team, and the value of `num` represents the game number that day (1 for the first game, 2 for the second game of a double

[8] By an astonishing coincidence, May 5 is my son's birthday.

Index of /components/game/mlb/year_2007/month_05/day_05

- Parent Directory
- batters/
- epg.xml
- gid_2007_05_05_bosmlb_minmlb_1/
- gid_2007_05_05_chamlb_anamlb_1/
- gid_2007_05_05_clemlb_balmlb_1/
- gid_2007_05_05_colmlb_cinmlb_1/
- gid_2007_05_05_detmlb_kcamlb_1/
- gid_2007_05_05_houmlb_slnmlb_1/
- gid_2007_05_05_lanmlb_atlmlb_1/
- gid_2007_05_05_nynmlb_arimlb_1/
- gid_2007_05_05_oakmlb_tbamlb_1/
- gid_2007_05_05_phimlb_sfnmlb_1/
- gid_2007_05_05_pitmlb_milmlb_1/
- gid_2007_05_05_sdnmlb_flomlb_1/
- gid_2007_05_05_seamlb_nyamlb_1/
- gid_2007_05_05_tormlb_texmlb_1/
- gid_2007_05_05_wasmlb_chnmlb_1/
- grid.json
- grid.xml
- master_scoreboard.json
- master_scoreboard.xml
- miniscoreboard.xml
- mobile_epg.xml
- multi_angle_epg.xml
- pitchers/
- pitching_staff/
- playertracker.xml
- scoreboard.xml
- uber_scoreboard.xml

Figure 2.8 Links to baseball games played on May 5, 2007

header). The links for each game contain a series of files, but the one I'm interested in is called boxscore.xml.

To retrieve the box score information I'll create a class called `GetGameData`. This class will have attributes for the base URL and the team abbreviations, as shown. The next listing shows a portion of this class.

Listing 2.5 A portion of `GetGameData`, showing the attributes and initialization

```
class GetGameData {
    def day
    def month
    def year

    String base = 'http://gd2.mlb.com/components/game/mlb/'
    Map stadiumMap = [:]

    Map abbrevs = [
        ana:'Los Angeles (A)', ari:'Arizona',     atl:'Atlanta',
        bal:'Baltimore',       bos:'Boston',      cha:'Chicago (A)',
        chn:'Chicago (N)',     cin:'Cincinnati',  cle:'Cleveland',
        col:'Colorado',        det:'Detroit',     flo:'Florida',
        hou:'Houston',         kca:'Kansas City', lan:'Los Angeles (N)',
```

Used as strings to download box scores

Map of team abbreviations to Stadium instances

```
        mil:'Milwaukee',        min:'Minnesota',    nya:'New York (A)',
        nyn:'New York (N)',     oak:'Oakland',      phi:'Philadelphia',
        pit:'Pittsburgh',       sdn:'San Diego',    sea:'Seattle',
        sfn:'San Francisco',    sln:'St. Louis',    tba:'Tampa Bay',
        tex:'Texas',            tor:'Toronto',      was:'Washington']

    GetGameData() {
        fillInStadiumMap()
    }
                                                    Read stadium data
    def fillInStadiumMap() {                   <--  from database
        Sql db = Sql.newInstance(
            'jdbc:h2:build/baseball',
            'org.h2.Driver'
        )

        db.eachRow("select * from stadium") { row ->
            Stadium stadium = new Stadium(
                name:row.name,
                team:row.team,
                latitude:row.latitude,
                longitude:row.longitude
            )

            stadiumMap[stadium.team] = stadium
        }
        db.close()
    }
```

The key-value pairs in the abbrevs map hold the three-letter abbreviations for each team and the city name, respectively.

The next step is to process the actual box scores. Here's some sample data, taken at random. The random date I've chosen is October 28, 2007.[9] The next listing shows the box score in XML form, truncated to show the typical elements without showing them all.

Listing 2.6 boxscore.xml: the box score from game 4 of the 2007 World Series

```
<boxscore game_id="2007/10/28/bosmlb-colmlb-1" game_pk="224026"
    home_sport_code="mlb" away_team_code="bos" home_team_code="col"
    away_id="111" home_id="115" away_fname="Boston Red Sox"
    home_fname="Colorado Rockies"
    away_sname="Boston" home_sname="Colorado" date="October 28, 2007"
    away_wins="5" away_loss="0" home_wins="0" home_loss="5" status_ind="F">
    <linescore away_team_runs="4" home_team_runs="3"
        away_team_hits="9" home_team_hits="7" away_team_errors="0"
        home_team_errors="0">
        <inning_line_score away="1" home="0" inning="1" />
        <inning_line_score away="0" home="0" inning="2" />
        ...
        <inning_line_score away="0" home="0" inning="9" />
    </linescore>
```

9 Just happens to be the day the Red Sox won the World Series in 2007.

```
    <pitching team_flag="away" out="27" h="7" r="3" er="3" bb="3"
        so="7" hr="2" bf="37" era="2.60">
        <pitcher id="452657" name="Lester" pos="P" out="17" bf="23"
            er="0" r="0" h="3" so="3" hr="0" bb="3" w="2" l="0" era="0.00"
            note="(W, 2-0)" />
        <pitcher id="434668" name="Delcarmen" pos="P" out="2" bf="4"
        er="1" r="1" h="2" so="1" hr="1" bb="0" w="0" l="0" era="9.00"
        note="(H, 2)" />
        ...
        <pitcher id="449097" name="Papelbon" pos="P" out="5" bf="5"
            er="0" r="0" h="0" so="1" hr="0" bb="0" w="0" l="0" era="0.00"
            note="(S, 4)" />
    </pitching>
    <batting team_flag="home" ab="34" r="3" h="7" d="2" t="0" hr="2"
        rbi="3" bb="3" po="27" da="18" so="7" avg=".216" lob="12">
        <batter id="430565" name="Matsui" pos="2B" bo="100" ab="4" po="3"
            r="0" bb="0" a="5" t="0" sf="0" h="1" e="0" d="1" hbp="0"
            so="1" hr="0" rbi="0" lob="2" fldg="1.000" avg=".286" />
        <batter id="466918" name="Corpas" pos="P" bo="101" ab="0" po="0"
            r="0" bb="0" a="1" t="0" sf="0" h="0" e="0" d="0" hbp="0"
            so="0" hr="0" rbi="0" lob="0" fldg="1.000" avg=".000" />
...
    </batting>
    <pitching team_flag="home" out="27" h="9" r="4" er="4" bb="1"
        so="4" hr="2" bf="34" era="6.91">
        <pitcher id="346871" name="Cook" pos="P" out="18" bf="23" er="3"
            r="3" h="6" so="2" hr="1" bb="0" w="0" l="2" era="4.50"
            note="(L, 0-2)" />
...
    </pitching>
    <batting team_flag="away" ab="33" r="4" h="9" d="2" t="0" hr="2"
        rbi="4" bb="1" po="27" da="8" so="4" avg=".322" lob="10">
        <batter id="453056" name="Ellsbury" pos="CF-LF" bo="100" ab="4"
            po="3" r="1" bb="0" a="0" t="0" sf="0" h="2" e="0" d="1"
            so="1" hr="0" rbi="0" lob="2" fldg="1.000" avg=".450" />
        <batter id="456030" name="Pedroia" pos="2B" bo="200" ab="4" po="1"
            r="0" bb="0" a="4" t="0" sf="0" h="0" e="0" d="0" hbp="0"
            so="0" hr="0" rbi="0" lob="2" fldg="1.000" avg=".227" />
...
    </batting>
...
</boxscore>
```

The root element is `<boxscore>`, which has several attributes. It has a child element called `<linescore>`, which shows the scoring in each inning. Then there are `<pitching>` and `<batting>` elements for the home team and away team, respectively.

This isn't a terribly complex XML file, but if you had to process it using Java the code would quickly get involved. Using Groovy, as shown previously, all you have to do is walk the tree.

Parsing this data uses the same approach as parsing the geocoded data in the last section. Here I need to assemble the URL based on the month, day, and year and then parse the box score file:

```
def url = base + "year_${year}/month_${month}/day_${day}/"
def game = "gid_${year}_${month}_${day}_${away}mlb_${home}mlb_${num}/
    boxscore.xml"
def boxscore = new XmlSlurper().parse("$url$game")
```

After parsing the file I can walk the tree to extract the team names and scores:

```
def awayName = boxscore.@away_fname
def awayScore = boxscore.linescore[0].@away_team_runs
def homeName = boxscore.@home_fname
def homeScore = boxscore.linescore[0].@home_team_runs
```

The dots represent child elements, as before, and this time the @ symbols imply attributes.

PARSING XML Dots traverse from parent elements to children, and @ signs represent attribute values.

XML, regular expressions, and the Groovy Truth

To do some slightly more interesting processing, consider determining the winning and losing pitchers. The XML contains that information in a `note` attribute of the `pitcher` element. I can process that using a regular expression, assuming it exists at all:

```
def pitchers = boxscore.pitching.pitcher
pitchers.each { p ->
    if (p.@note && p.@note =~ /W|L|S/) {
        println "  ${p.@name} ${p.@note}"
    }
}
```

First I select all the `pitcher` elements for both teams. Then I want to examine the `pitcher` elements to find out who won and lost and if anyone was assigned a save. In the XML this information is kept in a `note` annotation in the `pitcher` element, which may or may not exist.

In the `if` statement, therefore, I check to see if a `note` attribute is present. Here I'm using the "Groovy Truth," which means that non-null references evaluate to true. So do non-empty strings or collections, non-zero numbers, and, of course, the boolean literal `true`. If the `note` element is present, I then use the so-called "slashy" syntax to check to see if the note matches a regular expression: `p.@note =~ /W|L|S/`. If there's a match I print out the values.

GENERATING GAME RESULTS

Before I show the complete method I need one more section. For the Groovy Baseball application I'm not interested in console output. Rather, I want to assemble the game results into a format that can be processed in the view layer by JavaScript. That means I need to return an object that can be converted into XML (or JSON).

Here's a class called `GameResult` for that purpose:

```
class GameResult {
    String home
    String away
    String hScore
    String aScore
    Stadium stadium

    String toString() { "$home $hScore, $away $aScore" }
}
```

> **CLOSURE RETURN VALUES** The last expression in a closure is returned automatically.

This POGO is a simple wrapper for the home and away teams and the home and away scores, as well as for the stadium. The stadium is needed because it contains the latitude and longitude values I need for the Google Map. The following listing now shows the complete `getGame` method in the `GetGameData` class shown in listing 2.5.

Listing 2.7 The `getGame` method in `GetGameData.groovy`

```
def getGame(away, home, num) {
    println "${abbrevs[away]} at ${abbrevs[home]} on ${month}/${day}/
 ${year}"
    def url = base + "year_${year}/month_${month}/day_${day}/"
    def game = "gid_${year}_${month}_${day}_${away}mlb_${home}mlb_${num}/
 boxscore.xml"
    def boxscore = new XmlParser().parse("$url$game")                <- Parsing the XML data
    def awayName = boxscore.@away_fname                        <- Extract data
    def awayScore = boxscore.linescore[0].@away_team_runs
    def homeName = boxscore.@home_fname
    def homeScore = boxscore.linescore[0].@home_team_runs
    println "$awayName $awayScore, $homeName $homeScore (game $num)"
    GameResult result = new GameResult(home:homeName,          <- Create response object
        away:awayName,
        hScore:homeScore,
        aScore:awayScore,
        stadium:stadiumMap[home]                   <- Use home stadium
    )
    return result
}
```

The method uses an `XmlSlurper` to convert the XML box score into a DOM tree, extracts the needed information, and creates and returns an instance of the `GameResult` class.

There's one other method in the `GetGameData` class, which is the one used to parse the web page listing the games for that day. This is necessary because due to rain-outs and other postponements there's no way to know ahead of time which games will actually be played on a given day.

Parsing HTML is always a dicey proposition, especially because it may not be well-formed. There are third-partly libraries to do it,[10] but the mechanism shown here

[10] See, for example, the NekoHTML parser at http://nekohtml.sourceforge.net/.

works. It also demonstrates regular-expression mapping in Groovy. The getGames method from GetGameData is shown in the next listing.

Listing 2.8 The getGames method from GetGameData

```
def getGames() {
    def gameResults = []
    println "Games for ${month}/${day}/${year}"
    String url = base + "year_$year/month_$month/day_$day/"
    String gamePage = url.toURL().text
    def pattern =
        /\"gid_${year}_${month}_${day}_(\w*)mlb_(\w*)mlb_(\d)/

    Matcher m = gamePage =~ pattern          <-- Using the Matcher class from Java
    if (m) {
        m.count.times { line ->
            String away = m[line][1]     |  Extracted from
            String home = m[line][2]     |  the Matcher
            String num = m[line][3]      |
            try {
                GameResult gr = this.getGame(away,home,num)
                gameResults << gr
            } catch (Exception e) {
                println "${abbrevs[away]} at ${abbrevs[home]} not started
 yet"
            }
        }
    }
    return gameResults
}
```

The =~ method in Groovy returns an instance of java.util.regex.Matcher. The parentheses in the regular expression are groups, which let me extract the away team abbreviation, the home team abbreviation, and the game number from the URL. I use those to call the getGames method from listing 2.7 and put the results into a collection of GameResult instances.

TESTING

All that's left is to test the complete GetGameData class. A JUnit test to do so is shown in the next listing.

Listing 2.9 GetGameDataTests.groovy: a JUnit 4 test case

```
class GetGameDataTest {
    GetGameData ggd = new GetGameData(month:10,day:28,year:2007)

    @Test
    void testFillInStadiumMap() {
        assert 0 == ggd.stadiumMap.size()          <-- Before and after
        ggd.fillInStadiumMap()                         populating
        def stadiums = ggd.stadiumMap.values()         stadium map
        assert 30 == ggd.stadiumMap.size()         <--
        stadiums.each { Stadium stadium ->
            assert stadium.latitude > 25 && stadium.latitude < 48
```

```
            assert stadium.longitude > -123 && stadium.longitude < -71
        }
    }

    @Test
    void testGetGame() {                                          Check the World
        GameResult gr = ggd.getGame 'bos','col','1'          <--  Series game
        assert 'Boston Red Sox' == gr.away
        assert 'Colorado Rockies' == gr.home
        assert 4 == gr.aScore.toInteger()
        assert 3 == gr.hScore.toInteger()
    }
}
```

This is a standard JUnit 4 test case. I have much more to say about Groovy testing capabilities in chapter 6 on testing, but here's a simple example. There's nothing inherently Groovy about this class except that (1) I used the map-based constructor to instantiate the fixture, (2) optional parentheses were left out wherever possible, and (3) no explicit `public` or `private` keywords were needed. Otherwise, this is just a regular test case, and it works as usual.

What have I discussed in this section?

- Groovy has a convenient syntax for maps.
- XML parsing and extracting data are easy, as in the previous section.
- Groovy has a slashy syntax for regular expressions.
- Groovy classes work with JUnit tests.

There's one final piece of the puzzle needed, which is the driver used to call the system for each date. I use a "groovlet" for this purpose in the next section.

2.3.3 HTML builders and groovlets

The classes used so far access XML box score information and convert it into a series of game result objects. For the view layer, however, I need objects in a form that can be processed by JavaScript. There are several ways to accomplish this, but one of them is to use an XML builder to write out the information in XML form.[11]

GENERATING XML

The standard Groovy library includes a class called `groovy.xml.MarkupBuilder`,[12] which is one of several builders (much like the `SwingBuilder` shown at the beginning of this chapter) in the standard library. Each of the builders intercepts method calls that don't exist (so-called *pretended* methods) and constructs nodes out of them to make a tree structure. The tree is then exported appropriately for that kind of builder.

This is actually easier to see than to explain. Consider the `GameResult` class from the previous section, which held the home and away team names and scores and a reference to a `Stadium` object. Here's the syntax for creating XML out of that object:

---

[11] The data could just as easily be written in JSON format. Other JSON examples are used throughout the book.

[12] I would bet that if this class were created today, it would be called `XmlBuilder` instead.

```
MarkupBuilder builder = new MarkupBuilder()
builder.games {
    results.each { g ->
        game(
            outcome:"$g.away $g.aScore, $g.home $g.hScore",
            lat:g.stadium.latitude,
            lng:g.stadium.longitude
        )
    }
}
```

After instantiating the MarkupBuilder and calling the reference builder, the second line invokes the games method on it. It may not look like a method, but recall that in Groovy, if a closure is the last argument to a method it can be placed outside the parentheses, and here I'm using optional parentheses. Of course, there's no method called games in MarkupBuilder. That makes it a pretended method, and the builder intercepts that method call and creates a node out of it. In a MarkupBuilder that means it will ultimately create an XML element called games. The closure syntax implies that the next elements will be child elements of games.

Inside the closure the code iterates over each contained result, assigning it to the dummy variable g. For each GameResult g, the builder creates an element called game. The parentheses on game imply that game will contain attributes. In this case, each game has an outcome, a lat, and a lng.

Here's the output of the MarkupBuilder:

```
<games>
  <game outcome='Boston Red Sox 4, Colorado Rockies 3'
    lat='39.7564956' lng='-104.9940163' />
</games>
```

If there had been a dozen games that day there would a <game> element for each one of them. The bottom line is that in Groovy, generating XML is about as easy as parsing it.

SERVER-SIDE PROCESSING WITH GROOVLETS

To drive the whole system I need a server-side component that receives the needed date and calls the GetGameData class to retrieve the games, which are then returned in XML form. Groovy has a component known as a *groovlet* to make that all easy.

A groovlet is a script that is executed by a class called groovy.servlet.GroovyServlet. This class is part of the Groovy standard library. Like any servlet, it needs to be declared in the web.xml deployment descriptor for a web application and mapped to a particular URL pattern. In this case I chose the pattern *.groovy. Here's the excerpt from the deployment descriptor:

```
<servlet>
    <servlet-name>GroovyServlet</servlet-name>
    <servlet-class>groovy.servlet.GroovyServlet</servlet-class>
</servlet>
```

```
<servlet-mapping>
    <servlet-name>GroovyServlet</servlet-name>
    <url-pattern>*.groovy</url-pattern>
</servlet-mapping>
```

The Groovy Baseball application will therefore send all URLs ending in .groovy through the `GroovyServlet`, which will execute them. Groovlets executed this way are deployed as source code rather than as compiled classes under WEB-INF.[13] Groovlets also contain a set of implicit objects representing the request, response, input parameters, and more.

The following listing contains the complete content of the groovlet that drives the Groovy Baseball system.

Listing 2.10 `GameServlet.groovy`: a groovlet for Groovy Baseball

```
import beans.GameResult;
import beans.Stadium;
import service.GetGameData;

response.contentType = 'text/xml'              // Set the content type of the response
def month = params.month                        // Extract input parameters
def day = params.day
def year = params.year

m = month.toInteger() < 10 ? '0' + month : month
d = day.toInteger() < 10 ? '0' + day : day
y = year.toInteger() + ''

ggd = new GetGameData(month:m,day:d,year:y)    // Retrieve games for that date
results = ggd.games

html.games {                                    // Use a builder to generate XML
    results.each { g ->
        game(
            outcome:"$g.away $g.aScore, $g.home $g.hScore",
            lat:g.stadium.latitude,
            lng:g.stadium.longitude
        )
    }
}
```

The groovlet can set response headers, here setting the output to XML. Input parameters populate a map of strings called `params`, which can be accessed in the usual way. The URL requires two-digit days and two-digit months, so a zero is prepended when necessary. After retrieving the games for that date the output is generated using the implicit `MarkupBuilder`. There's no need to instantiate a `MarkupBuilder` in this case, because groovlets already contain one, called `html`.

The groovlet is called from a regular web page, using a URL of the form http://.../groovybaseball/GroovyService.groovy?month=10&day=28&year=2007. The XML data is written to the output stream, which can then be processed by JavaScript.

[13] The details are discussed in chapter 10 on web applications.

Lessons learned (Groovy Baseball)

1. POGOs have private attributes and public methods by default. Public getters and setters are auto-generated for each attribute.
2. POGOs include a map-based constructor that can be used to set any or all of the attributes in any combination.
3. Closures and methods in Groovy return their last evaluated expressions automatically.
4. The `XmlSlurper` class makes parsing XML simple and returns the root of the resulting DOM tree. Values can be extracted by walking the tree.
5. The `MarkupBuilder` class produces XML.
6. The `groovy.sql.Sql` class is a simple façade for dealing with relational databases.
7. Groovlets are simple Groovy scripts that respond to HTTP requests.
8. All Groovy exceptions are unchecked.

The rest of the system is just HTML and JavaScript, so it's beyond the scope of a Groovy discussion. The complete source code for the application is contained in the GitHub repository for the book.

2.4 Summary

This chapter is a tutorial on Groovy for Java developers, using example applications rather than a series of features. What's remarkable is how much Groovy simplifies the code. POGOs are a minimal yet more flexible version of POJOs. The `groovy.sql.Sql` class makes JDBC practical for reasonably small applications. The Groovy JDK adds many convenience methods, like `toURL` and `getText`, which make existing Java classes easier to use. The combination of maps, closures, and the `join` method makes it simple to build URLs for web services. Finally, the difference between working with XML in Java and working with XML in Groovy is staggering. Whenever I have to work with XML in any form I always look for a way to add a Groovy module to handle the details.

In the next chapter we'll examine mechanisms to integrate Java and Groovy together in more detail.

3 Code-level integration

This chapter covers

- Calling Groovy scripts from Java using JSR 223
- Calling Groovy scripts from Java using Groovy library classes

In chapter 1 I reviewed many of Java's arguable weaknesses and drawbacks and suggested ways that Groovy might help ameliorate them. Because that chapter was intended to be introductory, I only suggested how Groovy can help, without showing a lot of code examples.

This chapter begins an examination of Java and Groovy integration in detail. In this chapter I'll start using Groovy and Java together in fundamental ways, without worrying about frameworks or addressing any particular use case. A guide to the techniques discussed in this chapter is shown in figure 3.1.

3.1 Integrating Java with other languages

Combining Java with other languages has always been a challenge. Java historically hasn't played well with others.[1] The only API designed from the beginning for Java

---

[1] Of course, this is true of most languages.

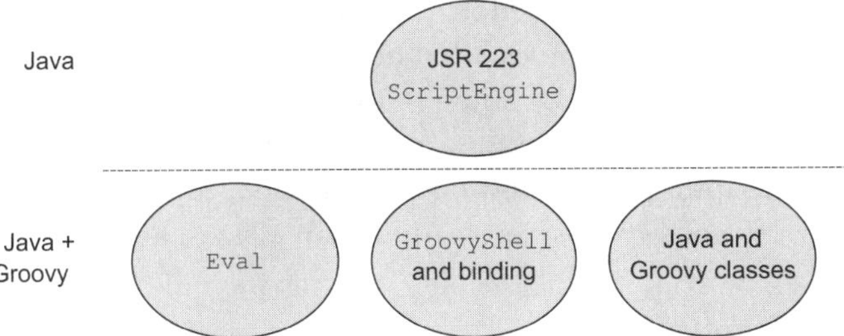

Figure 3.1 Guide to integration features. Groovy can be accessed with Java classes alone using the JSR 223 script engine. If you are willing to add some Groovy library classes to Java, the `Eval`, `GroovyShell`, and `Binding` classes make working with scripts easy. The best way to combine Groovy and Java is using classes for both languages.

to call functions written in other languages is JNI, the Java Native Interface, which is awkward to use even in the best of circumstances.[2] The past few years, however, have seen the rise of entire families of languages that compile directly to bytecodes that run on the JVM, from Groovy to Scala to Clojure, as well as bridge languages like Jython or JRuby that allow you to run code written in Python or Ruby on the JVM. From the point of view of these "alternative" JVM-based languages, Java's real contribution isn't the language itself, but rather the virtual machine and the associated Java libraries. JVM-based languages take advantage of the Java infrastructure and try to handle any Java-specific drawbacks.

> **JVM** Ultimately, Java's biggest contribution isn't the language; it's the virtual machine.

Whenever a new capability is integrated into Java's basic infrastructure, a Java Specification Request (JSR) is created to provide a standard implementation mechanism. In the integration case, the JSR in question is JSR 223, Scripting for the Java Platform (http://jcp.org/en/jsr/detail?id=223). The purpose of the JSR is to allow other (presumably scripting) languages to be invoked from Java. Although most of this book will assume that you're mixing Java and Groovy on a class-by-class basis, for the sake of completeness I'll review here how to call a Groovy script from Java, both using the JSR technique and using library classes provided by Groovy for that purpose.

Groovy is much closer to Java than the script integration story suggests, however. As I'll demonstrate in the section on calling Java from Groovy rather than the other way around, virtually every Groovy program of any size uses Java already. Groovy code can instantiate a Java class, call a method Groovy added to it (the so-called

[2] Once, back in the late 1990s, I had to build a Java Swing user interface in front of an engineering system written in Fortran. I used JNI to go from Java to C and then from C to Fortran. The results were like putting a notch into a wooden beam and saying, "I want you to break right here."

Groovy JDK highlighted in chapter 4, section 4.3), and call additional Java methods on the result. The question then becomes, what does Groovy bring to Java? How can you simplify your development tasks by adding Groovy to Java systems? I'll address that question in the rest of the chapter (and, indeed, in the rest of the book). Let's start, though, with the scripting story. How do you combine Java and Groovy in the same system when Groovy consists of scripts rather than classes, and you want to isolate any Java integration code?

3.2 Executing Groovy scripts from Java

The assumption in the first couple of sections of this chapter is that you've written or acquired some Groovy scripts and wish to use them in your Java system in a way that's minimally invasive. Perhaps you're using the scripts to implement business logic in Groovy because it changes so frequently (a technique referred to as Liquid Heart by Dierk Koenig, lead author of *Groovy in Action* [Manning, 2007]). Perhaps you're replacing Perl scripts with Groovy because anything you can do in Perl you can do in Groovy, with the added bonus that you can integrate with existing Java systems. Perhaps you're following one of the original intents of the JSR, which is to use a scripting language to generate user interfaces while letting Java handle the back-end functionality. In any case, I want to demonstrate how to invoke those scripts from a Java system as easily as possible.

One of the interesting features of Groovy is that, unlike in Java, you don't have to put all Groovy code into a class. You can just put all your Groovy code into a file called practically anything you like, as long as the file extension is .groovy, and then you can execute the scripts with the `groovy` command. One possible sweet spot for Groovy is to write short, simple programs without the clutter of creating a class with a `main` method in it, and here I'll show how to incorporate scripts like that into a Java application.

In keeping with the standard I'll start with a technique based on JSR 223, Scripting for the Java Platform, which allows you to invoke Groovy purely from Java library calls. Then I'll show that if you use a couple of classes from the Groovy API you can simplify the integration. Finally, I'll show that if you can change from scripts to classes for your Groovy code, nearly all the complexity can be eliminated.

Incidentally, assuming any Groovy scripts are compiled, at runtime treat the combined application as though it's all Java. All the integration strategies I plan to discuss in this chapter involve deciding where and how to use Groovy to make your life easier. Once you have the combined system, though, the deployment story is really simple, as the sidebar demonstrates.

Groovy and Java together at runtime

At *runtime*, compiled Groovy and compiled Java both result in bytecodes for the JVM. To execute code that combines them, all that's necessary is to add a single JAR file to the system. Compiling and testing your code requires the Groovy compiler and libraries, but at runtime all you need is one JAR.

(continued)

That JAR comes with your Groovy distribution in the embeddable subdirectory. Suppose, for example, your Groovy installation is version 2.1.5. Then on your disk in the Groovy installation directory you have the structure shown in the following figure, and the JAR file you need is groovy-all-2.1.5.jar.

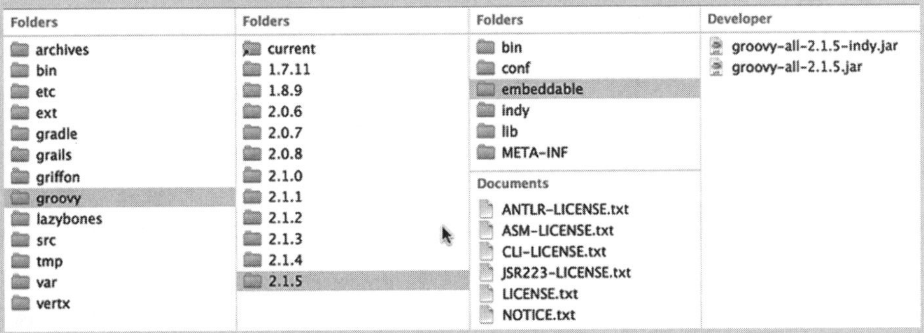

Add the groovy-all JAR to your system, and you can run it with the `java` command.

In the rest of the text, I'll refer to this JAR file as the "groovy-all" JAR. If this JAR is added to your classpath you can execute combined Groovy and Java applications with the standard `java` command. If you add a Groovy module to a web application, add the groovy-all JAR to the WEB-INF//lib directory and everything will work normally.

Here's a minimal demonstration just to prove the point. Consider the "Hello, World!" application written in Groovy, which, unlike in Java, is a one-liner:

```
println 'Hello, Groovy!'
```

If I saved this into a file called hello_world.groovy I could execute the script using the `groovy` command, which would compile it and run it all in one process. To run it using the `java` command, however, first I have to compile it with `groovyc` and then execute the resulting bytecodes, making sure the groovy-all JAR is in the classpath. The two-step process is shown. Note that the `java` command should be all on one line:

```
> groovyc hello_world.groovy
> java -cp
    .:$GROOVY_HOME/embeddable/groovy-all-2.1.5.jar
    hello_world
→ Hello, Groovy!
```

I needed the `groovyc` command in order to compile the script, but I was able to execute it using plain old `java` (as long as the groovy-all JAR was in the execution classpath).

At the API level, to call a Groovy script from Java you have a few alternatives. I'll first show the "hardest" way possible, using the JSR-223 API. The API associated with JSR 223 is designed to allow Java programs to invoke scripts written in other languages.

I'm calling this "the hard way" because it doesn't take advantage of anything provided by Groovy other than the script itself. I'll use the layers of indirection provided by the Java API, which separates the Groovy code from the Java code that invokes it. Later you'll start mixing Java and Groovy by combining classes and methods, and you'll find that's much easier. Still, it's worth seeing how to use the JSR, especially because, after all, it is the standard. Also, even if it's technically the hard way, it's really not all that hard.

3.2.1 Using JSR223 scripting for the Java Platform API

Built into Java SE 6 and above, the API for JSR 223, Scripting for the Java Platform, is a standard mechanism you can use to call scripts written in other languages. The advantage to this approach is that it avoids introducing anything specific to Groovy into the calling Java program. If you already have Groovy scripts and you just want to call them from inside Java, this is a good way to go.

JSR 223 The JSR allows you to call Groovy scripts using purely Java classes.

The JSR defines an API based on a `javax.script.ScriptEngine` instance. As is common with many Java libraries, the API also includes a factory interface, in this case called `javax.script.ScriptEngineFactory`, for retrieving `ScriptEngine` instances. The API also specifies a `javax.script.ScriptEngineManager` class, which retrieves metadata about the available `ScriptEngineFactory` instances.

In many Java APIs you use a factory to acquire the object you need. For example, parsing XML with a SAX parser is done by first getting an instance of the `SAXParserFactory` and then using it to acquire a new SAX parser. The same is true for DOM builders, XSLT transformation engines, and many others. In each case, if you want to use a particular implementation other than the built-in default, you need to specify an environment variable, a method argument, or some other way of letting Java know you're planning to do something different. You also need to make the alternative implementation available in your classpath.

The first issue, therefore, is to determine whether the script engine used for Groovy code is available by default and, if not, how to acquire it. Using the Java 7 JDK from Oracle I can determine which factories are already embedded. The following listing retrieves all the available factories from the manager and prints some of their properties.

Listing 3.1 Finding all the available script engine factories

```
public class ScriptEngineFactories {
    private static Logger log =                                   // A standard logger
        Logger.getLogger(ScriptEngineFactories.class.getName());

    public static void main(String[] args) {
        List<ScriptEngineFactory> factories =
            new ScriptEngineManager().getEngineFactories();       // Looping over the available factories
        for (ScriptEngineFactory factory : factories) {
```

```
            log.info("lang name: " + factory.getLanguageName());
            log.info("engine name: " + factory.getEngineName());
            log.info(factory.getNames().toString());
        }
    }
}
```

With a nod toward better practices than simply using `System.out.println` statements, I set up a simple logger. Then I retrieved all the available factories from the manager and printed the language name and engine name. Finally, I printed all the available names for each factory, which shows all the available aliases that can be used to retrieve them.

The results are shown here, truncated for readability:

```
INFO: lang name: ECMAScript
INFO: lang version: 1.8
INFO: engine version: 1.7 release 3 PRERELEASE
INFO: engine name: Mozilla Rhino
INFO: [js, rhino, JavaScript, javascript, ECMAScript, ecmascript]
```

The output shows that by default there's only one factory available, and its purpose is to execute JavaScript (or, more formally, ECMAScript). This factory can be retrieved using any of the names on the last line, but there's only one factory available, and it has nothing to do with Groovy.

Fortunately, making a Groovy script engine factory available is easy. One of the features of the `ScriptEngineManager` class is that it detects new factories using the same extension mechanism used for JAR files. In other words, all you have to do is to add the Groovy libraries to your classpath via the groovy-all JAR. Once you do that, the same program produces the additional output shown here:

```
INFO: lang name: Groovy
INFO: lang version: 2.1.3
INFO: engine version: 2.0
INFO: engine name: Groovy Scripting Engine
INFO: [groovy, Groovy]
```

In this case the script engine reports that the Groovy language version is 2.1.3 and the engine version is 2.0.[3]

In this particular API, even though a factory is now available, you don't need to use it to acquire the script engine. Instead, the `ScriptEngineManager` class has a method to retrieve the factory by supplying its name (either `groovy` or `Groovy`, as shown in the previous output) in the form of a `String`. From the `ScriptEngine` I can then execute Groovy scripts using the script engine's `eval` method. The process is illustrated in figure 3.2.

The next listing demonstrates the API in action in a simple "Hello, World!" Groovy script.

[3] I did use the Groovy 2.1.5 compiler, but the script engine still reports 2.1.3. It doesn't affect the results, though.

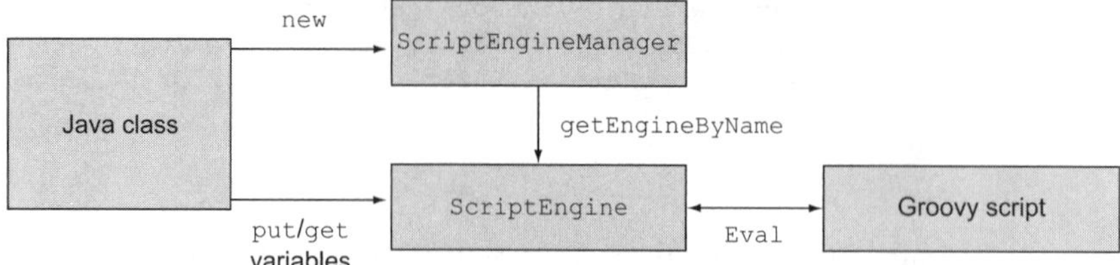

Figure 3.2 Using the JSR 223 `ScriptEngine` to invoke a Groovy script. Java creates a `ScriptEngineManager`, which then yields a `ScriptEngine`. After supplying parameters to the engine, its `eval` method is invoked to execute a Groovy script.

Listing 3.2 Using the `ScriptEngine` to execute a simple Groovy script

```
public class ExecuteGroovyFromJSR223 {
    public static void main(String[] args) {
        ScriptEngine engine =
            new ScriptEngineManager().getEngineByName("groovy");      Retrieve script engine
        try {
            engine.eval("println 'Hello, Groovy!'");                  Evaluate script code
            engine.eval(new FileReader("src/hello_world.groovy"));    Execute external script
        } catch (ScriptException e) {
            e.printStackTrace();
        } catch (FileNotFoundException e) {
            e.printStackTrace();
        }
    }
}
```

I retrieve the Groovy script engine by calling the `getEngineByName` method. I then use two different overloads of the `eval` method: one that takes a `String` argument and one that takes an implementation of the `java.io.Reader` interface. In the first case, the supplied string needs to be the actual scripting code. For the reader, though, I use a `FileReader` wrapped around the "Hello, Groovy!" script. The output is what you would expect in each case.

SUPPLYING PARAMETERS TO A GROOVY SCRIPT

What if the Groovy script took input parameters and returned data? In the Groovy scripting world this is handled through a *binding*. When I discuss the `GroovyShell` in the next section I'll show that there's actually a class in the Groovy API called `Binding`, but here I'll do the binding implicitly through the Java API.

A binding is a collection of variables at a scope that makes them visible inside a script. In the JSR 223 API, the `ScriptEngine` class itself acts as a binding. It has both a `put` and a `get` method that can be used to add variables to scripts and retrieve the results from them.

To illustrate this, let's do something a bit less trivial and possibly more practical. Instead of doing a simple "Hello, World!" script, consider the Google geocoder, in its version 2 form.

> **GROOVY SWEET SPOT** Groovy scripts are an easy way to experiment with new libraries.

A geocoder is an application that converts addresses to latitude/longitude pairs. Google has had a publicly available geocoder for years. In this section I'll use version 2, which requires a key (available through a free registration), but which gives me the chance to show some interesting Groovy features. When I discuss XML processing later in this chapter I'll use version 3 of the geocoder instead. That version no longer requires a key, but it doesn't make the results available in the same comma-separated form I'll use here.

The documentation for version 2 of the Google geocoder can be found at http://mng.bz/Pg8S. Version 2 is currently deprecated but still works. I'm using it here because it's familiar from the previous chapter, so you can focus on the input/output parts of the script, and because it also lets me demonstrate multiple return values.[4]

In order to use the geocoder, the basic idea is to transmit an address as a parameter in an HTTP `GET` request and process the results. As shown in chapter 2, using the Google geocoder takes the following steps:

1. Convert a list containing the street, city, and state into a URL-encoded string whose values are separated by ",".
2. Convert a map with the key's address and sensor into a query string.
3. Transmit the resulting URL to the Google geocoder.
4. Parse the results into the desired values.

The first step uses the `collect` method from Groovy, which takes a closure as an argument, applies the closure to each element of a collection, and returns a new collection containing the results. I take the resulting collection and joined each of its elements into a single string, using "," as a separator:

```
String address = [street,city,state].collect {
    URLEncoder.encode(it,'UTF-8')
}.join(',')
```

> **UNDECLARED VARIABLES** The street, city, and state are not declared in the script. This adds them to the binding, making them available to the caller.

To build a query string I add all the required parameters to a map called `params`. I'm also requesting comma-separated values for the output, which is not available in the version 3 geocoder:

```
def params = [q:address, sensor:false, output:'csv', key:'ABQIAAAAaUT...']
```

The value of `sensor` should be `true` if this request is coming from a GPS-enabled device and `false` otherwise. The `key` is determined at registration (version 3 doesn't

---

[4] Another reason to show the version 2 geocoder is because the Google Maps API for Android still uses it.

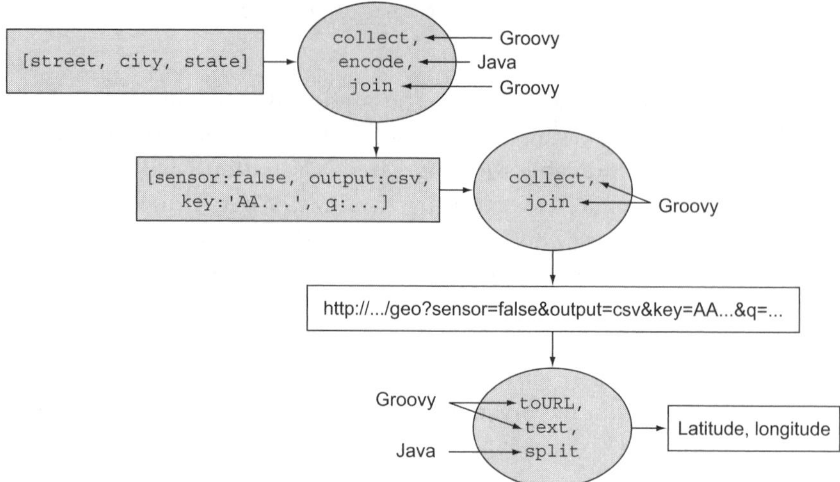

Figure 3.3 The Groovy script for accessing the Google V2 geocoder

require a key). The `output` is here set to CSV, so that the result is a string of comma-separated values composed of the response code (hopefully 200), the magnification level, and the latitude and longitude.

To convert the map into a query string, the `collect` method is used again. On a map, if a `collect` is applied with a two-argument closure, the method automatically separates the keys from the values. What I want here is to replace expressions like `key:value` with strings like `key=value`. The complete URL is then found by concatenating the query string to the base URL:

```
String url = base + params.collect { k,v -> "$k=$v" }.join('&')
```

Finally, I take advantage of the Groovy JDK. In the Groovy JDK the `String` class contains a method called `toURL`, which converts the `String` into an instance of `java.net.URL`. The `URL` class in the Groovy JDK includes a `getText` method, which I can invoke as a `text` property.

PROPERTY ACCESS In Groovy, the standard idiom is to access a property, which is automatically converted to a getter or setter method.

The code to retrieve the desired CSV string is

```
url.toURL().text
```

Now I can use the `split` method on String, which divides the string at the commas and returns a list containing the elements. I can then take advantage of Groovy's cool multivalued return capability to assign each value to an output variable.

The complete script is shown next and displayed graphically in figure 3.3:

```
String address = [street,city,state].collect {
    URLEncoder.encode(it,'UTF-8')
}.join(',+')
```

```
def params = [q:address,sensor:false,output:'csv',key:'ABQIAAAAaUT...']
String base = 'http://maps.google.com/maps/geo?'
String url = base + params.collect { k,v -> "$k=$v" }.join('&')
(code,level,lat,lng) = url.toURL().text.split(',')
```

Running this script requires me to supply the street, city, and state information, and then retrieve the output latitude and longitude. I want to use Java to supply the input values and process the output, but first I'll show a typical result, which can then be used as a test case. To avoid being too U.S.-centric I'll use the address for the Royal Observatory in Greenwich, England. That makes the values for `street`, `city`, and `state` "Blackheath Avenue," "Greenwich," and "UK," respectively.[5] Executing the script results in the output

```
(code,level,lat,lng) = (200,6,51.4752654,0.0014324)
```

The Royal Observatory was originally the arbitrarily chosen location of the prime meridian, so the value of the longitude should be pretty close to zero, and it is. The input address isn't as precise as it might be, and the observatory address doesn't define the actual prime meridian any more, but the results are pretty impressive anyway. The resulting test case as part of a JUnit 4 test is shown in the next listing.

Listing 3.3 A JUnit test case to check the JSR 223 script engine results

```
@Test
public void testLatLngJSR223() {
    ScriptEngine engine = new
     ScriptEngineManager().getEngineByName("groovy");
    engine.put("street", "Blackheath Avenue");         // Set binding variables
    engine.put("city", "Greenwich");
    engine.put("state", "UK");
    try {
        engine.eval(new FileReader("src/geocode.groovy"));      // Invoke Groovy script from Java
    } catch (ScriptException e) {
        e.printStackTrace();
    } catch (FileNotFoundException e) {
        e.printStackTrace();
    }
    assertEquals(51.4752654,
        Double.parseDouble((String) engine.get("lat")),0.01);   // Retrieve results from binding
    assertEquals(0.0014342,
        Double.parseDouble((String) engine.get("lng")),0.01);
```

The result is the same as running the Groovy script by itself using Groovy. Setting the values of the input variables is trivial. The output variables need to be cast to the `String` type and then converted to `doubles`, but again the process is straightforward. If your goal is to execute an external Groovy script from Java without introducing any Groovy dependencies at all (other than adding the groovy-all JAR to your classpath), this mechanism works just fine.

---

[5] Clearly the word "state" is to be interpreted broadly. Supply a country name for state, and it works all over the world.

In the next section I want to relax that requirement. If you're willing to use some classes from the Groovy standard library, life gets simpler.

3.2.2 Working with the Groovy Eval class

There are two special classes in the Groovy library, `groovy.util.Eval` and `groovy.lang.GroovyShell`, specifically designed for executing scripts. In this section I'll show examples using the `Eval` class, and in the next section I'll show `GroovyShell`. In each case, the goal is still to invoke external Groovy scripts from Java.

The `Eval` class is a utility class (all its methods are static) for executing operations that take none, one, two, or three parameters. The relevant methods are shown in table 3.1.

Table 3.1 Static methods in `groovy.util.Eval` for executing Groovy from Java

`Eval.me`	Overloaded to take a `String` expression or an expression with a `String` symbol and an `Object`
`Eval.x`	One argument: the value of `x`
`Eval.xy`	Two arguments, `x` and `y`
`Eval.xyz`	Three arguments, `x`, `y`, and `z`

To demonstrate the methods I'll add additional tests to the JUnit test case. The test is written in Java, so I'll automatically call Groovy from Java.

The following listing shows four tests, one for each of the static methods in the `Eval` class.

Listing 3.4 JUnit 4 test class verifying results of calling `Eval` methods from Java

```
public class ScriptingTests {
    @Test
    public void testEvalNoParams() {
        String result = (String) Eval.me("'abc' - 'b'");      // Zero-argument me method
        assertEquals("ac",result);
    }

    @Test
    public void testEvalOneParam() {
        String result = (String) Eval.x("a", "'abc' - x");    // One-argument x method
        assertEquals("bc",result);
    }

    @Test
    public void testEvalTwoParams() {
        String result = (String) Eval.xy("a", "b", "'abc' - x - y");   // Two-argument xy method
        assertEquals("c",result);
    }

    @Test
    public void testEvalThreeParams() {
        String result =
            (String) Eval.xyz("a", "b", "d", "'abc' - x - y + z");    // Three-argument xyz method
```

```
        assertEquals("cd",result);
    }
}
```

In each test the Groovy script to be evaluated is included as a string. Unlike the `ScriptEngine` there's no overload for instances of `Reader`, so to execute a script in a separate file would require reading the file into a string. The methods also assume that the input variables are called `x`, `y`, and `z`, which might be asking too much. Still, it's interesting that this mechanism exists at all.

In addition to illustrating the mechanics of calling Groovy scripts from Java, the tests also demonstrate operator overloading in the `String` class. The minus operator in Groovy corresponds to the `minus` method in `String`. Its implementation to remove the first instance of its argument from the given string is used with strings to remove instances of substrings. In Groovy, strings can be contained within either single or double quotes. Single-quoted strings are regular Java strings, and double-quoted strings are parameterized strings, diplomatically called Groovy strings, but formally called, unfortunately, `GStrings`.[6]

The process of using `Eval` from Java is shown in figure 3.4.

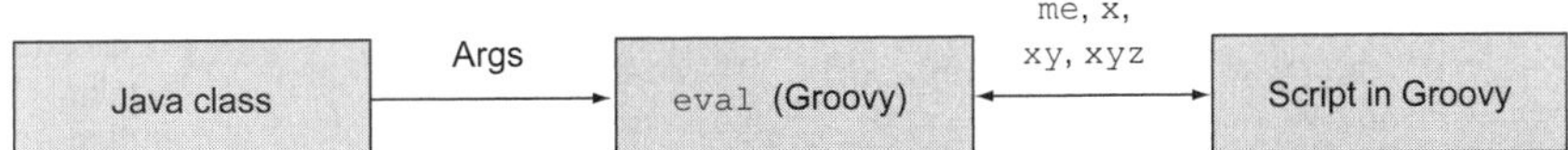

Figure 3.4 Java calls the `me`, `x`, `xy`, or `xyz` method in the Groovy `Eval` class to execute a script.

The `Eval` class is convenient and simple, but often it's too simple. It rests on a more powerful foundation, the `GroovyShell` class, which I'll discuss next.

3.2.3 Working with the GroovyShell class

The `GroovyShell` class is used for scripts that aren't restricted to the special cases described in the previous section on `Eval`. The class `groovy.lang.GroovyShell` can be used to execute scripts, particularly when combined with a `Binding`.

Unlike `Eval`, the `GroovyShell` class does not contain only static methods. It needs to be instantiated before invoking its `evaluate` method. As a simple example, consider adding the following test to the previous set of test cases:

```
@Test
public void testEvaluateString() {
    GroovyShell shell = new GroovyShell();
```

[6] To make matters worse, simple parameters are injected into `GStrings` using a dollar sign. This has led to far too many "insert a $ into a GString" jokes. To me, this is a clear demonstration that we don't have enough women in computer science. Don't you think that if there had been one woman on the team at the time, she could have said, "Hey, that's a funny joke, but let's not build it into the standard library that's going to be used by everybody forever?" After all, it's hard enough to get a language named Groovy taken seriously by the Fortune 500 without going there, too. For my part, I call them Groovy strings, which is what the class should have been called all along. It is a funny joke, though—for about 10 minutes.

```
    Object result = shell.evaluate("3+4");
    assertEquals(7, result);
}
```

The evaluate method is heavily overloaded. The version I'm using here takes a string representing the script to be evaluated. Other overloads take a java.io.File or a java.io.Reader instance, with various additional arguments. There are overloads that take a java.io.InputStream as well, but they're deprecated due to possible encoding issues.

So far, using the GroovyShell looks a lot like using the ScriptEngine class, though you can instantiate it directly in this case. To deal with input and output variables, however, the GroovyShell uses the groovy.lang.Binding class to provide a map of input and output variables.

The next listing shows the Binding and GroovyShell classes in action. It's another test to add to the growing JUnit 4 test case.

Listing 3.5 Using GroovyShell and Binding to invoke the Google geocoder

```
@Test
public void testLatLng() {
    Binding binding = new Binding();
    binding.setVariable("street", "Blackheath Avenue");
    binding.setVariable("city", "Greenwich");
    binding.setVariable("state", "UK");
    GroovyShell shell = new GroovyShell(binding);
    try {
        shell.evaluate(new File("src/geocode.groovy"));
        assertEquals(51.475,
            Double.parseDouble(
                (String) binding.getVariable("lat")),0.001);
        assertEquals(0.00143,
            Double.parseDouble(
                (String) binding.getVariable("lng")),0.001);
    } catch (CompilationFailedException e) {
        e.printStackTrace();
    } catch (IOException e) {
        e.printStackTrace();
    }
}
```

Create and populate the binding

Use binding in GroovyShell

Execute script using binding

Retrieve output variables

Passing parameters into the script is easy enough using the setVariable method on the Binding. The binding is then used as an argument to the GroovyShell constructor. The script is run from Java using the evaluate method as usual, and the results are extracted by getting the output variables from the shell. Using a GroovyShell and Binding is illustrated in figure 3.5.

There's more to the GroovyShell than I'm presenting here. I can use the parse method, rather than evaluate, to parse the script and retrieve a reference to the generated Script object. That way I can set the binding variables and rerun the script without having to recompile every time. GroovyShell also works with a hierarchy of classloaders and configurations. Allthough all of that is interesting, it doesn't really

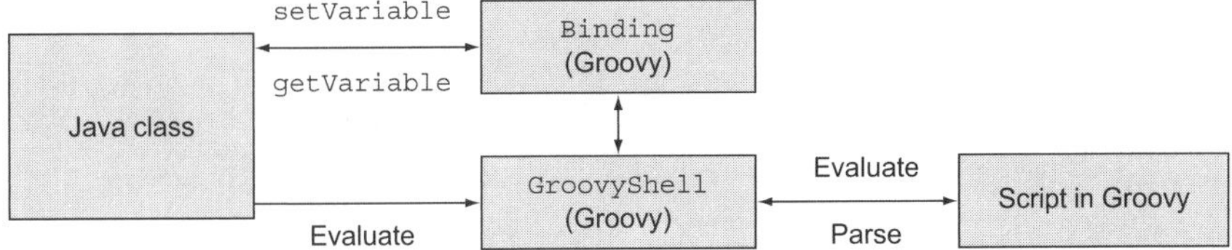

Figure 3.5 Java code sets variables in the `Binding`, which is used in the `GroovyShell` to execute Groovy code. The results are returned via the `getVariable` method in the `Binding`.

add a lot to the integration story, so I'll refer you to Dierk Koenig's most excellent *Groovy in Action* for details.

> **THE HARD WAY** Use the `ScriptEngine` class from Java, or the `Eval` and `GroovyShell` classes from Groovy, along with a `Binding` if necessary, to call Groovy scripts from Java.

Between the `ScriptEngine`, `Eval`, and `GroovyShell` classes, hopefully you'll agree that there are a variety of ways to execute Groovy scripts from Java. Collectively I still refer to this as "the hard way," though it isn't terribly hard, but it's awfully indirect compared to the easy way. From now on I'll stop trying to maintain the artificial separation of Java code from Groovy code. In order to make progress all I need to do is put the Groovy code into a class.

3.2.4 Calling Groovy from Java the easy way

All the techniques I've discussed so far—using the JSR 223 `ScriptEngine`, or using the Groovy API classes `Eval` and `GroovyShell`—work just fine but feel overly complicated. Groovy is supposed to simplify your life, so although the mechanisms shown in the previous section all work, for most use cases there's an easier way.

The easiest way to call Groovy from Java is to put the Groovy code in a class and compile it. Then Java code can instantiate the class and invoke its methods the normal way.

> **THE EASY WAY** To call Groovy from Java, put the Groovy code in a class, compile it as usual, and then instantiate it and invoke methods as though it was Java.

Let's return, once again, to the geocoder. This time, however, I'll refactor it into a class that can be instantiated, with methods that can be invoked from outside. The process is shown in figure 3.6.

As the figure shows, the Java application will use a `Location` class to store all the needed attributes. It will supply the `street`, `city`, and `state` fields as input parameters, but the `Location` class will also include `latitude` and `longitude` fields that will be updated by the Groovy geocoder. The geocoder itself will be written in Groovy, because it's easy to write the RESTful web service client code that way.[7]

[7] Note this is just like the geocoder with the `Stadium` class used in chapter 2 when I discussed the Groovy Baseball application. The differences here are the CSV output and that I'm invoking the Groovy implementation from Java.

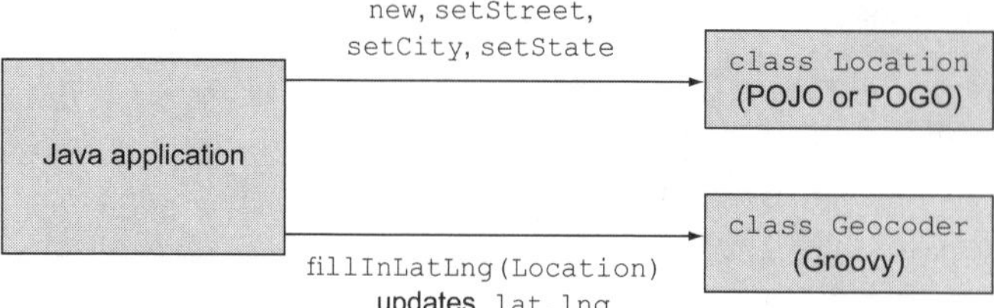

Figure 3.6 Mixing Java and Groovy classes. The Java app instantiates a Location and supplies it with street, city, and state values. It sends the new Location to the Groovy geocoder, whose `fillInLatLng` method supplies the latitude and longitude, which can then be retrieved by Java again.

Here's the new `Location` class, which could be written in either Java or Groovy. This time, to keep the code simple I'll use a Groovy POGO:

```
class Location {
    String street
    String city
    String state

    double latitude
    double longitude
}
```

The `Location` class encapsulates the address information in strings and provides double variables for the latitude and longitude values that will be set using the geocoder. Speaking of the geocoder, the next listing shows a revised version that wraps the script into a class.

Listing 3.6 A Groovy class for geocoding

```
class Geocoder {
    def base = 'http://maps.google.com/maps/geo?'

    void fillInLatLong(Location loc) {
        def addressFields = loc.street ?
            [loc.street,loc.city,loc.state] : [loc.city,loc.state]
        def address = addressFields.collect {
            URLEncoder.encode(it,'UTF-8')
        }.join(',')
        def params = [q:address,sensor:false,
            output:'csv',key:'ABQIAAAAa...']
        def url = base + params.collect { k,v -> "$k=$v" }.join('&')
        def (code,level,lat,lng) = url.toURL().text.split(',')
        loc.latitude = lat.toDouble()
        loc.longitude = lng.toDouble()
    }
}
```

The `fillInLatLong` method takes a `Location` as an argument. Strictly speaking, I didn't have to declare a type for the parameter at all. I could have relied on duck typing within the method and just been careful not to call it with anything other than an object with street, city, and state properties. Still, I'm building the service with a `Location` in mind, so it doesn't hurt to say so.

The `addressFields` variable uses the ternary operator to determine whether or not a street has been supplied when returning the collection of address components. Note that I'm appealing to the so-called "Groovy truth" here, in that I don't need to compare `loc.street` to `null` or an empty string explicitly. Any non-blank value of the `street` field as part of the `loc` argument will return true, so it will be added to the collection.

The rest of the class is the same as the previous script, though to make the class more useful I went to the trouble of converting the string results to doubles before returning the location.

One final issue is notable, and it highlights an important difference between a script and a class. All of the variables, whether they are local variables or attributes, have to be declared. There are no undefined variables, so there's also no binding to worry about any more.

How do I use these classes (`Geocoder` and `Location`) from Java? Just instantiate them and call methods as usual. In the previous section I started accumulating JUnit 4 tests into a test class. Here's another test to add to that set:

```
@Test
public void testGeocoder() {
    Location loc = new Location();
    loc.setState("1600 Pennsylvania Avenue");
    loc.setCity("Washington");
    loc.setState("DC");
    Geocoder geocoder = new Geocoder();
    geocoder.fillInLatLong(loc);
    assertEquals(38.895,loc.getLatitude(),0.001);
    assertEquals(-77.037,loc.getLongitude(),0.001);
}
```

It doesn't get much easier than that. I don't need to instantiate a script engine or worry about Groovy shells or class loaders. Just instantiate and populate a `Location`, instantiate a `Geocoder`, and invoke the desired method.

From now on all of the examples I show will do integration the easy way. Again, this isn't a value judgment against all the techniques demonstrated earlier in the chapter. If you want to call an existing Groovy script from Java, or you're required to keep Java and Groovy code separate in your application, the previous mechanisms all work. Freely intermixing classes the way this script does, however, is very easy.

One last issue remains before I start looking at how Groovy might help Java. So far in this chapter the goal was always to call Groovy from Java. What about the other direction? How do you call Java from Groovy?

3.2.5 Calling Java from Groovy

Actually, this is so easy it hardly deserves a section at all. I've already shown it more than once. Remember the earlier example using the Google V2 geocoder (reproduced here for convenience)?

```
def address = [street,city,state].collect {
    URLEncoder.encode(it,'UTF-8')                      <-- Java SE library code
}.join(',')
def params = [q:address,sensor:false,output:'csv',key:'ABQIAAAAaUT...']
def base = 'http://maps.google.com/maps/geo?'
def url = base + params.collect { k,v -> "$k=$v" }.join('&')
(code,level,lat,lng) = url.toURL().text.split(',')
```

The integration is already here through the use of the library class and various Java methods. I needed to pass the address to Google in URL-encoded form. To do that I ran each element of the address (street, city, and state) through the `java.net.URLEncoder`, using its `encode` method. In other words, the Groovy script used a Java library class and called one of its methods.

Lessons learned (integration)

1. Groovy scripts can be called with Java alone using the JSR 223 script engine.
2. The Groovy `Eval` class makes calling scripts involving zero, one, two, or three arguments simple.
3. The `GroovyShell` and `Binding` classes are used to programmatically set input variables, invoke a script, and retrieve its result.
4. The easiest way to call Groovy from Java is to make a Groovy class, compile it, instantiate it in Java, and call the methods as usual.

The combination of Java and Groovy is also emphasized in Figure 3.3, shown with the original listing. In that figure each Java method and each Groovy method is indicated with arrows.

The fact that the script mixes both Java and Groovy is true of practically any Groovy script. Groovy rests on the foundation of the Java libraries. It enhances those libraries, as you'll see in section 4.3 on the Groovy JDK, but there's no need to re-invent the flat tire.[8] Groovy is perfectly happy to use any Java classes you supply, and it makes many of them better.

COMPILE WITH GROOVYC Whenever you mix Java and Groovy, compile everything with `groovyc`. Let `groovyc` handle all the cross-compiler issues.

In the next chapter I'll look at some of the ways Groovy improves Java.

[8] Re-inventing the flat tire is what happens when you try to re-invent the wheel and get it wrong.

Don't separate Groovy and Java classes

The natural tendency when using two different languages is to separate the two codebases and compile them independently. With Groovy and Java that can lead to all sorts of problems, especially when cyclic dependencies are involved (in other words, Java class `A` uses Groovy class `B`, which invokes another method from Java class `A`, and so on). Maven projects in particular lead you down this path, because their default layouts naturally suggest putting Java code under src/main/java and Groovy code under src/main/groovy. The idea then is to use `javac` to compile the Java code and `groovyc` to compile the Groovy code.

Although you probably can get that to work, it makes life much more difficult than it needs to be. The developers of Groovy have worked hard on the cross-compilation issue for years. It's better for us, as users of both languages, to take advantage of their progress.

The simplest way to compile Groovy and Java in the same project is to let the `groovyc` compiler handle both codebases. Groovy knows all about Java and is quite capable of handling it. Any compiler flags you would normally send to `javac` work just fine in `groovyc` as well. This is actually a good general principle.

In the projects in this book I'll let `groovyc` do all the work. I'll show specific examples of this in chapter 5, but you can safely assume I'm using `groovyc` throughout.

3.3 Summary

This chapter is about basic Groovy / Java integration, regardless of use case. After reviewing all the different ways to call Groovy from Java, from the JSR-223 `ScriptEngine` to the `GroovyShell` and `Eval` classes in Groovy, I switched to the easy way, which is to put Groovy in a class and use it like any other library class. This easy blend of Java and Groovy will be used from now on.

Next I reviewed many ways that Groovy can help Java at the basic level, from POJO enhancements to AST transformations to building XML and more. I'll use these techniques in future chapters wherever they can help. I'll also review other helpful techniques along the way, though these are most of the major ones.

4 Using Groovy features in Java

This chapter covers

- Basic code-level simplifications
- Useful AST transformations
- XML processing

In chapter 1 I reviewed many of Java's arguable weaknesses and drawbacks and suggested ways that Groovy might help ameliorate them. Because that chapter was intended to be introductory I only suggested how Groovy can help, without showing a lot of code examples. Now that I've established how easy it is to add Groovy classes to Java applications, when is it helpful to do so? What features, if any, does Groovy bring to Java systems that make them easier to develop?

A guide to the techniques covered in this chapter is shown in figure 4.1. I'll review several Groovy advantages, like POGOs, operator overloading, the Groovy JDK, AST transformations, and how to use Groovy to work with XML and JSON data. To start, I'll show that from Groovy code POJOs can be treated as though they were POGOs.

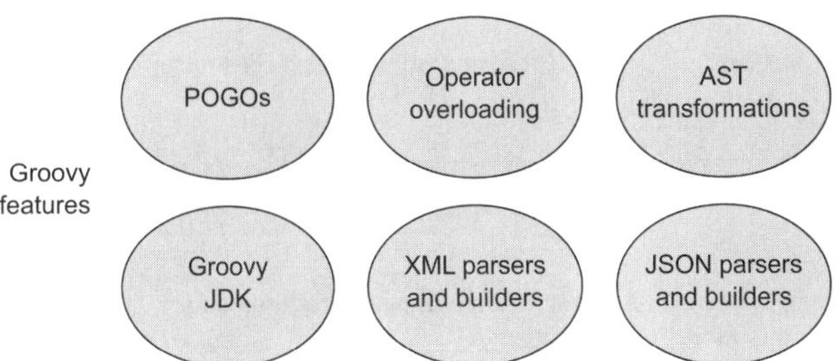

Figure 4.1 Groovy features that can be added to Java classes

4.1 Treating POJOs like POGOs

POGOs have more capabilities than POJOs. For example, all POGOs have a map-based constructor that's very convenient for setting properties. The interesting thing is that even if a class is written in Java, many of the same conveniences apply as long as it's accessed from Groovy.

Consider a simple POJO representing a person, possibly created as part of a domain model in Java, shown in the next listing. To keep it simple I'll only include an ID and a name. I'll put in a `toString` override as well but won't include the inevitable `equals` and `hashCode` overrides.

Listing 4.1 A simple POJO representing a person

```
public class Person {
    private int id;
    private String name;

    public Person() {}

    public Person(int id, String name) {
        this.id = id;
        this.name = name;
    }

    public void setId(int id) { this.id = id; }
    public int getId() { return id; }
    public void setName(String name) { this.name = name; }
    public String getName() { return name; }

    @Override
    public String toString() {
        return "Person [id=" + id + ", name=" + name + "]";
    }
}
```

Any typical Java persistence layer has dozens of classes just like this, which map to relational database tables (figure 4.2).

If I instantiate this class from Groovy I can use a map-based[1] constructor to do so, even though the Java version already specifies two constructors and neither is the one

[1] The term *map-based* refers to the fact that the attributes are set using the key-value notation used in Groovy maps. The constructor doesn't actually use a map to do its job.

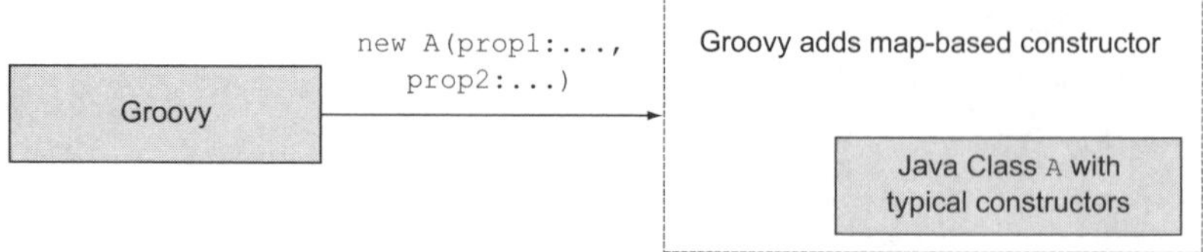

Figure 4.2 Groovy adds a map-based constructor to Java classes, regardless of what constructors are already included.

I want. The following Groovy script creates some `Person` instances using three different mechanisms, none of which appear in the Java class:

```
def buffy = new Person(name:'Buffy')
assert buffy.id == 0
assert buffy.name == 'Buffy'

def faith = new Person(name:'Faith',id:1)
assert faith.id == 1
assert faith.name == 'Faith'

def willow = [name:'Willow',id:2] as Person
assert willow.getId() == 2
assert willow.getName() == 'Willow'
```

The instances `buffy` and `faith` are created using the map-based constructor, first setting only the `name`, and then setting both the `name` and the `id`. I'm then able to verify, using Groovy's built-in `assert` method (omitting its optional parentheses), that the person's properties are set correctly.

Incidentally, all the `assert` statements that seem to be accessing private properties of the class directly really aren't. Groovy goes through the getter and setter methods provided in the Java class when it looks like properties are being accessed or assigned. I can prove this by modifying the implementation of the getter method to return more than just the name:

```
public String getName() {
    return "from getter: " + name;
}
```

Now I have to modify each of the asserts to include the string `"from getter: "` for them to still return true.

The third person, `willow`, is constructed using the `as` operator in Groovy. This operator has several uses, one of which is to coerce a map into an object as shown here. In this case the operator instantiates a person and supplies the map as properties for the resulting instance.

Moving on, I can also add the person instances to a Groovy collection, which isn't all that surprising but has some nice additional benefits. For example, Groovy collections support operator overloading, making it easy to add additional persons and have additional methods for searching:

```
def slayers = [buffy, faith]
assert ['Buffy','Faith'] == slayers*.name
assert slayers.class == java.util.ArrayList

def characters = slayers + willow
assert ['Buffy','Faith','Willow'] == characters*.name

def doubles = characters.findAll { it.name =~ /([a-z])\1/ }
assert ['Buffy','Willow'] == doubles*.name
```

Groovy has a native syntax for collections, which simplifies Java code. Putting the references inside square brackets creates an instance of the `java.util.ArrayList` class and adds each element to the collection. Then, in the `assert` statement, I used the so-called "spread-dot" operator to extract the `name` property from each instance and return a list of the results (in other words, the spread-dot operator behaves the same way `collect` does). By the way, I restored the `getName` method to its original form, which returns just the attribute value.

I was able to use operator overloading to add `willow` to the `slayers` collection, resulting in the `characters` collection. Finally, I took advantage of the fact that in Groovy, the `java.util.Collection` interface has been augmented to have a `findAll` method that returns all instances in the collection matching the condition in the provided closure. In this case the closure contains a regular expression that matches any repeated lowercase letter.

Many existing Java applications have extensive domain models. As you can see, Groovy code can work with them directly, even treating them as POGOs and giving you a poor-man's search capability.

Now to demonstrate a capability Groovy can add to Java that Java doesn't even support: operator overloading.

4.2 Implementing operator overloading in Java

So far I've used the fact that both the + and – operators have been overloaded in the `String` class. The overloaded + operator in `String` should be familiar to Java developers, because it's the only overloaded operator in all of Java; it does concatenation for strings and addition for numerical values. Java developers can't overload operators however they want.

That's different in Groovy. In Groovy all operators are represented by methods, like the `plus` method for + or the `minus` method for—. You can overload[2] any operator by implementing the appropriate method in your Groovy class. What isn't necessarily obvious, though, is that you can implement the correct method in a Java class, too, and if an instance of that class is used in Groovy code, the operator will work there as well (see figure 4.3).

[2] Incidentally, changing the behavior of operators this way is normally called operator *overloading*, because the same operator has different behavior in different classes. Arguably, though, what I'm actually doing is operator *overriding*. Effectively they're the same thing here, so I'll use the terms interchangeably.

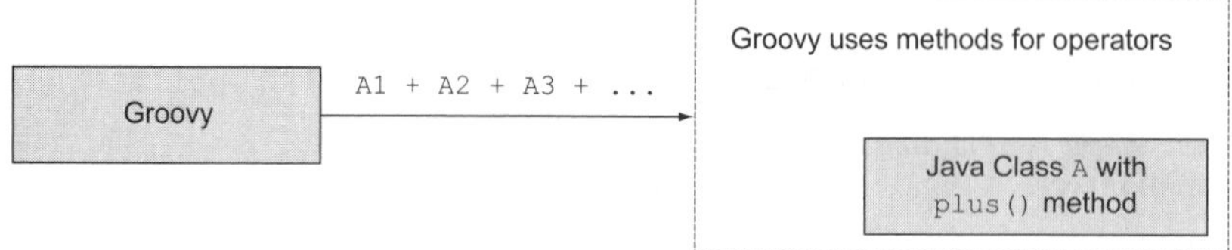

Figure 4.3 Groovy operators are implemented as methods, so if the Java class contains the right methods, Groovy scripts can use the associated operators on their instances.

To demonstrate this I'll create a Java class that wraps a map. A `Department` contains a collection of `Employee` instances and will have a `hire` method to add them and a `layOff` method to remove them (hopefully not very often). I'll implement operator overloading through three methods: `plus`, `minus`, and `leftShift`. Intuitively, `plus` will add a new employee, `minus` will remove an existing employee, and `leftShift` will be an alternative way to add. All three methods will allow chaining, meaning that they'll return the modified `Department` instance.

Here's the `Employee` class, which is just the `Person` POJO by another name:

```
public class Employee {
    private int id;
    private String name;

    public String getName() { return name; }
    public void setName(String name) { this.name = name; }
    public int getId() { return id; }
    public void setId(int id) { this.id = id; }
}
```

Now for the `Department` class, shown in the following listing, which maintains the employee collection in a `Map` keyed to the employee `id` values.

Listing 4.2 A `Department` with a map of `Employees` and operator overriding

```
public class Department {
    private int id;
    private String name;
    private Map<Integer, Employee> empMap =
        new HashMap<Integer, Employee>();                     // Employees indexed by ID

    public int getId() { return id; }
    public void setId(int id) { this.id = id; }
    public String getName() { return name; }
    public void setName(String name) { this.name = name; }

    public Collection<Employee> getEmployees() { return empMap.values(); }

    public void hire(Employee e) { empMap.put(e.getId(), e); }
    public void layOff(Employee e) { empMap.remove(e.getId()); }   // Business methods to add and remove Employees

    public Department plus(Employee e) {                      // Overriding operator methods
        hire(e);
        return this;
    }
```

```
    public Department minus(Employee e) {        <--
        layOff(e);                                   Overriding
        return this;                                 operator
    }                                                methods

    public Department leftShift(Employee e) {    <--
        hire(e);
        return this;
    }
}
```

By the way, notice that the `plus` method doesn't add two `Department` instances; rather, it adds an `Employee` to a `Department`. Groovy only cares about the name of the method for the operator.[3]

To test this I'll use the Spock testing framework. As in chapter 1, I'll present the test without going into much detail about the Spock framework itself, which I'll deal with in chapter 6. Fortunately, Spock tests are easy to read even if you don't know the details. The next listing shows a Spock test that's focused on just the operator methods.

Listing 4.3 A Spock test to check the operator overloading methods in a Java class

```
class DepartmentTest extends Specification {
    private Department dept;

    def setup() { dept = new Department(name:'IT') }

    def "add employee to dept should increase total by 1"() {
        given: Employee fred = new Employee(name:'Fred',id:1)

        when: dept = dept + fred

        then:
        dept.employees.size() == old(dept.employees.size()) + 1
    }

    def "add two employees via chained plus"() {
        given:
        Employee fred = new Employee(name:'Fred',id:1)
        Employee barney = new Employee(name:'Barney',id:2)

        when:
        dept = dept + fred + barney

        then:
        dept.employees.size() == 2
    }

    def "subtract emp from dept should decrease by 1"() {
        given:
        Employee fred = new Employee(name:'Fred',id:1)
        dept.hire fred
```

3 As an example from the Groovy JDK, the `java.util.Date` class has a `plus` method that takes an integer representing the number of days. See also the `multiply` method in `Collection` that takes an integer.

```
        when:
        dept = dept - fred

        then:
        dept.employees.size() == old(dept.employees.size()) - 1
    }

    def "remove two employees via chained minus"() {
        given:
        Employee fred = new Employee(name:'Fred',id:1)
        Employee barney = new Employee(name:'Barney',id:2)
        dept.hire fred; dept.hire barney

        when: dept = dept - fred - barney

        then: dept.employees.size() == 0
    }

    def "left shift should increase employee total by 1"() {
        given:
        Employee fred = new Employee(name:'Fred',id:1)

        when:
        dept = dept << fred

        then:
        dept.employees.size() == old(dept.employees.size()) + 1
    }

    def "add two employees via chained left shift"() {
        given:
        Employee fred = new Employee(name:'Fred',id:1)
        Employee barney = new Employee(name:'Barney',id:2)

        when:
        dept = dept << fred << barney

        then:
        dept.employees.size() == 2
    }
}
```

The Spock test is written in Groovy, so I can use +, –, and << and know that the associated methods will be used, even though they're implemented in a Java class.

The list of operators that can be overridden in Groovy includes `plus`, `minus`, and `leftShift`, as shown in the listing, and many others as well. You can implement array-like access through an index by implementing `getAt`, for example. Pre- and post-increment are implemented through the `next` and `previous` methods, respectively. The spaceship operator, <=>, is implemented through `compareTo`. You can even override the dot operator, believe it or not. The cool part is that you can implement these methods in either POJOs or POGOs, and Groovy will take advantage of them either way.

The next feature of Groovy that simplifies Java is one I've taken advantage of several times already: the Groovy JDK.

4.3 Making Java library classes better: the Groovy JDK

Every Groovy class contains a metaclass. In addition to providing information about a class, the metaclass contains methods that come into play if a method or property that doesn't exist is accessed through an instance. By intercepting those method or property "missing" failures, developers can provide whatever they want.

One application of this is for Groovy to add methods to existing classes. This is especially useful when you want to add methods to classes where you cannot change the source code. As mentioned earlier, Groovy makes extensive use of the existing Java standard libraries. It does not, however, simply use them as it finds them. In many cases, a range of new methods has been added to the Java libraries to make them easier and more powerful.

Collectively the set of enhanced Java libraries is known as the Groovy JDK. Groovy has two sets of Javadoc documentation. One is the Groovy API, which contains information about the included Groovy libraries. The other is the Groovy JDK, which shows only those methods and properties that have been added to the standard Java libraries, in order to, as the saying goes, make them groovier (see figure 4.4).

For example, Groovy adds many methods to the `java.util.Collection` interface, including `collect`, `count`, `find`, `findAll`, `leftShift`, `max`, `min`, `sort`, and `sum`. These methods are then available in any Groovy collection, whether they include objects from Java or Groovy.

I've already spent a fair amount of time on collections, though, and I'll revisit them frequently in the book. So to choose an example from a different Java class, let's illustrate why it's a bad idea to use basic authentication over HTTP.

In basic authentication a username and password are transmitted in encoded form to a server. Basic authentication concatenates the username and the password

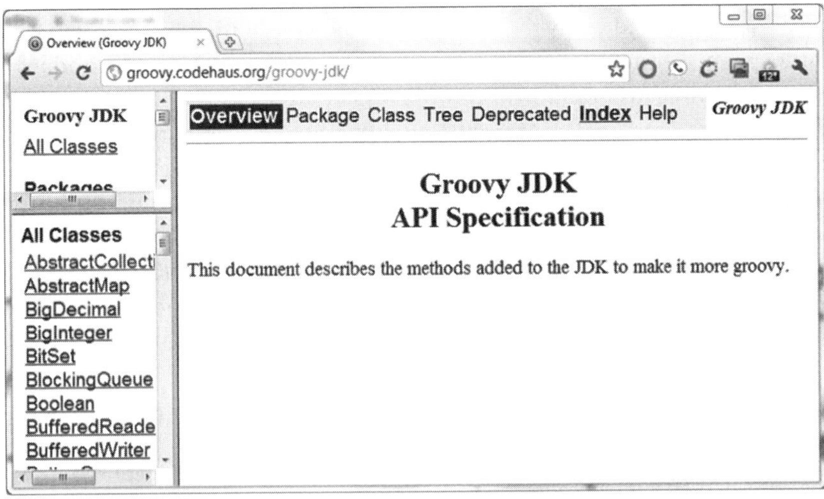

Figure 4.4 Groovy adds convenience methods to classes in the Java standard library.

together, separated by a colon, performs a Base 64 encoding on the resulting string, and sends the result as part of the authenticated HTTP request header.

There's a big difference, however, between encoding and encrypting. Encoded strings can just as easily be decoded. Groovy makes it easy to demonstrate this, because the Groovy JDK adds a method called `encodeBase64` to, of all things, byte arrays. It also adds a `decodeBase64` method to `String`. The following listing demonstrates both.

Listing 4.4 Base 64 encoding and decoding username/password information

```
def u = 'username'
def p = 'password'
def encoded = "$u:$p".getBytes().encodeBase64().toString()     <- Mixing Java and Groovy methods
println "$u:$p -> $encoded"
assert encoded == 'dXNlcm5hbWU6cGFzc3dvcmQ='
def (user,pass) = new String(encoded.decodeBase64()).split(':')     <- Reversing the encoding
println "(user,pass) = ($user,$pass)"
assert user == u
assert pass == p
```

There's a lot going on in this short script. First, a username and password are assembled into a Groovy string. Then the `getBytes` method is invoked on the combined string, which encodes the string into a sequence of bytes using the default character encoding. That method is from Java. The result is a byte array. Check the Groovy JDK and you'll find that Groovy has added the method `encodeBase64` to `byte[]`, which returns an instance of `groovy.lang.Writable`. Here I just use its `toString` method (from Java, of course, though it's overridden in the Groovy class) to see the resulting values. In effect I went from Java to Groovy to Java in one chained method call.

To go the other direction, first I use the `decodeBase64` method that Groovy adds to `java.lang.String`, which returns a `byte[]` again. Then `String` has a constructor that takes a byte array, and I use the `split` method from Java to separate the username from the password again and verify that they haven't been modified by the transformations.

Other than showing how the Groovy JDK adds new methods to standard Java data types, this example also demonstrates that encoded text isn't encrypted. Anyone who intercepts the request and accesses the encoded header can extract the username and password. Using basic authentication therefore is not at all secure if the requests are transmitted over an unencrypted connection, like HTTP. At a minimum the request should be sent over HTTPS instead.[4]

There are lots and lots of useful methods in the Groovy JDK. As another example, date manipulation is always painful in Java.[5] Groovy doesn't necessarily fix the many problems, but the Groovy JDK adds several methods to make date-related classes more

---

4 For several years Twitter supported basic authentication as part of its RESTful API. Hopefully all the many Twitter clients who used it transmitted their authentication over secure sockets. If not you might want to consider changing your password. These days Twitter has switched to OAuth, which may be overly complicated but is much better than basic authentication.

5 Java 8 is supposed to fix this, at long last. In the meantime, the open source date/time library of choice in the Java world is Joda time: http://joda-time.sourceforge.net/.

powerful. Here's an example, which hopefully will be both interesting and at least mildly amusing to some readers.

In the United States and Canada, February 2 is known as Groundhog Day. On Groundhog Day, the groundhog is supposed to emerge from his hole and look for his shadow. If he doesn't see it he'll stay out of the burrow, and winter is nearly over. If he sees his shadow, he goes back to sleep in his burrow, and we'll sadly have to suffer through six more weeks of winter.

Let's check the math on that, though, as shown in the next listing.

Listing 4.5 GroundHog Day—an example of `Date` and `Calendar` in the Groovy JDK

```
println 'Groundhog sees shadow --> 6 more weeks of Winter'
def c = Calendar.instance
c.set 2013, Calendar.FEBRUARY, 2                    <-- Set method from Java
def groundHogDay = c.time                           <-- Invokes getTime to return a Date
c.set 2013, Calendar.MARCH, 20                      <-- Set method from Java
def firstDayOfSpring = c.time                       <-- Invokes getTime to return a Date
def days = firstDayOfSpring - groundHogDay          <-- Subtracting dates
assert days == (firstDayOfSpring..groundHogDay).size() - 1   <-- Dates as a range
println """
There are ${(int)(days/7)} weeks and ${days % 7} days between GroundHog Day
and the first day of Spring (March 20), so Spring
comes early if the groundhog sees his shadow.
"""
```

I get an instance of the `Calendar` class by accessing its `instance` property. Of course, there's no instance property in `Calendar`, but the syntax actually means that I invoke the static `getInstance` method with no arguments. Then I call `set` with the appropriate arguments for Groundhog Day and the first day of spring. Extracting a `Date` instance from the `Calendar` is done through the `getTime` method (sigh[6]), which again is invoked by accessing the `time` property. So far this is straight Java, except that I'm invoking methods via properties and omitting optional parentheses.

I can subtract dates, though, because the Groovy JDK shows that the `minus` method in `Date` returns the number of days between them. The `Date` class has a `next` method and a `previous` method and implements `compareTo`. Those are the requirements necessary for a class to be used as part of a range, so I can check the math by invoking the `size` method on a range. The size of a range counts both ends, so I have to correct for the potential off-by-one error by subtracting one.

The bottom line is that there are six weeks and four days between Groundhog Day and the first day of spring (March 20). In other words, if the groundhog sees his shadow the resulting six more weeks of winter is actually a (slightly) early spring anyway.[7]

One last convenience should be noted here. In Java, arrays have a `length` property, strings have a `length` method, collections have a `size` method, `NodeLists` have

---

[6] Seriously, couldn't the method `getDate` have been used to extract a `Date` from a `Calendar`?

[7] Yes, that's a long way to go for a gag, but it does clearly show a mix of Java and Groovy that takes advantage of both Groovy JDK methods and operator overloading. The joke is just a side benefit.

a `getLength` method, and so on. In Groovy you can invoke `size` on all of them to get the proper behavior. In this case the Groovy JDK has been used to correct a historical inconsistency in Java.

The Groovy JDK is full of helpful methods. Even if your application is planning to use only Java library classes I encourage you to check the Groovy JDK for possible simplifications and enhancements.

I mentioned runtime metaprogramming, which is done through the metaclass. One of the more interesting features of Groovy, though, is compile-time metaprogramming done through AST transformations, which is the subject of the next section.

4.4 Cool AST transformations

Groovy 1.6 introduced Abstract Syntax Tree (AST) transformations. The idea is to place annotations on Groovy classes and invoke the compiler, which builds a syntax tree as usual and then modifies it in interesting ways. Writing AST transformations is done through various builder classes, but that's not my primary concern here. Instead I want to show some of the AST transformations that Groovy provides in the standard library and demonstrate that they can be applied to Java classes, too.

4.4.1 Delegating to contained objects

Let's start with delegation. Current design principles tend to favor delegation over inheritance, viewing inheritance as too highly coupled. Instead of extending a class in order to support all its methods, with delegation you wrap an instance of one class inside another. You then implement all the same methods in the outer class that the contained class provides, delegating each call to the corresponding method on the contained object. In this way your class has the same interface as the contained object but is not otherwise related to it.

Writing all those "pass-through" methods can be a pain, though. Groovy introduced the `@Delegate` annotation to take care of all that work for you.

Phones keep getting more and more powerful, so that the term *phone* is now something of a misnomer. The current generation of "smart phones" includes a camera, a browser, a contact manager, a calendar, and more.[8] If you've already developed classes for all the components, you can then build a smart phone by delegation. The interesting part is that the component classes can be in Java, and the container in Groovy.

Consider a trivial `Camera` class in Java:

```
public class Camera {
    public String takePicture() {
        return "taking picture";
    }
}
```

[8] Here's a good quote attributed to Bjarne Stroustrup, inventor of C++: "I've always wished for my computer to be as easy to use as my telephone; my wish has come true because I can no longer figure out how to use my telephone."

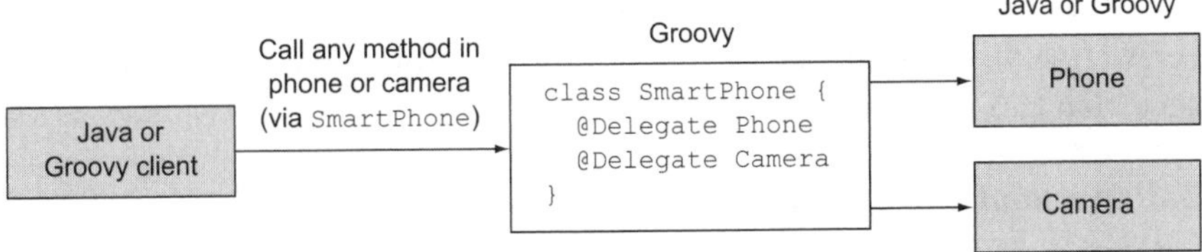

Figure 4.5 The `@Delegate` AST transformation exposes all methods in the delegates through the composite object. The transformation only works in Groovy classes, but the delegates themselves can be in Groovy, Java, or both.

Here also is a `Phone` class, in Java.

```
public class Phone {
    public String dial(String number) {
        return "dialing " + number;
    }
}
```

Now here's a `SmartPhone` class in Groovy that uses the `@Delegate` annotation to expose the component methods through the `SmartPhone` class (see figure 4.5):

```
class SmartPhone {
    @Delegate Camera camera = new Camera()
    @Delegate Phone phone = new Phone()
}
```

A JUnit test (written in Groovy this time) demonstrates the delegated methods in the next listing.

Listing 4.6 A JUnit test in Groovy to demonstrate the delegated methods

```
class SmartPhoneTest {
    SmartPhone sp = new SmartPhone()

    @Test
    void testPhone() {
        assert 'dialing 555-1234' == sp.dial('555-1234')
    }

    @Test
    void testCamera() {
        assert 'taking picture' == sp.takePicture()
    }
}
```

Simply add whatever components are needed, and the `@Delegate` annotation will expose their methods through the `SmartPhone` class. I could also add smart phone-specific methods as desired. The `@Delegate` annotation makes including capabilities easy, and the components themselves can be written in Java or Groovy, whichever is more convenient. The only requirement is that the `SmartPhone` class itself must be written in Groovy, because only the Groovy compiler understands the AST transformation.

I'll have another practical example of `@Delegate` later, in appendix C on SOAP-based web services (available for free download), but for now let's move on to making objects that can't be changed.

4.4.2 Creating immutable objects

With the rise of multi-core machines, programs that handle concurrency well are becoming more and more important. One mechanism for handling operations in a thread-safe manner is to use immutable objects as much as possible whenever shared information is required.

Unlike C++, Java has no built-in way to make it impossible to modify an object. There's no "const" keyword in Java, and applying the combination of `static` and `final` to a reference only makes the reference a constant, not the object it references. The only way to make an object immutable in Java is to remove all ways to change it.

This turns out to be a lot harder than it sounds. Taking out all setter methods is a good first step, but there are other requirements. Making a class support immutability requires that

- All mutable methods (setters) must be removed.
- The class should be marked `final`.
- Any contained fields should be `private` and `final`.
- Mutable components like arrays should defensively be copied on the way in (through constructors) and the way out (through getters).
- `equals`, `hashCode`, and `toString` should all be implemented through fields.

That sounds like work. Fortunately Groovy has an `@Immutable` AST transformation, which does everything for you (see figure 4.6).

The `@Immutable` transformation can only be applied to Groovy classes, but those classes can then be used in Java applications. I'll start by showing how the `@Immutable` annotation works and what its limitations are, and then use an immutable object in a Java class.

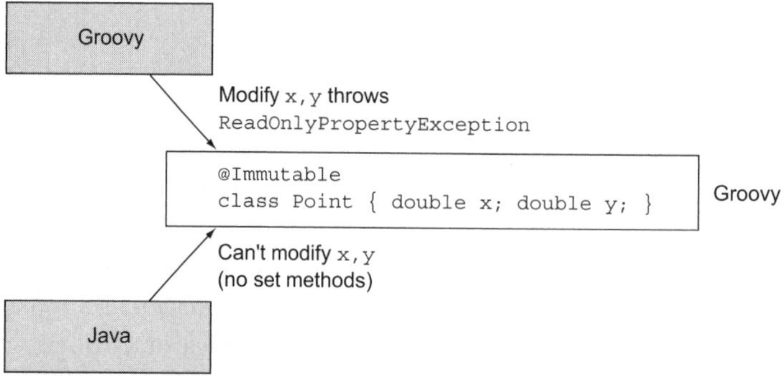

Figure 4.6 The `@Immutable` AST transformation results in an immutable object that can be used in both Java and Groovy clients.

Here's an immutable point class. It contains two fields, x and y, which represent the location of the point in a two-dimensional space:

```
@Immutable
class ImmutablePoint {
    double x
    double y

    String toString() { "($x,$y)" }
}
```

The `@Immutable` annotation is applied to the class itself. It still allows the properties to be set through a constructor, but once set the properties can no longer be modified. The next listing shows a Spock test to demonstrate that fact.

Listing 4.7 Testing the `ImmutablePoint` class

```
class ImmutablePointTest extends Specification {
    ImmutablePoint p = new ImmutablePoint(x:3,y:4)          <-- Set properties through constructor

    def "can use map ctor for immutables"() {
        expect: [3,4] == [p.x, p.y]                         <-- Access properties
    }

    def "can't change x"() {
        when: p.x = 5
        then: thrown(ReadOnlyPropertyException)             <-- Attempts to change throw exception
    }

    def "can't change y"() {
        when: p.y = 5
        then: thrown(ReadOnlyPropertyException)
    }
}
```

In the test the `ImmutablePoint` class is instantiated by specifying the values of x and y as constructor arguments. This is necessary, because there are no set methods available. I can access the properties through the regular dynamically generated get methods, but if I try to modify a property the attempt will throw a `ReadOnlyPropertyException`.

The `@Immutable` annotation is very powerful, but it has limitations. You can only apply it to classes that contain primitives or certain library classes, like `String` or `Date`. It also works on classes that contain properties that are also immutable. For example, here's an `ImmutableLine`, which contains two `ImmutablePoint` instances:

```
@Immutable
class ImmutableLine {
    ImmutablePoint start
    ImmutablePoint end

    def getLength() {
        double dx = end.x - start.x
        double dy = end.y - start.y
        return Math.sqrt(dx*dx + dy*dy)
    }
```

```
    String toString() { "from $start to $end" }
}
```

The `start` and `end` fields are both of type `ImmutablePoint`. I've added a method to return a dependent `length` property, which is computed using the Pythagorean theorem in the usual manner. This means I can access the `length` property of an `ImmutableLine` and the access will go through the `getLength` method, but because there's no setter I can't change the value from outside. The corresponding test for this class is shown in the following listing.

Listing 4.8 A Spock test for the `ImmutableLine` class

```
class ImmutableLineTest extends Specification {
    ImmutableLine line

    def setup() {
        ImmutablePoint p1 = new ImmutablePoint(x:3,y:0)
        ImmutablePoint p2 = new ImmutablePoint(x:0,y:4)
        line = new ImmutableLine(start:p1,end:p2)            <-- The line contains ImmutablePoints
    }

    def "points should be set properly"() {
        expect:
        line.start.x == 3; line.end.x == 0
        line.start.y == 0; line.end.y == 4
        (line.length - 5).abs() < 0.0001                     <-- Check the getLength computation
    }

    def "can't change start"() {
        when: line.start = new ImmutablePoint(x:1,y:1)
        then: thrown(ReadOnlyPropertyException)              <-- Once assigned start and end can't be changed
    }

    def "can't change end"() {
        when: line.end = new ImmutablePoint(x:1,y:1)
        then: thrown(ReadOnlyPropertyException)
    }
}
```

In order to create an `ImmutableLine` I need to first create a pair of `ImmutablePoint` instances that can be used in the `ImmutableLine` constructor. The first test checks that the contained points are set properly and then checks the `getLength` implementation by accessing the `length` "field." Finally, I make sure that I can't reassign the `start` or `end` properties of the line.

Taking this one step further, what happens if the class contains a collection? The `@Immutable` annotation will cause the collection to be wrapped by one of its unmodifiable alternatives. For example, let's say that a path is a collection of lines, so here's the definition of an `ImmutablePath`:

```
@Immutable
class ImmutablePath {
    List<ImmutableLine> segments = []
}
```

This time I can't just declare the segments variable using `def`. If I want the `@Immutable` annotation to work I need to specify that I'm using some sort of collection. On the right-hand side of the `segments` definition I still just have `[]`, which normally means an instance of `java.util.ArrayList`. In this case, however, what I actually get (by printing `segments.class.name`) is `java.util.Collections$UnmodifiableRandomAccessList`, believe it or not. The `Collections` class has utility methods like `unmodifiableList` that take a regular list and return a new list that can't be changed, but to be honest I wouldn't have necessarily expected it to be a `RandomAccessList` in this case. It doesn't make any difference what the actual class is, of course, as long as the contract is maintained.

Speaking of that contract, those unmodifiable methods in `Collections` don't remove the available mutator methods. Instead, they wrap them and throw an `UnsupportedOperationException` if they're accessed. That's arguably a strange way to implement an interface, but so be it. The Spock test for this class is shown in the following listing.

Listing 4.9 A Spock test for the `ImmutablePath` class

```
class ImmutablePathTest extends Specification {
    ImmutablePath path

    def setup() {
        def lines = []
        ImmutablePoint p1 = new ImmutablePoint(x:0,y:0)
        ImmutablePoint p2 = new ImmutablePoint(x:3,y:0)
        ImmutablePoint p3 = new ImmutablePoint(x:0,y:4)
        lines << new ImmutableLine(start:p1,end:p2)
        lines << new ImmutableLine(start:p2,end:p3)
        lines << new ImmutableLine(start:p3,end:p1)

        path = new ImmutablePath(segments:lines)
    }

    def "points should be set through ctor"() {
        expect:
        path.segments.collect { line -> line.start.x } == [0,3,0]
        path.segments.collect { line -> line.start.y } == [0,0,4]
        path.segments.collect { line -> line.end.x } == [3,0,0]
        path.segments.collect { line -> line.end.y } == [0,4,0]
    }

    def "cant add new segments"() {
        given:
        ImmutablePoint a = new ImmutablePoint(x:5,y:5)
        ImmutablePoint b = new ImmutablePoint(x:4,y:4)

        when:
        path.segments << new ImmutableLine(start:a,end:b)

        then:
        thrown UnsupportedOperationException
    }
}
```

Everything works as expected. It takes some doing to build up all the immutable objects needed to create an `ImmutablePath` instance, but once everything is set it all works.

Everything I've shown about the `@Immutable` annotation so far falls in the category of the good news. Now for the bad news, though again it's not all that bad. First, the `@Immutable` annotation, like many of the AST transformations, wreaks havoc on Integrated Development Environments (IDEs). The transformations occur at compile time, which the IDEs have a hard time anticipating. Even though everything I've done so far is legal and works just fine, my IDE[9] continually struggled with it. At this point the IDE issues are mostly annoying, but fixing them is legitimately a Hard Problem and probably won't go away soon.

The next problem occurs when I try to use my `ImmutablePoint` in a Java program. How am I supposed to assign the `x` and `y` values? Groovy gives me a map-based constructor that I've been using so far, but Java won't see that.

Fortunately, the developers of `@Immutable` anticipated that problem. The transformation also generates a tuple constructor that takes each of the properties in the order they're defined. In this case, it's as though the `ImmutablePoint` class has a two-argument constructor that takes doubles representing `x` and `y` in that order.

Here's a JUnit 4 test (written in Java, so it's an example of Java/Groovy integration itself) that takes advantage of that constructor:

```
public class ImmutablePointJUnitTest {
    private ImmutablePoint p;

    @Test
    public void testImmutablePoint() {
        p = new ImmutablePoint(3,4);
        assertEquals(3.0, p.getX(), 0.0001);
        assertEquals(4.0, p.getY(), 0.0001);
    }
}
```

This, again, works just fine. At the moment, my IDE even understands that the two-argument constructor exists, which is pretty sweet. I'm using the three-argument version of the `Assert.assertEquals` method, by the way, because I'm comparing doubles, and for that you need to specify a precision.

There's also no need to try to check for immutability, because from the Java point of view the class has no methods to invoke that might change `x` or `y`. Unlike the `getX` and `getY` methods shown, there are no corresponding setters.

As I say, this all works, but if you're trying to use the generated constructor and your system refuses to believe that one exists, there's a simple workaround. Simply add a factory class in Groovy that can instantiate the points in the usual way:

```
class ImmutablePointFactory {
    ImmutablePoint newImmutablePoint(xval,yval) {
```

9 Most of the code in this chapter was written using Groovy / Grails Tool Suite (STS) version 3.2.

```
        return new ImmutablePoint(x:xval,y:yval)
    }
}
```

Now the Java client can instantiate ImmutablePointFactory and then invoke the newImmutablePoint factory method, supplying the desired x and y values.

Everything works, that is, until you succumb to the temptation to follow standard practices in the Java API and make the factory class a singleton. That's the subject of the next subsection.

4.4.3 Creating singletons

When a new Java developer first discovers the wide, wonderful world of design patterns, one of the first ones they tend to encounter is Singleton. It's an easy pattern to learn, because it's easy to implement and only involves a single class. If you only want one instance of a class, make the constructor private, add a static final instance variable of the class type, and add a static getter method to retrieve it. How cool is that?

Unfortunately, our poor new developer has wandered into a vast jungle, full of monsters to attack the unwary. First of all, implementing a true singleton isn't nearly as easy as it sounds. If nothing else, there are thread safety issues to worry about, and because it seems no Java program is every truly thread-safe the results get ugly fast.

Then there's the fact that a small but very vocal contingent of developers view the whole Singleton design pattern as an anti-pattern. They trash it for a variety of reasons, and they tend to be harsh in their contempt for both the pattern and anyone foolish or naïve enough to use it.

Fortunately I'm not here to resolve that issue. My job is to show you how Groovy can help you as a Java developer, and I can do that here. As you may have anticipated based on the title of this section, there's an AST transformation called @Singleton.

To use it all I have to do is add the annotation to my class. Here I've added it to the ImmutablePointFactory from earlier:

```
@Singleton
class ImmutablePointFactory {
    ImmutablePoint newImmutablePoint(xval,yval) {
        return new ImmutablePoint(x:xval,y:yval)
    }
}
```

Again, I can't resist saying it: that was easy. The result is that the class now contains a static property called instance, which contains, naturally enough, the one and only instance of the class. Also, everything is implemented in as correct a manner as possible by the author[10] of the transformation. In Groovy code I can now write the following:

```
ImmutablePoint p = ImmutablePointFactory.instance.newImmutablePoint(3,4)
```

---

[10] Paul King, one of the coauthors of *Groovy in Action* (Manning, 2007) and a fantastic developer. Let me be blunt about this: everything Paul King writes is good. He tends to add his presentations to SlideShare.net as well, so go read them as soon as humanly possible.

That works just fine. It's when I try to do the same thing in Java that I run into problems. Again, the compiler understands, but I've never been able to coax my IDE into believing that the factory class has a `public static` field called `instance` in it.

Still, the annotation works and the IDEs will eventually understand how to deal with it. In fact, all the cool new AST transformations work, and I encourage you to consider them significant shortcuts to writing applications.

There are other AST transformations available and more being written all the time. I encourage you to keep an eye on them in case one comes along that can simplify your code the same way the ones just discussed do.

As cool as AST transformations are, though, our last task is so much easier to do in Groovy than in Java that it practically sells Groovy to Java developers all by itself. That issue is parsing and generating XML.

4.5 Working with XML

Way back in the late 90s, when XML was young, new, and still popular (as hard to imagine as that may be now), the combination of XML and Java was expected to be a very productive one. Java was the portable language (write once, run anywhere, right?), and XML was the portable data format. Unfortunately, if you've ever tried working with XML through the Java built-in APIs you know the results have fallen far short of the promise. Why are the Java APIs for working with XML so painful to use?

Here's a trivial example. I have a list of books in XML format, as shown here:

```
<books>
    <book isbn="...">
        <title>Groovy in Action</title>
        <author>Dierk Koenig</author>
        <author>Paul King</author>
        ...
    </book>
    <book isbn="...">
        <title>Grails in Action</title>
        <author>Glen Smith</author>
        <author>Peter Ledbrook</author>
    </book>
    <book isbn="...">
        <title>Making Java Groovy[11]</title>
        <author>Ken Kousen</author>
    </book>
</books>
```

Now assume that my task is to print the title of the second book. What could be easier? Here's one Java solution, based on parsing the data into a document object model (DOM) tree and finding the right element:

---

[11] I had to find some way to include my book in that august company, just to bask in the reflected glory.

```
public class ProcessBooks {
    public static void main(String[] args) {
        DocumentBuilderFactory factory =
            DocumentBuilderFactory.newInstance();
        Document doc = null;
        try {
            DocumentBuilder builder = factory.newDocumentBuilder();
            doc = builder.parse("src/jag/xml/books.xml");
        } catch (ParserConfigurationException e) {
            e.printStackTrace();
        } catch (SAXException e) {
            e.printStackTrace();
        } catch (IOException e) {
            e.printStackTrace();
        }
        if (doc == null) return;
        NodeList titles = doc.getElementsByTagName("title");
        Element titleNode = (Element) titles.item(1);
        String title = titleNode.getFirstChild().getNodeValue();
        System.out.println("The second title is " + title);
    }
}
```

This is actually the short version of the required program. To make it any shorter I'd have to collapse the exception handling into catching just `Exception`, or add a `throws` clause to the `main` method.

Many APIs in Java are designed around a set of interfaces, with the assumption that there will be many different alternative implementations. In the Java API for XML Processing (JAXP) world there are many parsers available, so the API is dominated by interfaces. Of course, you can't instantiate an interface, so using the API comes down to factories and factory methods.

To parse the XML file using a simple DOM parser, therefore, I first need to acquire the relevant factory, using its `newInstance` method. Then I use the factory method `newDocumentBuilder`, which is admittedly a really good name for a factory method. Parsing the file is then done through the `parse` method, as expected. Inside the DOM parser the tree is constructed using, interestingly enough, a SAX parser, which is why I need to prepare for SAX exceptions.

Assuming I get that far, the result at that point is a reference to the DOM tree. Finding my answer by traversing the tree is quite frankly out of the question. Traversals are highly sensitive to the presence of white-space nodes, and the available methods (`getFirstChild`, `getNextSibling`, and the like) aren't really a direct method to my answer. If whoever put together the XML file had been kind enough to assign each element an ID I could have used the great `getElementByID` method to extract the node I need, but no such luck there. Instead I'm reduced to collecting the relevant nodes using `getElementsByTagName`, which doesn't return something from the `Collections` framework as you might expect, but a `NodeList` instead. The `NodeList` class has an `item` method that takes an integer representing the zero-based index of the node I want, and at long last I have my title node.

Then there's the final indignity, which is that the value of a node is not the character content I want. No, I have to retrieve the first text child of the node, and only then can I get the value, which returns the text I needed.

> **XML and Groovy**
>
> I was once teaching a class about Java and XML, and one of the exercises was to extract a nested value. After taking the students through the awkward, ugly, Java solution, a woman in the back raised her hand.
>
> "I kept waiting for you to say, 'this is the hard way,'" she said, "and now here's the easy way, but you never got to the easy way."
>
> In reply I had to say, "Want to see the easy way? Let's look at the Groovy solution to this problem."
>
> ```
> def root = new XmlSlurper().parse('books.xml')
> println root.book[1].title
> ```
>
> How's that for easy? I instantiated an `XmlSlurper`, called its `parse` method on the XML file, and just walked the tree to the value I want.
>
> If I ever need to parse or generate XML I always add a Groovy module to do it.

Let's look at another, somewhat more practical, example. Remember the Google geocoder used in chapter 3? When the geocoder went to version 3, Google removed the requirement to register for a key (good) but also removed the CSV output type (unfortunate). Now the only available output types are either JSON or XML. Google also changed the URL for accessing the web service (pretty typical when versioning a web service, actually), embedding the two available output types into the new URLs. In chapter 9 on RESTful web services I'll have a lot more to say about the choice of output types (formally known as *content negotiation*), but here the type is embedded in the URL.

From a Java point of view, working with JSON output is a bit of a complication because it requires an external library to parse the JSON data. That's not too much of a burden because there are several good JSON libraries available, but you still have to pick one and learn to use it. We've already talked about how involved it is to work with XML data in Java, so that's not a great alternative either.

Groovy, however, eats XML for lunch. Let's see just how easy it is for Groovy to access the new geocoder and extract the returned latitude and longitude data.

First, here's a sample of the XML output returned from the web service for the input address of Google's home office:

```
<GeocodeResponse>
 <status>OK</status>
 <result>
  <type>street_address</type>
  <formatted_address>1600 Amphitheatre Pkwy, Mountain View, CA 94043, USA</
    formatted_address>
```

```
...
  <geometry>
   <location>
    <lat>37.4217550</lat>
    <lng>-122.0846330</lng>
   </location>
   ...
  </geometry>
 </result>
</GeocodeResponse>
```

A lot of child elements have been omitted from this response in order to focus on what I actually want. The latitude and longitude values are buried deep inside the output. Of course, digging to that point is easy enough for Groovy. Here's a script that creates the required HTTP request, transmits it to Google, and extracts the response, all in less than a dozen lines:

```
String street = '1600 Ampitheatre Parkway'
String city = 'Mountain View'; state = 'CA'
String base = 'http://maps.google.com/maps/api/geocode/xml?'
String url = base + [sensor:false,
    address:[street, city, state].collect { v ->
         URLEncoder.encode(v,'UTF-8')
    }.join(',')].collect {k,v -> "$k=$v"}.join('&')
def response = new XmlSlurper().parse(url)
latitude = response.result[0].geometry.location.lat
longitude = response.result[0].geometry.location.lng
```

The code strongly resembles the version 2 client presented earlier, in that I have a base URL for the service (note that it includes the response type, XML, as part of the URL) and a parameters map that I convert into a query string. Transmitting the request and parsing the result is done in one line of code, because the `XmlSlurper` class has a `parse` method that takes a URL. Then extracting the latitude and longitude is simply a matter of walking the tree.

Several times I've written applications that took this script, after converting it to a class that used a `Location` like before, and added it as a service. The code savings over the corresponding Java version is just too great to ignore.

Parsing is one thing, but what about generation? For that, Groovy provides a builder class called `groovy.xml.MarkupBuilder`.

Consider another POJO representing a `Song`, as shown here:

```
public class Song {
    private int id;
    private String title;
    private String artist;
    private String year;

    public Song() {}

    public Song(int id, String title, String artist, String year) {
        this.id = id;
        this.title = title;
```

```
        this.artist = artist;
        this.year = year;
    }

    public int getId() { return id;  }
    public void setId(int id) { this.id = id; }
    public String getTitle() { return title; }
    public void setTitle(String title) { this.title = title; }
    public String getArtist() { return artist; }
    public void setArtist(String artist) { this.artist = artist; }
    public String getYear() { return year; }
    public void setYear(String year) { this.year = year; }
}
```

The Song class, implemented in Java, contains an id and strings for the title, artist, and year. The rest is just constructors, getters, and setters. In a real system the class would also probably have overrides of toString, equals, and hashCode, but I don't need that here.

How should Song instances be represented in XML? One simple idea would be to treat the ID as an attribute of the song, and have title, artist, and year as child elements. In the following listing I show part of a Groovy class that converts Song instances to XML and back.

Listing 4.10 Converting songs to XML and back

```
class SongXMLConverter {
    String song2xml(Song s) {
        StringWriter sw = new StringWriter()                  // Output buffer for XML
        MarkupBuilder builder = new MarkupBuilder(sw)
        builder.song(id:s.id) {                               // Script the XML using Groovy builder
            title s.title
            artist s.artist
            year s.year
        }
        return sw.toString()
    }

    Song xml2song(String xml) {
        def root = new XmlSlurper().parseText(xml)
        return new Song(id:root.@id.toInteger(),
            title:root.title, artist:root.artist, year:root.year)
    }

    String songlist2xml(songs) {
        StringWriter sw = new StringWriter()
        MarkupBuilder builder = new MarkupBuilder(sw)
        builder.songs {                                       // Script the XML using Groovy builder
            songs.each { s ->
                song(id:s.id) {
                    title s.title
                    artist s.artist
                    year s.year
                }
            }
```

```
        }
        return sw.toString()
    }

    List<Song> xml2songlist(String xml) {
        def result = []
        def root = new XmlSlurper().parseText(xml)
        root.song.each { s ->
            result << new Song(id:s.@id.toInteger(),title:s.title,
                artist:s.artist,year:s.year)
        }
        return result
    }
}
```

The `SongXMLConverter` class has four methods: one to convert a single song to XML, one to convert XML to a single song, and two to do the same for a collection of songs. Converting from XML to `Song` instances is done with the `XmlSlurper` illustrated earlier. The only new part is that the slurper accesses the song ID value using the `@id` notation, where the `@` is used to retrieve an attribute. Figure 4.7 shows the job of the `XmlSlurper`, or its analogous class, `XmlParser`.

Going the other direction, from song to XML, is done with a `MarkupBuilder`. The `MarkupBuilder` class writes to standard output by default. In this class I want to return the XML as a string, so I used the overloaded `MarkupBuilder` constructor that takes a `java.io.Writer` as an argument. I supply a `StringWriter` to the constructor, build the XML, and then convert the output to a `String` using the normal `toString` method.

Once I have a `MarkupBuilder` I write out the song's properties as though I was building the XML itself. Let's focus on the conversion of a single song to XML form, as shown next:

```
MarkupBuilder builder = new MarkupBuilder(sw)
builder.song(id:s.id) {
    title s.title
    artist s.artist
    year s.year
}
```

The job of the `MarkupBuilder` is illustrated in figure 4.8.

This is an example of Groovy's metaprogramming capabilities, though it doesn't look like it at first. The idea is that inside the builder, whenever I write the name of a

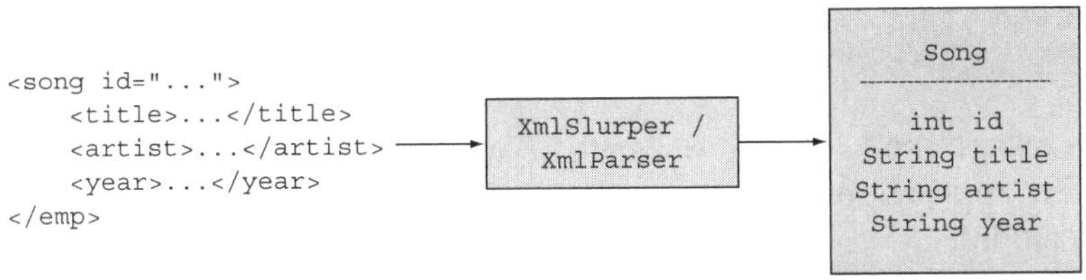

```
<song id="...">
    <title>...</title>
    <artist>...</artist>   --->  XmlSlurper /  --->  Song
    <year>...</year>             XmlParser           ----------
</emp>                                               int id
                                                     String title
                                                     String artist
                                                     String year
```

Figure 4.7 Using an `XmlSlurper` or `XmlParser` to populate an object from XML data

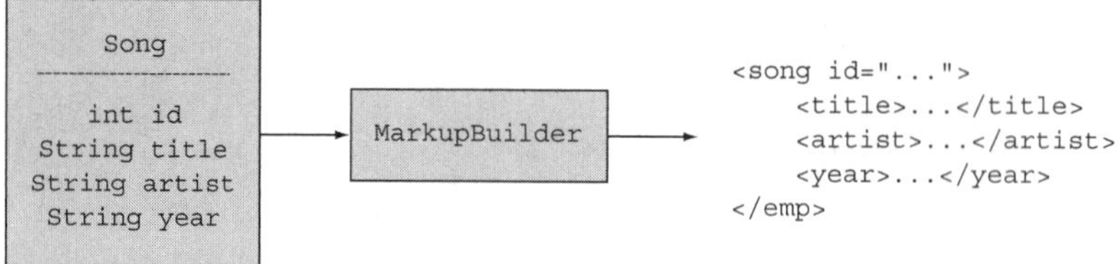

Figure 4.8 Generating an XML representation of an object using a `groovy.xml.MarkupBuilder`

method that doesn't exist, the builder interprets it as an instruction to create an XML element. For example, I invoke the `song` method on the builder with the argument being a map with a key called `id` and a value being the song's ID. The builder doesn't have a `song` method, of course, so it interprets the method call as a command to build an element called `song`, and the argument is an instruction to add an `id` attribute to the `song` element whose value is the song ID. Then, when it encounters the curly brace it interprets that as an instruction to begin child elements.

I have three more method calls: one to `title`, one to `artist`, and one to `year`. The lack of parentheses can be misleading in this case, but each is actually a method call. Once again the builder interprets each of the non-existent methods as commands to create XML elements, and the arguments this time, because they're not in map form, become character data contained in the elements. The result of the builder process is the XML shown next:

```
<song id="...">
    <title>...</title>
    <artist>...</artist>
    <year>...</year>
</song>
```

The method that converts a list of songs into a larger XML file just does the same thing for each song.

Lessons learned (XML)

1. Groovy's `XmlParser` and `XmlSlurper` make parsing XML trivial, and values can be extracted by walking the resulting DOM tree.
2. Generating XML is just as easy, using `MarkupBuilder`.

GROOVY SWEET SPOT Groovy is excellent at parsing and generating XML. If your Java application works with XML, strongly consider delegating to a Groovy module.

4.6 Working with JSON data

Groovy processes JSON data as easily as it processes XML. To conclude this chapter, let me present a trivial example of JSON response data from a web service.

The service is known as ICNDB: the Internet Chuck Norris Database. It is located at http://icndb.com and has a RESTful API for retrieving the associated jokes. If you send an HTTP GET request to http://api.icndb.com/jokes/random?limitTo=[nerdy] you get back a string in JSON form.

Groovy makes it easy to send a GET request. In the Groovy JDK the `String` class has a `toURL` method, which converts it to an instance of `java.net.URL`. Then the Groovy JDK adds a method to the URL class called `getText`. Accessing the web service is therefore as simple as

```
String url = 'http://api.icndb.com/jokes/random?limitTo=[nerdy]'
String jsonTxt = url.toURL().text
println jsonTxt
```

Executing this returns a JSON object of the form

```
{ "type": "success", "value": { "id": 563, "joke": "Chuck Norris causes the
    Windows Blue Screen of Death.", "categories": ["nerdy"] } }
```

In all the Google geocoder demonstrations I've used so far in this book I introduced the `XmlSlurper` class, whose `parse` method takes the URL in string form and automatically converts the result to a DOM tree. Since version 1.8, Groovy also includes a `JsonSlurper`, but it doesn't have as many overloads of the `parse` method as the `XmlSlurper` does. It does, however, contain a `parseText` method, which can process the `jsonTxt` returned from the previous code.

If I add that to the earlier lines, the complete ICNDB script is shown in the next listing.

Listing 4.11 `chuck_norris.groovy`, which processes data from ICNDB

```
import groovy.json.JsonSlurper

String url = 'http://api.icndb.com/jokes/random?limitTo=[nerdy]'
String jsonTxt = url.toURL().text
def json = new JsonSlurper().parseText(jsonTxt)
def joke = json?.value?.joke
println joke
```

The `parseText` method on `JsonSlurper` converts the JSON data into Groovy maps and lists. I then access the `value` property of the `json` object, which is a contained JSON object. It has a `joke` property, which contains the string I'm looking for.

The result of executing this script is something like this:

```
Chuck Norris can make a method abstract and final
```

Just as generating XML is done by scripting the output through a `MarkupBuilder`, generating JSON data uses the `groovy.json.JsonBuilder` class. See the GroovyDocs for `JsonBuilder` for a complete example.

Lessons learned (JSON)

1. The `JsonSlurper` class has a `parseText` method for working with JSON formatted strings.
2. The `JsonBuilder` class generates JSON strings using the same mechanism as the `XmlSlurper`.

This completes the tour of Groovy features that can be added to Java applications regardless of use case.

Lessons learned (Groovy features used in Java)

1. When Groovy access a POJO it can use the map-based constructor as though it were a POGO.
2. Every operator in Groovy delegates to a method, and if that method is implemented in a Java class the operator in Groovy will still use it. This means you can do operator overloading even in a Java class.
3. The Groovy JDK documents all the methods that Groovy adds to the Java standard API through metaprogramming.
4. Groovy AST transformations can only be applied to Groovy classes, but the classes can be mixed with Java in interesting ways. This chapter includes examples of `@Delegate`, `@Immutable`, and `@Singleton`.

4.7 Summary

This chapter reviewed many ways that Groovy can help Java at the basic level, from POJO enhancements to AST transformations to building XML and more. I'll use these techniques in future chapters wherever they can help. I'll also review other helpful techniques along the way, though these are most of the major ones.

The next couple of chapters, however, change the focus. Although mixing Java and Groovy is easy and is a major theme of this book, some companies are reluctant to add Groovy to production code until their developers have a certain minimum comfort level with the language. As it happens, there are two major areas where Groovy can strongly impact and simplify Java projects without being integrated directly. The first of those is one of the major pain points in enterprise development: the build process. The other is testing, which is valued more highly the better the developer.

By covering these two techniques early in the book I can then use, for example, Gradle builds and Spock tests when I attack the use cases Java developers typically encounter, like web services, database manipulation, or working with the Spring framework.

Part 2

Groovy tools

Welcome to part 2: "Groovy tools." In these two chapters, I address two of the major ways Groovy is often introduced into an organization: namely, build processes and testing.

Chapter 5 on build processes reviews the dominant build tools in the Java world, Ant and Maven, and shows how to add Groovy dependencies to each. It also covers the Ant tasks that work with Groovy and the major Groovy plugins for Maven. Finally, it provides an introduction to Gradle, one of the most important projects in the Groovy world, and includes examples covering several interesting build tasks.

Chapter 6 on testing starts with JUnit tests in both Java and Groovy and then looks at the JUnit subclass `GroovyTestCase` and its descendants and what additional capabilities they bring. Then it covers the `MockFor` and `StubFor` classes in the Groovy library, which are great ways to build mock objects and also provide some insight into Groovy metaprogramming. Finally, the chapter ends with a good overview of the Spock testing framework, which includes mocking capabilities of its own.

5 Build processes

This chapter covers

- Adding Groovy to Ant builds
- Using Maven with Groovy
- Groovy Grapes and `@Grab`
- The future: Gradle

Building source code is almost always a pain point in development organizations. An ideal build process is automated end-to-end, including compilation, running tests, generating reports, and producing any required artifacts. The process needs to be fast enough that it can be done frequently, especially given modern agile approaches, and yet flexible enough to adapt to the exigencies of individual teams.

In the Java world two primary approaches to automated builds have emerged over time. Both are open source projects from Apache. The first is Ant (http://ant.apache.org), which uses a library of tasks configured in XML backed by Java classes. The other is Maven (http://maven.apache.org), which offers a rich array of options and promises to make the entire process simple, but uses a highly opinionated API that requires a degree of mastery to use effectively.

To start I want to address the goals of any build process, and then see how the various tools attempt to meet them.

5.1 The build challenge

A software build combines several features that individually seem like they ought to be easy but in practice become complicated. To build your code you must

- Download any necessary dependencies.
- Compile the source code with the dependencies properly resolved, handling any cross-language issues that may arise.
- Run the unit, integration, and/or functional tests.
- Produce the desired artifacts, whatever they may be.

Optionally, other tasks might include checking code out of source code control, generating documentation, and even deploying the results into production.

> **The IDE build**
>
> Some companies still do their builds inside integrated development environments (IDEs). Although this is not in itself a bad thing, it often leads to long-term problems. Sooner or later such companies wind up with a special computer that no one is allowed to touch, even though the original owner left or transferred to another division long ago, because it's the only system where the build still works.
>
> Current thinking is that the source code control system should manage all aspects of a build, from the required scripts to the JAR dependencies. That way you can always be sure the build is correct and self-sufficient, which avoids the whole "at least it works on my machine" problem.

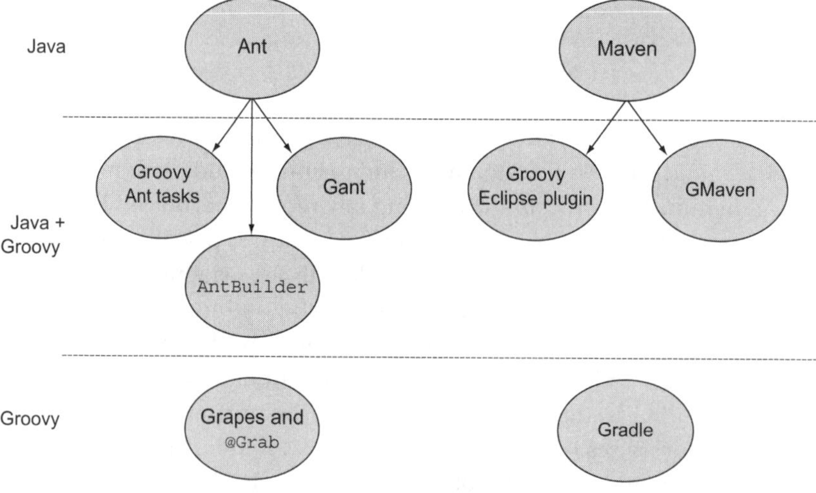

Figure 5.1 Guide to technologies in this chapter. Java approaches are based on Ant or Maven. Groovy supplies Ant tasks for compilation and executing scripts. Gant is used by Grails but will eventually be replaced by Gradle. The `AntBuilder` class is useful and built into Gradle. There are two separate plugins available for Maven builds. Groovy Grapes make it easy to deliver code (normally scripts) to a client without compiling it first. Ultimately, though, the future belongs to Gradle.

In fact, the recent trend in development processes is toward continuous delivery, where a single command performs the whole sequence from build to deployment in one motion.[1]

There are two primary build tools in the Java world: Ant and Maven. Ant is older and is gradually being replaced, but it is still common in the industry and is the foundation of everything that came afterward. Maven is used extensively in the Java industry but tends to trigger strong feelings in developers.

A guide to the technologies covered in this chapter is shown in figure 5.1. I'll start with the Apache Ant project in the next section.

5.2 The Java approach, part 1: Ant

Apache Ant is a Java-based build tool, based on the older "make" technology but without many of its difficulties. The name Ant represents either "another neat tool" or a tool that lifts far more than its own weight, depending on whom you ask. Ant build files are written in XML, so they are inherently cross-platform, and because Java classes implement the XML tasks, a single API suffices for all operating systems.

That's the good news. The (somewhat) bad news is that Ant is an extremely low-level API, so many build files consist of lots of twisty little tasks, all alike.[2]

Let me start with a "Hello, World" example in the next listing, based on a sample from the Ant tutorial provided by Apache at the Ant website.

Listing 5.1 build.xml: A simple Ant build file for a "Hello, World" Java application

```
<project name="HelloWorld" basedir="." default="main">

    <property name="src.dir"     value="src"/>
    <property name="build.dir"   value="build"/>
    <property name="classes.dir" value="${build.dir}/classes"/>
    <property name="jar.dir"     value="${build.dir}/jar"/>
    <property name="main-class"  value="mjg.HelloWorld"/>

    <target name="clean">
        <delete dir="${build.dir}"/>
    </target>

    <target name="compile">
        <mkdir dir="${classes.dir}"/>
        <javac srcdir="${src.dir}" destdir="${classes.dir}"
            includeantruntime="false"/>
    </target>

    <target name="jar" depends="compile">
        <mkdir dir="${jar.dir}"/>
        <jar destfile="${jar.dir}/${ant.project.name}.jar"
```

---

1 See Jez Humble and Dave Farley's book *Continuous Delivery* (Addison Wesley, 2010) for details. (Available through its companion website, http://continuousdelivery.com/.)

2 Yes, an Adventure (or Zork) reference. I just mean they're small, they're many, and they're easy to get lost in.

```
            basedir="${classes.dir}">
            <manifest>
                <attribute name="Main-Class" value="${main-class}"/>
            </manifest>
        </jar>
    </target>

    <target name="run" depends="jar">
        <java jar="${jar.dir}/${ant.project.name}.jar" fork="true"/>
    </target>

    <target name="clean-build" depends="clean,jar"/>

    <target name="main" depends="clean,run"/>

</project>
```

By default, this file is called build.xml and resides in the root directory of the project. The root element of the project file is called `<project>`, which is given a `name`, a base directory, and the name of a default task to run if none is supplied on the command line.

At the top of the file a series of properties are set, including the locations of various directories. Note that one property can refer to another by using the `${...}` syntax.

A series of `<task>` elements (`clean`, `compile`, `jar`, `run`, `clean-compile`, and `main`) are defined to represent individual actions during the build process. Some tasks depend on others, which is expressed using the `depends` attribute of the `<task>` element.

All the defined tasks ultimately delegate to a library of predefined Ant tasks. Here those tasks include file-based tasks like `mkdir` and `delete`, and Java-related tasks like `javac`, `jar`, and `java`.

Executing this build without arguments means typing `ant` at the command line, which will execute the default `main` task. Because `main` depends on `clean` and `run` it will execute those tasks first, which will execute their own individual dependencies, and so on. The result looks like the following listing.

Listing 5.2 Execution of the default task in the "Hello, World" Ant build

```
Buildfile: /.../build.xml
clean:
   [delete] Deleting directory /.../build
compile:
    [mkdir] Created dir: /.../build/classes
    [javac] Compiling 1 source file to /.../build/classes
jar:
    [mkdir] Created dir: /.../build/jar
      [jar] Building jar: /.../build/jar/HelloWorld.jar
run:
     [java] Hello, World!
main:
BUILD SUCCESSFUL
Total time: 1 second
```

Each task outputs its own name, followed by the included built-in Ant tasks indented underneath. The build completed successfully, though that can be misleading. The `BUILD SUCCESSFUL` statement at the end means that Ant finished all the tasks. The individual tasks may or may not have worked.

The tasks chosen here are typical, but there is no standard. Each organization (and even each developer) is free to choose their own. Reusing tasks between different builds also requires an `import` statement (or copy-and-paste reuse), plus some effort to make sure the tasks are not tied to a particular project structure.

Again, the benefit here is that this is all completely portable. The Ant build should work just as well on Mac OS X as it does on Windows or Linux. The downside is that this is a trivial Hello World application and the build file is already over 35 lines long. Once you add in the `junit` and `junitreport` tasks, to say nothing of customizing the classpath with third-party libraries, the size of this file will grow quickly. A more extensive build file, including the JUnit 4 libraries and a test case, can be found in the chapter source code.

Rather than do that here, however, let me show you how to introduce Groovy into this system.

5.3 Making Ant Groovy

Ant is not as common in Java builds as it used to be, but switching build tools is a major decision for most organizations and not to be undertaken lightly. If you're working with a large installed base of Ant builds, then Groovy can still contribute.

Four approaches are available:

- Groovy scripting code can be added directly to an Ant build file.
- Groovy scripts and classes can be compiled and executed in Ant builds using special Ant tasks for that purpose.
- The Groovy standard library contains a special class called `groovy.util.AntBuilder` that can replace the XML build file with Groovy scripting code that does the same thing.
- There's a Groovy DSL available, called Gant, which provides an alternative to `AntBuilder`.

ANTBUILDER Even if you don't use Ant, the `AntBuilder` class is worth knowing about because it's embedded in other build tools, like Gant and Gradle.

The following subsections will tackle each of these Groovy and Ant topics in turn.

5.3.1 The <groovy> Ant task

Ant has two hooks that allow you to add Groovy to a standard build file. The `<groovy>` and `<groovyc>` tasks use the Groovy libraries to execute Groovy scripts and compile Groovy source files, respectively.

Starting first with <groovy>, defining the associated task in an Ant build lets you write Groovy code directly into the build file. The following listing shows a trivial example.

Listing 5.3 A trivial Ant build that executes Groovy code in a task

```
<?xml version="1.0" encoding="UTF-8"?>
<project name="Groovy Ant" basedir="." default="info">
    <property environment="env" />                          <!-- Access environment variables -->

    <path id="groovy.classpath">
    <fileset dir="${env.GROOVY_HOME}/embeddable" />         <!-- Use the groovy-all JAR file -->
    </path>

    <taskdef name="groovy"                                  <!-- Define the groovy task -->
           classname="org.codehaus.groovy.ant.Groovy"
           classpathref="groovy.classpath" />

    <target name="info">
        <groovy>                                            <!-- Use the groovy task -->
             println 'Hello, World!'
             ant.echo 'Hello, World!'
        </groovy>
    </target>
</project>
```

The environment property allows the build to access system properties in the operating system. Here the env variable is used to access the current value of GROOVY_HOME, the installation directory for Groovy. The <path> element assigns the groovy-all JAR file (found in the embeddable directory) to the groovy.classpath ID.

The <taskdef> element then defines the groovy task as a reference to the org.codehaus.groovy.ant.Groovy class, which is resolved in the groovy-all JAR file. Once the groovy task has been defined it can be used to execute arbitrary Groovy code. A straight print of "Hello, World!" is executed, and then the Ant echo task is also called.

It's therefore easy enough to add Groovy code to an existing Ant build file, which can be useful if looping or conditional logic is needed in the build. It's notoriously difficult to "program" in XML, and technologies that tend that direction (like Ant and XSLT) often result in awkward, complex build files. Adding Groovy scripting code might help the build file without modifying the underlying source code.

5.3.2 The <groovyc> Ant task

Say you follow the advice in this book and decide to add Groovy modules to your implementation code. If you're still going to build with Ant you'll need a compilation task, similar to <javac>, for Groovy. That task is <groovyc>.

The basic <groovyc> task definition is simple enough:

```
<taskdef name="groovyc"
    classname="org.codehaus.groovy.ant.Groovyc"
    classpathref="groovy.classpath"/>
```

The name of the task is <groovyc>, and it's backed by the Groovyc class in the org.codehaus.groovy.ant package. This class is part of the Groovy Ant JARs referenced in the earlier build file.

The result of this task definition is that you can compile Groovy classes with <groovyc> while you compile Java classes with <javac>. This enforced separation of code bases can lead to difficulties, however, if there are cross dependencies. For example, a Groovy class may implement a Java interface and reference a Java class, which in turn uses a Groovy class, and so on.

A good way to resolve these issues is to use the *joint-compilation* approach. Ant lets you embed the <javac> task inside the <groovyc> task. The nested tag approach results in a <groovyc> task that looks like this:

```
<groovyc srcdir="${src.dir}" destdir="${classes.dir}"
    classpathref="classpath">
    <javac source="1.5" target="1.5" />
</groovyc>
```

The nested <javac> task doesn't imply the Java compiler is running. As a child of the <groovyc> task it lets the Groovy joint compiler do all the work.

The source directory, destination directory, and classpath variables defined in the <groovyc> task are passed down to the nested <javac> task. The joint-compilation approach means that Groovy will compile the Groovy sources and create stubs for them, then call the Java compiler to do the same for the Java sources, and resume the compilation process with the Groovy compiler. The result is that you can mix Java and Groovy sources without a problem.

Therefore, to extend the Ant build file presented section 5.2 to include Groovy files, make the additions and changes shown in the next listing.

Listing 5.4 Extending the "Hello, World" build to mix Java and Groovy sources

```
    <path id="groovy.classpath">
       <fileset dir="${env.GROOVY_HOME}/embeddable" />
    </path>

    <path id="classpath">
        <fileset dir="${lib.dir}" includes="**/*.jar" />
    </path>

    <taskdef name="groovyc"
        classname="org.codehaus.groovy.ant.Groovyc"
        classpathref="groovy.classpath" />
...
    <target name="compile">
        <mkdir dir="${classes.dir}" />
           <groovyc srcdir="${src.dir}" destdir="${classes.dir}"
               classpathref="classpath">
               <javac source="1.5" target="1.5" />
           </groovyc>
       </target>
```

The rest is the same as before.

If you're committed to Ant builds using XML, that's all there is to it. If, however, you're willing to switch your build language to Groovy, there are a couple of other alternatives. The next two subsections use Groovy for the build language but are still fundamentally based on Ant.

5.3.3 Writing your build in Groovy with AntBuilder

The standard Groovy library includes a class called `groovy.util.AntBuilder`. To use it you need to add the Java-based Ant JAR library files to your classpath, but once you do, `AntBuilder` lets you replace the XML syntax with Groovy.

Any task defined by Ant can be used through the `AntBuilder` class. For example, the following listing shows a simple script that makes a copy of its own source, verifies that it worked, and then deletes the copy.

Listing 5.5 `antbuilder.groovy`, which copies itself

```
def ant = new AntBuilder()
String dir = 'src/main/groovy'

assert !(new File("$dir/antbuildercopy.groovy").exists())

ant.echo 'about to copy the source code'
ant.copy file:"$dir/antbuilder.groovy",
    tofile:"$dir/antbuildercopy.groovy"

assert (new File("$dir/antbuildercopy.groovy").exists())

ant.echo 'deleting the copied file'
ant.delete file:"$dir/antbuildercopy.groovy"
```

Builder code and regular Groovy code are freely intermixed in this example. The Ant tasks used here are `echo`, `copy`, and `delete`, but it would be easy enough to use others like `javac`, `junitreport`, or even optional Ant tasks like `mail`. As long as the required Ant libraries are in the classpath, each will work.

There's actually a simplification available. The `with` syntax is available as a part of Groovy's metaprogramming capabilities. It can simplify the previous listing down to that shown in the next listing.

Listing 5.6 Simplifying the build script using the `with` method

```
ant.with {
    echo 'about to copy the source code'
    copy file:"$dir/antbuilder.groovy",
        tofile:"$dir/antbuildercopy.groovy"
    echo 'deleting the copied file'
    delete file:"$dir/antbuildercopy.groovy"
}
```

The `with` method invokes the contained methods on the Ant builder.

AntBuilder can be used to script entire build files. It's useful for creating a build file quickly, especially if you already know the corresponding Ant tasks well. Because AntBuilder is part of the standard Groovy library it can be used wherever you need to do build-related tasks. Even better, Gradle build files include an instance of AntBuilder, making the migration path from Ant to Gradle much simpler.

A more interesting example is given in the next listing, which is a port of the original Ant build shown in listing 5.1.

Listing 5.7 A Groovy AntBuilder script port of the build.xml file from listing 5.1

```
AntBuilder ant = new AntBuilder()                        Instantiate the builder

String srcDir = 'src'
String buildDir = 'build'                                Port of
String classesDir = "${buildDir}/classes"                <property>
String jarDir = "${buildDir}/jar"                        elements
String reportDir = "${buildDir}/reports"
String libDir = 'lib'

ant.with {                                               Use builder as delegate
    path(id:'classpath') {                               for unrecognized
        fileset dir:libDir, includes:"**/*.jar"          methods in block
    }

    path id:'application', location:"$jarDir/HelloAntBuilder.jar"

    delete dir:buildDir
    mkdir dir:classesDir                                 Compile Java
    javac(srcdir:srcDir, destDir:classesDir,
        includeantruntime:false, classpathref:'classpath')

    mkdir dir:jarDir
    jar(destfile:"${jarDir}/HelloAntBuilder.jar", basedir:classesDir) {
        manifest {                                       Build JAR
            attribute name:'Main-Class', value:'mjg.HelloWorld'
        }
    }

    mkdir dir:reportDir
    junit(printsummary:'yes') {
        classpath {
            path refid:'classpath'
            path refid:'application'
        }                                                Run tests
        formatter type:'xml'
        batchtest(fork:'yes', todir:reportDir) {
            fileset dir:srcDir, includes:"**/*Test.java"
        }

    }

    junitreport(todir:reportDir) {
        fileset dir:reportDir, includes:"TEST-*.xml"     Generate
        report todir:reportDir                           test report
    }
```

```
        java(jar:"$jarDir/HelloAntBuilder.jar", fork:'true') {
            classpath {
                path refid:'classpath'
                path refid:'application'
            }
        }
    }
```

Execute main method

You execute this script with the groovy command. Inside the with block, all methods like mkdir, javac, and junit are passed to the builder instance. Formally this means that the delegate property for the with block is the AntBuilder instance. Because this is a Groovy script you could add any code you wish to do other processing. It's notoriously awkward do arrange loops and conditionals inside XML files, for instance, but here that would be easy.

For all of its simplicity, though, AntBuilder is still just Ant under the hood. Groovy wouldn't be Groovy if there wasn't a domain-specific language (DSL) alternative. The best of breed is Gradle, which is discussed later in this chapter. There's another approach, however, which you may encounter in practice. For completeness the next subsection contains a brief discussion of Groovy Ant, known as Gant.

5.3.4 Custom build scripts with Gant

Although the future of build files in Groovy belongs to Gradle, Gant still occupies one special niche in the Groovy ecosystem. As of this writing, the latest version of the Grails framework (2.3)[3] still implements its build scripts in Gant.[4] If you need to create a custom build script for a Grails application, Gant is still useful. If you're not planning to do that, you can comfortably skip this subsection.

> **GANT USE CASE** Grails commands are implemented as Gant scripts, so if you need to customize a Grails command or create a new one, Gant is the tool of choice.

The Gant scripts in Grails are also an excellent choice of sample code. To keep this section simple I'll review parts of an existing Grails Gant script, called Clean.groovy. The script can be found in the scripts directory under the root of the Grails distribution. As with all Grails Gant scripts, it's invoked using the script name in lowercase, substituting dashes for camel case; so for the Clean script the command would be grails clean, and for the CreateDomainObject script the command is grails create-domain-object.

Here's the Clean script in its entirety (minus the copyright statement):

```
includeTargets << grailsScript("_GrailsClean")
setDefaultTarget("cleanAll")
```

[3] Grails is discussed in chapter 8 on databases and chapter 10 on web development. The home page for Grails is http://grails.org.

[4] Gant will continue to be included in Grails through at least version 2.3.

The grailsScript command loads a different Gant script, called _GrailsClean. By convention (and Grails is all about conventions), scripts that begin with an underscore are internal scripts that can't be executed from the command line. The first line thus loads a series of tasks, and the second line makes the cleanAll task the default.

Turning now to the _GrailsClean script, let me highlight a couple of small sections from it:

```
includeTargets << grailsScript("_GrailsEvents")

target (cleanAll: "Cleans a Grails project") {
    clean()
    cleanTestReports()
    grailsConsole.updateStatus "Application cleaned."
}

target (clean: "Implementation of clean") {
    depends(cleanCompiledSources, cleanWarFile)
}
```

The resemblance to Ant is not accidental. Gant scripts contain targets, and targets can be invoked as though they were method calls. Here the target defined with the name cleanAll invokes two other tasks (clean and cleanTestReports) and then invokes the updateStatus method on the predefined grailsConsole object.

The clean task uses the depends method (again analogous to the same functionality in Ant) to make sure that the cleanCompiledSources and cleanWarFile tasks are invoked when the clean task is invoked. Here's a snippet from the cleanCompiledSources task:

```
target (cleanCompiledSources: "Cleans compiled Java and Groovy sources") {
    def webInf = "${basedir}/web-app/WEB-INF"
    ant.delete(dir:"${webInf}/classes")
    ant.delete(file:webXmlFile.absolutePath, failonerror:false)
    ant.delete(dir:"${projectWorkDir}/gspcompile", failonerror:false)
```

The task goes on to delete many more items, delegating to an internal AntBuilder object in each case. The cleanWarFile task shows how you can mix in Groovy logic code inside a script:

```
target (cleanWarFile: "Cleans the deployable .war file") {
    if (buildConfig.grails.project.war.file) {
        warName = buildConfig.grails.project.war.file
    }
    else {
        def fileName = grailsAppName
        def version = metadata.'app.version'
        if (version) {
            fileName += "-$version"
        }
        warName = "${basedir}/${fileName}.war"
    }
```

```
    ant.delete(file:warName, failonerror:false)
}
```

This is straightforward Groovy code that simply defines some variables and sets their properties based on the current configuration, and then invokes the `delete` method on the `ant` object.

That's enough Gant for this book.[5]

5.3.5 Ant summary

That also concludes the discussion of Ant and Ant-based approaches, both in Java and Groovy. The "Lessons learned" sidebar shows the details.

Lessons learned (Ant)

1. If you have an existing Ant build, you can add `<groovyc>` and `<groovy>` tasks to it.
2. Gant is only used by Grails, and not for very much longer.
3. `AntBuilder` is rare by itself but is built into and useful in Gradle

It's time now to examine the other major build tool in the Java world: Maven.

Ant limitations

When it was released Ant was a major improvement over previous build processes. Still, it has major issues that complicate life, especially in larger builds. Here's a brief list of complexities associated with using Ant. This is not intended to be a criticism of Ant, but rather to highlight the issues that lead to the next-generation tools.

Ant builds are based on XML, and XML is not a scripting language. Builds inevitably need to be customized and usually vary depending on whether the project is in development, test, or production mode. Ant allows you to set properties, but properties aren't variables. It's especially difficult to do complex branching logic in an XML file.

Ant says nothing about dependency management. It assumes you have all the required libraries available and that you can build a file set to hold them and use that as your classpath. The Ivy project (also from Apache) fills that gap, and the combination of Ant and Ivy is much more common now than Ant alone.

XML was designed to be processed by programs, not people. Reading a short XML file isn't hard. Reading a long, involved one is, and even the trivial build file presented in this section is over 50 lines long when a few basic tasks are included.

---

[5] Additional information on Gant can be found at the Groovy website. There's also a decent tutorial in the book *Grails in Action* (Manning, 2009), by Peter Ledbrook and Glen Smith. Finally, the Grails user guide has a section on creating Gant scripts specifically for Grails.

> ***(continued)***
>
> *The built-in Ant tasks are very low level.* As a result, Ant build files quickly grow long and complex and involve a lot of repetition.
>
> For all these reasons and others Ant was ripe for a higher-level replacement. That role was filled by the Maven project, which is either a blessing or a curse depending on your experiences with it.

5.4 The Java approach, part 2: Maven

I'm going to confess up front that Maven is hard to talk about rationally. Its best features (establishing a conventional project layout, managing dependencies, providing a rich plugin architecture) are also considered some of its worst features (difficult to work outside its conventions, hard to manage transitive dependencies, the whole "download the internet" problem). I can honestly say I've never encountered a technology that's both common in the industry and yet loathed with the white-hot intensity of a thousand suns.[6] Bring up Maven in a group of developers, and someone will refuse to discuss "the M word." Yet, at the same time, somebody else will quietly say that they can make it do anything and don't understand what all the fuss is about.

My own experience isn't so black-and-white. I find that if a project was designed using Maven from the beginning, it tends to work well with the system. It's also hard to use that system without Maven. On the other hand, adding Maven to a system that wasn't started with it can be quite painful. In addition, friends have also assured me that once a system gets above a certain size, the whole process becomes an unmanageable mess.

Perhaps the best way to stay above the fray is to say that Maven has a highly opinionated API. To be successful you have to do things the Maven way. Plus, like Ant, you're coding your build in XML, which is never easy. The multi-project build capabilities are awkward, too.[7]

I will note that the standard Maven project layout (shown in figure 5.2) has become common throughout the industry. Also, people may complain about Maven's approach to dependency management, but I haven't seen anything dramatically better. Gradle (the proposed replacement, discussed later in this chapter) uses Maven repositories and Ivy dependency management and suffers from the same "download the internet" problem. Dependency management is just hard, no matter how you approach it.

Returning (at last) to the core theme of this book, the goal of this section is to show you how to incorporate Groovy into Maven builds. There are two ways to do that. I'll start with the Groovy-Eclipse plugin and then build the same application using the GMaven project.

---

6 Except possibly for every Microsoft technology ever.

7 Admittedly that doesn't sound terribly "above the fray," but at least I'm trying.

Figure 5.2 Standard Maven project structure used for the application in this section. Compiled sources are in src/main/java, and tests reside in src/test/java.

5.4.1 The Groovy-Eclipse plugin for Maven

The Groovy-Eclipse compiler plugin (http://mng.bz/2rHY) is a standard compiler plugin for Maven. It emerged from the effort to build a good Eclipse plugin for Groovy that worked with combined Groovy and Java projects. The Maven plugin is a way to take advantage of that effort, whether you plan to use the Eclipse IDE or not.

To demonstrate its use I'll build a small project that accesses the Yahoo! Weather web service and reports on the current conditions. This is easy enough to do in Java but becomes particularly simple in Groovy.

The Yahoo! Weather web service (http://developer.yahoo.com/weather/) provides weather information in the form of an RSS feed. The web service is accessed from a URL of the form

```
http://weather.yahooapis.com/forecastrss
```

The URL has two parameters, one required and one optional. The required parameter is `w`, a so-called WOEID (Where On Earth ID), that Yahoo uses to identify a location. The other parameter is `u`, which is used to specify the temperature units in Fahrenheit (`f`, the default) or Celsius (`c`). For unknown reasons, there's no way to programmatically look up a WOEID. Instead Yahoo! directs you to its own weather page and suggests you search for your city.

A simple HTTP GET request to the proper URL returns an XML response in RSS form. A sample is included on Yahoo!'s web page.

Suppose I decided to build a simple application to retrieve the current weather conditions based on this service. Maven recommends that you specify a particular artifact to begin the project, so I'll start with the classic `maven-archetype-quickstart`:

```
> mvn archetype:generate -DgroupId=mjg -DartifactId=weather
    -DarchetypeArtifactId=maven-archetype-quickstart
    -Dversion=1.0-SNAPSHOT -Dpackage=mjg
```

MAVEN ARCHETYPES The Groovy-Eclipse plugin uses regular Java archetypes and adds Groovy functionality. The GMaven approach in the next section includes a basic archetype to get started.

This generates a Java project with the standard layout, meaning the source code directory is src/main/java and the testing directory is src/test/java. The quick start archetype includes a trivial App.java and AppTest.java in those directories, respectively. The generator also adds a standard Maven POM file in the root directory, whose only dependency is on JUnit, as shown in the next listing.

Listing 5.8 The Maven pom.xml file for a standard Java project

```
<project xmlns="http://maven.apache.org/POM/4.0.0"
  xmlns:xsi="http://www.w3.org/2001/XMLSchema-instance"
  xsi:schemaLocation="http://maven.apache.org/POM/4.0.0
                      http://maven.apache.org/maven-v4_0_0.xsd">
  <modelVersion>4.0.0</modelVersion>
  <groupId>mjg</groupId>
  <artifactId>weather</artifactId>
  <packaging>jar</packaging>
  <version>1.0-SNAPSHOT</version>
  <name>weather</name>
  <url>http://maven.apache.org</url>
  <dependencies>
    <dependency>
      <groupId>junit</groupId>
      <artifactId>junit</artifactId>
      <version>4.10</version>
      <scope>test</scope>
    </dependency>
  </dependencies>
</project>
```

The only change I've made so far from the standard is to upgrade the JUnit dependency to 4.10 from 3.8.1.

To do the actual work I need a class to send the request to Yahoo and parse the response, and a POJO to hold the resulting weather information. Starting with the POJO, for a given city, region, and country I want to store the condition, temperature, wind chill, and humidity. The web service returns a lot more information than this, but this will suffice to get started.

POJOs are simple containers for data, so the constructors, getter and setter methods, and any necessary overrides are mostly clutter. I can therefore simplify my life if I use a POGO instead, as shown in the following listing.

Listing 5.9 `Weather.groovy`, a POGO to hold weather results from the web service

```
package mjg

class Weather {
    String city
    String region
    String country
    String condition
    String temp
```

```
    String chill
    String humidity

    String toString() {
        """
        Weather for $city, $region, $country:
        Condition   : $condition
        Temperature: $temp
        Wind Chill  : $chill
        Humidity    : $humidity
        """
    }
}
```

The toString method is a way to produce formatted output. Groovy's multiline string makes it particularly easy.

The other class I need is a parser for the web service. Because all I need is a GET request I can use the parse method in the XmlSlurper class as usual and drill down the resulting DOM tree to get the results I want. That's pretty simple, too, as shown in the following listing.

Listing 5.10 `YahooParser.groovy`, which accesses and parses the weather service

```
package mjg

class YahooParser {
    final static String BASE = 'http://weather.yahooapis.com/forecastrss?'

    Weather getWeather(String woeid) {
        def root = new XmlSlurper().parse(BASE + "w=$woeid")
        Weather w = new Weather(
            city:root.channel.location.@city,
            region:root.channel.location.@region,
            country:root.channel.location.@country,
            condition:root.channel.item.condition.@text,
            temp:root.channel.item.condition.@temp,
            chill:root.channel.wind.@chill,
            humidity:root.channel.atmosphere.@humidity
        )
    }
}
```

Given a WOEID, the service builds the URL and accesses the web service, parses the resulting RSS, and returns an instance of the Weather class with all the relevant fields populated.

To complete the program I need a driver, which I can write as a Groovy script. That's a one-liner, unless I want to allow the client to specify a WOEID on the command line:

```
def woeid = args.size() ? args[0] : '2367105'
println new YahooParser().getWeather(woeid)
```

The default WOEID in the script is for Boston, MA, and it's stored in `RunDemo.groovy`. In order to demonstrate the differences when both Java and Groovy sources are present together, I also added a Java class to access the web service in the file RunInJava.java:

```
public class RunInJava {
    public static void main(String[] args) {
        String woeid = "2367105";
        if (args.length > 0) woeid = args[0];
        YahooParser yp = new YahooParser();
        System.out.println(yp.getWeather(woeid));
    }
}
```

Now comes the interesting part: how do I get Maven to handle all the Groovy code? The Groovy-Eclipse plugin requires two additions to the POM file. First I need to add Groovy as a dependency:

```
<dependencies>
...
    <dependency>
        <groupId>org.codehaus.groovy</groupId>
        <artifactId>groovy-all</artifactId>
        <version>2.1.5</version>
    </dependency>
  </dependencies>
```

Next I need to add the Groovy-Eclipse plugin in a `build` section below the dependencies:

```
<build>
    <plugins>
        <plugin>
            <artifactId>maven-compiler-plugin</artifactId>
            <version>2.3.2</version>
            <configuration>
                <compilerId>groovy-eclipse-compiler</compilerId>
            </configuration>
            <dependencies>
                <dependency>
                    <groupId>org.codehaus.groovy</groupId>
                    <artifactId>groovy-eclipse-compiler</artifactId>
                    <version>2.7.0-01</version>
                </dependency>
            </dependencies>
        </plugin>
    </plugins>
</build>
```

With both of these additions Maven will compile and use Groovy code appropriately, except for one rather strange oddity. Normally I would add my Groovy classes to src/main/groovy and any Groovy tests to src/test/groovy. According to the plugin documentation, I can do that only if (1) there's at least one Java class in src/main/java or (2) I add a lot more XML to specify the additional source directories.

SOURCE DIRECTORIES For the Groovy-Eclipse plugin, put Java and Groovy sources in the src/main/java and src/test/java directories by default.

I put my Groovy files in src/main/java and src/test/java. Now I can build the project using

```
mvn clean install
```

I can even execute the project using the `exec:java` (!) task, both using the default WOEID and with a supplied command-line argument:

```
> mvn exec:java -Dexec.mainClass=mjg.RunDemo
...
        Weather for Boston, MA, United States:
        Condition   : Cloudy
        Temperature: 58
        Wind Chill : 58
        Humidity    : 84
```

I can supply a command-line argument using `-Dexec.args`:

```
> mvn exec:java -Dexec.mainClass=mjg.RunDemo -Dexec.args='44418'
...
        Weather for London, , United Kingdom:
        Condition   : Cloudy
        Temperature: 54
        Wind Chill : 54
        Humidity    : 82
```

A guiding principle in this book is that Java is good at tools, libraries, and (existing) infrastructure, and that Groovy is good at everything else. It's hard to imagine a better demonstration of that than the current example. The entire application was written in Groovy, at a code savings on the order of 10 to 1. The infrastructure treated the code as though it was all Java, and I was even able to use the Java `exec` task to execute the Groovy script to drive the application.

The Groovy-Eclipse compiler plugin is a funded project, because it's used inside the IDEs provided by SpringSource (a division of VMware).[8] The quality of the plugin, especially for cross-compilation, is therefore quite high. Just because it has the name "Eclipse" wired into it, there's no reason not to use it in a Maven project. There's no implication that the plugin is exclusive to the IDE. You can use it anywhere, as I did with the Maven project in this section.

The other way to add Groovy to a project built with Maven is to use the GMaven project, discussed in the next section.

5.4.2 The GMaven project

GMaven is an alternative approach for adding Groovy into Maven projects. It works with combined Java and Groovy sources by generating stubs for the Groovy files as part of the build sequence.

[8] Now part of Pivotal, which is owned by VMware, which is owned by EMC...

To help users get started, the project provides a Maven archetype called gmaven-archetype-basic. To use the archetype, execute the following at the command line:

```
> mvn archetype:generate -DgroupId=mjg -DartifactId=weather
    -DarchetypeArtifactId=gmaven-archetype-basic
    -Dversion=1.0-SNAPSHOT -Dpackage=mjg
```

This again produces a project in standard Maven structure, in which the sources are in src/main/groovy and the tests are in src/test/groovy. The plugin expects both Java and Groovy sources to reside in those directories.

The generated POM is shown in the following listing, with some modifications discussed in the listing.

Listing 5.11 The Maven pom.xml file produced by the GMaven project

```
<project xmlns="http://maven.apache.org/POM/4.0.0"
  xmlns:xsi="http://www.w3.org/2001/XMLSchema-instance"
  xsi:schemaLocation="http://maven.apache.org/POM/4.0.0
                      http://maven.apache.org/maven-v4_0_0.xsd">
    <modelVersion>4.0.0</modelVersion>

    <groupId>mjg</groupId>
    <artifactId>weather</artifactId>
    <name>weather project</name>
    <version>1.0-SNAPSHOT</version>

    <dependencies>
        <dependency>
            <groupId>junit</groupId>
            <artifactId>junit</artifactId>
            <version>4.10</version>
            <scope>test</scope>
        </dependency>
        <dependency>
            <groupId>org.codehaus.groovy</groupId>            Groovy 2.0
            <artifactId>groovy-all</artifactId>               dependency
            <version>2.1.5</version>
        </dependency>
      </dependencies>

    <build>
        <plugins>
            <plugin>
                <groupId>org.codehaus.gmaven</groupId>
                <artifactId>gmaven-plugin</artifactId>
                <version>1.4</version>                                    Groovy 2
                <configuration>                                           support for
                    <providerSelection>2.0</providerSelection>            GMaven
                </configuration>
                <executions>
                    <execution>
                        <goals>
                            <goal>generateStubs</goal>                    Stub
                            <goal>compile</goal>                          generation
                            <goal>generateTestStubs</goal>
```

```
                        <goal>testCompile</goal>
                    </goals>
                </execution>
            </executions>
        </plugin>
    </plugins>
</build>
</project>
```

The POM needs a Groovy dependency. It doesn't have to be global, but it was just as easy to add it that way here. The provider was adjusted to 2.1.5 in order to use Groovy version 2.

Building the system is done with a standard Maven `install`:

```
> mvn clean install
```

During the build process, Java stubs are generated for each Groovy file. The stubs themselves are quite minimal; they're only used to resolve the inter-language dependencies rather than execution. As an example, here's a portion of the stub generated for the `Weather` class, whose Groovy implementation was shown in the previous section.

Listing 5.12 Part of the Java stub generated from `Weather.groovy`

```
public class Weather
  extends java.lang.Object
    implements groovy.lang.GroovyObject {
    public  groovy.lang.MetaClass getMetaClass() {
        return (groovy.lang.MetaClass)null;}
    public  void setMetaClass(groovy.lang.MetaClass mc) { }
    public  java.lang.Object invokeMethod(
        java.lang.String method, java.lang.Object arguments) { return null;}
    public  java.lang.Object getProperty(java.lang.String property) {
        return null;}
    public  void setProperty(
        java.lang.String property, java.lang.Object value) { }
    public  java.lang.String getCity() { return (java.lang.String)null;}
    public  void setCity(java.lang.String value) { }
    // ... remaining getter and setter methods
}
```

Treat Java class as Groovy

Business methods (getters and setters)

Any Java class can be treated as though it was Groovy source by implementing the `GroovyObject` interface, as the stub does here. The first five methods in the stub provide no-op implementations for all the methods in that interface. The rest of the stub consists of empty implementations for the remaining methods, which in this case are the getters and setters and the `toString` method.

The stub generated for the `RunDemo` class is slightly different, in an interesting way. The Groovy implementation is just a couple lines of scripting code. As noted in the demonstration in chapter 3 where I executed a compiled Groovy script from the `java` command, every Groovy script is ultimately converted to a class by the compiler, and the corresponding RunDemo.java stub illustrates this:

```
public class RunDemo extends groovy.lang.Script {
  public RunDemo() {}
  public RunDemo(groovy.lang.Binding context) {}
  public static  void main(java.lang.String... args) { }
  public  java.lang.Object run() { return null;}
}
```

The class extends `groovy.lang.Script`, has a default constructor and a constructor that takes a `groovy.lang.Binding`, a standard Java `main` method, and a `run` method. All Groovy scripts look like this to the JVM. Running the script is like executing the `main` method, which delegates to the `run` operation here.

As before, to run the program using the Maven you call the `exec:java` task with the right arguments. In this case that means the main class is either `RunDemo` or `RunInJava`:

```
> mvn exec:java -Dexec.mainClass=mjg.RunDemo

> mvn exec:java -Dexec.mainClass=mjg.RunInJava
```

Either way, the result is the same as in the previous section.

The GMaven project has been quiet recently, but it's still alive. As demonstrated, the archetype works and the stub generation allows the plugin to delegate compilation to the standard Maven tools.

Lessons learned (Maven)

1. There are two separate ways to add Groovy to Maven builds, each with benefits and drawbacks: the "Groovy Eclipse" plugin and GMaven.
2. If at all possible, consider moving to Gradle.

5.4.3 Maven summary

There are two ways to add Groovy dependencies to a Maven project: the Groovy-Eclipse plugin and the GMaven project. My advice (which may change as the projects evolve) is

1. For an already existing Maven build, add the Groovy-Eclipse plugin. It works, and a company that has a significant interest in the success of Groovy financially supports development of the plugin itself. The fact that the name includes the word *Eclipse* is irrelevant.
2. For new projects either plugin will work, but the existence of a Maven archetype makes it particularly easy to get started with GMaven.
3. It's quite interesting that both plugins expect Java and Groovy sources to reside together. There's a significant integration lesson there somewhere.

Moving now from hybrid approaches to purely Groovy solutions, I'll address first the short and sweet Grapes approach before moving to the real destination: Gradle.

5.5 Grapes and @Grab

The Grape mechanism allows you to declare library dependencies directly inside a Groovy script. This is useful when you need to deliver a script to a client that doesn't already have the required dependencies but is willing to download them as part of the build process.

The overall API is called Grape (Groovy Adaptable/Advanced Packaging Engine) and starts with the `groovy.lang.Grab` annotation. It uses an Ivy resolver to identify and download dependencies. Its primary use case is on scripts, so that they can be delivered to a client without any setup requirements other than having Groovy installed. At runtime Groovy will download and install any declared libraries and their transitive dependencies as part of the execution process.

> **GRAPE USE CASE** Grape allows you to deliver a simple script that can be executed by a client without any setup necessary other than installing Groovy, making it particularly convenient for testers or QA people.

To demonstrate the Grape system, let me choose the Math library from the Apache Commons project (http://commons.apache.org/math/). Specifically, I want to work with the complex numbers package. The package includes a class called `Complex`, which represents complex numbers. Although the class is interesting in itself, it also makes for a nice demonstration of Groovy's metaprogramming capabilities.

In Maven syntax the library has a group ID of `org.apache.commons`, an artifact ID of `commons-math3`, and a version of 3.0. Therefore, the format of the `@Grab` annotation is as shown in the following script:

```
import org.apache.commons.math3.complex.*

@Grab('org.apache.commons:commons-math3:3.0')
Complex first = new Complex(1.0, 3.0);
Complex second = new Complex(2.0, 5.0);
```

The `@Grab` annotation downloads both the given library and its dependencies. The syntax uses Maven structure, using colons to connect the group ID, the artifact ID, and the version number. Alternatively, you can specify the sections individually:

```
@Grab(group='org.apache.commons', module='commons-math3', version='3.0')
```

The behavior is equivalent in either case.

There isn't much more to Grapes than this. In order to show an interesting example that requires an external Java library, let me present a simple case of Groovy metaprogramming. There's nothing about it that requires Grapes in particular, but it shows how a small amount of metaprogramming can make a Java library class groovier. Using Grapes in the script allows me to send it to a client without compiling it or providing the library dependencies. The Grape annotations will handle the rest.

The Complex class represents a complex number, which combines real and imaginary parts. The class contains a two-argument constructor, as shown, that takes the real and imaginary parts as parameters. Many methods are defined on the class, so that it generalizes basic numerical computations to the complex domain.

Recall that in Groovy every operator delegates to a method call. Interestingly enough, the Complex class already has a method called multiply for computing the product of two complex numbers. Because the * operator in Groovy uses the multiply method, that operator can be used immediately:

```
assert first.multiply(second) == first * second
```

Again, this is a Java class. Fortunately, the developers of the class chose to include a method called multiply, so Groovy can use the * operator with complex numbers.

What about all the other mathematical operations? Most don't line up as cleanly. For example, the class uses add instead of plus and subtract instead of minus. It's easy to connect them, however, by adding the appropriate methods to the metaclass associated with Complex when viewed through Groovy.

As a reminder, every class accessed through Groovy contains a metaclass, and the metaclass is an Expando. This means that methods and properties can be added to the metaclass as desired, and the resulting members will be part of any instantiated object. Here's how to add several mathematical operations to Complex:

```
Complex.metaClass.plus = { Complex c -> delegate.add c }
Complex.metaClass.minus = { Complex c -> delegate.subtract c }
Complex.metaClass.div = { Complex c -> delegate.divide c }
Complex.metaClass.power = { Complex c -> delegate.pow c }
Complex.metaClass.negative = { delegate.negate() }
```

That takes care of the +, -, /, **, and negation operators, respectively. In each case, the relevant method is defined on the metaclass by setting it equal to a closure. The associated closure takes a Complex argument (in the case of binary operators) and invokes the desired existing method on the closure's delegate, passing along the argument.

> **CLOSURE DELEGATES** Every closure has a delegate property. By default the delegate points to the object that the closure was invoked on.

After adding those methods to the metaclass, the operators can be used in the Groovy script:

```
assert new Complex(3.0, 8.0) == first + second
assert new Complex(1.0, 2.0) == second - first
assert new Complex(0.5862068965517241, 0.03448275862068969) ==
    first / second
assert new Complex(-0.007563724861696302, 0.01786136835085382) ==
    first ** second
assert new Complex(-1.0, -3.0) == -first
```

To complete this part of the story I want to demonstrate the famous equation known as Euler's identity,[9] which is expressed as

$$e^{i\pi} = -1$$

This equation connects the imaginary numbers (i) and the transcendental numbers (e and π) to the negative numbers (–1). Euler found this expression so profound he had it inscribed on his tombstone.

The `java.lang.Math` class contains constants `Math.E` and `Math.PI`, and the `Complex` class has the constant `Complex.I`. To make the formula look better I'll use static imports for all of them.

One final addition is necessary to make this work. `Math.E` in Java is of type double, and I want to raise it to a `Complex` power. The easiest way to do that is to convert the double to an instance of the `Complex` class and then use the `pow` method in the `Complex` class. Returning to Groovy metaprogramming, I need a `power` method (which corresponds to the `**` operator) on `Double` that takes a `Complex` argument:

```
Double.metaClass.power = { Complex c -> (new Complex(delegate,0)).pow(c) }
```

With all that machinery in place the resulting code is a bit anticlimactic, but that's a good thing:

```
Complex result = E ** (I * PI)
assert result.real == -1
assert result.imaginary < 1.0e-15
```

As usual in Groovy, accessing the `real` or `imaginary` property is equivalent to calling the `getReal` or `getImaginary` method, respectively. The expression does generate a real part of –1, but the imaginary part isn't exactly zero due to the round-off error associated with Java doubles. On my machine it evaluates to a number less than the bound shown, which is certainly close enough.

There are a few additional annotations available in the Grapes system. One is `@GrabConfig`, used in the next example when loading a database driver. The following script uses the `groovy.sql.Sql` class to generate an H2 database and add some data to it:

```
import groovy.sql.Sql

@GrabConfig(systemClassLoader=true)
@Grab(group='com.h2database', module='h2', version='1.2.140')
Sql sql = Sql.newInstance(url:'jdbc:h2:mem:',driver:'org.h2.Driver')
```

The annotations provide the driver, so the `Sql` class can be used normally.

Because a member of a class can only have a single instance of a particular annotation, the `@Grapes` annotation is used to combine multiple `@Grab` annotations. The next listing computes complex values and stores them in a database table.

---

[9] Leonhard Euler (1707 – 1783) was one of the most brilliant mathematicians of all time. His work spanned virtually every field of math and science, and his collected works filled between 60 and 80 quarto volumes. The transcendental number e is named after him.

Listing 5.13 Using Apache Commons Math and a database driver together

```
@GrabConfig(systemClassLoader=true)
@Grapes([
    @Grab('org.apache.commons:commons-math3:3.0'),
    @Grab(group='com.h2database', module='h2', version='1.2.140')
])

import static java.lang.Math.*
import org.apache.commons.math3.complex.Complex
import org.apache.commons.math3.complex.ComplexUtils
import groovy.sql.Sql

Sql sql = Sql.newInstance(url:'jdbc:h2:mem:',driver:'org.h2.Driver')

sql.execute '''
    create table coordinates (
        id bigint generated by default as identity,
        angle double not null,
        x double not null,
        y double not null,
        primary key (id)
    )
'''

int n = 20
def delta = 2*PI/n
(0..<n).each { num ->
    Complex c = ComplexUtils.polar2Complex(1, num*delta)
    sql.execute """
    insert into coordinates(id,angle,x,y)
        values(null, ${i*delta}, $c.real, $c.imaginary)
    """
}

sql.rows('select * from coordinates').each { row ->
    println "$row.id, $row.angle, $row.x, $row.y"
}
```

The script creates a table to hold x and y coordinates at 20 points along a circle. The `ComplexUtils.polar2Complex` method takes a radius (here using one for simplicity) and an angle (in radians) along the circle and generates a complex number, which is then stored in the database.

The Grapes system is simple and effective, but limited in practice. The additions work in a script, but for a larger system it's more common to use a full-scale build tool, like Gradle, which is the subject of the next section.

5.6 The Gradle build system

Gradle is proposed as a next-generation build solution. Gradle combines the flexibility of Groovy builds with a powerful domain-specific language (DSL) that configures a rich set of classes.

As with virtually all Groovy projects of any significant size, Gradle is written in both Java and Groovy. Gradle is essentially a DSL for builds.[10] It defines a language of syntax and semantics that allows you to write a build file quickly and easily.

Gradle doesn't come with an installer. Instead you just download a ZIP file, set the `GRADLE_HOME` environment variable to wherever you unzip it, and add the $GRADLE_HOME/bin directory to your path, and you're ready to go. In fact, you don't even need to install Groovy first, because Gradle comes with its own version of Groovy.

How projects in the Groovy ecosystem include Groovy

One of the dirty little secrets of Groovy is that the major versions are not always binary compatible. Code compiled with one version doesn't necessarily work with any other.

This means that projects in the Groovy ecosystem have a choice. They can either be compiled with different versions of Groovy and make the Groovy version number part of their own version, or they can bundle in a particular version of Groovy.

The Spock framework (discussed in chapter 6) takes the former approach. Spock versions are in the form 0.7-groovy-2.0, meaning Spock version 0.7 compiled with Groovy version 2.0.

The Grails and Gradle projects take the other approach. Grails 1.3.9, for example, includes a copy of Groovy 1.7.8, Grails 2.0.3 includes Groovy 1.8.6, and Grails 2.2.1 includes Groovy 2.0.8. To see the Groovy version included in your Gradle distribution, run the `gradle -v` command.

For Grails, the bundled Groovy version locks you into that version for the entire application. For Gradle, however, the bundled Groovy version is used only to execute the build script itself. You're free to use any version of Groovy in your own projects, and Gradle will correctly build them.

When you run the `gradle -v` command, in addition to showing the Gradle and Groovy versions, Gradle also reports the included versions of Ant and Ivy, as well as the JVM and OS.

Gradle builds range from extremely simple to quite powerful. I'll start with the simplest possible example and build from there.

5.6.1 Basic Gradle builds

Gradle is a plugin-based architecture. Most Gradle tutorials start by defining what a task is and showing how to call one. Rather than do that here, let me instead show you a minimal build file and go from there.

[10] Mandatory DSL jokes: "JavaScript is a DSL for finding browser bugs"; "Java is a DSL for generating stack traces"; "Maven is a DSL for downloading the internet."

Here's the smallest possible Gradle build for a Java project, in a file called build.gradle:

```
apply plugin:'java'
```

The `apply` syntax indicates that the build is using the Java plugin. When you run the `build` command using this file, Gradle executes tasks in several stages, as shown:

```
:compileJava UP-TO-DATE
:processResources UP-TO-DATE
:classes UP-TO-DATE
:jar
:assemble
:compileTestJava UP-TO-DATE
:processTestResources UP-TO-DATE
:testClasses UP-TO-DATE
:test
:check
:build

BUILD SUCCESSFUL
```

Each word after the colon is a Gradle *task*. Gradle constructs a Directed Acyclic Graph (DAG) out of the specified tasks, paying attention to their dependencies, and then executes them in order. This minimal project has no source code, so the compile tasks are up to date without running at all. In fact, the only task that does anything is the `jar` task, which creates a JAR file in the build/libs directory.

If you're doing any testing your project will need to include the JUnit dependency. Consider a simple project that uses standard Maven structure, so that any Java classes are contained in src/main/java, and any tests are in src/test/java. The next listing shows a POJO called `Greeting` with a single `String` property called `message`.

Listing 5.14 A `Greeting` POJO to demonstrate a Gradle build

```
public class Greeting {
    private String message = "Hello, World!";

    public String getMessage() {
        return message;
    }

    public void setMessage(String message) {
        this.message = message;
    }
}
```

The following listing is a JUnit test called `GreetingTest`, which checks the getter and setter.

Listing 5.15 A JUnit test for the `Greeting` POJO

```
import static org.junit.Assert.*;
import org.junit.Test;

public class GreetingTests {
    private Greeting greeting = new Greeting();
```

```
    @Test
    public void testGetGreeting() {
        assertEquals("Hello, World!", greeting.getMessage());
    }

    @Test
    public void testSetGreeting() {
        greeting.setMessage("What up?");
        assertEquals("What up?", greeting.getMessage());
    }
}
```

The next listing shows a Gradle build file with a JUnit dependency during the testing phase. It's still a "Hello, World" example, but it does introduce some essential concepts.

Listing 5.16 A build.gradle file for the POJO application with testing

```
apply plugin:'java'

repositories {
    mavenCentral()
}

dependencies {
    testCompile 'junit:junit:4.10'
}
```

Maven notation 'group:artifact:version'

The terms `repositories` and `dependencies` are part of the Gradle DSL. Any required libraries are listed in the `dependencies` block. There are several legal forms for listing dependencies. The one used here is a string separated by colons. Using Maven syntax is not an accident, as shown in the `repositories` section. Many different types of repositories can be used, but here the standard Maven central repository is declared.

Executing the build this time runs the same series of tasks, but now any tests are executed and a JUnit report in HTML form is produced in the build/reports/tests directory.

That demonstrated that a Gradle build can be applied to a Java project with no Groovy dependencies. To show that the same process works on mixed Java/Groovy projects, I'll add a Groovy test case, called `GroovyGreetingTests`, in the src/test/groovy directory. The test case is shown in the next listing.

Listing 5.17 A Groovy test for the POJO, making this a mixed Java/Groovy project

```
import static org.junit.Assert.*
import org.junit.Test

class GroovyGreetingTests {
    Greeting greeting = new Greeting()

    @Test
    void testGetMessage(){
        assert 'Hello, World!' == greeting.message
    }
```

```
    @Test
    void testSetMessage() {
        greeting.message = 'Yo, dude'
        assert 'Yo, dude' == greeting.message
    }
}
```

The new build.gradle file requires a Groovy dependency. Prior to Gradle version 1.6 the name of the dependency was "groovy". Now the preferred notation is to declare the Groovy dependency as a standard compile-time requirement. The complete build.gradle file is shown in the following listing.

Listing 5.18 A build.gradle file for a mixed Java/Groovy project

```
apply plugin:'groovy'

repositories {
    mavenCentral()
}

dependencies {
    compile 'org.codehaus.groovy:groovy-all:2.1.5'
    testCompile 'junit:junit:4.10'
}
```

The other change to the build file is that the Java plugin has been replaced by the Groovy plugin, which includes the Java tasks already. The new plugin adds a couple of tasks to the build, as shown here:

```
:compileJava
:compileGroovy UP-TO-DATE
:processResources UP-TO-DATE
:classes
:jar
:assemble
:compileTestJava
:compileTestGroovy
:processTestResources UP-TO-DATE
:testClasses
:test
:check
:build

BUILD SUCCESSFUL
```

Both the `compileGroovy` and `compileTestGroovy` tasks are new, but everything else proceeds normally. The classes are compiled, the tests run, and the HTML test report is produced.

That's the basic structure of a Gradle build file when dealing with Java, Groovy, or mixed Java/Groovy projects. Similar files are shown throughout this book. To illustrate some interesting Gradle features I'll now consider several use cases that often come up in practice.

5.6.2 Interesting configurations

Gradle builds are used throughout this book. I'll bring up lots of different options when discussing specific examples in context, but here I can discuss a few interesting ideas.

CUSTOM SOURCE SETS

First, one of the running themes in this book is that separating Groovy source code from Java source code is rather artificial. What if you wanted to use the same source folder for both, as an Eclipse project might do? Here's an easy customized project layout to do so:

```
sourceSets {
        main {
            java { srcDirs = [] }
            groovy { srcDir 'src' }
        }
        test {
            java { srcDirs = [] }
            groovy { srcDir 'src' }
        }
    }
```

Source sets are collections of source code in a Gradle build. Here, by assigning the `srcDirs` property of both the src/main/java and src/test/java folders to an empty list, the Java compiler won't run at all. Instead, the Groovy compiler is used for all classes in the src directory, which will presumably hold both Java and Groovy classes.

COPYING JARS

Another useful tactic is to make a local copy of the dependent libraries. The following task does that:

```
task collectJars(type: Copy) {
    into "$buildDir/output/lib"
    from configurations.testRuntime
}
```

The `collectJars` task is a kind of `Copy` task—one of the built-in task types in Gradle. Running `collectJars` copies the JAR files in the runtime classpath into the output/lib folder in the build directory. Spock uses this task to make a complete distribution.

INPUTS AND OUTPUTS

Another neat capability of Gradle is that it can skip tasks that aren't necessary. It does this by creating hashes of files and directories and checking whether or not they have changed. The following listing shows an example taken from the samples[11] that come with Gradle.

[11] See the userguide/tasks/incrementalBuild/inputsAndOutputs directory in the download distribution. Gradle comes with a huge number of very simple samples like this one.

Listing 5.19 Inputs/outputs example from the `incrementalBuilds` Gradle sample

```
task transform {
    ext.srcFile = file('mountains.xml')
    ext.destDir = new File(buildDir, 'generated')
    inputs.file srcFile
    outputs.dir destDir
    doLast {
        println "Transforming source file."
        destDir.mkdirs()
        def mountains = new XmlParser().parse(srcFile)
        mountains.mountain.each { mountain ->
            def name = mountain.name[0].text()
            def height = mountain.height[0].text()
            def destFile = new File(destDir, "${name}.txt")
            destFile.text = "$name -> ${height}\n"
        }
    }
}
```

External properties for the source and destination files

Time-stamped file and directory

Executed only if inputs or outputs have changed

The `srcFile` and `destDir` properties of the script are assigned to the `ext` map, which puts them in the project but avoids any potential conflict with existing `Project` properties. The `inputs` and `outputs` properties can be assigned to either files or directories (in other words, the word `file` is interpreted as a `java.io.File`). If both properties are the same as during the previous run, the code inside the `doLast` block is skipped.

ANT INTEGRATION

One of the nice features of Gradle is that it includes an instance of `groovy.ant.AntBuilder` as part of the build. That means that anything that can be done with Ant can be handled inside a Gradle build. That has a couple of consequences. First, if you already have an Ant build file, you can invoke its tasks inside a Gradle build. You can even make the Gradle tasks dependent on the Ant tasks.

Consider this example, from the Gradle samples.[12] The Ant build file is build.xml, and it contains a single task called `hello`:

```
<project>
    <target name="hello">
        <echo>Hello, from Ant</echo>
    </target>
</project>
```

The Gradle build is in the file build.gradle:

```
ant.importBuild 'build.xml'

task intro(dependsOn: hello) << {
    println 'Hello, from Gradle'
}
```

[12] See userguide/ant/dependsOnAntTarget in the distribution.

The `intro` task depends on the `hello` task from the Ant build, which is imported using the `ant` variable (an instance of `AntBuilder`). Running `gradle intro` executes both tasks:

```
:hello
[ant:echo] Hello, from Ant
:intro
Hello, from Gradle

BUILD SUCCESSFUL
```

THE WRAPPER TASK

Finally, a client can execute a Gradle build even if they don't have Gradle installed. Gradle comes with a special `Wrapper` task, which has a version property:

```
task wrapper(type: Wrapper) {
    gradleVersion = '1.6'
}
```

Running this task generates scripts for both Windows and Unix, called `gradlew.bat` and `gradlew`, respectively, along with a minimal Gradle JAR distribution. When executed the wrappers first download and install a local copy of Gradle and then execute the build.

Gradle is a very powerful system, and a thorough investigation is well beyond the scope of this book.[13] Hopefully this section will provide you with enough of an introduction to get you started.

> **Lessons learned (Grapes and Gradle)**
>
> 1 `@Grab` is helpful for Groovy scripts.
> 2 Gradle uses Groovy build files to configure your build but downloads the internet like Maven.
> 3 Gradle does not have artifacts like Maven, but people are working on ways to create standard builds for various goals.
> 4 In addition to the discussion in this chapter, every project in this book includes a Gradle build highlighting a variety of capabilities.

5.7 Summary

This chapter looked at build tools useful for both Groovy and Java projects. Ant is very common but low level. Groovy provides both a raw `groovy` task and a `groovyc` compiler task, which can be useful in combined projects.

Maven is a higher-level tool, but it can be difficult to customize. In this chapter I presented both the GMaven project as a way to add Groovy to Maven and the Groovy-Eclipse plugin approach, which tends to be more robust for cross-compilation issues.

---

[13] The book *Gradle in Action* (Manning, 2013) by Benjamin Muschko is both well written and thorough. I highly recommend it.

Groovy includes an `@Grab` annotation with its so-called Grapes capability, which can be used to add dependencies directly to a Groovy script. It's powerful, but it's restricted to Groovy builds.

Finally, I presented the Gradle build tool. This chapter included a basic discussion of Gradle and mentioned several more advanced capabilities. Gradle is used throughout this book to demonstrate interesting mechanisms in each chapter.

6 Testing Groovy and Java projects

This chapter covers

- Using `GroovyTestCase` and its subclasses
- Testing scripts as well as classes
- The `MockFor` and `StubFor` classes in the Groovy library
- The Spock testing framework

The rise of automated testing is one of the most significant software development productivity improvements in the past 20 years. Automated tests, running as part of your build process, are very easy to set up, catch problems right away, and give you the freedom to refactor your code without worrying that you're breaking something unrelated.

Testing is the cornerstone of many of the "agile" development processes, from more modern techniques like SCRUM to Kanban back to the original Extreme Programming (XP) movement. There are two other benefits of automated testing, however, that aren't nearly as publicized:

1. *Tests are executable documentation.*

   Any major open source project is a communal effort by some of the best developers in the world, many of whom are working on their own time.

They're highly motivated to write code, not documentation. The result is that the documentation quality tends to be inferior to the code quality, if it's even up to date in the first place.

My own experience is that the better the developer, the more he or she cares about testing. The best developers write complete tests, and these tests run all the time as part of a continuous integration system. If a test breaks, the system notifies the project committers right away. As a result, the tests are excellent examples of how the developers intend the system to be used.

Whenever you work with a major open source project, download the source. You may or may not look at the details, but the tests are invaluable.

2 *Tests aren't part of production code.*

This isn't as big a deal from a developer point of view, but it's a huge issue for managers. One of the reasons companies are reluctant to adopt new languages is that they aren't sure how well they work in a production environment. Production code often involves complex approval processes and performance assessments that can be extremely conservative.

If you would like to try Groovy in your system, testing is one easy way to do it. Groovy has many testing capabilities built into the language, all of which work with both Groovy and Java code. Best of all from a management point of view, at runtime Groovy's just another JAR file.

This chapter reviews the Groovy APIs and libraries that make testing easier. First I'll review how Java developers normally test applications, focusing on the JUnit library. Then I'll show how Groovy enhances that process through its `GroovyTestCase` extension. Next I'll show how to test scripts written in Groovy, using subclasses of

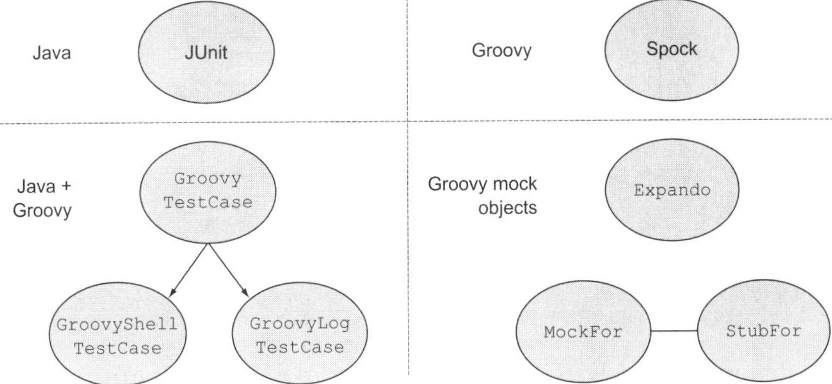

Figure 6.1 Java tests in this chapter are from JUnit. The standard Groovy library includes a subclass of JUnit's `TestCase` called `GroovyTestCase`, and its subclasses are useful as well. The Spock framework is a very popular alternative testing API that includes a JUnit test runner. Groovy makes it easy to create mock objects through library classes like `Expando`, `MockFor`, and `StubFor`.

GroovyTestCase. From there I'll discuss testing classes in isolation using mocks and stubs. This involves the built-in mock and stub capabilities in Groovy, both through the Expando class and through Groovy's MockFor and StubFor classes. Finally I'll show you a glimpse of the future in the form of the powerful Spock framework, a pure Groovy library that simplifies testing for both Java and Groovy projects.

Figure 6.1 is a guide to the technologies discussed in this chapter.

6.1 Working with JUnit

The agile development community created JUnit (http://junit.org) as a great tool for automating tests. While other Java testing tools exist, JUnit has been so influential that nearly every Java developer I encounter has either used it or heard of it. JUnit's success has spawned an entire family of comparable tools for other languages (known collectively as "xUnit"). JUnit is simple, easy to use, and ubiquitous in the Java world. As I'll show in this chapter, the available Groovy tools also are easy to use and easy to learn, and some of them are based directly on JUnit. [1]

Adding JUnit to your projects (a review from chapter 5)

JUnit is an open source project created by two of the founders of Extreme Programming,[1] Erich Gamma and Kent Beck. The JUnit library can be downloaded from the home site (http://junit.org), but it's built into most of the common IDEs, including Eclipse, NetBeans, and IntelliJ IDEA. It also can be retrieved from the Maven central repository, using a POM dependency of the form

```
<dependency>
    <groupId>junit</groupId>
    <artifactId>junit</artifactId>
    <version>4.10</version>
</dependency>
```

As an alternative, JUnit version 4.5 and above enables the artifact ID junit-dep instead, which does not include the so-called Hamcrest matchers (http://code.google.com/p/hamcrest/) that simplify the syntax in certain cases. Like most cool projects, the source code for JUnit now resides at GitHub, at https://github.com/junit-team/junit.

Most of the Gradle build files in this book (especially for the projects in this chapter) include JUnit as a "test-compile" dependency. That means classes in the API (like org.junit.TestCase and org.junit.Assert) are only available for test classes.

When writing JUnit tests in Groovy, you have two options. You can write a JUnit test with annotations as usual, but implement it in Groovy, or you can extend the

[1] Now known more commonly as "agile" development, because most Fortune 500 companies don't want to be associated with "extreme" anything.

GroovyTestCase class. The only difference is that GroovyTestCase adds a few additional methods to the TestCase class from JUnit.

Because this book is all about integration, I'd like to examine the following cases:

- Use a standard Groovy JUnit test to check a Java implementation.
- Use a standard Java JUnit test to check a Groovy implementation.
- Write a Groovy test that extends GroovyTestCase to see what additions it provides.

In each case I need something to test. Because I plan to mix the languages, one way I've found that makes that easier is to declare my methods in a Java interface and then implement it in both languages. That's actually a pretty general rule.

> **GROOVY IMPLEMENTS JAVA** Groovy classes can implement Java interfaces as easily as Java classes can.

The next listing shows a Java interface, called UtilityMethods, containing three method declarations.

Listing 6.1 A Java interface with three methods

```
public interface UtilityMethods {
    int[] getPositives(int... values);
    boolean isPrime(int x);
    boolean isPalindrome(String s);
}
```

In true test-driven development (TDD) I would now write the tests, watch them fail, and then write the correct implementations. Because the subject of this chapter is the tests rather than the implementations, let me present the implementations first.[2]

The following listing is the Java implementation of the UtilityMethods interface.

Listing 6.2 The Java implementation of the UtilityMethods interface

```
import java.util.ArrayList;
import java.util.List;

public class JavaUtilityMethods implements UtilityMethods {

    public int[] getPositives(int... values) {
        List<Integer> results = new ArrayList<Integer>();
        for (Integer i : values) {
            if (i > 0) results.add(i);
        }
        int[] answer = new int[results.size()];
        for (int i = 0; i < results.size(); i++) {
            answer[i] = results.get(i);
        }
```

[2] I try to use TDD, but more often I use GDD, which stands for Guilt-Driven Development. If I write code and it's not tested, I feel guilty and write a test for it.

```
        return answer;
    }

    public boolean isPrime(int x) {
        if (x < 0) throw new IllegalArgumentException("argument must be >
     0");
        if (x == 2) return true;
        for (int i = 2; i < Math.sqrt(x) + 1; i++) {
            if (x % i == 0) return false;
        }
        return true;
    }

    public boolean isPalindrome(String s) {
        StringBuilder sb = new StringBuilder();
        for (char c : s.toCharArray()) {
            if (Character.isLetter(c)) {
                sb.append(c);
            }
        }
        String forward = sb.toString().toLowerCase();
        String backward = sb.reverse().toString().toLowerCase();
        return forward.equals(backward);
    }
}
```

The implementations will not be surprising to anyone with a Java background. The Groovy implementation, shown in the next listing, is somewhat shorter.

Listing 6.3 The Groovy implementation of the `UtilityMethods` interface

```
class GroovyUtilityMethods implements UtilityMethods {

    @Override
    int[] getPositives(int... values) {
        values.findAll { it > 0 }
    }

    @Override
    boolean isPrime(int x) {
        if (x < 0) throw new IllegalArgumentException('argument must be > 0')
        if (x == 2) return true
        (2..< Math.sqrt(x) + 1).each { num ->
            if (x % num == 0) return false // DANGER! THIS IS A BUG!
        }
        return true
    }

    @Override
    boolean isPalindrome(String s) {
        String str = s.toLowerCase().replaceAll(/\W/,'')
        str.reverse() == str
    }
}
```

findAll returns all values satisfying the closure

A range with an open upper bound

The Groovy JDK adds a reverse method to String

There is, in fact, a subtle bug in the implementation of the `isPrime` method. The tests will detect it and give me a chance to explain the trap.

In the next subsection I'll use Java to test the Groovy implementation and fix the bug. Then I'll use Groovy to test the Java implementation, and finally I'll write the test as a subclass of `GroovyTestCase` to see how that can help.

6.1.1 A Java test for the Groovy implementation

The following listing contains a JUnit 4 test, written in Java, to test the Groovy implementation. It includes a static import for the methods in the `org.junit.Assert` class and `@Test` annotations for the individual tests.

Listing 6.4 A Java JUnit test to check the Groovy implementation

```
package mjg;

import static org.junit.Assert.assertFalse;
import static org.junit.Assert.assertTrue;

import java.util.ArrayList;
import java.util.List;

import org.junit.Test;

public class GroovyImplJavaTest {
    private UtilityMethods impl = new GroovyUtilityMethods();

    @Test
    public void testGetPositives() {
        int[] testValues = {-3, 1, 4, -1, 5, -2, 6};
        List<Integer> testList = new ArrayList<Integer>();
        testList.add(1);  testList.add(4);
        testList.add(5);  testList.add(6);
        int[] results = impl.getPositives(testValues);
        for (int i : results) {
            assertTrue(testList.contains(i));
        }
    }

    @Test
    public void testIsPrime() {
        int[] primes = {2, 3, 5, 7, 11, 13, 17, 19, 23, 29};
        for (int p : primes) {
            assertTrue(impl.isPrime(p));
        }
        assertFalse("9 is not prime", impl.isPrime(9));
    }

    @Test(expected=IllegalArgumentException.class)
    public void testNegativePrime() {
          impl.isPrime(-3);
    }
```

Static import so assert methods don't start with Assert

Results in List in order to use contains method

Test passes if exception thrown

```
    @Test
    public void testIsPalindrome() {
        assertTrue(impl.isPalindrome("Step on no pets!"));
        assertTrue(impl.isPalindrome("Lisa Bonet ate no basil"));
        assertTrue(impl.isPalindrome(
            "Are we not drawn onward, we few, drawn onward to new era!"));
        assertFalse(impl.isPalindrome("This is not a palindrome"));
    }
}
```

In JUnit 3 tests extended the `org.junit.TestCase` class, and test methods were detected by reflection. `TestCase` had all the needed assert methods in it. Now, in JUnit 4, tests don't have a superclass and are detected through the `@Test` annotation. The assert methods are now static methods in the `Assert` class, leading to probably the most common use of static imports in all of Java. If you do a static import on the `Assert` class you can write the assert methods the same way they looked in the older version.

The only other interesting part of this is the use of the `expected` property of the `@Test` annotation, which declares that the test only passes if the expected exception is thrown. Figure 6.2 shows the result.

The test detected that the Groovy implementation is returning true for all cases. The Groovy implementation divides the given number by all the integers from 2 up to the square root of the number minus 1, looking for any that come out even. That

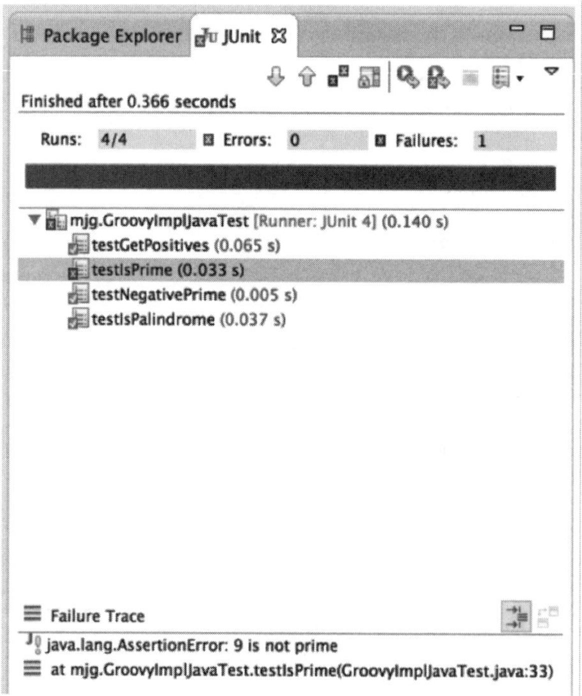

Figure 6.2 The `isPrime` method has a bug, but the rest are fine.

algorithm is fine. The problem is that if a composite (non-prime) number is detected, the method is supposed to return false.

Unfortunately, a return from inside a closure doesn't behave the way a regular Java developer expects. In fact, when you return from a closure it's like you're returning from a method within another method. It only returns from the closure, not the method containing it.

That's a trap worthy of a callout:

> **RETURN FROM CLOSURE** A return from inside a closure only returns from the closure, not the method that contains it.

Probably the easiest fix is to switch to a loop, where returns work as expected. Here's one proper implementation:

```
boolean isPrime(int x) {
    if (x < 0) throw new IllegalArgumentException('argument must be > 0')
    if (x == 2) return true

    for (num in 2..< Math.sqrt(x) + 1) {
        if (x % num == 0) {
            return false
        }
    }
    return true
}
```

Now the test passes. Next I'll show a Groovy test for the Java implementation.

6.1.2 A Groovy test for the Java implementation

You can implement JUnit tests using Groovy as easily as Java, with the attendant code simplifications. The next listing shows such a test.

Listing 6.5 A Groovy JUnit test for a Java implementation

```
import org.junit.Test

class JavaImplGroovyTest {
    UtilityMethods impl = new JavaUtilityMethods()

    @Test
    void testGetPositives() {
        def correct = [1, 2, 3]
        def results = impl.getPositives(-3..3 as int[])
        assert results.every { it > 0 }
    }

    @Test
    void testIsPrime() {
        def primes = [2, 3, 5, 7, 11, 13, 17, 19, 23]
        primes.each { num ->
```

Coercion of a range into an int array (annotation on `def results = impl.getPositives(-3..3 as int[])`)

Every method returns true if closure is true for all elements (annotation on `assert results.every { it > 0 }`)

```
            assert impl.isPrime(num)
        }
        assert !impl.isPrime(9)
    }

    @Test(expected=IllegalArgumentException)          <-- Same mechanism
    void testIsPrimeWithNegative() {                       as in Java test
        impl.isPrime(-3)
    }

    @Test
    void testIsPalindrome() {
        assert impl.isPalindrome('No cab, no tuna nut on bacon')
        assert impl.isPalindrome('Do geese see God?')
        assert impl.isPalindrome("Go hang a salami; I'm a lasagna hog!")
        assert !impl.isPalindrome('This is not a palindrome')
    }
}
```

There are some code simplifications here, but this is still recognizably a standard JUnit test. Initial data can be provided by coercing a range into an array of integers. The every method in `Collection` lets me check all the return values in one statement. Otherwise this is the same as before.

One other note: due to the Groovy Truth,[3] `assert` in Groovy is the same as `assertTrue` and `assertNotNull`. Also, the Groovy `assert` has excellent debugging output. As a result, most Groovy developers use `assert` in their tests rather than any of the assert methods from the `org.junit.Assert` class.

Finally, let me show a test class that extends `GroovyTestCase` and see what extra capabilities that brings.

6.1.3 A GroovyTestCase test for a Java implementation

Groovy provides the class `groovy.util.GroovyTestCase` as part of its standard library. As mentioned earlier, it extends `org.junit.TestCase`. The following listing shows one such test for the Java implementation.

Listing 6.6 A `GroovyTestCase` test for the Java implementation

```
class JavaImplGTCTest extends GroovyTestCase {
    UtilityMethods impl = new JavaUtilityMethods()

    void testGetPositives() {                                Protected log
        log.info('inside testGetPositives')             <-- property
        def correct = [1, 2, 3]
        def results = impl.getPositives(-3..3 as int[])
        assertLength(3, results)
        assertArrayEquals(correct as Integer[], results as Integer[])     Additional
        correct.each { assertContains(it, results) }                      methods
    }
```

[3] Non-null references are true, non-zero numbers are true, non-empty collections are true, non-empty strings are true, and so on.

```
void testIsPrime() {
    def primes = [2, 3,5, 7, 11, 13, 17, 19, 23, 29]
    primes.each { num ->
        assert impl.isPrime(num)
    }
    assert !impl.isPrime(9)
}

void testIsPrimeWithNegative() {
    shouldFail(IllegalArgumentException) {        <-- Additional shouldFail method
        impl.isPrime(-3)
    }
}

void testIsPalindrome() {
    assert impl.isPalindrome('A Santa pets rats, as Pat taps a star step
 at NASA.')
    assert impl.isPalindrome('Oy, Oy, a tonsil is not a yo-yo.')
    assert impl.isPalindrome('''
    A man, a plan, a caret, a ban, a myriad, a sum, a lac, a liar,
    a hoop, a pint, a catalpa, a gas, an oil, a bird, a yell, a vat,
    a caw, a pax, a wag, a tax, a nay, a ram, a cap, a yam, a gay,
    a tsar, a wall, a car, a luger, a ward, a bin, a woman, a vassal,
    a wolf, a tuna, a nit, a pall, a fret, a watt, a bay, a daub,
    a tan, a cab, a datum, a gall, a hat, a fag, a zap, a say, a jaw,
    a lay, a wet, a gallop, a tug, a trot, a trap, a tram, a torr,
    a caper, a top, a tonk, a toll, a ball, a fair, a sax, a minim,
    a tenor, a bass, a passer, a capital, a rut, an amen, a ted,
    a cabal, a tang, a sun, an ass, a maw, a sag, a jam, a dam, a sub,
    a salt, an axon, a sail, an ad, a wadi, a radian, a room, a rood,
    a rip, a tad, a pariah, a revel, a reel, a reed, a pool, a plug,
    a pin, a peek, a parabola, a dog, a pat, a cud, a nu, a fan, a pal,
    a rum, a nod, an eta, a lag, an eel, a batik, a mug, a mot, a nap,
    a maxim, a mood, a leek, a grub, a gob, a gel, a drab, a citadel,
    a total, a cedar, a tap, a gag, a rat, a manor, a bar, a gal,
    a cola, a pap, a yaw, a tab, a raj, a gab, a nag, a pagan, a bag,
    a jar, a bat, a way, a papa, a local, a gar, a baron, a mat, a rag,
    a gap, a tar, a decal, a tot, a led, a tic, a bard, a leg, a bog,
    a burg, a keel, a doom, a mix, a map, an atom, a gum, a kit,
    a baleen, a gala, a ten, a don, a mural, a pan, a faun, a ducat,
    a pagoda, a lob, a rap, a keep, a nip, a gulp, a loop, a deer,
    a leer, a lever, a hair, a pad, a tapir, a door, a moor, an aid,
    a raid, a wad, an alias, an ox, an atlas, a bus, a madam, a jag,
    a saw, a mass, an anus, a gnat, a lab, a cadet, an em, a natural,
    a tip, a caress, a pass, a baronet, a minimax, a sari, a fall,
    a ballot, a knot, a pot, a rep, a carrot, a mart, a part, a tort,
    a gut, a poll, a gateway, a law, a jay, a sap, a zag, a fat, a hall,
    a gamut, a dab, a can, a tabu, a day, a batt, a waterfall, a patina,
    a nut, a flow, a lass, a van, a mow, a nib, a draw, a regular,
    a call, a war, a stay, a gam, a yap, a cam, a ray, an ax, a tag,
    a wax, a paw, a cat, a valley, a drib, a lion, a saga, a plat,
    a catnip, a pooh, a rail, a calamus, a dairyman, a bater,
    a canal - Panama!
    ''')
```

```
        assert !impl.isPalindrome('This is not a palindrome')
    }
}
```

There are a few new features here. First, `GroovyTestCase` includes a static, protected property called `log` of type `java.util.logging.Logger`. It's not exactly difficult to add a logger to a test yourself, but providing one automatically is a convenience.

Next, the class adds an `assertLength` method. It has three overloads. In each, the first argument is the expected length of the array. The second argument is an array of integers, an array of characters, or an array of type `Object`. Here I'm using the method to check that the number of positive integers returned is as expected.

The class also provides an `assertArrayEquals` method, which takes two `Object` arrays as arguments. The docs say that this method checks that the arrays are equivalent and contain the same elements.[4]

Another added method is `assertContains`. That method has two overloads, one for characters and one for integers, so it's only useful in those cases.

Finally, the superclass also provides the `shouldFail` method, which takes either an exception type and a closure or just a closure. It expects an exception when the closure is run, so it behaves much as the `@Test` annotation with an expected property.

The `GroovyTestCase` class has a few additional methods that don't appear here, like `assertScript`, `shouldFailWithCause`, and the ever-popular `notYetImplemented`. See the GroovyDocs for details.

The interesting part is that this test can be run from the command line. The `groovy` command acts as a text-based JUnit runner for `GroovyTestCase` subclasses. The result looks similar to this:

```
$ groovy -cp bin src/test/groovy/mjg/JavaImplGTCTest.groovy
.Jun 23, 2013 5:53:05 PM java_util_logging_Logger$info call
INFO: inside testGetPositives
...
Time: 0.179

OK (4 tests)
```

The Java interface and implementation classes are compiled and reside in the project's bin directory, so they need to be added to the classpath when running the Groovy script.

Lessons learned (JUnit)[5]

1. JUnit is the most common Java unit-testing framework in the industry.
2. Normal JUnit tests are based on annotations. The `@Test` annotation has a property called `expected`. Such tests only pass if the expected exception is thrown.

---

4 That sounds like it's from the Department of Redundancy Department, but it's not.

5 Before I leave this section, I should mention that the palindromes used in the examples come from the Gigantic List of Palidromes page at www.derf.net/palindromes/old.palindrome.html.

(continued)

3. Version 4 tests do not have a superclass. Instead, all of the assert methods are static methods in the `org.junit.Assert` class.
4. By the Groovy truth, `assert`, `assertTrue`, and `assertNotNull` are all the same.
5. Because the Groovy `assert` provides so much debugging information when it fails, it's normally preferred over the standard JUnit `assertEquals` methods.
6. `GroovyTestCase` extends `TestCase` from JUnit and adds a handful of convenience methods, like `assertLength` and `shouldFail`.

Testing a script written in Groovy involves special circumstances, especially if input data is supplied from outside. That's the subject of the next section.

6.2 Testing scripts written in Groovy

Testing scripts is a bit different from testing classes. You don't normally instantiate a script and call a method on it, although you can. Instead, it's easiest just to execute the script and let its own internal `assert` statements do any correctness checks.

USING ASSERT When Groovy developers write scripts, they typically add asserts to demonstrate that the script works properly.

Running a script inside a test case is easy enough if no input or output variables are involved. Because scripts normally contain `assert` statements that verify their correctness, the key is simply to execute the script programmatically. That's what the `GroovyShell` class is for.

Here's a simple example. Consider a short but powerful script that accesses the Internet Chuck Norris Database,[6] reproduced from chapter 4:

```
import groovy.json.JsonSlurper

def result = 'http://api.icndb.com/jokes/random'.toURL().text
def json = new JsonSlurper().parseText(result)
def joke = json?.value?.joke
assert joke
println joke
```

This script, when executed, accesses the RESTful web service at the URL shown, retrieves a random joke in JavaScript Object Notation (JSON) form, parses (or, rather, slurps) it, and prints the resulting joke. The script uses the safe dereference operator to avoid `NullPointerExceptions` in case something goes wrong, but it has an `assert` statement to check that something actually was retrieved. When executed, the result is something like

```
Chuck Norris can instantiate an interface
```

[6] Arguably, this is why the internet was invented.

To test this script all I need to do is execute it and let the embedded assert statement do the work. I can execute it programmatically as in the following listing.

Listing 6.7 A class to hold all the script tests

```
class ScriptTests {
    @Test
    void testChuckNorrisScript() {
        GroovyShell shell = new GroovyShell()
        shell.evaluate(new File('src/main/groovy/mjg/chuck_norris.groovy'))
    }
}
```

The GroovyShell class, discussed in chapter 3 on Groovy and Java integration, has an evaluate method that takes a File argument. I simply point the File to the script in question, and the evaluate method on the shell executes it.

What if I want to check the results? In this case the result is random, but if my script has an actual result based on input values, is there something that can be done then?

To handle this I'm going to need a binding for the script (again discussed in chapter 3). A binding is an object that allows input and output variables to be accessed from the script.

SCRIPT BINDING Any variable that isn't declared in a script is part of the binding and can be accessed from outside.

Consider the classic "Hello, World!" script in Groovy. I'll put it in a package in the next listing, but other than that it's the same script described in appendix B, "Groovy by Feature."

Listing 6.8 The "Hello, World!" script

```
package mjg
println 'Hello, World!'
```

This script doesn't contain any assert statements, but because it prints to the console I'd like to be able to check the output. To do so I can assign the out property of the corresponding binding to a StringBuffer, which I can access after the script executes.[7] The following test has been added to the ScriptTests class started in listing 6.7.

Listing 6.9 A test that captures script output

```
@Test
void testHelloWorld() {
    Binding binding = new Binding()
```

[7] This isn't documented well at all, so consider it more value added for you by reading this book. Guillaume Laforge told me about it (and wrote it, too), so he gets the real credit.

```
    def content = new StringWriter()
    binding.out = new PrintWriter(content)
    GroovyShell shell = new GroovyShell(binding)
    shell.evaluate(new File('src/main/groovy/mjg/hello_world.groovy'))
    assert "Hello, World!" == content.toString().trim()
}
```

The out property of the binding is assigned to a PrintWriter wrapped around a StringWriter, so that when the println method in the script is executed, the output goes to the writer instead of the console. Then, after executing the script using the shell, I can check that the proper statement was printed by accessing the writer and trimming its output.

Normally a binding is used to pass input variables into a script. Here's a slight variation on the previous example, using a name variable.

Listing 6.10 A script with a binding variable

```
package mjg
println "Hello, $name!"
```

Again, the only real difference here is that the print statement uses a name variable that is not declared inside the script. That means it can be passed in from outside, as shown in the following test.

Listing 6.11 Setting a binding variable to test a script

```
@Test
void testHelloName() {
    Binding binding = new Binding()
    binding.name = 'Dolly'
    def content = new StringWriter()
    binding.out = new PrintWriter(content)
    GroovyShell shell = new GroovyShell(binding)
    shell.evaluate(new File('src/main/groovy/mjg/hello_name.groovy'))
    assert "Hello, Dolly!" == content.toString().trim()
}
```

The name variable is set to Dolly, and the result is confirmed as before.

6.2.1 Useful subclasses of GroovyTestCase: GroovyShellTestCase

The combination of script and binding is sufficiently common that the Groovy API now includes the class groovy.util.GroovyShellTestCase. This is a subclass of GroovyTestCase that instantiates a GroovyShell inside the setUp method. The shell is provided as a protected attribute, but the class also includes a withBinding method that takes a Map of parameters and a closure to execute. The following listing shows tests for the Groovy scripts in this section.

Listing 6.12 Testing Groovy scripts using `GroovyShellTestCase`

```
class ScriptShellTests extends GroovyShellTestCase {
    String base = 'src/main/groovy'

    void testChuckNorris() {
        shell.evaluate(new File("$base/mjg/chuck_norris.groovy"))
    }

    void testHelloWorld() {
        def content = new StringWriter()
        withBinding([out:new PrintWriter(content)]) {
            shell.evaluate(new File("$base/mjg/hello_world.groovy"))
            assert "Hello, World!" == content.toString().trim()
        }
    }

    void testHelloName() {
        def content = new StringWriter()
        withBinding([out:new PrintWriter(content), name:'Dolly']) {
            shell.evaluate(new File("$base/mjg/hello_name.groovy"))
            assert "Hello, Dolly!" == content.toString().trim()
        }
    }
}
```

Executing a script, which includes assert statements

Changing the out variable in the binding

Adding an input parameter

The first test finds the script to run and executes it using the shell instantiated in the superclass. The other tests use the `withBinding` method to override the `out` variable and provide an input parameter. The results are the same as instantiating the `GroovyShell` and `Binding` classes directly.

The previous example showed how to capture standard output from a script, but normally scripts return concrete values. The `withBinding` method returns whatever the script returns. As a trivial example, consider the following powerful Groovy calculator, saved in a file called `calc.groovy`:

```
z = x + y
```

Because none of the three variables (x, y, and z) are declared, they can all be accessed through the script's binding. The next listing shows a test for this script that validates the returned value.

Listing 6.13 A test for the addition script, `calc.groovy`

```
void testAddition() {
    def result = withBinding( [x:3,y:4] ) {
        shell.evaluate(new File('src/main/groovy/mjg/calc.groovy'))
        shell.context.z
    }
    assert 7 == result
}
```

The last line of the closure accesses the `z` variable, whose value is retrieved from the binding.

There's one other subclass of GroovyTestCase available in the standard library, called GroovyLogTestCase, which helps when testing logging. That class is the subject of the next subsection.

6.2.2 Useful subclasses of GroovyTestCase: GroovyLogTestCase

Good developers don't rely on capturing standard output. Instead they use loggers to direct output to locations that can be accessed later. For some time now Java has had a basic logging capability built into it, which can act as the front end on logging API implementations.

The Java logging classes, like Logger and Level, reside in the java.util.logging package. As an example of their use, consider the following minor variation on the calculator script from the previous section, stored in a file called calc_with_logger.groovy.

Listing 6.14 A script that uses a logger

```
import java.util.logging.Logger

Logger log = Logger.getLogger(this.class.name)
log.info("Received (x,y) = ($x,$y)")
z = x + y
```

The static getLogger method from the Logger class is a factory method that creates a Logger instance for this particular component. Here I'm using the name of the script, which becomes the name of the generated class. Once again, the variables x, y, and z are part of the script binding. The logger provides methods corresponding to various log levels. In the standard, the built-in levels include finest, finer, fine, info, warning, and severe. In this particular case, the input parameters are being logged at info level. To execute this script with x and y set to 3 and 4, use the following code:

```
Binding b = new Binding(x:3, y:4)
GroovyShell shell = new GroovyShell(b)
shell.evaluate(new File('src/main/groovy/mjg/calc_with_logger.groovy'))
println shell.context.z
```

The result is similar to this (dates and times may vary):

```
Jun 24, 2013 12:21:19 AM
     org.codehaus.groovy.runtime.callsite.PojoMetaMethodSite$PojoCachedMethod
     SiteNoUnwrap invoke
INFO: Received (x,y) = (3,4)
7
```

The default logger includes a console "appender," which directs all log output to the console. The mechanisms for capturing standard output don't work here, though. Instead, Groovy provides a class called GroovyLogTestCase, which includes a static method called stringLog for that purpose. The next listing shows a test demonstrating its use.

Listing 6.15 Capturing log output in a test case

```
class CalcWithLoggerTests extends GroovyLogTestCase {

    void testAddition() {
        def result = stringLog(Level.INFO, calc_with_logger.class.name) {
            Binding b = new Binding()
            b.x = 3; b.y = 4
            GroovyShell shell = new GroovyShell(b)
            shell.evaluate(
                new File('src/main/groovy/mjg/calc_with_logger.groovy'))
            assert 7 == shell.context.z
        }
        assert result.contains('INFO: Received (x,y) = (3,4)')
    }
}
```

The `stringLog` method returns the log output as a string, which is used to check that the logger is working correctly.

Most of the scripts in this book are tested using the techniques described in this section. If the script (or any class, for that matter) has dependencies, however, there's a bit more work to be done.

Lessons learned (testing scripts)

1. Groovy scripts provide their own challenges, especially when trying to capture input or output data and logging results.
2. Groovy source code can be executed programmatically through the `GroovyShell` and `Binding` classes, which then execute any contained `assert` methods.
3. Special subclasses of `GroovyTestCase` are available to simplify script testing.

True unit testing means testing an isolated class. The success or failure of the test should not rely on any associated objects. Any dependent objects should be replaced by mocks or stubs that return predetermined values when accessed.

This is another area that's significantly easier to handle when using Groovy than it is when using Java. Groovy has several built-in mechanisms for creating mock or stub objects, which I'll review in the next section.

6.3 Testing classes in isolation

In object-oriented programs no class is an island. Classes normally have dependencies. An integration test uses all of the dependencies together with the class under test (often called the CUT for that reason), but to truly test a given class you need to isolate it from its environment.

To isolate a class you need to provide it with what it needs from the dependencies in order to do its job. For example, if a class processes data it extracts from the rest of the system, you need to supply that data in a controlled manner that doesn't involve the rest of the system.

Formally, the class being tested is known as the *caller*, and the classes it depends on are known as *collaborators*. The goal is to provide controlled implementations of all the collaborators so the caller can be tested by itself.

In this section we'll look at an example similar to the one shown in chapter 7 on Spring. It's simple enough to follow without being totally artificial. The example is a classic bank account. There's an `Account` class, an `AccountDAO` interface, a `FileAccountDAO` implementation, and an `AccountService` class. The layout is shown in figure 6.3. The idea is that the service will have a method called `transferFunds` that sets transaction boundaries, the DAO class does persistence for the `Account`, and the `Account` itself is just an entity that will be saved and restored from some persistence structure.

In this case I'll use a simple file for persistence. Normally I would use a database, but I want to illustrate how to do a unit test in Groovy with a stub representing the file. In the process I'll get to discuss the difference between unit tests and integration tests. So far the tests in this chapter haven't tried to mock any dependent objects, so they can be considered integration tests. Now I'll look at doing true unit tests.

In addition to the basic classes, figure 6.3 also shows where the techniques in the following subsections (coerced closures and expandos) will be used for testing.

A (programmatic) client would use the banking system by invoking methods on the service class, `AccountService`, which presumably would be transactional. The service class uses implementations of the `AccountDAO` interface to work with individual accounts. The `Account` class itself is a simple POJO.

The next sections show the implementation code for the service and DAO, and illustrate how to use coerced closures and expandos to represent dependent objects. Specifically, when testing the logic in the service class a closure is used to represent the DAO. When testing the DAO implementation an expando stands in for the `File` class.

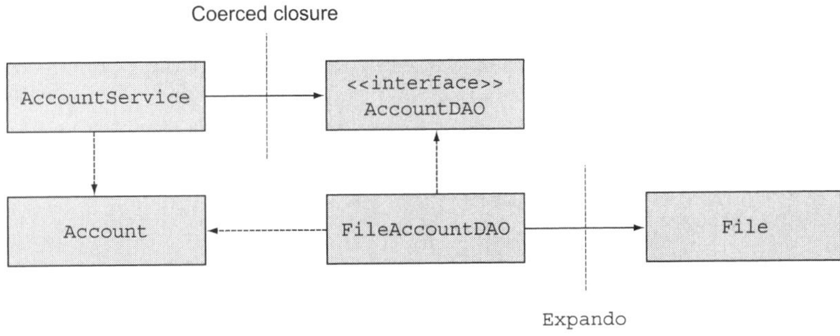

Figure 6.3 A UML diagram of a simple banking system that uses a service, and a DAO implementation based on flat files. Dashed open arrows represent dependencies, solid open arrows are associations, and the dashed closed arrow indicates implementation.

6.3.1 Coerced closures

Let me start with the AccountService, as shown in the next listing.

Listing 6.16 AccountService (in Java): uses the AccountDAO to find Accounts

```
public class AccountService {
    private AccountDAO dao;

    public void setDao(AccountDAO dao) {          // Insert the DAO
        this.dao = dao;
    }

    public void transferFunds(int from, int to, double amount) {
        Account fromAccount = dao.findAccountById(from);
        Account toAccount = dao.findAccountById(to);

        fromAccount.withdraw(amount);
        toAccount.deposit(amount);
    }

    public double getBalance(int id) {
        return dao.findAccountById(id).getBalance();   // Using the DAO
    }
}
```

Again, to keep things simple, the AccountService has only two business methods: a transferFunds method to move money from one account to another, and a getBalance method that delegates to the corresponding method in Account. Both methods take integer ids as arguments and use the AccountDAO to look up the corresponding accounts. Therefore, in order to do its job the AccountService needs an AccountDAO instance.

The AccountService is tied to the AccountDAO. A true unit test would test this class in isolation, meaning I need to provide some kind of stub for the AccountDAO class. AccountDAO is actually an interface, as shown in the next listing.

Listing 6.17 The AccountDAO interface, with CRUD methods for the Account class

```
public interface AccountDAO {
    Account findAccountById(int id);
    Collection<Account> findAllAccounts();
    int createNewAccount(double balance);
    void deleteAccount(int id);
}
```

If I create a stub implementation of the AccountDAO interface, I need to implement all these methods. Notice, however, that the AccountService only uses one method out of the interface: findAccountById. That's the only method I actually need. Unfortunately, I can't implement only that method. When implementing an interface I need to implement all its methods, whether I plan to use them or not.

I can use a Groovy technique to avoid all the extra work. If I provide a closure with the same argument list as the method I care about, I can then "coerce" the closure into the interface. The closure becomes the implementation of all the methods in the interface with the same argument list.

In this case I want to provide an implementation for the findAccountById method, which takes an integer id and returns an Account. I'm going to use a map to accomplish this:

```
Account a1 = new Account(1,100)
Account a2 = new Account(2,100)
def accounts = [1:a1, 2:a2]
```

The Account class (not shown, but it's a simple POJO contained in the book source code) has a two-argument constructor that takes an id and an initial balance. I instantiated two accounts with IDs 1 and 2 and added them to a map under the ID values. Now I need the closure that implements my method:

```
{ id -> accounts[id] }
```

That's a one-argument closure whose dummy variable, again called id, returns the Account stored under that ID. With that machinery in place I can provide a stub implementation for the DAO to the service class, as shown in the next listing.

Listing 6.18 A JUnit 4 test case for the AccountService, in Groovy, with a stubbed DAO

```
class AccountServiceTest {
    AccountService service = new AccountService()
    Account a1 = new Account(1,100)
    Account a2 = new Account(2,100)
    def accounts = [1:a1, 2:a2]

    @Before
    void setUp() throws Exception {
        service.dao = { id -> accounts[id] } as AccountDAO    <-- Closure as interface implementation
    }

    @Test
    void testTransferFunds() {
        assertEquals 100, a1.balance, 0.01
        assertEquals 100, a2.balance, 0.01

        service.transferFunds(1, 2, 50)    <-- Service method that uses the dao

        assertEquals 50, a1.balance, 0.01
        assertEquals 150, a2.balance, 0.01
    }
}
```

In the setUp method (with the @Before annotation), I use the as operator to treat the closure as an AccountDAO interface. That means the closure will be used as an implementation for all the methods in the interface. Because the only method used in the DAO interface was findAccountById, I can assign a single coerced closure to the dao property in the service (which goes through the setDao method, as usual), and I'm done. The testTransferFunds method verifies that the initial balances of the two accounts are as expected, does the transfer, and then checks that the updated balances are correct, keeping in mind that comparing doubles requires a third argument representing the precision.

If I need to implement multiple methods in the interface using a closure, I can supply a map of closures to method names, where each closure has the proper argument list. For example, the following listing shows a map of closures representing the entire `AccountDAO` interface and a few tests showing how it works.

Listing 6.19 Using a map of closures to implement an interface

```
Account a1 = new Account(1, 100)
Account a2 = new Account(2, 100)
def accounts = [1:a1, 2:a2]
int nextId = 3

def mock = [findAccountById: { int id -> accounts[id] },
            findAllAccounts: { -> accounts.values() },
            createNewAccount: { double bal -> nextId++ },
            deleteAccount: { int id -> } ] as AccountDAO

assert mock.findAccountById(1) == a1
mock.findAllAccounts().each {
    assert accounts.containsValue(it)
}
assert 3 == mock.createNewAccount(200)
assert !mock.deleteAccount(3)
```

Coercing a map of closures into an interface

The bottom line is that closures can be used as the implementation of an interface, and that this is an easy and very powerful technique for providing stub implementations of collaborators.

Next I want to test the DAO implementation class that uses a flat file to store the accounts. The goal in this case will be to provide a stub that stands in for the `java.io.File` class.

6.3.2 The Expando class

I'm going to use a file as my persistence mechanism, but for the testing environment I'm going to keep a cache of accounts in a map. This means that when I initialize the DAO I need to read the file and store the accounts found there in a map, and any time I make a change to an account I need to write the results back to a file. When reading the data I can just use the map—unless the file has been changed, in which case I'll have to re-read the file.[8]

To start, here are the attributes in my `FileAccountDAO` class:

```
def accountsFile
Map<Integer, Account> accounts = [:]
private static int nextId
boolean dirty
```

[8] I got the idea of using an expando this way from Jeff Brown, indefatigable coauthor of *Definitive Guide to Grails 2* (Apress, 2013).

I deliberately declared the variable representing the accounts file to be of type def rather than File, for reasons I'll explain when I create the stub. The other attributes are a map to represent the accounts cache (using generics, which Groovy compiles successfully but doesn't enforce[9]), a private static integer that will be my primary key generator, and a Boolean flag to indicate whether the accounts cache needs to be refreshed.

Here's the method used to read the accounts from the file:

```
void readAccountsFromFile() {
    accountsFile.splitEachLine(',') { line ->
        int id = line[0].toInteger()
        double balance = line[1].toDouble()
        accounts[id] = new Account(id:id,balance:balance)
    }
    nextId = accounts?.keySet().max() ?: 0
    nextId++
    dirty = false
}
```

Each account is stored as plain text, with a comma separating the id from the balance. Reading accounts uses the splitEachLine method that takes two arguments: the delimiter (a comma in this case) and a closure that defines what to do with the resulting list. The closure says to parse the ID and balance into the proper data types, instantiate an account with the resulting values, and save it in the map. Then I need to set the nextId variable to one more than the max of the IDs used so far, which gives me an opportunity to use the cool Elvis operator.[10] Finally, because this method refreshes the cache, I can set the dirty flag to false.

The corresponding method to write out the accounts is shown next:

```
void writeAccountsToFile() {
    accountsFile.withWriter { w ->
        accounts.each { id, account ->
            w.println("$id,$account.balance")
        }
    }
    dirty = true
}
```

The withWriter method is from the Groovy JDK and is added to the java.io.File class. It provides an output writer wrapped around the file that closes automatically when the closure argument completes. The closure writes the ID and balance of each account to a single line in the file, separated by a comma. Because this method changes the file, it sets the dirty flag to true so that the class knows the cache needs to be refreshed.

---

[9] That's another subtle trap. The syntax for Java generics compiles in Groovy, but just because you declared a List<Integer> doesn't mean you can't add instances of String, Date, or Employee if you want to. In Groovy, think of the generic declaration as nothing more than documentation.

[10] I don't really go out of my way to find excuses to use the cool Elvis operator, but I don't pass them up when they present themselves either.

With those methods in place, the next listing shows the complete DAO implementation.

Listing 6.20 The complete `FileAccountDAO` implementation, in Groovy

```
class FileAccountDAO implements AccountDAO {
    def accountsFile
    Map<Integer, Account> accounts = [:]
    private static int nextId
    boolean dirty

    private void readAccountsFromFile() {
        accountsFile.splitEachLine(',') { line ->
            int id = line[0].toInteger()
            double balance = line[1].toDouble()
            accounts[id] = new Account(id:id,balance:balance)
        }
        nextId = accounts?.keySet().max() ?: 0
        nextId++

        dirty = false
    }

    private void writeAccountsToFile() {
        accountsFile.withWriter { w ->
            accounts.each { id, account ->
                w.println("$id,$account.balance")
            }
        }
        dirty = true
    }

    @Override
    Account findAccountById(int id) {
        if (dirty) readAccountsFromFile()
        return accounts[id]
    }

    @Override
    Collection<Account> findAllAccounts() {
        if (dirty) readAccountsFromFile()
        return accounts.values()
    }

    @Override
    int createNewAccount(double balance) {
        int newId = nextId++
        accounts[newId] = new Account(id:newId,balance:balance)
        writeAccountsToFile()
        return newId;
    }

    @Override
    void deleteAccount(int id) {
        accounts.remove(id)
        writeAccountsToFile()
    }
}
```

Refresh the cache if necessary (annotating `if (dirty) readAccountsFromFile()` in `findAccountById` and `findAllAccounts`)

Cache changed, so persist it (annotating `writeAccountsToFile()` in `createNewAccount` and `deleteAccount`)

The business methods are straightforward, based on the accounts cache (the map). The only complication is determining whether or not the cache needs to be refreshed before returning a value. Methods that change the accounts force a write to the file. Methods that retrieve them just need to check if a read is necessary.

That's a fair amount of code, and I would feel very uncomfortable if it wasn't tested. An integration test would simply supply an actual file to the DAO, and I have such a test in the book's source code. A unit test, however, would remove the dependency on the `File` class. That's where the `Expando` comes in.

The `groovy.util.Expando` class creates an object with no attributes or methods of its own, other than the ones it inherits. The cool part is that you can treat an instance of `Expando` as though it was a map, where the keys are the names of properties or methods, and the values are the property values or method implementations.

> **EXPANDO** A `groovy.util.Expando` is a class that creates an empty object to which you can add properties and methods as desired.

To see this in action, let me create an `Expando` to act as a replacement for the file in my DAO. First I have to see what methods in `File` need to be represented.

Here are the methods in `AccountDAO` that use the `accountsFile` dependency. The methods I need to mock are in bold:

```
private void readAccountsFromFile() {
    accountsFile.splitEachLine(',') { line ->
        int id = line[0].toInteger()
        double balance = line[1].toDouble()
        accounts[id] = new Account(id:id,balance:balance)
    }
    nextId = accounts?.keySet().max() ?: 0
    nextId++

    dirty = false
}

private void writeAccountsToFile() {
    accountsFile.withWriter { w ->
        accounts.each { id, account ->
            w.println("$id,$account.balance")
        }
    }
    dirty = true
}
```

Examining the previous listing shows that I'm using `splitEachLine` and `withWriter` in the `File` class and the `println` method from the `Writer` class, so these methods need to be implemented in the `Expando`.

All of those methods are already implemented in the `String` class. Therefore, why not use a string to represent the file? I'll add a string property to the `Expando` and then implement all the needed methods so that they delegate to the corresponding methods on the string. Here's the resulting code:

```
Expando ex = new Expando()
ex.data = ''
ex.println = { data.append(it) }
ex.withWriter = { new StringWriter() }
ex.splitEachLine = { pattern, clos ->
    data.splitEachLine(pattern, clos) }
```

First I instantiate the Expando. Next I add a data property to it and assign it to an empty string. The println method is then implemented through the append method on String. The withWriter method is assigned a closure that returns a new StringWriter. Finally, the splitEachLine method is assigned to a two-argument closure that delegates to the corresponding existing method on String.

All that's left is to substitute the Expando for the file in the DAO:

```
FileAccountDAO dao = new FileAccountDAO(accountsFile:ex)
```

Here at last is the reason I needed to declare the accountsFile variable with def rather than File. An Expando isn't a file and isn't related to the File class in any way, so a File reference would be a problem. If I use def to declare the variable instead, I can freely assign the Expando variable to my variable. Duck typing does the rest; every time a method is invoked on the variable, the corresponding method is called on the Expando.

> **DYNAMIC TYPING TO THE RESCUE** If I declare a reference using def, I can assign it to anything. When I invoke methods on it I'm relying on the methods being there in whatever class I've used.

The next listing shows the complete unit test for the file DAO.

Listing 6.21 FileAccountDAO unit test, using an Expando to stub the File

```
class FileAccountDAOUnitTests {
    FileAccountDAO dao

    @Before
    void setUp() {
        Expando ex = new Expando()
        ex.data = ''
        ex.splitEachLine = { pattern, clos ->
            data.splitEachLine(pattern, clos) }
        ex.withWriter = { new StringWriter() }
        ex.println = { data.append(it) }
        dao = new FileAccountDAO(accountsFile:ex)
    }

    @Test
    void testCreateAndFindNewAccount() {
        int id = dao.createNewAccount(100.0)
        Account local = new Account(id:id,balance:100.0)
        Account fromDao = dao.findAccountById(id)
        assertEquals local.id, fromDao.id
        assertEquals local.balance, fromDao.balance, 0.01
    }
```

```
    @Test
    void testFindAllAccounts() {
        (1..10).each { num -> dao.createNewAccount(num*100) }
        def accounts = dao.findAllAccounts()
        assertEquals 10, accounts.size()
        accounts*.balance.each { it in (100..1000) }
    }

    @Test
    void testDeleteAccount() {
        (1..10).each { num -> dao.createNewAccount(num*100) }
        def accounts = dao.findAllAccounts()
        assertEquals 10, accounts.size()
        accounts.each { account -> dao.deleteAccount(account.id) }
        assert 0 == dao.findAllAccounts().size()
    }
}
```

In a way, I got lucky with this example. The variable I needed to stub, `accountsFile`, was exposed as a property, so I could assign the `Expando` to it from outside. What if that's not the case? What if the variable is instantiated inside the class? Can anything be done then?

If I'm limited to Java, I'm out of luck.[11] In fact, even mocking frameworks have trouble with this situation. Fortunately, Groovy has a built-in mechanism for handling exactly this problem. The classes I need are called `StubFor` and `MockFor`.

6.3.3 StubFor and MockFor

A typical Groovy developer doesn't necessarily spend a lot of time metaprogramming, but they sure reap the benefits of it. I use builders in several places in this book. Domain-specific languages (DSLs) like GORM, are built through metaprogramming techniques. The whole Groovy JDK is created through metaclass manipulation. In the last section I used an `Expando` to create a test object, and that only works in a language that supports metaprogramming. After a while you get used to metaprogramming capabilities and aren't really surprised by their benefits any more.

In this section I'm going to show a technique that, even after all my years of programming in Groovy, still feels like magic. I know it works, and I use it wherever I can, but every time it happens I have to take a moment to sit back and smile at how cool it is.

Let me go directly to the example I want to show and then explain the stub technique. Rather than use the bank account system described so far, let me remind you of the geocoder example I've used in several chapters of this book. The next listing shows the `Geocoder` class that's part of the Groovy Baseball system described in chapter 2.

---

[11] Unless I have AspectJ available, but even then the solution is complicated.

Listing 6.22 The Groovy Baseball Geocoder class, revisited

```
class Geocoder {
    String base = 'http://maps.googleapis.com/maps/api/geocode/xml?'

    void fillInLatLng(Stadium stadium) {
        String urlEncodedAddress =
            [stadium.street, stadium.city, stadium.state].collect {
                URLEncoder.encode(it,'UTF-8')
            }.join(',')
        String url = base + [sensor:false,
            address: urlEncodedAddress].collect {k,v -> "$k=$v"}.join('&')
        def response = new XmlSlurper().parse(url)          // What if I'm not online?
        String latitude =
            response.result[0].geometry.location.lat ?: "0.0"
        String longitude =
            response.result[0].geometry.location.lng ?: "0.0"
        stadium.latitude = latitude.toDouble()
        stadium.longitude = longitude.toDouble()
    }
}
```

I have a test for this class, but it's most definitely an integration test. The following listing shows a JUnit 4 test for the geocoder, written in Groovy.

Listing 6.23 GeocoderIntegrationTests.groovy: a JUnit 4 test for the geocoder

```
import static org.junit.Assert.*;
import org.junit.Test;

class GeocoderIntegrationTest {
    Geocoder geocoder = new Geocoder()

        @Test
    public void testFillInLatLng() {
        Stadium google = new Stadium(
            street:'1600 Ampitheatre Parkway',
            city:'Mountain View',state:'CA')                // Google headquarters

        geocoder.fillInLatLng(google)                       // Access Google's geocoder online

        assertEquals(37.422, google.latitude, 0.01)         // Comparing doubles
        assertEquals(-122.083, google.longitude, 0.01)      // requires a precision
    }
}
```

A `Stadium` has a street, city, state, latitude, and longitude, and the geocoder's job is to take the address, invoke Google's geocoder service using it, and use the result to update the latitude and longitude. After setting up a `Stadium` instance corresponding to Google's home office, the test invokes the `fillInLatLng` method and checks that the updated latitude and longitude values are within tolerances.

This works just fine, but to do its job it has to access the Google geocoder service. That's why it's an integration test.[12]

[12] See http://en.wikipedia.org/wiki/Integration_testing for the definition of an integration test.

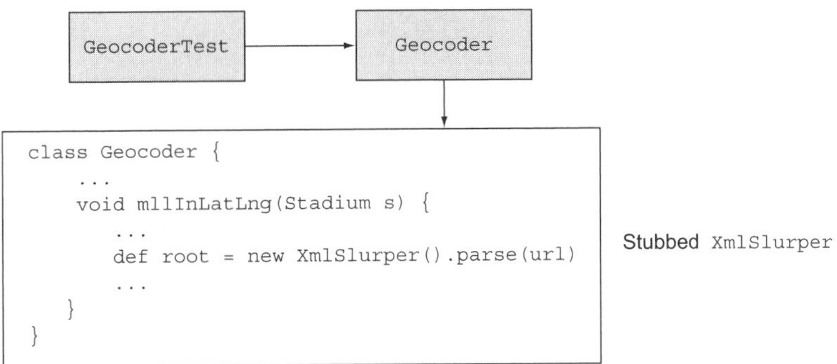

Figure 6.4 The geocoder relies on an `XmlSlurper` instantiated locally to do its job. The goal is to modify its `parse` method to return the needed value, even though the slurper is a local variable in the test method.

What happens if I'm not online? More formally, is there any way I can test the logic in the `fillInLatLng` method without relying on the external URL?

The online access is being handled through the `parse` method of `XmlSlurper`. That method takes a URL, accesses it, downloads the XML response, parses it into a DOM tree, and returns the root element. In a normal mock I'd like to replace the expression "`new XmlSlurper().parse(url)`" with a pre-defined DOM tree. If the slurper had been supplied from outside this class, I could create a stub and force the `parse` method to return what I want. Unfortunately, the slurper is instantiated right inside the method.

Here's where Groovy's `MockFor` and `StubFor` classes come in.

> **Stubs vs. mocks**
>
> Mocks have strong expectations, while stubs do not. That means that a test involving a mock fails if the collaborator methods are not called the proper number of times and in the proper order. With stubs, expectations are looser; you don't need to call the methods in the proper order, though it does enforce the multiplicity requirement.
>
> Conceptually, a stub is simply a stand-in for the collaborator, so the focus is on the caller. Because a mock's expectations are strong, you're effectively testing the interaction between the caller and the collaborator, known as the *protocol*.

Figure 6.4 shows how I want the stub to work.

I want the `parse` method of the slurper to return the root of a DOM tree that looks like what the Google geocoder would have returned had I been able to access it. The easiest way to get that value is to set up the proper XML tree and parse it ahead of time:

```
String xml = '''
<root><result><geometry>
    <location>
        <lat>37.422</lat>
```

```
        <lng>-122.083</lng>
    </location>
</geometry></result></root>'''

def correctRoot = new XmlSlurper().parseText(xml)
```

The XML string has the proper latitude and longitude for the Google home office. To get the proper root value I invoke the parseText method of the XmlSlurper. My Geocoder class can take that root and walk the tree as usual to get the latitude and longitude.

The challenge is this: how do I get my own Geocoder to use this implementation when there's no obvious way to inject it? The solution is to use the StubFor class and set the expectations around it:

```
def stub = new StubFor(XmlSlurper)
stub.demand.parse { correctRoot }
```

The StubFor constructor takes a class reference and builds a stub around it. Then I "demand" that the parse method return the root of the tree calculated in the previous fragment.

To get Groovy to use the new stub, invoke the test inside a closure argument to the use method:

```
stub.use {
   geocoder.fillInLatLng(stadium)
}
```

The use closure is the key. Through the magic of Groovy metaprogramming, when the parse method of XmlSlurper is accessed inside the fillInLatLng method, the demanded version is used rather than the actual implementation. The result is that the business logic of the fillInLatLng method is tested, without relying on the slurper itself.

The next listing shows the complete test. To make absolutely sure that the online version of the geocoder is not being used, I created a stadium with the wrong address. The only way the test passes is if the slurper returns the rigged values.

Listing 6.24 GeocoderUnitTest.groovy: tests geocoder even if not online

```
import static org.junit.Assert.*
import groovy.mock.interceptor.StubFor

import org.junit.Test

class GeocoderUnitTest {
    Geocoder geocoder = new Geocoder()

    @Test
    public void testFillInLatLng() {
        Stadium wrongStadium = new Stadium(          <-- Deliberately using the wrong address
            street:'1313 Mockingbird Lane',
            city:'New York',state:'NY')
```

```
        String xml = '''
        <root><result><geometry>
            <location>
                <lat>37.422</lat>
                <lng>-122.083</lng>
            </location>
        </geometry></result></root>'''

        def correctRoot = new XmlSlurper().parseText(xml)      <-- The correct DOM tree

        def stub = new StubFor(XmlSlurper)                     | Setting
        stub.demand.parse { correctRoot }                      | expectations

        stub.use {
            geocoder.fillInLatLng(wrongStadium)                <-- Use the stub
        }
        assertEquals(37.422, wrongStadium.latitude, 0.01)
        assertEquals(-122.083, wrongStadium.longitude, 0.01)
    }
}
```

The test sets up a `Stadium` instance that deliberately has the wrong address. The correct root of the DOM tree is generated using the string data, and the `demand` property of the stub is used to return it. By executing the test inside the `use` block, the correct answer is supplied at the proper moment, and the test succeeds.

The `StubFor` and `MockFor` APIs are far more extensive than what's being shown here. You can demand that a method returns different preset values each time you call it. You can verify that the methods are called the proper number of times in the proper order by using the `verify` method on `StubFor` (`MockFor` does that automatically). See the API for details.

The only real limitation on the `StubFor` and `MockFor` classes is that they can only be used to replace Groovy implementations. You can't supply a Java class and have it work. Still, if your service is implemented in Groovy, they are an invaluable addition to your testing arsenal.[13]

Lessons learned (mocking dependencies)

1. To easily create a stub of an interface, use closures to implement the methods. This is known as *closure coercion*.
2. The `Expando` class has no properties or methods, but both can be added at runtime to configure an object to do what you want.
3. The `StubFor` and `MockFor` classes in the standard library can be used to create mock objects *even when they're replacing local variables* in the test fixture.[14]

[13] Candor compels me to admit that I worked out how to use `StubFor` and `MockFor` over a few days, and then did what I should have done originally: looked them up in *Groovy in Action*. GinA (as it was then known; the second edition is ReGinA) had it all laid out over a few pages, nice and neat. There's a reason that *Groovy in Action* is still my all-time favorite technical book.

[14] If you read nothing else in this chapter, take a look at that.

So far every technique in this chapter has been based on existing classes in the Groovy standard library. One new testing library, however, has been gaining momentum in the Groovy community, and not just because it has a clever name. The Spock framework is simple to learn, easy to use, and the subject of the next section.

6.4 The future of testing: Spock

The Spock framework yields more productivity for less effort than any other framework I've encountered. Spend a small amount of time with Spock (for example, through the discussions in this section), and you can immediately be productive. Spock provides both tests and a solid mocking capability in an easy-to-use package.

According to the developer of the framework,[15] the name Spock is a blend of "specification" and "mock." That may even be true. It seems more likely, however, that somebody just liked the name Spock and the rest is clever rationalization.[16] The result, inevitably, is that any discussion of the framework results in a series of *Star Trek*-related puns. My original plan was to avoid them, but it's practically impossible.[17]

6.4.1 The Search for Spock

The main site for Spock is http://spockframework.org, which actually redirects to a Google code project at https://code.google.com/p/spock/. There you'll find wiki pages with lots of good information. Like most cool projects these days, the source code is hosted at GitHub at https://github.com/spockframework/spock. You can clone the repository and do a manual build, or you can install the distribution from the standard Maven repository.

Spock versions are tied to Groovy versions. The latest release version of Spock is 0.7-groovy-2.0. Don't let the low version number deter you.[18] The Spock API is simple and easy to use and understand, and its adoption has been very rapid.[19]

The Gradle file in the next listing shows the appropriate dependencies to build this chapter's source code.

Listing 6.25 Building and testing with Spock using Gradle

```
apply plugin: "groovy"

repositories {
    mavenCentral()
}
```

---

[15] Peter Niederweiser, who is active and helpful on the Spock email list.

[16] Of which I totally approve.

[17] For example, Spock is a *logical* framework for *enterprise* testing. Test well, and prosper. I have been, and always shall be, your friendly testing framework.

[18] Version 1.0 is due out by the time this book appears in print.

[19] The Spock plugin will be included in Grails by default starting in version 2.3.

```
dependencies {
    groovy "org.codehaus.groovy:groovy-all:2.1.5
    testCompile "org.spockframework:spock-core:0.7-groovy-2.0"
}
```

The repository at Maven central holds the Groovy distribution and the Spock release versions. The dependency is decoded in the usual way, with the group being "org.spockframework," the name (or artifact ID, in Maven speak) being "spock-core," and the version number of 0.7-groovy-2.0. Note that the Spock version is tied to a Groovy version.

6.4.2 Test well, and prosper

Spock tests all extend a superclass called `spock.lang.Specification`. In addition to its own methods, the `Specification` class includes the `@RunWith` annotation from JUnit. The result is that Spock tests can be run within the normal JUnit testing infrastructure.

The tests themselves all have a common form. Each test method (known as a *fixture*) is declared using the `def` keyword, followed by a string that describes what the test is supposed to accomplish. Fixture methods normally take no arguments.

Listing 6.26 shows a simple Spock test to verify some `String` behavior. By convention, Spock test cases end in `Spec`. That isn't a requirement,[20] but it does help to keep the Spock tests easily identifiable, especially when your system uses both Spock and JUnit tests together.

Listing 6.26 A specification verifying basic `java.lang.String` behavior

```
import spock.lang.Specification;

class StringSpec extends Specification {
    String llap

    def setup() { llap = "Live Long and Prosper" }

    def "LLaP has 21 characters"() {
        expect: llap.size() == 21
    }

    def "LLaP has 4 words"() {
        expect: llap.split(/\W/).size() == 4
    }

    def "LLaP has 6 vowels"() {
        expect: llap.findAll(/[aeiou]/).size() == 6
    }
}
```

The class extends `spock.lang.Specification`, which is what makes it a Spock test. The spec is testing a `String`, so it has an attribute named `llap`. In the `setup` method, the `llap` variable is assigned to the string "Live Long and Prosper." The `setup` method runs before each test, similar to `@Before` in JUnit 4. JUnit 3 contains a method called

[20] Spock tests in Grails *do* have to end in `Spec`.

setUp that does the same thing, but in Spock the setup method is written in lowercase, with a def keyword.

The test methods, known as feature methods in the Spock documentation, are written in block structure. In each of the test methods shown here, there's a single block called expect. The expect block consists of a series of Boolean expressions, each of which must evaluate to true for the test to pass.

The three sample tests check (1) the number of characters in the test string; (2) that there are four words in the test string, based on splitting the string at non-word boundaries; and (3) that the test string has a total of six vowels, again based on a regular expression.

Like JUnit 4, Spock tests can verify that exceptions are thrown. Spock tests can also verify that exceptions are not thrown. Consider the following two tests, which are added to the previous listing:

```
def "Access inside the string doesn't throw an exception"() {
    when: s.charAt(s.size() - 1)
    then: notThrown(IndexOutOfBoundsException)
}

def "Access beyond the end of the string throws exception"() {
    when: s.charAt(s.size() + 1)
    then: thrown(IndexOutOfBoundsException)
}
```

These tests use the when/then blocks, which are used as a stimulus/response pair. Any code can be added to the when block, but the then block must consist of Boolean expressions, as with expect. The expressions are evaluated automatically, using the Groovy Truth. This means that non-null references, non-empty strings, and non-zero numbers all evaluate to true.

The charAt method in String throws an exception if its argument is negative or beyond the end of the string. The previous two tests show both conditions, using the thrown() and notThrown() methods. The thrown method can return the exception if you want to process it further, using one of two variations in syntax

```
Exception e = thrown()
```

or

```
e = thrown(Exception)
```

where the Exception can be any specific exception class.

Consider the following test, which also introduces the extremely useful old method.

Listing 6.27 Another spec, illustrating the old method

```
class QuoteSpec extends Specification {
    String quote = """I am endeavoring, ma'am, to construct a
        mnemonic memory circuit, using stone knives and bear skins."""

    List<String> strings

    def setup() { strings = quote.tokenize(" ,.") }
```

```
    def "test string has 16 words"() {
        expect: strings.size() == 16
    }

    def "adding a word increases total by 1"() {
        when: strings << 'Fascinating'
        then: strings.size() == old(strings.size()) + 1
    }
}
```

The `tokenize` method takes a set of delimiters as arguments and divides the string at those positions. The result is an `ArrayList` of words. That's interesting enough, but the cool part is in the test that appends a new word to the list. In this case, the size of the list is evaluated twice, once before the `when` block is executed and once afterward. The expression shows that the result afterward is equal to the result beforehand, plus one.

6.4.3 Data-driven specifications

Spock tests have one additional feature beyond what appears in other testing frameworks: data-driven[21] specifications. The idea is that if you provide a collection of data in a format that Groovy can iterate over, then the test will run each entry through any supplied Boolean conditions.

This is easier to show than to describe. Consider the test shown on the main page of the Spock website, repeated in the next listing. It feeds names from a data table into `expect`, using three different sources of data.

Listing 6.28 Data-driven Spock test

```
class HelloSpock extends spock.lang.Specification {
    @Unroll
    def "#name should be #length"() {
        expect:
        name.size() == length

        where:
        name     | length
        "Spock"  | 5
        "Kirk"   | 4
        "Scotty" | 6
        'McCoy'  | 5
    }

    def "check lengths using arrays"() {
        expect: name.size() == length

        where:
        name << ["Spock","Kirk","Scotty"]
        length << [5,4,6]
    }
```

[21] Shouldn't Data run on Android? (Yeah, that was particularly bad. Sorry.)

```
    def "check lengths using pairs"() {
        expect: name.size() == length
        where:
        [name,length] << [["Spock",5],["Kirk",4],["Scotty",6]]
    }
}
```

The where block in the first test contains a data table. The column names (name and length) are variables, which are referenced in the expect block. Groovy takes each row of the table and evaluates the expect condition. It's an elegant system that's easy to understand and quite powerful. While the data table is a powerful construct, in fact any collection that Groovy knows how to iterate over works as well.

The second and third tests illustrate the same process but supply the data via collections. The second test uses separate lists for the name and length values. This means that to understand the test data you have to match up the collection indexes. For example, "Spock" goes with 5, "Kirk" goes with 4, and so on. The third test is a bit easier to visualize, because the data is organized into ordered pairs. Which mechanism you use (data table, sets of pairs, individual collections, and so on) is purely a question of style.

Another interesting part of Spock is the @Unroll annotation. Without it, the name listed in the test output would be the name of the test itself. With it, each row of the where block creates a different name.

Figure 6.5 shows the results of executing this test in the Groovy and Grails Tool Suite (which is just Eclipse plus lots of plugins) as a JUnit test. In addition to demonstrating that Spock tests run with the existing JUnit infrastructure, the test also shows the difference in output that results with the @Unroll annotation. The second and third tests use the name of the method as their output. The first test, marked with @Unroll, shows up under "unrooted tests," where each test gets its own unique name based on the test data.

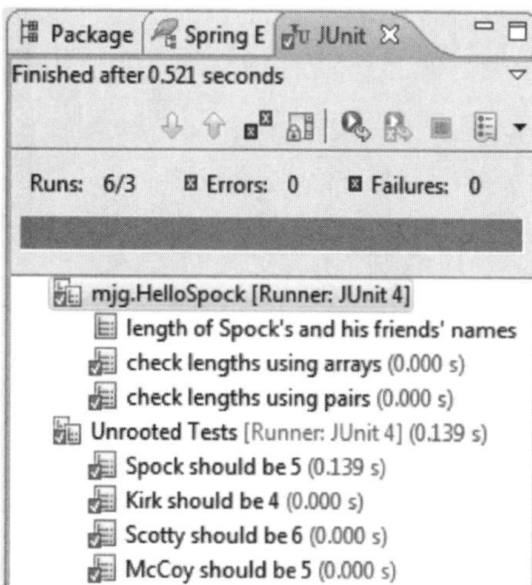

Figure 6.5 Results of the Spock data-driven tests. The test with the @Unroll annotation is shown in the Eclipse output as "unrooted," showing different output messages for each set of data.

What if the class you plan to test has dependencies? Those dependencies need to be stubbed or mocked, as discussed earlier. Fortunately, Spock has its own mocking capabilities built in.

6.4.4 The trouble with tribbles

The `Specification` class from Spock contains a method called `Mock` that is used to create mock objects. If your dependency is based on an interface, the `Mock` method can generate a mock object directly, using Java's dynamic proxy mechanism. If it's a class, `Mock` will extend the class using the CGLIB library.

It's time for a relatively simple (and relatively silly) example. A tribble[22] is a small, furry animal that breeds prolifically, likes Vulcans, and hates Klingons. Here's a `Tribble` class, written in Groovy.

Listing 6.29 A `Tribble` class in Groovy

```
class Tribble {

    String react(Vulcan vulcan) {
        vulcan.soothe()
        "purr, purr"
    }

    String react(Klingon klingon) {
        klingon.annoy()
        "wheep! wheep!"
    }

    def feed() {
        def tribbles = [this]
        10.times { tribbles << new Tribble() }
        return tribbles
    }
}
```

What do you get when you feed a tribble? Not a fat tribble, but rather a lot of hungry little tribbles. The `feed` method returns a list containing the original tribble plus 10 more.

The overloaded `react` method takes either a Vulcan or a Klingon as an argument. If it's a Vulcan, the tribble soothes the Vulcan and purrs contentedly. If it's a Klingon, the tribble annoys the Klingon and reacts badly. The `Tribble` class has a dependency on both `Vulcan` and `Klingon`.

To keep things simple, both `Vulcan` and `Klingon` are interfaces. The `Vulcan` interface is shown here:

```
interface Vulcan {
    def soothe()
    def decideIfLogical()
}
```

[22] See http://en.wikipedia.org/wiki/The_Trouble_With_Tribbles for details, in the unlikely event you haven't seen that particular *Star Trek* (original series) episode. It holds up remarkably well after 35 (!) years.

Vulcans have a soothe method, called by the tribble, and a decideIfLogical method that isn't necessary for this test. That's one of the problems with implementing stubs, by the way; you have to implement all the interface methods, even the ones that aren't relevant to the test in question.

Klingons are a bit different:

```
interface Klingon {
    def annoy()
    def fight()
    def howlAtDeath()
}
```

Tribbles annoy Klingons. Klingons also fight and howlAtDeath,[23] two methods that aren't needed here. To test the Tribble class, I need to create mock objects for both the Vulcan and Klingon classes, set their expectations appropriately, and test that the tribble behaves appropriately around each.

Let me show the tests one by one. First I'll check to see that the feed method works properly:

```
def "feed a tribble, get more tribbles"() {
    when:
    def result = tribble.feed()

    then:
    result.size() == 11
    result.every {
        it instanceof Tribble
    }
}
```

The when block invokes the feed method. The then block checks that there are 11 elements in the returned collection and that each is a tribble. There's nothing new or unusual about this test. Moving on to the test for reacting to Vulcans, however, I need to mock the Vulcan interface.[24]

```
def "reacts well to Vulcans"() {
    Vulcan spock = Mock()

    when:
    String reaction = tribble.react(spock)

    then:
    reaction == "purr, purr"
    1*spock.soothe()
}
```

There are two ways to use the Mock method in Spock. The first is shown here: instantiate the class, and assign it to a variable of the proper type. The method will implement

---

[23] Klingons in *Star Trek: The Next Generation* howl at death. They didn't in the original series, as far as I know.

[24] When I mock a Vulcan, I feel like Dr. McCoy.

the interface of the declared type. The second way is to use the interface type as an argument to the Mock method, which isn't shown here.

Once the mock has been created, the when block uses the mock as the argument to the react method. In the then block, first the proper reaction is checked, and then comes the interesting part. The last line says that the test passes only if the soothe method is called on the mock exactly one time, ignoring any returned value.

This is a very flexible system. The cardinality can be anything, including using an underscore as a wild card (for example, (3.._) means three or more times).

Moving on to the Klingon interface, the following test does multiple checks:

```
def "reacts badly to Klingons"() {
    Klingon koloth = Mock()

    when:
    String reaction = tribble.react(koloth)

    then:
    1 * koloth.annoy() >> {
        throw new Exception()
    }
    0 * koloth.howlAtDeath()
    reaction == null
    Exception e = thrown()
}
```

After mocking the Klingon[25] and invoking the react method, the then block first checks to see that the annoy method on the mock is invoked exactly once and, using the right-shift operator, implements the method by throwing an exception. The next line checks that the howlAtDeath method is not invoked at all. Because the annoy method throws an exception, there is no returned reaction. The last line then verifies that annoying the Klingon did in fact throw the expected exception.

The idea is that even if the mock is configured to throw an exception, the tribble test still passes. The test verifies that the exception is thrown without making the test itself fail.

6.4.5 Other Spock capabilities

The capabilities shown so far hopefully provide a teaser for Spock. There are more features in Spock that go beyond the scope of this chapter. For example, the @Ignore annotation on a test skips that test, but there's also an @IgnoreRest annotation that skips all the other tests instead. The @IgnoreIf annotation checks a Boolean condition and skips the test if the condition evaluates to true. There's also a @Stepwise annotation for tests that have to be executed in a particular order, and a @Timeout annotation for tests that are taking too long to execute.

[25] How do you mock a Klingon? From a galaxy far, far away (rimshot).

Lessons learned (Spock)

1. Spock tests extend `spock.lang.Specification`.
2. The `Specification` class has a JUnit runner, so Spock tests run in your existing JUnit infrastructure.
3. Spock test names are descriptive sentences. The framework uses AST transformations to convert them to legal Groovy.
4. The tests are composed of blocks, like `expect` or `when/then`. Expressions in an `expect` or `then` block are evaluated for the Groovy Truth automatically.
5. The `old` method from `spock.lang.Specification` evaluates its argument before the `when` block is executed.
6. The `where` block is used to iterate over test data, either from a table, a database result, or any data structure over which Groovy can iterate.
7. Spock has its own built-in mocking capabilities.

The wiki for Spock contains many examples, as well as detailed documentation about mock details (called *interactions*) and more. The source code also comes with a Spock example project that you can use as a basis for your project. Spock is built with Gradle, which configures all the dependencies, and can plug into other APIs like Spring. See the docs and APIs for details.[26]

6.5 Summary

This chapter covered a lot of ground in the testing arena. Groovy brings a simple `assert` statement into play that can be used for scripts and includes the `GroovyTestCase` class that extends JUnit's capabilities. When it comes to managing dependencies, you can build a stub implementation of an interface using closures, and you can build a more complete stub using the `Expando` class.

Groovy also has the `StubFor` and `MockFor` classes, which can be used to test interactions. They can even create mock objects for classes that are instantiated as local variables, which is pretty amazing.

Finally, if you're willing to add an additional library, the Spock testing framework provides a simple yet versatile API that still runs on your existing JUnit-based infrastructure. It also has its own mock abilities and integrates with other libraries, like Spring and Tapestry.

Adding Groovy also adds a wide variety of options for testing Java and mixed Java/Groovy projects. Hopefully the techniques in this chapter will help you decide where you can get the most benefit from them.

---

[26] See also the Manning book *Spock in Action*, by Ken Sipe, coming soon.

Part 3

Groovy in the real world

In part 3, "Groovy in the real world," I try to address the sorts of challenges Java developers face on a regular basis.

I start with the Spring framework, which is probably the most commonly used open source project in the Java world. Spring and Groovy are old friends and work together beautifully. Chapter 7 shows how to use Groovy classes as Spring beans anywhere in your system, including aspects. It then shows Spring capabilities unique to dynamic languages, like refreshable beans, inline scripted beans, and the `BeanBuilder` class from Grails.

Chapter 8 covers Groovy interactions with persistent storage. Groovy includes a very useful façade over JDBC known as the `groovy.sql.Sql` class, which is effective when working with relational databases. The chapter also provides an example of working with the GMongo project, a Groovy wrapper around the Java API for working with MongoDB. This is a typical Groovy idiom—taking a Java library and making it easier to use. Finally, the chapter discusses many of the issues associated with GORM, the Grails Object Relational Mapping layer from Grails, which is probably the most common domain-specific language in Groovy used today.

Chapter 9 focuses on RESTful web services, with an emphasis on the JAX-RS 2.0 specification. Most of the JAX-RS capabilities operate the same way under Groovy as under Java, but examples are provided to show how to work with hypermedia applications as well.

The last chapter in this section is about web application development. Chapter 10 starts with a nice example of Groovy metaprogramming using categories. Specifically, the `ServletCategory` class is presented as an example of what can be done quickly and easily with Groovy. Next comes a discussion of groovlets, which are Groovy scripts executed through a servlet that make it easy to get a simple application running. The chapter concludes with a demonstration of the Grails framework as a beautiful combination of Groovy DSLs that combine and configure Spring/Hibernate-based web applications.

7 The Spring framework

This chapter covers

- Using Groovy classes in Spring applications
- Refreshable beans
- Inline scripted beans
- The Grails `BeanBuilder` class
- Spring AOP with Groovy classes

As Java frameworks go, Spring is one of the most successful. Spring brought the ideas of dependency injection, complex object lifecycle management, and declarative services for POJOs to the forefront of Java development. It's a rare project that doesn't at least consider taking advantage of all Spring has to offer, including the vast array of Spring "beans" included in its library. Spring touches almost every facet of enterprise Java development, in most cases simplifying them dramatically.

In this chapter I'll look at how Groovy interacts with the Spring framework. As it turns out, Groovy and Spring are old friends. Spring manages Groovy beans as easily as it handles Java. Spring includes special capabilities for working with code from dynamic languages, however, which I'll review here.

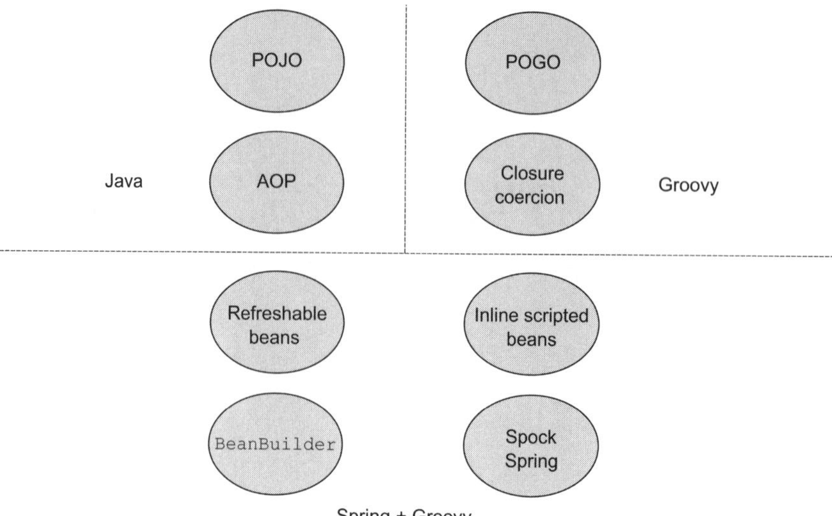

Figure 7.1 Guide to the Spring technologies with Groovy. Spring manages POGOs as easily as POJOs, so the examples include Groovy implementations of both normal beans and aspects. Closure coercion is used to implement the `RowMapper` interface in a `JdbcTemplate`. Refreshable beans are Groovy source files that can be modified at runtime. Inline scripted beans are included inside XML configuration files. Grails provides a `BeanBuilder` class for configuring beans. Finally, Spock has a library that allows it to be used with Spring's test context feature.

Groovy can be used to implement beans or to configure them. In this chapter I'll try to review all the ways Groovy can help Spring. Figure 7.1 contains a guide to the technologies discussed in this chapter.

To show how Groovy helps Spring, I need to review what Spring is all about and how it's used and configured. I'll start with a simple, but non-trivial, sample application. Rather than show all the pieces (which are in the source code repository for the book), I'll highlight the overall architecture and the Groovy parts.

7.1 A Spring application

For all its benefits, Spring is a hard framework to demonstrate to developers unfamiliar with it. The "Hello, World" application in Spring makes you question why you'd ever want it, because it replaces a couple of lines of simple, easy-to-understand, strongly typed Java with several additional lines of code, plus about 20 lines of XML. That's not exactly a ringing endorsement.

To see the real value of Spring you have to see a real application, even if it's simplified in various ways. The following application models the service and persistence layers of an account management application. The presentation layer is arbitrary, so the following code could be used in either a client-side or a server-side application. In this case, I'll demonstrate the functionality through both unit and integration tests.

JAVA AND GROOVY SPRING BEANS Rather than build the entire application in Java and then convert it to Groovy as in other chapters, to save space this application mixes both languages. The point is that Spring managed beans can be implemented in either Java or Groovy, whichever is most convenient.

Consider an application that manages bank accounts. I'll have a single entity class representing an account, with only an `id` and a `balance`, along with `deposit` and `withdraw` methods.

The next listing shows the `Account` class in Groovy, which has a serious advantage over its Java counterpart: it makes it easy to work with a `java.math.BigDecimal`.

Listing 7.1 An `Account` POGO in Groovy that uses `BigDecimal`

```
import groovy.transform.EqualsAndHashCode
import groovy.transform.ToString

@EqualsAndHashCode(includes=['id'])          // AST transformations
@ToString(includeNames=true)
class Account {
    Integer id
    BigDecimal balance

    def deposit(amount) {
        balance += amount                    // Using operators with BigDecimal
    }

    def withdraw(amount) {
        balance -= amount
    }
}
```

Financial calculations are one of the reasons we need `java.math.BigDecimal` and `java.math.BigInteger`. Using `BigDecimal` keeps round-off errors from being sent into an account where it can accumulate over time.[1] It's easy to show how quickly round-off errors can become a problem. Consider the following two lines:

```
println 2.0d - 1.1d
println 2.0 - 1.1
```

The first line uses doubles, while the second line uses `java.math.BigDecimal`. The first evaluates to 0.8999999999999999, while the second evaluates to 0.9. In the `double` case I've only done a single calculation and already I have enough error to show up.

When coding in Java working with `BigDecimal` is awkward because it's a class rather than a primitive. That means you can't use your normal +, *, - operators and have to use the class's API instead.

1 If you haven't seen *Office Space* yet (http://mng.bz/c6o8), you have a real treat ahead of you.

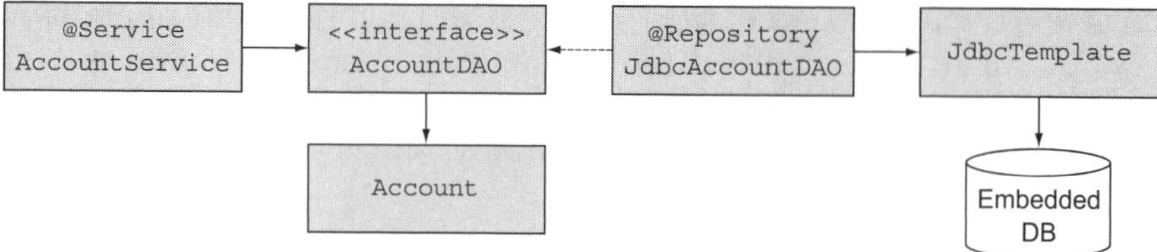

Figure 7.2 A simple account management application. Transactions are demarcated in the service layer. The persistence layer consists of a single DAO class that implements an interface and uses the Spring `JdbcTemplate` to access an embedded database.

Because Groovy has operator overloading, however, none of that is necessary. I can simply declare the balance to be a `BigDecimal`, and everything else just works, even if I use the `Account` class from Java.

One additional comment about the `Account`: at the moment no constraints are being applied to ensure that the balance stays positive. This is as simple as I can make it, just for exposition purposes.

The overall design for using the `Account` class is shown in figure 7.2. This is a very simple form of a layered architecture, with transactional support in the service layer and a persistence layer that consists of an interface and a DAO class, discussed shortly.

The persistence layer follows the normal Data Access Object design pattern. The next listing shows a Java interface, called `AccountDAO`, written in Java.

Listing 7.2 The `AccountDAO` interface, in Java

```
package mjg.spring.dao;

import java.util.List;

import mjg.spring.entities.Account;

public interface AccountDAO {
    int createAccount(double initialBalance);
    Account findAccountById(int id);
    List<Account> findAllAccounts();
    void updateAccount(Account account);
    void deleteAccount(int id);
}
```

The interface contains typical methods for transferring `Account` objects to the database and back. There's a method to create new accounts, update an account, and delete an account; a method to find an account by `id`; and one to return all the accounts.

The implementation of the interface, using a Groovy class called `JdbcAccountDAO`, works with the `JdbcTemplate` from Spring. Rather than show the whole class (which is available in the book source code), let me present just the structure and then emphasize the Groovy aspect afterward. An outline of the class is shown in the following listing.

Listing 7.3 Implementing the AccountDAO using JdbcTemplate, in Groovy

```
@Repository
class JdbcAccountDAO implements AccountDAO {
    JdbcTemplate jdbcTemplate                                    // Template that simplifies JDBC

    @Autowired
    JdbcAccountDAO(DataSource dataSource) {
        jdbcTemplate = new JdbcTemplate(dataSource)
    }

    int createAccount(double initialBalance) { ... }
    void updateAccount(Account account) { ... }
    void deleteAccount(int id) { ... }

    Account findAccountById(int id) {
        String sql = "select * from accounts where id=?"
        jdbcTemplate.queryForObject(sql,
            accountMapper as RowMapper<Account>, id)
    }

    List<Account> findAllAccounts() {
        String sql = "select * from accounts"
        jdbcTemplate.query(sql, accountMapper as RowMapper<Account>)
    }

    def accountMapper = { ResultSet rs, int row ->
        new Account(id:rs.getInt('id'),balance:rs.getDouble('balance'))
    }
}
```

Closure coercion implementing the interface

The various query methods take an argument of type `RowMapper<T>`, whose definition is

```
public interface RowMapper<T> {
    T mapRow(ResultSet rs, int rowNum) throws SQLException
}
```

When you execute one of the query methods in `JdbcTemplate`, Spring takes the `ResultSet` and feeds each row through an implementation of the `RowMapper` interface. The job of the `mapRow` method is then to convert that row into an instance of the domain class. The normal Java implementation would be to create an inner class called, say, `AccountMapper`, whose `mapRow` method would extract the data from the `ResultSet` row and convert it into an `Account` instance. Providing an instance of the `AccountMapper` class to the `queryForObject` method would then return a single `Account`. The same instance can be supplied to the `query` method, which then returns a collection of `Accounts`.

This is exactly the type of closure coercion demonstrated in chapter 6. A variable called `accountMapper` is defined and assigned to a closure with the same arguments as the required `mapRow` method. The variable is then used in both the `findAccountById` and `findAllAccounts` methods.

There are two uses for Groovy here:

1 A Groovy class implemented a Java interface, which makes integration easy and simplifies the code.
2 Closure coercion eliminated the expected inner class.

In the example in the book source code I also included the service class referenced in figure 7.2. It uses Spring's `@Transactional` annotation to ensure that each method operates in a required transaction. There is nothing inherently Groovy about it, so again I'll just show an outline of the implementation in the next listing.

Listing 7.4 A portion of the `AccountService` class in Java

```
@Service
@Transactional                                  <- Declarative transactional behavior
public class AccountService {
    @Autowired                                  <- Injecting the DAO
    private AccountDAO dao;

    public double getAccountBalance(int id) { ... }
    public double depositIntoAccount(int id, double amount) { ... }
    public double withdrawFromAccount(int id, double amount) { ... }

    public boolean transferFunds(int fromId, int toId, double amount) {
        Account from = dao.findAccountById(fromId);
        Account to = dao.findAccountById(toId);
        from.withdraw(amount);
        to.deposit(amount);
        dao.updateAccount(from);
        dao.updateAccount(to);
        return true;
    }

}
```

The `@Autowired` annotation is used by Spring to plug in (*inject*) an instance of a class implementing the `AccountDAO` interface into the service class. See the Spring documentation[2] for more details on autowiring.

The service implementation is in Java mostly because there's no great advantage to implementing it in Groovy, though I could easily have done so.

The last piece of the puzzle is the Spring bean configuration file. The configuration in the book source code uses a combination of XML and a component scan for the repository and service classes. Again, nothing in it uses Groovy, so I won't present it here. For the record, the sample uses Spring's `<embedded-database>` tag to set up a sample H2 database in memory that is reinitialized on each run. The rest is as described.

Returning now to Groovy, I want to show the Gradle build file in the next listing.

---

2 http://mng.bz/m9M3

Listing 7.5 The Gradle build file for the account application

```
apply plugin:'groovy'
apply plugin:'eclipse'

repositories {
    mavenCentral()
}

def springVersion = '3.2.2.RELEASE'
def spockVersion = '0.7-groovy-2.0'

dependencies {
    compile "org.codehaus.groovy:groovy-all:2.1.5"
    compile "org.springframework:spring-context:$springVersion"
    compile "org.springframework:spring-jdbc:$springVersion"
    runtime "com.h2database:h2:1.3.172"
    runtime "cglib:cglib:2.2"

    testCompile "org.springframework:spring-test:$springVersion"
    testCompile "org.spockframework:spock-core:$spockVersion"
    testCompile "org.spockframework:spock-spring:$spockVersion"
}
```

The build file is typical of projects presented in this book so far. It declares both the Groovy and Eclipse plugins. It uses Maven central for the repository. The dependencies include Groovy and Spock, as usual. Spring is added by declaring the `spring-context` and `spring-jdbc` dependencies. Those dependencies wind up adding several other Spring-related JARs. The `h2database` dependency is used for the H2 driver needed by the embedded database.

One interesting addition is the `spock-spring` dependency. Spring includes a powerful testing framework of its own, which is based on JUnit and automatically caches the Spring application context. The `spock-spring` dependency lets Spock tests work with the Spring testing context.

The first test class is a Spock test for the `JdbcAccountDAO`. The following listing shows some of the tests from the complete set.

Listing 7.6 Spock tests for the `JdbcAccountDAO` implementation

```
import spock.lang.Specification;

@ContextConfiguration("classpath:applicationContext.xml")
@Transactional
class JdbcAccountDAOSpec extends Specification {
    @Autowired
    JdbcAccountDAO dao

    def "dao is injected properly"() {
        expect: dao
    }

    def "find 3 accounts in sample db"() {
        expect: dao.findAllAccounts().size() == 3
    }
```

```
    def "find account 0 by id"() {
        when:
        Account account = dao.findAccountById(0)

        then:
        account.id == 0
        account.balance == 100.0
    }
    // tests for other methods as well
}
```

The `@ContextConfiguration` annotation tells the test runner how to find the Spring bean configuration file. Adding `@Transactional` means that each test runs in a required transaction that (and this is the cool part) rolls back automatically at the end of each test, implying that the database is reinitialized at the beginning of each test. The DAO is autowired into the test class. The individual tests check that all the methods in the DAO work as expected.

The next listing shows the tests for the service class, which includes using the `old` method from Spock described in chapter 6 on testing.

Listing 7.7 Spock tests for the service class

```
import spock.lang.Specification

@ContextConfiguration("classpath:applicationContext.xml")
@Transactional
class AccountServiceSpec extends Specification {
    @Autowired
    AccountService service

    def "balance of test account is 100"() {
        expect: service.getAccountBalance(0) == 100.0
    }

    // ... other tests as necessary ...

    def "transfer funds works"() {
        when:
        service.transferFunds(0,1,25.0)

        then:
        service.getAccountBalance(0) ==
            old(service.getAccountBalance(0)) - 25.0
        service.getAccountBalance(1) ==
            old(service.getAccountBalance(1)) + 25.0
    }
}
```

As before, the annotations let the Spock test work with Spring's test framework, which caches the application context. I used the `old` operation from Spock to check changes in the account balance after a deposit or withdrawal. No other additions are needed to use Spock with the Spring test context.

This application, though simple, illustrates a lot of Spring's capabilities, from declarative transaction management to autowiring to simplified JDBC coding to effective testing. From Spring's point of view, Groovy beans are just bytecodes by another name. As long as the groovy-all JAR file is in the classpath, Spring is quite happy to use beans written in Groovy.

Spring manages beans from Groovy as easily as it manages beans from Java. There are special capabilities that Spring offers beans from dynamic languages, though. I'll illustrate them in the next sections, beginning with beans that can be modified in a running system.

7.2 Refreshable beans

Since version 2.0, Spring has provided special capabilities for beans from dynamic languages like Groovy. One particularly interesting, if potentially dangerous, option is to deploy what are known as *refreshable* beans.

For refreshable beans, rather than compile classes as usual, you deploy the actual source code and tell Spring where to find it and how often to check to see if it has changed. Spring checks the source code at the end of each refresh interval, and if the file has been modified it reloads the bean. This gives you the opportunity to change deployed classes even while the system is still running.[3]

I'll demonstrate a somewhat contrived but hopefully amusing example. In the previous section I presented an application for managing accounts. Let me now assume that the account manager, presumably some kind of bank, decides to get into the mortgage business. I now need a class representing a mortgage application, which a client would submit for approval. I'm also going to need a mortgage evaluator, which I'll implement both in Java and in Groovy. The overall system is shown in figure 7.3.

To keep this example simple, the mortgage application class only has fields representing the loan amount, the interest rate, and the number of years desired, as shown in the next listing.

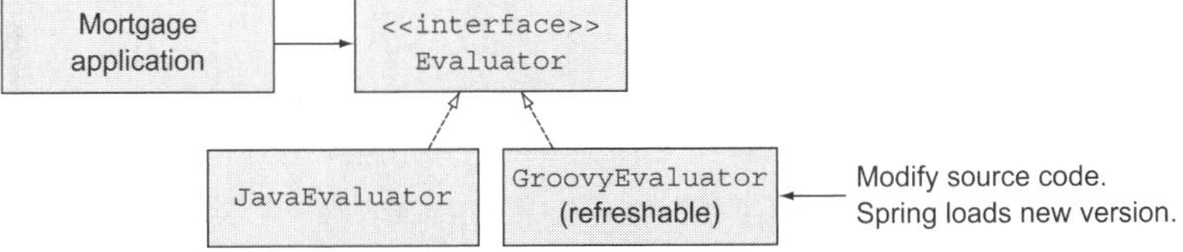

Figure 7.3 The `GroovyEvaluator` is a refreshable bean. The source code is deployed, and Spring checks it for changes after each refresh interval. If it has changed, Spring reloads the bean.

[3] Yes, that's a scary notion to me, too. The Spider-Man corollary applies: With Great Power Comes Great Responsibility.

Listing 7.8 A trivial mortgage application class in Groovy

```
class MortgageApplication {
    BigDecimal amount
    BigDecimal rate
    int years
}
```

As before, Groovy is used just to reduce the amount of code and to make it easier to work with `BigDecimal` instances. An instance of this class is submitted to the bank, which runs it through a mortgage evaluator to decide whether or not to approve it. The following listing shows a Java interface representing the evaluator, which will be implemented in both Java and Groovy.

Listing 7.9 The `Evaluator` interface in Java

```
public interface Evaluator {
    boolean approve(MortgageApplication application);
}
```

The interface contains only one method, approve, which takes a mortgage application as an argument and returns `true` if the application is approved and `false` otherwise.

Pretend now that it is currently the summer of 2008. The general public is blissfully unaware of terms like *credit default swaps*, and banks are eager to loan as much money as possible to as many people as possible. In other words, here's a Java implementation of the `Evaluator` interface.

Listing 7.10 A Java evaluator, with a rather lenient loan policy

```
public class JavaEvaluator implements Evaluator {
    public boolean approve(MortgageApplication application) {
        return true;
    }

}
```

That's a very forgiving loan policy, but if everyone else is doing it, what could go wrong?

What went wrong, of course, is that in the late summer and early fall of 2008, Bear Stearns collapsed, Lehman Brothers went bankrupt, and the U.S. economy nearly collapsed. The bank needs to stop the bleeding as soon as possible. If the evaluator in place is the Java evaluator just shown, then the system has to be taken out of service in order to modify it. The fear is that if the system is taken offline, then customers might worry that it will never come back again.[4]

There's another possibility, however. Consider the Groovy version of the mortgage evaluator, whose behavior is equivalent to the Java version, as shown in the following listing.

---

[4] That's an *It's a Wonderful Life* reference: "George, if you close those doors, you'll never open them again!"

Listing 7.11 A Groovy mortgage evaluator deployed as source code

```
class GroovyEvaluator implements Evaluator {
    boolean approve(MortgageApplication application) { true }
}
```

Again, it simply returns `true`, just as the Java version did. Rather than compiling this class and deploying it as usual, however, this time I want to create a refreshable bean. To do so, I need to work with the `lang` namespace in the Spring configuration file (assuming I'm using XML; alternatives exist for Java configuration files). I also need to deploy the source code itself, rather than the compiled version of this file.

> **DEPLOYING SOURCE** Note that for refreshable beans you deploy the source, not the compiled bean.

The next listing shows the bean configuration file with both evaluators. Note the addition of the `lang` namespace and the Groovy bean.

Listing 7.12 The bean configuration file with the refreshable Groovy evaluator bean

```
<?xml version="1.0" encoding="UTF-8"?>
<beans xmlns="http://www.springframework.org/schema/beans"
    xmlns:xsi="http://www.w3.org/2001/XMLSchema-instance"
    xmlns:lang="http://www.springframework.org/schema/lang"            <-- Namespace
    xsi:schemaLocation="                                                    for dynamic
        http://www.springframework.org/schema/beans                        languages
        http://www.springframework.org/schema/beans/spring-beans.xsd
        http://www.springframework.org/schema/lang
        http://www.springframework.org/schema/lang/spring-lang.xsd">

    <bean id="javaEvaluator" class="mjg.spring.JavaEvaluator" />

    <lang:groovy id="groovyEvaluator"                                   <-- Refreshable
        script-source="file:resources/GroovyEvaluator.groovy"               bean
        refresh-check-delay="1000" />

</beans>
```

Groovy provides a namespace for beans from dynamic languages, including Groovy, BeanShell, and JRuby. One of the elements declared in that namespace is `<lang:groovy>`, whose `script-source` attribute is used to point to the source code of a Groovy class. Note that unlike the Java evaluator bean in the same file, this attribute points to the actual source file, rather than the compiled bean. The other important attribute for the element is `refresh-check-delay`, which indicates the time period, in milliseconds, after which Spring will check to see if the source file has changed. Here the delay has been set to one second.

Now comes the fun part.[5] The next listing shows a demo application that loads the Groovy evaluator bean and calls the `approve` method 10 times, sleeping for one second between each call.

---

[5] Seriously. This is a fun demo to do in front of a live audience. Try it and see.

Listing 7.13 A demo application that loads the Groovy bean and calls `approve` 10 times

```
public class Demo {
    public static void main(String[] args) {
        ApplicationContext ctx =
            new FileSystemXmlApplicationContext(
                 "resources/applicationContext.xml");
        Evaluator e = null;
        boolean ok;

        for (int i = 0; i < 10; i++) {
            e = (Evaluator) ctx.getBean("groovyEvaluator");    // Load refreshable bean
            ok = e.approve(null);                              // Check approval
            System.out.println(ok ? "approved" : "denied");

            try {
                Thread.sleep(1000);                            // Gives time to change the implementation of approve
            } catch (InterruptedException ie) {
                ie.printStackTrace();
            }
        }
    }
}
```

The idea is to start the demo running and then, while the iteration is going, edit the source code to change the return value of the `approve` method from `true` to `false`.[6] The output of the program resembles

The source code is changed halfway through the loop to stop the bleeding. If Congress should then spring[7] into action and award a massive government bailout, it can be changed back.[8]

The ability to change the implementation of a bean inside a running system is powerful, but obviously risky. Spring only makes it available to beans from dynamic languages like Groovy.

---

6 Did you notice that the `approve` method was invoked with a null argument, acknowledging that the mortgage application doesn't matter at all? That's part of the gag, so be sure to chuckle when you do it.

7 Ouch. Yes, a bad pun, but an irresistible one.

8 Or not.

A real use case for refreshable beans

As much fun as the banking application illustrated in this section is, few companies will allow you to deploy source code into production and then edit it while the system is running. So when would you actually use this capability?

Some problems only occur when a system is under load. Think of a refreshable bean as an adaptable probe that can be inserted into a Spring-based system by a server-side developer in a controlled fashion. You have the freedom to do more than just change a log level or some other property (which you could in principle do with JMX, the Java Management Extensions). You can change what the probe is doing in real time and diagnose what's actually going on.

Dierk Koenig, lead author of *Groovy in Action* (Manning, 2007), calls this pattern "keyhole surgery." It's used as a minimally invasive procedure when you don't know what you're going to find when you go in.[9]

Before discussing the other Spring capability restricted to beans from dynamic languages, namely inline scripted beans, let me introduce another idea. One of the great features of Spring is that it provides a convenient infrastructure for aspect-oriented programming. I want to discuss what that means and how to use Groovy to implement an aspect.

7.3 Spring AOP with Groovy beans

Many of Spring's capabilities are implemented using aspect-oriented programming (AOP). Spring provides the infrastructure for developing aspects. The interesting part is that aspects can be written as easily in Groovy as in Java.

AOP is a big subject, but I can summarize a few of the key features here.[10] Aspects are designed to handle *crosscutting concerns*, which are features that apply to many different locations. Examples of crosscutting concerns include logging, security, and transactions. Each of them needs to be applied at multiple locations in a system, which results in considerable duplication, as well as tangling of different kinds of functionality in the same feature.

Crosscutting concerns are written as methods, known as *advice*. The next issue is where to apply the advice. The generic term for all available locations where advice can be applied is *joinpoints*. The set of selected joinpoints for a given aspect is known as a *pointcut*. The combination of an advice and a pointcut is what defines an *aspect*.

The sample application for this section and the next is shown in figure 7.4.

---

9 Check out Dierk's presentation "Seven Groovy Usage Patterns for Java Developers" on www.slideshare.net for more details.

10 A complete discussion of AOP can be found in *AspectJ in Action*, 2nd edition (Manning, 2009), by Ramnivas Laddad, www.mannin10g.com/laddad2/.

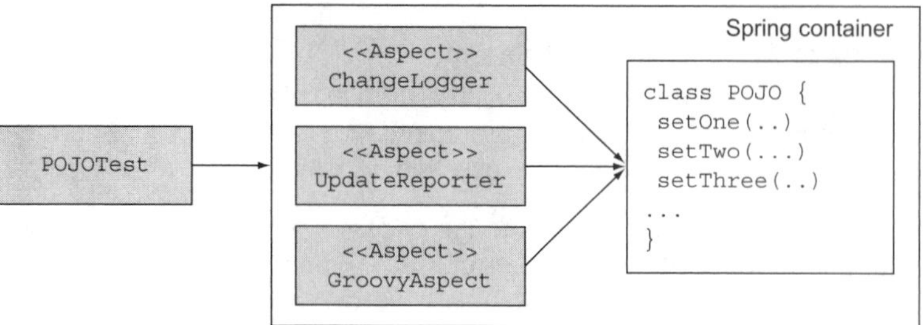

Figure 7.4 Spring AOP in action. `ChangeLogger` is a Java aspect that logs a message before each `set` method. `UpdateReporter` does the same in Groovy but reports on existing values. The `GroovyAspect` is an inline scripted bean defined inside the configuration file.

The following listing shows an example of an aspect, using Spring annotations, written in Java. This aspect is applied whenever a `set` method is about to be called, and it logs which method is being invoked and what the new value will be.

Listing 7.14 A Java aspect that logs changes to properties

```
package mjg.aspects;

import java.util.logging.Logger;

import org.aspectj.lang.JoinPoint;
import org.aspectj.lang.annotation.Aspect;
import org.aspectj.lang.annotation.Before;

@Aspect
public class ChangeLogger {
    private Logger log = Logger.getLogger(
         ChangeLogger.class.getName());

    @Before("execution(void set*(*))")
    public void trackChange(JoinPoint jp) {
        String method = jp.getSignature().getName();
        Object newValue = jp.getArgs()[0];
        log.info(method + " about to change to " +
            newValue + " on " + jp.getTarget());
    }
}
```

The `@Aspect` annotation tells Spring this is an aspect. The `@Before` annotation defines the pointcut using AspectJ pointcut language.[11] This particular pointcut applies at all methods that begin with the letters `set` that take a single argument and return `void`. The `trackChange` method is the advice. The `JoinPoint` argument is supplied by Spring when the aspect is called. It provides context for the execution. In this case,

[11] The documentation for AspectJ is hosted with Eclipse, of all places. See http://www.eclipse.org/aspectj/ for details.

the JoinPoint has methods to retrieve the signature of the method being advised, as well as the arguments supplied to the method and the target object.

To demonstrate this aspect in action, I need to configure Spring to apply the aspect, and I need an object to advise. The latter is easy enough. The next listing shows a simple class with three properties.

Listing 7.15 A simple POJO with three set methods

```
package mjg;

public class POJO {
    private String one;
    private int two;
    private double three;

    public String getOne() { return one; }
    public void setOne(String one) { this.one = one; }

    public int getTwo() { return two; }
    public void setTwo(int two) { this.two = two; }

    public double getThree() { return three; }
    public void setThree(double three) { this.three = three; }

    @Override
    public String toString() {
        return "POJO [one=" + one + ", two=" + two +
            ", three=" + three + "]";
    }
}
```

The class is called POJO, and it has three properties, called one, two, and three. Each has a getter and a setter. The aspect will run before each of the set methods.

Spring's AOP infrastructure has some restrictions compared to full AOP solutions. Spring restricts pointcuts to only public method boundaries on Spring-managed beans. I therefore need to add the POJO bean to Spring's configuration file. I also need to tell Spring to recognize the @Aspect annotation and to generate the needed proxy. The resulting bean configuration file is presented in the following listing.

Listing 7.16 The Spring bean configuration file for AOP

```
<?xml version="1.0" encoding="UTF-8"?>
<beans xmlns="http://www.springframework.org/schema/beans"
    ... namespace declarations elided ... >

    <aop:aspectj-autoproxy />

    <bean id="tracker" class="mjg.aspects.ChangeLogger" />
    <bean id="pojo" class="mjg.POJO" p:one="1" p:two="2" p:three="3"/>
</beans>
```

The aop namespace provides the <aspect-autoproxy> element, which tells Spring to generate proxies for all classes annotated with @Aspect. The tracker bean is the Java aspect shown previously. The pojo bean is the POJO class just discussed.

Now I need to call the set methods in order to see the aspect in action. The next listing shows a test case based on JUnit 4 that uses Spring's JUnit 4 test runner, which caches the application context in between tests.

Listing 7.17 A JUnit 4 test case to exercise the POJO

```
package mjg;

import static org.junit.Assert.*;

import org.junit.Test;
import org.junit.runner.RunWith;
import org.springframework.beans.factory.annotation.Autowired;
import org.springframework.test.context.ContextConfiguration;
import org.springframework.test.context.junit4.SpringJUnit4ClassRunner;

@ContextConfiguration("classpath:applicationContext.xml")
@RunWith(SpringJUnit4ClassRunner.class)
public class POJOTest {
    @Autowired
    private POJO pojo;

    @Test
    public void callSetters() {
        pojo.setOne("one");
        pojo.setTwo(22);
        pojo.setThree(333.0);
        assertEquals("one", pojo.getOne());
        assertEquals(22, pojo.getTwo());
        assertEquals(333.0, pojo.getThree(),0.0001);
    }
}
```

Spring injects an instance of the POJO into the test and executes the test, which simply calls the three setters and checks that they work properly. The interesting part is in the console output, which shows the aspect in play:

```
INFO: setOne about to change to one on POJO [one=1, two=2, three=3.0]
INFO: setTwo about to change to 22 on POJO [one=one, two=2, three=3.0]
INFO: setThree about to change to 333.0 on POJO [one=one, two=22, three=3.0]
```

The aspect reports the name of each set method and its argument when it's called. Everything works as advertised.

There's one issue, though. What if you want to know the current value of each property before the setter changes it? There's no obvious way to find out. The joinpoint gives access to the target, and I know that a set method is being called, but while I know conceptually that for every setter there's a getter, figuring out how to invoke it isn't trivial. Determining the proper get method could probably be done with a combination of reflection and string manipulation, but there's work involved.

At least, there's work involved unless I appeal to Groovy. I can do everything I just described in a handful of lines of Groovy, as the next listing demonstrates.

Listing 7.18 A Groovy aspect for printing property values before they are changed

```
package mjg.aspects

import java.util.logging.Logger

import org.aspectj.lang.JoinPoint
import org.aspectj.lang.annotation.Aspect
import org.aspectj.lang.annotation.Before

@Aspect
class UpdateReporter {
    Logger log = Logger.getLogger(UpdateReporter.class.name)

    @Before("execution(void set*(*))")
    void reportOnSet(JoinPoint jp) {
        String method = jp.signature.name
        String base = method - 'set'
        String property = base[0].toLowerCase() + base[1..-1]
        def current = jp.target."$property"
        log.info "About to change $property from $current to ${jp.args[0]}"
    }
}
```

The `UpdateReporter` class is written in Groovy. It has the `@Aspect` and `@Before` annotations exactly as the Java aspect did. The method being invoked is computed the same way the Java aspect did, with the only minor difference being that Groovy accesses the `signature` and `name` properties rather than explicitly invoking the associated `getSignature` and `getName` methods. That's a case of foreshadowing, actually, because it means that all I really need to do is to figure out the name of the property.

The property is found by taking the name of the `set` method, subtracting out the letters `set`, and converting the result to standard property syntax. Now that I have the name of the property, I just need to access it from the target, which is done on the next line. I used a Groovy string to make sure that the property is evaluated. The result is that in three lines of Groovy I now know what the original value of the property is. All that remains is to log it to standard output.

To run this aspect I just added a corresponding bean to the configuration file:

```
<bean id="updater" class="mjg.aspects.UpdateReporter" />
```

Now if I run the same test case the output is as shown here:

```
INFO: About to change one from 1 to one
INFO: setOne about to change to one on POJO [one=1, two=2, three=3.0]
INFO: About to change two from 2 to 22
INFO: setTwo about to change to 22 on POJO [one=one, two=2, three=3.0]
INFO: About to change three from 3.0 to 333.0
INFO: setThree about to change to 333.0 on POJO [one=one, two=22, three=3.0]
```

Both the Groovy aspect and the Java aspect are executing on the `set` methods of the POJO. The advantage of the Groovy aspect is that it's easily able to determine the existing value of the property before changing it.

Life isn't quite as simple as I'm describing it. The string manipulation that processed the set method determined a property name. If the property doesn't actually exist (or, rather, the get method doesn't exist), accessing it isn't going to work. Still, asking that each setter has a corresponding getter doesn't seem to be too much to expect, especially because Groovy POGOs do that automatically.

To finish this section, listing 7.19 shows an aspect added to the banking example from the beginning of this chapter, tracing methods in the Account class. Because Account is a POGO, I don't have explicit setter methods. I don't necessarily want to track all the getters, either, because one of them is getMetaClass, and that's not a business method.

One way around that is to use a Java interface implemented by the POGO. Instead, here I'm going to use explicit pointcuts and put them together.

Here's the complete AccountAspect listing with the pointcuts and advice.

Listing 7.19 An aspect tracking methods in the Account POGO

```
import java.util.logging.Logger

import org.aspectj.lang.JoinPoint
import org.aspectj.lang.annotation.Aspect
import org.aspectj.lang.annotation.Before
import org.aspectj.lang.annotation.Pointcut

@Aspect
class AccountAspect {
    Logger log = Logger.getLogger(AccountAspect.class.name)

    @Pointcut("execution(* mjg..Account.deposit(*))")
    void deposits() {}

    @Pointcut("execution(* mjg..Account.withdraw(*))")
    void withdrawals() {}

    @Pointcut("execution(* mjg..Account.getBalance())")
    void balances() {}

    @Before("balances() || deposits() || withdrawals()")
    void audit(JoinPoint jp) {
         String method = jp.signature.name
         log.info("$method called with ${jp.args} on ${jp.target}")
    }
}
```

The @Pointcut annotation is how you create a *named* pointcut. The name is set by the name of the method on which it's applied. The three pointcuts here match the deposit, withdraw, and getBalance methods in the Account class. The @Before advice combines them using an or expression and logs the method calls. When running the AccountSpec tests, the (truncated) output is similar to this:

```
Jun 28, 2013 12:03:29 PM
INFO: getBalance called with [] on mjg.spring.entities.Account(id:4,
    balance:100.0)
Jun 28, 2013 12:03:29 PM
```

```
INFO: deposit called with [100] on mjg.spring.entities.Account(id:8,
     balance:100.0)
INFO: withdraw called with [100] on mjg.spring.entities.Account(id:9,
     balance:100.0)
Jun 28, 2013 12:03:29 PM
INFO: getBalance called with [] on mjg.spring.entities.Account(id:9,
     balance:0.0)
```

The `JoinPoint` can be used to get more information, but those are AOP details rather than Groovy.

In both of these examples the aspect was provided in its own class. Spring provides an alternative, however, in the form of beans defined right in the bean definition file.

7.4 Inline scripted beans

Another capability Spring provides to beans from dynamic languages is that they can be coded right inside the XML configuration.[12]

Here's an example. The following sections can be used in a bean configuration file, as shown in the next listing.

Listing 7.20 Additions to bean configuration file for an inline scripted aspect

```
<lang:groovy id="aspectScript">
    <lang:inline-script>
<![CDATA[
import org.aspectj.lang.JoinPoint
import java.util.logging.Logger

class GroovyAspect {
    Logger log = Logger.getLogger(GroovyAspect.getClass().getName())

    def audit(JoinPoint jp) {
        log.info "${jp.signature.name} on ${jp.target.class.name}"
    }
}
]]>
    </lang:inline-script>
</lang:groovy>

<aop:config>
    <aop:aspect ref="aspectScript">
        <aop:before method="audit" pointcut="execution(* *.*(*))"/>
    </aop:aspect>
</aop:config>
```

The `<inline-script>` tag wraps the source code for the Groovy bean. I took the added step of wrapping the code in a `CDATA` section, so the XML parser will leave the Groovy source alone when validating the XML.

---

[12] I have to admit that in several years of using Spring and Groovy I've never found a compelling use case for inline scripted beans that couldn't have been handled with regular classes. If you have one, please let me know.

Rather than use annotations, this time the code is written as though it was any other bean. As a result I had to add the `<config>` element as well. As usual, an aspect is a combination of a pointcut and an advice. In this case the pointcut is contained in the `<before>` element, but this time it applies to every one-argument method in the system. The advice is the `audit` method in the `aspectScript` bean, which just prints the name of the method being invoked and the name of the object containing it.

The resulting output adds more lines to the console:

```
INFO: setOne on mjg.POJO
INFO: setTwo on mjg.POJO
INFO: setThree on mjg.POJO
```

The original motivation for inline scripted beans was that you could do as much processing as you liked in the script before releasing the bean.[13] Now that Spring has moved to version 3.x, however, there are additional options for configuring beans.

7.5 Groovy with JavaConfig

Spring introduced a third way to configure beans in version 3.0. Originally all beans were configured using XML. Then version 2.0 introduced annotations (assuming JDK 1.5 is available) like `@Component`, `@Service`, and `@Repository` and component scans that picked them up.

In version 3.0 Spring introduced a Java configuration option. Instead of defining all your beans in a central location in XML, or spreading annotations throughout the code base in Java, now you can define the beans in a Java class annotated with `@Configuration`. Inside the configuration file, individual beans are annotated with `@Bean`.

One of the advantages of this approach is that the configuration information is strongly typed, because it's all written in Java. Another advantage, though, is that you're now free to write whatever code you want, as long as you ultimately return the proper object.

Consider the following example. In the account manager example discussed previously, say I want to charge a processing fee once a month.[14] To do so I create a class that processes accounts, called, naturally enough, `AccountProcessor`. I want the `AccountProcessor` to get all the accounts and charge each one a fee of one dollar.[15]

If I did this in the traditional way, I would inject the `AccountDAO` into the `AccountProcessor`. Then, in a `processAccounts` method, I would use the DAO to retrieve the accounts and charge the fee on each. With the Java configuration option, however, I have an alternative.

The following listing shows the `AccountProcessor` class, in Java this time.

[13] As I say, it's a reach. The Spring docs suggest that this is a good opportunity for scripted validators, but I don't see it.

[14] Gee, I feel more like a real banker already.

[15] It's not much, but it's a start.

Listing 7.21 An account processor that debits each account by one dollar

```
package mjg.spring.services;

import java.util.List;

import mjg.spring.entities.Account;

public class AccountProcessor {
    private List<Account> accounts;

    public void setAccounts(List<Account> accounts) {
        this.accounts = accounts;
    }

    public List<Account> getAccounts() { return accounts; }

    public double processAccounts() {
        double total = 0.0;
        for (Account account : accounts) {
            account.withdraw(1.0);
            total += 1.0;
        }
        return total;
    }
}
```

Instead of injecting the `AccountDAO` into the processor, I gave it a list of accounts as an attribute. The `processAccounts` method runs through them, withdrawing a dollar from each and returning the total. Without the dependency on the `AccountDAO`, this processor could be used on any collection of accounts from any source. This has the extra benefit of always retrieving the complete set of accounts from the DAO. Injecting the account list would initialize it when the application starts but not update it later.

So how does the collection of accounts get into my processor? The next listing shows the Java configuration file.

Listing 7.22 A Java configuration file that declares the `AccountProcessor` bean

```
package mjg.spring;

import mjg.spring.dao.AccountDAO;
import mjg.spring.services.AccountProcessor;

import org.springframework.beans.factory.annotation.Autowired;
import org.springframework.context.annotation.Bean;
import org.springframework.context.annotation.Configuration;

@Configuration
public class JavaConfig {
    @Autowired
    private AccountDAO accountDAO;

    @Bean
    public AccountProcessor accountProcessor() {
        AccountProcessor ap = new AccountProcessor();
```

```
        ap.setAccounts(accountDAO.findAllAccounts());
        return ap;
    }
}
```

The @Configuration annotation indicates that this is a Java configuration file that defines beans for Spring. Each bean is defined with the @Bean annotation. The name of the method is the name of the bean, and the return type is the class for the bean. Inside the method my job is to instantiate the bean, configure it appropriately, and return it.

The implementation of a bean method can be as simple as instantiating the bean and returning it, setting whatever properties are needed along the way. In this case, though, I decided to autowire in the AccountDAO bean (which was picked up in the component scan) and then use the DAO to retrieve all the accounts and put them in the processor.

The next listing shows a Spock test to prove that the system is working. It relies on the embedded database again, which, as you may recall, configures three accounts.

Listing 7.23 A Spock test to check the behavior of the AccountProcessor

```
package mjg.spring.services

import mjg.spring.dao.AccountDAO;

import org.springframework.beans.factory.annotation.Autowired;
import org.springframework.test.context.ContextConfiguration
import org.springframework.transaction.annotation.Transactional

import spock.lang.Specification

@ContextConfiguration("classpath:applicationContext.xml")
@Transactional
class AccountProcessorSpec extends Specification {
    @Autowired
    AccountProcessor accountProcessor

    @Autowired
    AccountDAO dao

    def "processing test accounts should yield 3"() {
        given: def accounts = dao.findAllAccounts()

        when: def result = accountProcessor.processAccounts()

        then:
        result == 3.0
        accounts.every { account ->
            account.balance.toString().endsWith "9"
        }
    }
}
```

Both the AccountProcessor and the AccountDAO beans are autowired into the test. The DAO is used to retrieve the accounts. Then, when the processor processes the accounts, three dollars are returned.

The other test condition relies on the fact that the initial balance for each account is divisible by 10. Therefore, after subtracting one from each account, the updated balances should all end in the digit 9. It's kind of kludgy, but it works.

The point of this exercise was to show that with the Java configuration option you can write whatever code you want to configure the bean before releasing it. There's not much Groovy can add to that, though it's worth proving that the Java configuration option works on a Groovy class as well.

Normally I wouldn't use Spring to manage basic entity instances. Spring specializes in managing back-end services, especially those that would normally be designed as singletons. Spring beans are all assumed to be singletons unless otherwise specified. Still, you can tell Spring to provide a new instance each time by making the scope of the bean equal to `prototype`.

Listing 7.24 shows a Java (actually, a Groovy) configuration file, with a single bean definition of type `Account` called `prototypeAccount`. It uses the `AccountDAO` to generate a new bean each time a `prototypeAccount` is requested, essentially making Spring a factory for `Account` beans, all of which start with an initial balance of 100.

Listing 7.24 A Spring configuration file in Groovy as a factory for `Accounts`

```
package mjg.spring.config

import mjg.spring.dao.AccountDAO
import mjg.spring.entities.Account

import org.springframework.beans.factory.annotation.Autowired
import org.springframework.context.annotation.Bean
import org.springframework.context.annotation.Configuration
import org.springframework.context.annotation.Scope

@Configuration
class GroovyConfig {
    @Autowired
    AccountDAO dao

    @Bean @Scope("prototype")
    Account prototypeAccount() {
        int newId = dao.createAccount(100.0)
        new Account(id:newId,balance:100.0)
    }
}
```

The `@Configuration` and `@Bean` annotations are the same as their counterparts in the Java configuration file. The `AccountDAO` is autowired in as before. This time, though, the `@Scope` annotation is used to indicate that the `prototypeAccount` is not a singleton. The implementation uses the DAO to create each new account with the given balance and then populates an `Account` object with the generated ID.

To prove this is working properly, here is another Spock test in the next listing.

Listing 7.25 A Spock test for the prototype Accounts

```
package mjg.spring.services

import mjg.spring.entities.Account

import org.springframework.beans.factory.annotation.Autowired
import org.springframework.context.ApplicationContext
import org.springframework.test.context.ContextConfiguration
import org.springframework.transaction.annotation.Transactional

import spock.lang.Specification

@ContextConfiguration("classpath:applicationContext.xml")
@Transactional
class AccountSpec extends Specification {
    @Autowired
    ApplicationContext ctx

    def "prototype accounts have consecutive ids and balance 100"() {
        when:
        Account a1 = (Account) ctx.getBean("prototypeAccount")
        Account a2 = (Account) ctx.getBean("prototypeAccount")
        Account a3 = (Account) ctx.getBean("prototypeAccount")

        then:
        a3.id == a2.id + 1
        a2.id == a1.id + 1
        a1.balance == 100.0
        a2.balance == 100.0
        a3.balance == 100.0
    }
}
```

This time the application context itself is autowired into the test, because I want to call its `getBean` method myself multiple times. The test then gets three instances of `prototypeAccount` and verifies first that their account numbers are consecutive and then that all three have the expected balance.

The bottom line is that you can use Groovy to create a Spring configuration file as easily as you can use Java, and in both cases you have the full power of the language to do whatever additional configuration you might want before releasing the beans.

All of the techniques so far have discussed how to use capabilities defined in Spring. There's one new capability, however, that allows you to define complex beans using a builder notation. This mechanism came from the Grails project but can be used anywhere.

7.6 Building beans with the Grails BeanBuilder

So far in this book I haven't said much about Grails, the powerful framework that combines Groovy DSLs with Spring MVC and Hibernate. I'll discuss Grails much more in chapter 10 on Groovy web applications, but part of it is relevant here. Normally innovations in Spring find their way into Grails, usually in the form of a plugin, but every once in a while a Grails innovation goes the other way.

The Grails `BeanBuilder` is an example. The `grails.spring.BeanBuilder` class uses Groovy's builder syntax to create Spring configuration files. Everything you can do in regular configuration files you can do using the Grails `BeanBuilder` class. The best part, and the part most relevant for discussion here, is that you don't need to be working on a Grails project to use the `BeanBuilder`.

NOTE Rumor has it that the Grails `BeanBuilder` class will be added to the core Spring libraries in version 4, which will make using it trivial. Still, the process described here is useful for any general external library.

The version of Spring used for the examples in this chapter is 3.2, which doesn't include the `BeanBuilder`. A few versions ago Grails was reformulated to split its dependencies into separate JARs as much as possible, the same way Spring was refactored in version 3. The Grails distribution thus contains a JAR file called grails-spring-2.2.2.jar, corresponding to Grails version 2.2.2.

The Grails-Spring JAR could simply be added to my projects as an external JAR dependency, but because the rest of my project was built with Gradle I prefer to list my additional dependency that way too. The Grails-Spring JAR itself depends on Simple Logging Framework for Java (SLF4J), so its dependencies must be added too.

The following listing shows the complete build file, which assumes the project is using traditional Maven structure.

Listing 7.26 The complete Gradle build file, including Grails-Spring dependencies

```
apply plugin:'groovy'
apply plugin:'eclipse'

repositories {
    mavenCentral()
}

def springVersion = '3.2.2.RELEASE'
def spockVersion = '0.7-groovy-2.0'

dependencies {
    compile "org.codehaus.groovy:groovy-all:2.1.5"
    compile "org.springframework:spring-context:$springVersion"
    compile "org.springframework:spring-jdbc:$springVersion"
    runtime "com.h2database:h2:1.3.172"
    testCompile "commons-dbcp:commons-dbcp:1.4"
    runtime "cglib:cglib:2.2"

    runtime "org.slf4j:slf4j-nop:1.5.8"
    runtime "org.slf4j:slf4j-api:1.5.8"
    testCompile "org.grails:grails-spring:2.2.2"

    compile "aopalliance:aopalliance:1.0"
    compile "org.aspectj:aspectjrt:1.6.10"
    compile "org.aspectj:aspectjweaver:1.6.10"

    testCompile "org.springframework:spring-test:$springVersion"
    testCompile "org.spockframework:spock-core:$spockVersion"
    testCompile "org.spockframework:spock-spring:$spockVersion"
}
```

Grails-Spring additions

The additions shown in the build file are all that's necessary to use the Grails `BeanBuilder` in a regular application. The Grails-Spring dependency (and SLF4J) are listed in the regular way. Any additional required JARs (and there are several) will then be downloaded automatically.

To demonstrate how to use the `BeanBuilder`, let me take a different approach from the earlier examples. The `BeanBuilder` is a class provided by an open source project. Open source projects by definition make their source code available. While browsing through the implementation of an open source project is certainly educational, I'd like to point out an oft-overlooked resource. The better open source projects are loaded with test cases. Because nobody is really fond of writing documentation,[16] sometimes it's hard to figure out exactly how to use a particular capability in a project. If you're lucky, whoever wrote the feature you want also wrote test cases for it. Then the tests demonstrate in great detail how the feature is intended to be used. Test cases are executable documentation, illustrating the ways the author meant for you to use the feature.

In the case of the Grails `BeanBuilder`, there's a test case called `grails.spring.BeanBuilderTests`, which has a couple of very nice properties:

- It was originally authored by Graeme Rocher, the head of the Grails project and possibly the best developer I've ever met.[17]
- The test case has nearly 30 different tests in it, demonstrating everything you might want to do with the class.

In this section I want to review some basic features of the `BeanBuilderTests` class. In fact, I copied the class into the book source code just to make sure everything worked. I needed to remove a couple of tests that weren't relevant to running `BeanBuilder` independently from Grails, but everything else tested successfully.

Before I continue, I should highlight this approach as a good general rule:

> **TEST CASES** Downloading the source code of an open source project is useful even if you never look at the implementation. The test cases alone are often more valuable than the actual documentation.

That advice might be more useful than anything else said in this book.

The next listing shows the first test case in the `BeanBuilderTests` class.

Listing 7.27 The `BeanBuilderTests` class with its first test case

```
class BeanBuilderTests extends GroovyTestCase {

    void testImportSpringXml() {
        def bb = new BeanBuilder()
```

[16] Other than in book form, I mean. Writing books is both fun and easy. That's my story, and I'm sticking to it.

[17] Except for maybe Guillaume Laforge, Dierk Koenig, Paul King, Andres Almiray, or a few others. The Groovy ecosystem is filled with wicked-smart developers.

```
        bb.beans {
            importBeans "classpath:grails/spring/test.xml"
        }

        def ctx = bb.createApplicationContext()

        def foo = ctx.getBean("foo")
        assertEquals "hello", foo
    }
}
```

To use `BeanBuilder` all you have to do is instantiate the class. This is similar to using `MarkupBuilder`, `SwingBuilder`, `AntBuilder`, or any of the wide range of builders written in Groovy. Here the builder is assigned to the variable `bb`, so using the builder starts with `bb.beans`, which is like creating a root `<beans>` element in a Spring configuration file. The curly braces then indicate child elements. Here the child element is an `importBeans` element, which reads the file test.xml from the classpath. Before proceeding, here's the text of test.xml:

```
<?xml version="1.0" encoding="UTF-8"?>
<beans xmlns="http://www.springframework.org/schema/beans"
    xmlns:xsi="http://www.w3.org/2001/XMLSchema-instance"
    xsi:schemaLocation="http://www.springframework.org/schema/beans
        http://www.springframework.org/schema/beans/spring-beans-2.0.xsd">

    <bean id="foo" class="java.lang.String">
        <constructor-arg value="hello" />
    </bean>
</beans>
```

This is a typical beans configuration file containing a single bean definition. The bean is an instance of `java.lang.String` whose value is `hello` and whose name is `foo`.

Returning to the test case, after importing the XML file the `createApplicationContext` method is invoked, which makes the beans available through the application context. Then the test calls `getBean` to return the `foo` bean and checks that its value is `hello`.

The conclusions to be drawn are that to use the `BeanBuilder` you must (1) instantiate the class, (2) define the beans using normal builder syntax, (3) create the application context from the builder, and (4) access and use the beans in the normal way.

The next listing contains another test in the test case that illustrates setting a bean's properties.

Listing 7.28 Setting bean properties in the `BeanBuilder`, from `BeanBuilderTests`

```
    void testSimpleBean() {
        def bb = new BeanBuilder()
        bb.beans {
            bean1(Bean1) {
                person = "homer"
                age = 45
                props = [overweight:true, height:"1.8m"]
                children = ["bart", "lisa"]
```

```
            }
        }
        def ctx  = bb.createApplicationContext()

        assert ctx.containsBean("bean1")
        def bean1 = ctx.getBean("bean1")

        assertEquals "homer", bean1.person
        assertEquals 45, bean1.age
        assertEquals true, bean1.props?.overweight
        assertEquals "1.8m", bean1.props?.height
        assertEquals(["bart", "lisa"], bean1.children)
    }
```

Inside the builder the syntax uses the bean name followed by the bean class in parentheses. In this case, `bean1` is the name or ID of an instance of the `Bean1` class. Near the bottom of the file you'll find the definition of `Bean1`:

```
class Bean1 {
    String person
    int age
    Properties props
    List children
}
```

In fact, several beans are defined at the bottom of the class. Unlike Java, Groovy source files can have multiple classes defined in them. The `Bean1` class contains attributes of type `String`, `int`, `Properties`, and `List`. The test case assigns the `name` to `homer` and the `age` to `45`, uses the map syntax to assign the `overweight` and `height` properties, and sets the list to the names of the children.[18] The tests then assert that the bean is in the application context and that, after retrieving it, all the properties have been set as described.

You're not limited to defining a single bean, of course. The next listing shows a test that creates several beans and sets their relationships.

Listing 7.29 Defining several related beans with the `BeanBuilder`

```
    void testBeanReferences() {
        def bb = new BeanBuilder()
        bb.beans {
            homer(Bean1) {
                person = "homer"
                age = 45
                props = [overweight:true, height:"1.8m"]
                children = ["bart", "lisa"]
            }
            bart(Bean1) {
                person = "bart"
                age = 11
            }
            lisa(Bean1) {
```

[18] Leaving out Maggie, who sadly always seems to be an afterthought.

```
            person = "lisa"
            age = 9
        }
        marge(Bean2) {
            person = "marge"
            bean1 = homer
            children = [bart, lisa]
        }
    }
    def ctx  = bb.createApplicationContext()

    def homer = ctx.getBean("homer")
    def marge = ctx.getBean("marge")
    def bart = ctx.getBean("bart")
    def lisa = ctx.getBean("lisa")

    assertEquals homer, marge.bean1
    assertEquals 2, marge.children.size()

    assertTrue marge.children.contains(bart)
    assertTrue marge.children.contains(lisa)
}
```

The beans named `homer`, `bart`, and `lisa` are all instances of the `Bean1` class. The `marge` bean is an instance of `Bean2`, which adds a reference of type `Bean1` called `bean1`. Here the `bean1` reference in `marge` is assigned to `homer`. The `Bean1` class also has a `children` attribute of type `List`, so it's assigned to a list containing `bart` and `lisa`.

I don't want to go through all the tests here, but there are a couple of features that should be highlighted. For example, you can define beans at different scopes, as shown in the next listing.

Listing 7.30 Defining beans at different scopes

```
void testScopes() {
    def bb = new BeanBuilder()
    bb.beans {
        myBean(ScopeTest) { bean ->
            bean.scope = "prototype"
        }
        myBean2(ScopeTest)
    }
    def ctx = bb.createApplicationContext()

    def b1 = ctx.myBean
    def b2 = ctx.myBean

    assert b1 != b2

    b1 = ctx.myBean2
    b2 = ctx.myBean2

    assertEquals b1, b2
}
```

By setting the `scope` attribute on `myBean` to `prototype`, retrieving the bean twice results in separate instances. The scope of `myBean2` is singleton by default, so asking for it twice results in two references to the same object.

You can also use tags from different Spring namespaces. Earlier in this chapter I created an aspect using Groovy. The following listing shows a similar case using the `BeanBuilder`.

Listing 7.31 Defining an aspect using `BeanBuilder`

```
void testSpringAOPSupport() {

    def bb = new BeanBuilder()

    bb.beans {
        xmlns aop:"http://www.springframework.org/schema/aop"

        fred(AdvisedPerson) {
            name = "Fred"
            age = 45
        }
        birthdayCardSenderAspect(BirthdayCardSender)

        aop.config("proxy-target-class":true) {
            aspect(id:"sendBirthdayCard",ref:"birthdayCardSenderAspect" ) {
                after method:"onBirthday", pointcut:
                    "execution(void grails.spring.AdvisedPerson.birthday())
                     and this(person)"
            }
        }
    }

    def appCtx = bb.createApplicationContext()
    def fred = appCtx.getBean("fred")
    assertTrue (fred instanceof SpringProxy )

    fred.birthday()

    BirthdayCardSender birthDaySender = appCtx.getBean(
        "birthdayCardSenderAspect")

    assertEquals 1, birthDaySender.peopleSentCards.size()
    assertEquals "Fred", birthDaySender.peopleSentCards[0].name
}
```

The aop namespace is declared using `xmlns`. In the builder that's interpreted as a (non-existent) method call, whose interpretation is to make the namespace available under the aop prefix. The `fred` bean is an instance of `AdvisedPerson`, whose definition is

```
@Component(value = "person")
class AdvisedPerson {
    int age
    String name

    void birthday() {
        ++age
    }
}
```

The `birthdayCardSenderAspect` is an instance of `BirthdayCardSender`, which is defined at the bottom of the file:

```
class BirthdayCardSender {
   List peopleSentCards = []
   void onBirthday(AdvisedPerson person) {
      peopleSentCards << person
   }
}
```

Using the `config` element from the `aop` namespace, the builder declares an aspect called `sendBirthdayCard` that references the aspect. After any execution of the birthday method in an advised person, the aspect's `onBirthday` method is executed, which adds the person to the `peopleSentCards` collection. The test then verifies that the aspect did in fact run.

Other tests illustrate other capabilities in `BeanBuilder`. For example, if the property you're trying to set requires a hyphen, you put the property in quotes. Some tests show examples like

```
aop.'scoped-proxy'()
```

or

```
jee.'jndi-lookup'(id:"foo", 'jndi-name':"bar")
```

See the test file for a wide range of examples. The bottom line is that anything you can do in a regular Spring bean configuration file, you can do with the Grails `BeanBuilder`.

> **Lessons learned (Spring with Groovy)**
>
> 1 Spring manages POGOs the same way it manages POJOs, so beans can be implemented in Groovy as easily as in Java.
> 2 Closure coercion eliminates the need for anonymous inner classes.
> 3 By adding a single JAR file, Spock tests work inside the Spring test context.
> 4 Refreshable beans allow you to modify the system without restarting it.
> 5 Inline scripted beans are embedded in configuration files.
> 6 The Grails `BeanBuilder` gives yet another way to configure Spring.

7.7 Summary

This chapter demonstrated all the places where Groovy can work productively with the Spring framework. In addition to writing Spring beans in Groovy, which sometimes results in significant code savings, there are features of Spring unique to beans from dynamic languages. I showed both refreshable beans, in which you deploy the source code and can revise it without stopping the system, and inline scripted beans, in which the beans are defined directly in the configuration file. Groovy beans can also be Spring AOP aspects, as shown. Finally, I reviewed tests from the `BeanBuilder` class from Grails, which can be used to create Spring bean definitions using the normal Groovy builder syntax, even outside of Grails.

In the next chapter, it's time to look at database development and manipulation. There, in addition to the cool capabilities of the `groovy.sql.Sql` class, I'll also use another contribution from the Grails project, the Grails Object Relational Mapping (GORM) capability.

8 Database access

This chapter covers

- JDBC and the Groovy `Sql` class
- Simplifying Hibernate and JPA using GORM
- Working with the NoSQL database

Virtually every significant application uses persistent data in one form or another. The vast majority of them save the data in relational databases. To make it easy to switch from one database to another, Java provides the JDBC[1] API. While JDBC does handle the required tasks, its low-level nature leads to many lines of code to handle even the simplest tasks.

Because the software is object-oriented and the database is relational, there's a mismatch at the boundary. The open source Hibernate project attempts to bridge that gap at a higher level of abstraction. Java includes the Java Persistence API (JPA) as a uniform interface to Hibernate and other object-relational mapping (ORM) tools.

[1] You would think that JDBC stands for Java Database Connectivity. Everyone would agree with you, except for the people at Sun (now Oracle) who created the API. They claim that JDBC is a trademarked acronym that doesn't stand for anything. Clearly lawyers were involved somewhere in the process. I'm not going to be bound by such silliness, and if I get sued as a result, I'll be sure to blog about it.

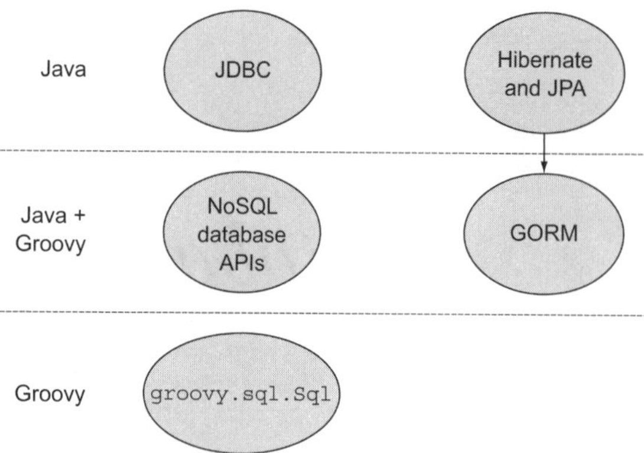

Figure 8.1 Java uses JDBC and JPA, with Hibernate being the most common JPA provider. Most NoSQL databases have a Java API that can be wrapped by Groovy; in this chapter GMongo is used to access MongoDB. GORM is a Groovy DSL on top of Spring and Hibernate. Finally, the `groovy.sql.Sql` class makes it easy to use raw SQL with a relational database.

Groovy, as usual, provides some simplifications to the Java APIs. For raw SQL, the Groovy standard library includes the `groovy.sql.Sql` class. For ORM tools like Hibernate, the Grails project created a domain-specific language (DSL) called GORM. Finally, many of the so-called "No SQL" databases that have become popular recently also provide Groovy APIs to simplify their use. Figure 8.1 shows the technologies covered in this chapter.

With relational databases everything ultimately comes down to SQL, so I'll start there.

8.1 The Java approach, part 1: JDBC

JDBC is a set of classes and interfaces that provide a thin layer over raw SQL. That's a significant engineering achievement, actually. Providing a unified API across virtually every relational database is no trivial task, especially when each vendor implements significantly different variations in SQL itself. Still, if you already have the SQL worked out, the JDBC API has classes and methods to pass it to the database and process the results.

The following listing shows a simple example, based on a single persistent class called `Product`.

Listing 8.1 The `Product` class, a POJO mapped to a database table

```
package mjg;

public class Product {
    private int id;
    private String name;
    private double price;

    public Product() {}

    public Product(int id, String name, double price) {
        this.id = id;
        this.name = name;
        this.price = price;
    }
```

```
    public int getId() { return id; }
    public void setId(int id) { this.id = id; }
    public String getName() { return name; }
    public void setName(String name) { this.name = name; }
    public double getPrice() { return price; }
    public void setPrice(double price) { this.price = price; }
}
```

The `Product` class has only three attributes, one of which (`id`) will represent the primary key in the database. The rest of the class is simply constructors, getters and setters, and (not shown) the normal `toString`, `equals`, and `hashCode` overrides. The complete version is available in the book source code.

The next listing shows the `ProductDAO` interface.

Listing 8.2 A DAO interface for the `Product` class

```
import java.util.List;
public interface ProductDAO {
    List<Product> getAllProducts();
    Product findProductById(int id);
    void insertProduct(Product p);
    void deleteProduct(int id);
}
```

To implement the interface I need to know the table structure. Again, to keep things simple, assume I only have a single table, called `product`. For the purposes of this example the table will be created in the DAO implementation class, using the H2 database.

The implementation class is `JDBCProductDAO`. A couple of excerpts are shown ahead. Java developers will find both the code and the attendant painful verbosity quite familiar.

The following listing shows the beginnings of the implementation, including constants to represent the URL and driver class.

Listing 8.3 A JDBC implementation of the DAO interface

```
public class JDBCProductDAO implements ProductDAO {
    private static final String URL = "jdbc:h2:build/test";
    private static final String DRIVER = "org.h2.Driver";

    public JDBCProductDAO() {
        try {
            Class.forName(DRIVER);
        } catch (ClassNotFoundException e) {
            e.printStackTrace();
            return;
        }
        createAndPopulateTable();
    }
// ... More to come ...
}
```

The import statements have been mercifully omitted. The private method to create and populate the table is shown in the next listing.

Listing 8.4 Adding creation and population of the Product table to the DAO

```
private void createAndPopulateTable() {
 Connection conn = null;
 Statement stmt = null;
 try {
     conn = DriverManager.getConnection(URL);
     stmt = conn.createStatement();
     stmt.execute("drop table product if exists;");
     stmt.execute("create table product (id int primary key, name " +
     "varchar(25), price double);");
     stmt.executeUpdate("insert into product values " +
     "(1,'baseball',4.99),(2,'football',14.95),(3,'basketball',14.99)");
 } catch (SQLException e) {
     e.printStackTrace();
 } finally {
     try {
         if (stmt != null) stmt.close();
         if (conn != null) conn.close();
 } catch (SQLException e) {
     e.printStackTrace();
 }
}
```

Declared outside try/catch, to access in finally

Everything in JDBC throws an SQLException

Only way to guarantee everything is closed

Yes, even close() throws an exception

A phrase often used when describing Java is that the essence is buried in ceremony. JDBC code is probably the worst offender in the whole API. The "essence" here is to create the table and add a few rows. The "ceremony" is all the boilerplate surrounding it. As the listing shows, `try/catch` blocks are needed because virtually everything in JDBC throws a checked `SQLException`. In addition, because it's absolutely necessary to close the database connection whether an exception is thrown or not, the connection must be closed in a `finally` block. To make matters even uglier, the `close` method itself also throws an `SQLException`, so it, too, must be wrapped in a `try/catch` block, and of course the only way to avoid a potential `NullPointerException` is to verify that the connection and statement references are not null when they're closed.

This boilerplate is repeated in every method in the DAO. For example, the following listing shows the implementation of the `findProductById` method.

Listing 8.5 The findProductById method with all the required ceremony

```
public Product findProductById(int id) {
    Product p = null;
    Connection conn = null;
    PreparedStatement pst = null;
    try {
        conn = DriverManager.getConnection(URL);
        pst = conn.prepareStatement(
            "select * from product where id = ?");
        pst.setInt(1, id);
```

The essence; everything else is ceremony

```
        ResultSet rs = pst.executeQuery();
        if (rs.next()) {
            p = new Product();
            p.setId(rs.getInt("id"));
            p.setName(rs.getString("name"));
            p.setPrice(rs.getDouble("price"));
        }
        rs.close();
    } catch (SQLException e) {
        e.printStackTrace();
    } finally {
        try {
            if (pst != null) pst.close();
            if (conn != null) conn.close();
        } catch (SQLException e) {
            e.printStackTrace();
        }
    }
    return p;
}
```

The essence; everything else is ceremony

As with so many things in Java, the best thing you can say about this code is that eventually you get used to it. All that's being done here is to execute a `select` statement with a `where` clause including the necessary product ID and converting the returned database row into a `Product` object. Everything else is ceremony.

I could go on to show the remaining implementation methods, but suffice it to say that the details are equally buried. See the book source code for details.

Lessons learned (JDBC)

1. JDBC is a very verbose, low-level set of classes for SQL access to relational databases.
2. The Spring `JdbcTemplate` class (covered in chapter 7) is a good choice if Groovy is not available.

Years ago this was the only realistic option for Java. Now other options exist, like Spring's `JdbcTemplate` (discussed in chapter 7 on Spring) and object-relational mapping tools like Hibernate (discussed later in this chapter). Still, if you already know SQL and you want to implement a DAO interface, Groovy provides a very easy alternative: the `groovy.sql.Sql` class.

8.2 The Groovy approach, part 1: groovy.sql.Sql

The `groovy.sql.Sql` class is a simple façade over JDBC. The class takes care of resource management for you, as well as creating and configuring statements and logging errors. It's so much easier to use than regular JDBC that there's never any reason to go back.

The next listing shows the part of the class that sets up the connection to the database and initializes it.

Listing 8.6 A `ProductDAO` implementation using the `groovy.sql.Sql` class

```
import groovy.sql.Sql

class SqlProductDAO implements ProductDAO {
    Sql sql = Sql.newInstance(url:'jdbc:h2:mem:',
        driver:'org.h2.Driver')

    SqlProductDAO() {
        sql.execute '''
            create table product (
                id int primary key,
                name varchar(25),
                price double
            )'''
        sql.execute """
            insert into product values
                (1,'baseball',4.99),
                (2,'football',14.95),
                (3,'basketball',14.99)"""
    }

    // ... more to come ...
}
```

Configure the database properties

Multiline strings to make reading easier

The `groovy.sql.Sql` class contains a static factory method called `newInstance` that returns a new instance of the class. The method is overloaded for a variety of parameters; see the GroovyDocs for details.

The `execute` method takes an SQL string and, naturally enough, executes it. Here I'm using a multiline string to make the `create table` and `insert into` statements easier to read. The `Sql` class takes care of opening a connection and closing it when finished.

THE SQL CLASS The `groovy.sql.Sql` class does everything raw JDBC does, and handles resource management as well.

The same `execute` method can be used to delete products:

```
void deleteProduct(int id) {
    sql.execute 'delete from product where id=?', id
}
```

The `execute` method not only creates the prepared statement, it also inserts the provided ID into it and executes it. It's hard to get much simpler than that.

Inserting products can use the same method, but with a list of parameters:

```
void insertProduct(Product p) {
    def params = [p.id, p.name, p.price]
    sql.execute
        'insert into product(id,name,price) values(?,?,?)', params
}
```

The class has another method called `executeInsert`, which is used if any of the columns are auto-generated by the database. That method returns a list containing the generated values. In this example the `id` values are supplied in the program. Autogenerated values will be considered in section 8.3 on Hibernate and JPA.

Retrieving products involves a minor complication. There are several useful methods for querying. Among them are `firstRow`, `eachRow`, and `rows`. The `firstRow` method is used when a single row is required. Either `eachRow` or `rows` can be used if there are multiple rows in the result set. In that case, `eachRow` returns a map of column names to column values, and the `rows` method returns a list of maps, one for each row.

The complication is that the returned column names are in all capitals. For example, the query

```
sql.firstRow 'select * from product where id=?', id
```

returns

```
[ID:1, NAME:baseball, PRICE:4.99]
```

for an `id` of `1`. Normally I'd like to use that map as the argument to the `Product` constructor, but because the `Product` attributes are all lowercase that won't work.

One possible solution is to transform the map into a new one with lowercase keys. That's what the `collectEntries` method in the `Map` class is for. The resulting implementation of the `findProductById` method is therefore

```
Product findProductById(int id) {
    def row = sql.firstRow('select * from product where id=?', id)
    new Product( row.collectEntries { k,v -> [k.toLowerCase(), v] } );
}
```

It would be easy enough to generalize this to the `getAllProducts` method by using `eachRow` and transforming them one at a time. A somewhat more elegant solution is to use the `rows` method and transform the resulting list of maps directly:

```
List<Product> getAllProducts() {
    sql.rows('select * from product').collect { row ->
        new Product(
            row.collectEntries { k,v -> [k.toLowerCase(), v] }
        )
    }
}
```

This solution is either incredibly elegant or too clever by half, depending on your point of view. Collecting[2] everything together (except for the initialization shown in the constructor already), the result is shown in the following listing.

[2] No pun intended.

Listing 8.7 The complete `SqlProductDAO` class, except for the parts already shown

```
class SqlProductDAO implements ProductDAO {
    Sql sql = Sql.newInstance(url:'jdbc:h2:mem:',driver:'org.h2.Driver')

    List<Product> getAllProducts() {
        sql.rows('select * from product').collect { row ->
            new Product(
                row.collectEntries { k,v -> [k.toLowerCase(), v] }
            )
        }
    }

    Product findProductById(int id) {
        def row = sql.firstRow('select * from product where id=?', id)
        new Product(
           row.collectEntries { k,v -> [k.toLowerCase(), v] } );
    }

    void insertProduct(Product p) {
        def params = [p.id, p.name, p.price]
        sql.execute
           'insert into product(id,name,price) values(?,?,?)', params
    }

    void deleteProduct(int id) {
        sql.execute 'delete from product where id=?', id
    }
}
```

By the way, there's one other option available,[3] but only if the `Person` class is implemented in Groovy. If so, I can add a constructor to the `Person` class that handles the case conversion there:

```
class Product {
    int id
    String name
    double price

    Person(Map args) {
        args.each { k,v ->
            setProperty( k.toLowerCase(), v)
        }
    }
}
```

With this constructor, the `getAllProducts` method reduces to

```
List<Product> getAllProducts() {
    sql.rows('select * from product').collect { new Product(it) }
}
```

It's hard to beat that for elegance.

[3] Thanks to Dinko Srkoc on the Groovy Users email list for this helpful suggestion.

Going meta

The "elegant" solution in the chapter breaks down if the class attributes use camel case, which is normal. The corresponding database table entries would then use underscores to separate the words.

As shown by Tim Yates on the Groovy Users email list,[4] you can use Groovy metaprogramming to add a `toCamelCase` method to the `String` class to do the conversion. The relevant code is

```
String.metaClass.toCamelCase = {->
  delegate.toLowerCase().split('_')*.capitalize().join('').with {
    take( 1 ).toLowerCase() + drop( 1 )
  }
}
```

Every Groovy class has a metaclass retrieved by the `getMetaClass` method. New methods can be added to the metaclass by assigning closures to them, as is done here. A no-arg closure is used, which implies that the new method will take zero arguments.

Inside the closure the `delegate` property refers to the object on which it was invoked. In this case it's the string being converted. The database table columns are in uppercase separated by underscores, so the delegate is converted to lowercase and then split at the underscores, resulting in a list of strings.

Then the spread-dot operator is used on the list to invoke the `capitalize` method on each one, which capitalizes only the first letter. The `join` method then reassembles the string.

Then comes the fun part. The `with` method takes a closure, and inside that closure any method without a reference is invoked on the delegate. The `take` and `drop` methods are used on lists (or, in this case, a character sequence). The `take` method retrieves the number of elements specified by its argument. Here that value is 1, so it returns the first letter, which is made lowercase. The `drop` method returns the rest of the elements after the number in the argument is removed, which in this case means the rest of the string.

The result is that you can call the method on a string and convert it. `'FIRST_NAME'.toLowerCase()` becomes `'firstName'`, and so on.

Welcome to the wonderful world of Groovy metaprogramming.

The advantages of `groovy.sql.Sql` over raw JDBC are obvious. If I have SQL code already written, I always use it.

[4] See http://groovy.329449.n5.nabble.com/Change-uppercase-Sql-column-names-to-lowercase-td5712088.html for the complete discussion.

Lessons learned (Groovy SQL[5])

1. The `groovy.sql.Sql` class makes working with raw SQL better in every way: resource management, multiline strings, closure support, and mapping of result sets to maps.
2. Related examples in this book can be found in chapter 7 on Spring and chapter 9 on REST.

Rather than write all that SQL, you can instead use one of the object-relational mapping (ORM) tools available, the most prevalent of which is still Hibernate. The Java Persistence API (JPA) specification acts as a front-end on ORM tools and is the subject of the next section.

8.3 The Java approach, part 2: Hibernate and JPA

One approach to simplifying JDBC is to automate as much of it as possible. The early years of Java saw attempts to add ORM tools directly to the specification, with varying degrees of success. First came Java Data Objects, which worked directly with compiled bytecodes and are largely forgotten today. Then came Enterprise JavaBeans (EJB) entity beans, which were viewed by the community as a mess in the first couple of versions.

As frequently happens when there's a need and only an unpopular specification available, the open source community developed a practical alternative. In this case the project that emerged was called Hibernate, which still aims to be the ORM tool of choice in the Java world when dealing with relational databases.

In regular JDBC a `ResultSet` is connected to the data source as long as the connection is open, and goes away when the connection is closed. In the EJB world, therefore, you needed two classes to represent an entity: one that was always connected, and one that was never connected. The former was called something analogous to `ProductEJB`, and the latter was a `ProductTO`, or transfer object.[6] When getting a product from the database the `ProductEJB` held the data for a single row, and its data was transferred to a `ProductTO` for display. The transfer object wasn't connected, so it could get stale, but at least it didn't use up a database connection, which is a scarce commodity. Transferring the data from the EJB to the TO was done by a session EJB, where the transaction boundaries occurred. The session EJBs formed the service layer, which also held business logic. The whole process was much like that shown in figure 8.2.

The result is that the `ProductEJB` class and the `ProductTO` class were essentially identical, in that they both contained the same method signatures, even though the implementations were different. Martin Fowler (author of *Patterns of Enterprise Application Architecture* [Addison-Wesley, 2002], *Refactoring* [Addision-Wesley, 1999],

---

[5] Worst SQL Joke Ever Told: SQL query walks into a bar, selects two tables and says, "Mind if I join you?" (rimshot). (Warning: NoSQL version later in this chapter.)

[6] Older terms included Data Transfer Object (DTO) and Value Object (VO).

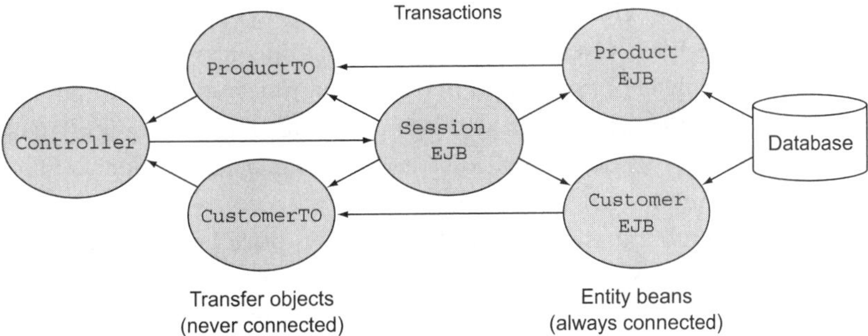

Figure 8.2 Controllers contact transactional session EJBs, which acquire database data through entity EJBs. The data is copied to transfer objects and returned to the controller.

and several other books) calls that an anti-pattern and says that it's a symptom of a flawed design.

One of the key differences between Hibernate and EJBs is the concept of a Hibernate session. The innovation was that, rather than one class of objects that were always connected and another class of objects that were never connected, what was needed was a set of objects that were sometimes connected and sometimes not. In Hibernate, when objects are part of a Hibernate session, the framework promises to keep them in sync with the database. When the session closes, the object is disconnected, thereby becoming its own transfer object. Any time an object is retrieved through Hibernate, it becomes part of a Hibernate session.

You retrieve a Hibernate session via a session factory. The session factory reads all the mapping metadata, configures the framework, and performs any necessary preprocessing. It's supposed to be instantiated only once, acting as a singleton.

Those readers who are familiar with the Spring framework (as discussed in chapter 7) should suddenly become interested, because managing singletons is one of the things that Spring is all about. Another of its capabilities is declarative transaction management, which fits in nicely too. The result is that designs in the EJB 2.x world were replaced by a combination of Spring for the declarative transactions and the session factory and Hibernate for the entity beans.

In version 3 of EJB the architecture was redesigned again to fit more closely with that used by Spring and Hibernate. The entity beans part led to the creation of the Java Persistence API. The JPA world uses the same concepts but labels them differently.[7] The Hibernate `Session` becomes an `EntityManager`. The `SessionFactory` is an `EntityManagerFactory`. Objects that are managed (that is, in the Hibernate session) compose a *persistence context*.

[7] Of course it does. Using the same terms would be too easy.

Finally, in the original Hibernate, mapping from entity classes to database tables was done through XML files. Over time XML has become less popular and has been replaced by annotations. Hibernate and JPA share many annotations, which is fortunate.

It's time for an example, which will bring Spring, Hibernate, and JPA together. Chapter 7 on the Spring framework discusses Spring in some detail. Here I'll just highlight the parts needed for the example.

To start I'll need a database. For that I'll use H2, a pure Java file- or memory-based database. Spring provides an embedded database bean to make it easy to work with H2. The relevant bean from the Spring configuration file is

```
<jdbc:embedded-database id="dataSource" type="H2">
    <jdbc:script location="classpath:schema.sql"/>
    <jdbc:script location="classpath:test-data.sql"/>
</jdbc:embedded-database>
```

The schema and test-data SQL files define a single table, called `PRODUCT`, with three rows:

```
create table PRODUCT (
    id bigint generated by default as identity (start with 1),
    name varchar(255), price double, primary key (id)
)
insert into PRODUCT(name, price) values('baseball', 5.99)
insert into PRODUCT(name, price) values('basketball', 10.99)
insert into PRODUCT(name, price) values('football', 7.99)
```

Spring provides a bean to represent the `EntityManagerFactory`, which has a handful of properties to set:

```
<bean id="entityManagerFactory" class=
    "org.springframework.orm.jpa.LocalContainerEntityManagerFactoryBean">
    <property name="dataSource" ref="dataSource" />
    <property name="persistenceUnitName" value="jpaDemo" />
    <property name="packagesToScan">
        <list>
            <value>mjg</value>
        </list>
    </property>
    <property name="jpaVendorAdapter">
        <bean class=
        "org.springframework.orm.jpa.vendor.HibernateJpaVendorAdapter">
            <property name="database" value="H2" />
        </bean>
    </property>
</bean>
```

The `LocalContainerEntityManagerFactoryBean`[8] class uses the data source bean defined previously, scans the given packages for entities, and uses Hibernate as its implementation.

---

[8] Extremely long class names are a Spring staple. My favorite is `AbstractTransactionalDataSourceSpring-ContextTests`, which has 49 characters and is even deprecated. What's yours?

The entity itself is the `Product` class, this time with a sprinkling of JPA (or Hibernate) annotations:

```
@Entity
public class Product {

    @Id
    private int id;
    private String name;
    private double price;

    // ... constructors ...
    // ... getters and setters ...
    // ... toString, equals, hashCode ...
}
```

The `@Entity` and `@Id` annotations declare `Product` to be a class mapped to a database table and identify the primary key, respectively. Because, by an amazing coincidence,[9] the `Product` attribute names and the database column names happen to match, I don't need the additional physical annotations like `@Table` and `@Column`.

The `ProductDAO` interface is the same as that shown in section 8.1 on JDBC, except that now the `insertProduct` method returns the new database-generated primary key. The `JpaProductDAO` implementation class is where the action happens, and it's shown in the next listing.

Listing 8.8 The `JpaProductDAO` class, which uses JPA classes to implement the DAO

```
@Repository                                                  <-- Spring bean detected
public class JpaProductDAO implements ProductDAO {               on a component scan
    @PersistenceContext                                      <-- Injected entity
    private EntityManager entityManager;                         manager

    public List<Product> getAllProducts() {
        return entityManager.createQuery("from Product p").getResultList();
    }

    public Product findProductById(int id) {
        return entityManager.find(Product.class, id);
    }

    public int insertProduct(Product p) {
        entityManager.persist(p);
        return p.getId();
    }

    public void deleteProduct(int id) {
        entityManager.remove(findProductById(id));
    }
}
```

[9] Not really.

The JPA implementation is wonderfully spare, but that's because it assumes the transaction management is handled elsewhere and that Spring will handle allocating and closing the necessary database resources.

I would never be comfortable writing that much code without a decent test case. Spring's test context framework manages the application context, allows the test fixture to be injected, and, if a transaction manager is supplied, automatically rolls back transactions at the end of each test.

To handle the transactions I used another Spring bean, `JpaTransactionManager`, which uses the entity manager factory previously specified:

```
<bean id="transactionManager"
    class="org.springframework.orm.jpa.JpaTransactionManager"
    p:entityManagerFactory-ref="entityManagerFactory" />
```

The resulting test case is shown in the following listing.

Listing 8.9 A Spring test case for the JPA DAO implementation

```
@RunWith(SpringJUnit4ClassRunner.class)
@ContextConfiguration(locations="classpath:applicationContext.xml")
@Transactional
public class JpaProductDAOTest {
    @Autowired
    private ProductDAO dao;

    @Test
    public void testFindById() {
        Product p = dao.findProductById(1);
        assertEquals("baseball", p.getName());
    }

    @Test
    public void testGetAllProducts() {
        List<Product> products = dao.getAllProducts();
        assertEquals(3, products.size());
    }

    @Test
    public void testInsert() {
        Product p = new Product(99, "racketball", 7.99);
        int id = dao.insertProduct(p);
        Product p1 = dao.findProductById(id);
        assertEquals("racketball", p1.getName());
    }

    @Test
    public void testDelete() {
        List<Product> products = dao.getAllProducts();
        for (Product p : products) {
            dao.deleteProduct(p.getId());
        }
        assertEquals(0, dao.getAllProducts().size());
    }
}
```

The tests check each of the DAO methods. My favorite is `testDelete`, which deletes every row in the table, verifies that they're gone, and *doesn't add them back in*, which has the side effect of giving any DBAs heart palpitations. Fortunately, Spring rolls back all the changes when the test is finished, so nothing is lost, but a good time is had by all.

The last piece of the puzzle is the Maven build file. You can see it, as usual, in the book source code.

That's a fair amount of code and configuration, and I've only got one class and one database table. Frankly, if I can't make that work, I might as well give it up. It's when you add relationships that life gets complicated.[10]

Lessons learned (Hibernate and JPA)

1. The Java Persistence API manages object-relational mapping providers that convert objects to table rows and back again.
2. Hibernate is the most common JPA provider in the industry.
3. ORM tools provide transitive persistence, persistence contexts, SQL code generation, and more.
4. Like all Java libraries, they're still pretty verbose.

Groovy can help this situation in a couple of ways, which will be discussed in the next section.

8.4 The Groovy approach, part 2: Groovy and GORM

Before getting into the Grails Object-Relational Mapping (GORM) part of Grails, let me identify a couple of places where Groovy can simplify the example application from the previous section.

8.4.1 Groovy simplifications

The entity class `Product` could be written as a POGO. That wouldn't change the behavior, but it would cut the size of the class by about two-thirds. That and the other Spring-related parts of the application could be converted to Groovy, which is shown in more detail in chapter 7 on Spring.

A Gradle build file is contained in the book source code. It looks like most of the build files shown in earlier chapters, but it's considerably shorter and easier to read than the corresponding Maven build.

8.4.2 Grails Object-Relational Mapping (GORM)

The Grails framework consists of a set of Groovy DSLs on top of Spring and Hibernate. Because the combination of Spring and Hibernate is a very common architecture in

[10] On many levels; sometimes the jokes just write themselves.

the Java world, Grails is a natural evolution that simplifies the coding and integration issues.

Grails is discussed in more detail in chapter 10 on web applications, but the Hibernate integration part is relevant here. Grails combines Groovy domain-specific languages (DSLs) to make configuring the domain classes easy.

DOMAIN CLASSES In Grails the term *domain* is like *entity* in JPA. Domain classes map to database tables.

Consider a small but nontrivial domain model based on the same `Product` class used earlier in this chapter. The next listing shows the `Product` class, now in Groovy.

Listing 8.10 The `Product` class, this time as a POGO in a Grails application

```
class Product {
    String name
    double price

    String toString() { name }

    static constraints = {
        name blank:false
        price min:0.0d
    }
}
```

In Grails each domain class implicitly has a primary key called `id` of some integer type, which isn't shown here but exists nevertheless. The `constraints` block here is part of GORM.[11] Each line in the constraints block is actually a method call, where the name of the method is the attribute name. The `blank` constraint implies, naturally enough, that the name of the product can't be an empty string. The `price` constraint sets a minimum value of 0, and the `d` makes it a double, because the constraint type must match the attribute data type.

This application will have three more domain classes, representing customers, orders, and lines on the orders. Next up is the `Customer` class, shown in the next listing.

Listing 8.11 The `Customer` class. Customers have many orders (hopefully).

```
class Customer {
    String name

    String toString() { name }

    static hasMany = [orders:Order]          <-- One-to-many relationship

    static constraints = {
        name blank:false
    }
}
```

[11] The lizard creature that Captain Kirk fought in the *Star Trek* original series episode "Arena" was a Gorn, not a GORM. I mean, who ever heard of Grails Object-Relational Napping, anyway? (Though there's probably a "lazy loading" joke in there somewhere.)

Customers have a `name` attribute and a `Set` representing their orders.

> **GRAILS HASMANY** In Grails the `hasMany` property implies a one-to-many relationship. By default, the contained objects form a set.

The `name` cannot be blank. The `Order` class is shown in the following listing.

Listing 8.12 The `Order` class, which has many orders and belongs to a customer

```
class Order {
    String number
    Date dateCreated
    Date lastUpdated

    static hasMany = [orderLines:OrderLine]
    static belongsTo = [customer:Customer]

    double getPrice() {
        orderLines*.price.sum()
    }

    static mapping = {
        table 'orders'
        orderLines fetch: 'join'
    }
}
```

Annotations:
- Automatically maintained by Hibernate (dateCreated, lastUpdated)
- One-to-many (hasMany)
- Bidirectional and cascade delete (belongsTo)
- Derived quantity; not saved (getPrice)
- Custom mapping (mapping)

There's a lot going on here. First, an order contains a `Set` of order lines. Orders also belong to a specific customer. The customer reference implies that you can navigate from an order to its associated customer. By assigning it to the `belongsTo` property in this way, a cascade-delete relationship exists between the two classes. If a customer is deleted from the system, all of its orders are deleted as well.

> **GRAILS BELONGSTO** In Grails, the word `belongsTo` implies a cascade-delete relationship.

The `getPrice` method computes the price of the order by summing up the prices on each order line. It too is a derived quantity and is therefore not saved in the database.

The `dateCreated` and `lastUpdated` properties are automatically maintained by Hibernate. When an order is first saved, its `dateCreated` value is set; and every time it's modified, `lastUpdated` is saved as well.

Finally, the `mapping` block is used to customize how the class is mapped to a database table. By default, Grails will generate a table whose name matches the class name. Because the word `order` is an SQL keyword, the resulting DDL statement would have problems. In the `mapping` block the generated table name is specified to be `orders`, rather than `order`, to avoid that problem. Also, Hibernate treats all associations as lazy. In this case, that means that if an order is loaded, a separate SQL query will be required to load the order lines as well. In the mapping block, the `fetch join` relationship means that all the associated order lines will be loaded at the same time as the order, via an inner join.

The OrderLine class contains the product being ordered and the quantity, as shown in the following listing.

Listing 8.13 The OrderLine POGO, which is assembled to build an Order

```
class OrderLine {
    Product product
    int quantity

    double getPrice() { quantity * product?.price }

    static constraints = {
        quantity min:0
    }
}
```

The getPrice method multiplies the quantity times the price of the product to get the price of the order line. This, in turn, is summed in order to get the total price, as you saw earlier.

Note also that the OrderLine class does not have a reference to the Order it belongs to. This is a unidirectional cascade-delete relationship. If the order is deleted, all the order lines go, but you cannot navigate from an order line to its associated order.

When you declare a hasMany relationship, Grails then provides methods for adding the contained objects to their containers. To illustrate one of those methods, here's the file BootStrap.groovy, which is a configuration file used in a Grails application for initialization code. The next listing shows code that instantiates a customer, two products, an order, and some order lines and saves them all to the database.

Listing 8.14 Initialization code in BootStrap.groovy

```
class BootStrap {

    def init = { servletContext ->
        if (!Product.findByName('baseball')) {
            Product baseball =
                new Product(name:'baseball', price:5.99).save()
            Product football =
                new Product(name:'football', price:12.99).save()
            Customer cb = new Customer(name:'Charlie Brown').save()
            Order o1 = new Order(number:'1', customer:cb)
                .addToOrderLines(product:baseball, quantity:2)
                .addToOrderLines(product:football, quantity:1)
                .save()
        }
    }

    def destroy = {
    }
}
```

The code in the init closure is executed when the application is started. The addToOrderLines method comes from declaring that an Order has many OrderLine

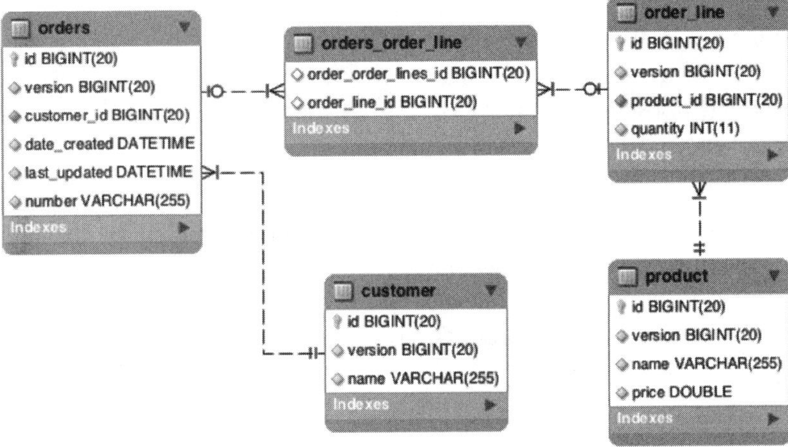

Figure 8.3 An entity relationship diagram for the generated database, given the domain classes listed in the text

instances. The `save` method first validates each object against its constraints and then saves it to the database.

Grails uses Hibernate's ability to generate a database schema. An entity relationship diagram (ERD) for the generated database is shown in figure 8.3.[12]

In this case the database is MySQL version 5, so the data type for `id` is `BIGINT`. It also converts the camel case properties `dateCreated` and `lastUpdated` into underscores in the table. Because the relationship between `Order` and `OrderLine` was unidirectional, Hibernate generates a join table between them called `orders_order_line`.

Grails also adds a column called `version` to each table. Hibernate uses this for optimistic locking. That means whenever a row of a table is modified and saved, Hibernate will automatically increment the version column by one. That's an attempt to get locking behavior without actually locking a row and paying the resulting performance penalty. If the application involves many reads but only a few writes, this works well. If there are too many writes, Grails also adds an instance method called `lock` to each domain class that locks the row. That's called *pessimistic locking* and will result in worse performance, so it's only used when necessary.

Grails does far more than this. For example, Grails uses Groovy to generate dynamic finder methods for each domain class. For the `Product` class, Grails generates static methods on the domain class that include

- `Product.list()`, which returns all product instances
- `Product.findByName(...)`, which returns the first product matching the name

[12] This diagram was generated using MySQL Workbench, which is a free tool available at www.mysql.com/products/workbench/.

- `Product.findAllByPriceGreaterThan(...)`, which returns all the products whose prices are greater than the argument
- `Product.findAllByNameIlikeAndPriceGreaterThan(...,...)`, which returns products whose names satisfy a case-insensitive SQL `like` clause and which have prices greater than the second argument

There are many more; see the Grails documentation[13] for details. In each case Grails uses the mappings to generate SQL code satisfying the desired conditions.

Grails also uses Groovy to provide a builder for criteria queries. Hibernate has an API for criteria queries that allows you to build up a query programmatically. The Java API works but is still quite verbose. Grails dramatically simplifies it so that you can write expressions like this:

```
Product.withCriteria {
  like('name','%e%')
  between('price', 2.50, 10.00)
  order('price','desc')
  maxResults(10)
}
```

This generates an SQL statement to find all products whose names include the letter *e* and whose prices are between $2.50 and $10.00. It returns the first 10 matching products in descending order by price.

One of the fundamental principles in Hibernate is the concept of a Hibernate session. As stated in the previous section, Hibernate ensures that any object inside a Hibernate session (what JPA calls a persistence context) will be kept in sync with the database. In Hibernate, objects can be in one of three states,[14] as shown in figure 8.4.

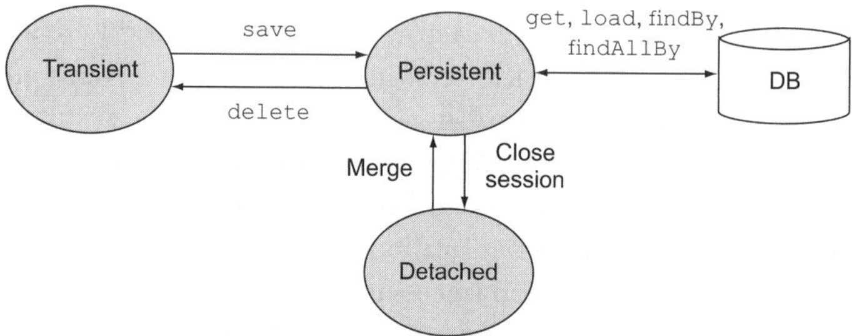

Figure 8.4 New and deleted objects are transient. When they are saved they become persistent, and when the session closes they become detached. Knowing the state of an object is key to understanding how it works in Hibernate.

[13] See http://grails.org/doc/latest/ for the Grails documentation. Chapter 6 in those docs discusses GORM in detail.

[14] The Hibernate docs defining the states can be found at http://mng.bz/Q9Ry.

Any object retrieved through Hibernate—for example, by using one of the dynamic finders or criteria queries—is placed in the persistent state and will stay in sync with the database while it remains in that state. Newly created objects that have not yet been saved are transient, and objects that are in memory when the Hibernate session is closed are then detached. Detached objects are no longer connected to the database.

The key question is, when is the Hibernate session created, and when is it closed? Over time a common practice has been established to scope the session to a single HTTP request. This is known in the Hibernate literature as the Open Session in View (OSIV) pattern, and it's implemented through a request interceptor. The Spring framework comes with a library class to do this automatically, which Grails uses by default.

> **OSIV BEAN** Grails uses an OSIV bean from Spring to scope the Hibernate session to each HTTP request. The bean intercepts incoming requests and creates the session, and then it intercepts the outgoing responses and closes the session.

Finally, transactions are managed using Spring's declarative transaction capabilities, using the `@Transactional` annotation. All Grails service methods are transactional by default, but their behavior can be customized using the annotation.

Setting up all this infrastructure—managing the sessions and transactions, mapping domain classes to tables, establishing relationships, handling optimistic locking, generating dynamic finders and criteria queries, and scoping the Hibernate session to each request—requires a lot of work when putting Spring and Hibernate together manually. Grails does all of this for you, and much more besides.

The Spring framework is one of the most common open source projects in all of Java, and Hibernate is still the most common ORM tool. Any project considering using them together owes it to itself to consider using Grails.

Lessons learned (Groovy and GORM)

1. Groovy simplifies all database access by using POGOs instead of POJOs, using closures for result set processing, and making building and testing easier.
2. The GORM API makes configuring Hibernate-based applications easy. When combined with Spring (as in Grails), transactions and the Hibernate session become simple, too.
3. It's not so easy to use GORM outside of Grails, which is tightly tied to Spring. Trying to do so is rare enough in the industry that the process wasn't covered in this chapter.

Recent versions of Grails can also map to non-relational databases, but you can also use regular Groovy to do that, as the next section shows.

8.5 Groovy and NoSQL databases

One of the most interesting trends in software development in the past few years[15] has been the growth of alternative, non-relational databases. The generic term NoSQL (which the majority of the community interpret as "Not Only SQL") refers to a range of schema-less databases that are not based on relational approaches.

The subject of NoSQL databases is already large and rapidly growing, and it's well beyond the scope of this book. But many of the databases have a Java API, and some of them also have Groovy wrappers that simplify them.

One of the most interesting is MongoDB,[16] whose Java API is rather awkward but is dramatically improved through a Groovy wrapper called GMongo. The GMongo project, whose GitHub repository is located at https://github.com/poiati/gmongo, is the product of Paulo Poiati and is the subject of this section.

MongoDB is a document-oriented database that stores its data in binary JSON (BSON) format. This makes it perfect for storing data downloaded from RESTful web services, which often produce JSON data on request.

8.5.1 Populating Groovy vampires

This example came about because I was wandering in a bookstore recently and noticed that while there was only one bookshelf labeled "Computer," there were three others labeled "Teen Paranormal Romance." Rather than lament the decline of Western Civilization I chose to take this as evidence that I needed to add Groovy vampires to my book.

Consider the web service provided by the movie review site Rotten Tomatoes, http://developer.rottentomatoes.com. If you register for an API key, you can make HTTP GET requests that search for movies, cast members, and more. The data is returned in JSON form. The base URL for the API is located at http://api.rottentomatoes.com/api/public/v1.0. All requests start with that URL.

For example, searching for information about the movie *Blazing Saddles*[17] is done by accessing http://api.rottentomatoes.com/api/public/v1.0/movies.json?q=Blazing%20Saddles&apiKey=... (supply the API key in the URL). The result is a JSON object that looks like the following listing.

Listing 8.15 A portion of the JSON object representing the movie *Blazing Saddles*

```
{
    "total": 1,
    "movies": [
        {
            "id": "13581",
            "title": "Blazing Saddles",
```

[15] Other than the rise of dynamic languages on the JVM, of course.

[16] See www.mongodb.org/ for downloads and documentation.

[17] That's not a vampire movie, obviously, but the urge to save Mongo in MongoDB is irresistible. "Mongo only pawn in game of life" is a brilliant line and arguably the peak of the Alex Karras oeuvre.

```
            "year": 1974,
            "mpaa_rating": "R",
            "runtime": 93,
            "release_dates": {
                "theater": "1974-02-07",
                "dvd": "1997-08-27"
            },
            "ratings": {
                "critics_rating": "Certified Fresh",
                "critics_score": 89,
                "audience_rating": "Upright",
                "audience_score": 89
            },
            "synopsis": "",
            ...,
            "abridged_cast": [
                {
                    "name": "Cleavon Little",
                    "id": "162693977",
                    "characters": [
                        "Bart"
                    ]
                },
                {
                    "name": "Gene Wilder",
                    "id": "162658425",
                    "characters": [
                        "Jim the Waco Kid"
                    ]
                },
                ...
            ],
            "alternate_ids": {
                "imdb": "0071230"
            },
...
}
```

In addition to the data shown, the JSON object also has links to the complete cast list, reviews, and more. Another reason to use a database like MongoDB for this data is that not every field appears in each movie. For example, some movies contain a critic's score and some do not. This fits with the whole idea of a schema-less database based on JSON.

First, to populate the MongoDB I'll use an instance of the `com.gmongo.GMongo` class. This class wraps the Java API directly. In fact, if you look at the class in `GMongo.groovy`, you'll see that it consists of

```
class GMongo {

  @Delegate
  Mongo mongo

  // ... Constructors and other methods ...
}
```

There follow various constructors and simple patch methods. The `@Delegate` annotation from Groovy is an Abstract Syntax Tree (AST) transformation[18] that exposes the methods in the `com.mongodb.Mongo` class, which comes from the Java API, through GMongo. The AST transformation means you don't need to write all the delegate methods by hand.

Initializing a database is as simple as

```
GMongo mongo = new GMongo()
def db = mongo.getDB('movies')
db.vampireMovies.drop()
```

MongoDB uses `movies` as the name of the database, and collections inside it, like `vampireMovies`, are properties of the database. The `drop` method clears the collection.

Searching Rotten Tomatoes consists of building a GET request with the proper parameters. In this case, the following code searches for vampire movies:

```
String key = new File('mjg/rotten_tomatoes_apiKey.txt').text
String base = "http://api.rottentomatoes.com/api/public/v1.0/movies.json?"
String qs = [apiKey:key, q:'vampire'].collect { it }.join('&')
String url = "$base$qs"
```

The API key is stored in an external file. Building the query string starts with a map of parameters, which is transformed into a map of strings of the form "key=value" and then joined with an ampersand. The full URL is then the base URL with an appended query string. Getting the movies and saving them into the database is almost trivial:

```
def vampMovies = new JsonSlurper().parseText(url.toURL().text)
db.vampireMovies << vampMovies.movies
```

The `JsonSlurper` receives text data in JSON form from the URL and converts it to JSON objects. Saving the results into the database is as simple as appending the whole collection.

The API has a limit of 30 results per page. The search results include a property called `next` that points to the next available page, assuming there is one. The script therefore needs to loop that many times to retrieve the available data:

```
def next = vampMovies?.links?.next
while (next) {
    println next
    vampMovies = slurper.parseText("$next&apiKey=$key".toURL().text)
    db.vampireMovies << vampMovies.movies
    next = vampMovies?.links?.next
}
```

That's all there is to it. Using a relational database would require mapping the movie structure to relational tables, which would be a bit of a challenge. Because MongoDB uses BSON as its native format, even a collection of JSON objects can be added with no work at all.

---

[18] Discussed in chapter 4 on integration and in appendix B, "Groovy by Feature," and used in many other places in this book.

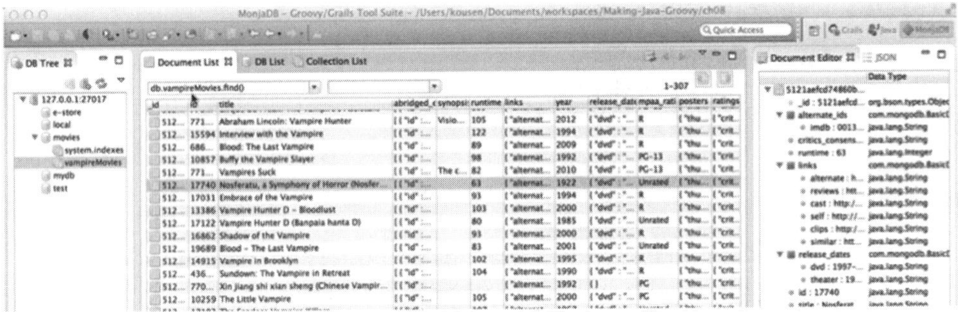

Figure 8.5 A portion of the vampire movies database, using the MonjaDB plugin for Eclipse

There's an Eclipse plugin, called MonjaDB, which connects to MongoDB databases. Figure 8.5 shows a portion of the vampireMovies database.

8.5.2 Querying and mapping MongoDB data

Now that the data is in the database I need to be able to search it and examine the results. This can be done in a trivial fashion, using the `find` method, or the data can be mapped to Groovy objects for later processing.

The `find` method on the collection returns all JSON objects satisfying a particular condition. If all I want is to see how many elements are in the collection, the following suffices:

```
println db.vampireMovies.find().count()
```

With no arguments, the `find` method returns the entire collection. The `count` method then returns the total number.

Mapping JSON to Groovy brings home the difference between a strongly typed language, like Groovy, and a weakly typed language, like JSON. The JSON data shown is a mix of strings, dates, integers, and enumerated values, but the JSON object has no embedded type information. Mapping this to a set of Groovy objects takes some work.

For example, the following listing shows a `Movie` class that holds the data in the JSON object.

Listing 8.16 `Movie.groovy`, which wraps the JSON data

```
@ToString(includeNames=true)
class Movie {
    long id
    String title
    int year
    MPAARating mpaaRating
    int runtime
    String criticsConsensus
```

```
    Map releaseDates = [:]
    Map<String, Rating> ratings = [:]
    String synopsis
    Map posters = [:]
    List<CastMember> abridgedCast = []
    Map links = [:]
}
```

The Movie class has attributes for each contained element, with the data types specified. It contains maps for the release dates, posters, ratings, and additional links, and a list for the abridged cast. A CastMember is just a POGO:

```
class CastMember {
    String name
    long id
    List<String> characters = []
}
```

A Rating holds a string and an integer:

```
class Rating {
    String rating
    int score
}
```

Just to keep things interesting, the MPAA rating is a Java enum, though it could just as easily have been implemented in Groovy:

```
public enum MPAARating {
    G, PG, PG_13, R, X, NC_17, Unrated
}
```

Converting a JSON movie to a Movie instance is done through a static method in the Movie class. A portion of the fromJSON method is shown in the next listing.

Listing 8.17 A portion of the method that converts JSON movies to Movie instances

```
static Movie fromJSON(data) {
    Movie m = new Movie()
    m.id = data.id.toLong()
    m.title = data.title
    m.year = data.year.toInteger()
    switch (data.mpaa_rating) {
        case 'PG-13' : m.mpaaRating = MPAARating.PG_13; break
        case 'NC-17' : m.mpaaRating = MPAARating.NC_17; break
        default :
            m.mpaaRating = MPAARating.valueOf(data.mpaa_rating)
    }
    m.runtime = data.runtime
    m.criticsConsensus = data.critics_consensus ?: ''
```

The complete listing can be found in the book source code but isn't fundamentally different from what's being shown here.

A test to prove the conversion is working is shown in the following listing.

Listing 8.18 A JUnit test to verify the JSON conversion

```
class MovieTest {
    @Test
    void testFromJSON() {
        def data = new JsonSlurper().parseText(
        new File('src/main/groovy/mjg/blazing_saddles.txt').text)
        Movie.fromJSON(data.movies[0]).with {
            assert id == 13581
            assert title == 'Blazing Saddles'
            assert year == 1974
            assert mpaaRating == MPAARating.R
            assert runtime == 93
            assert releaseDates ==
                ['theater':'1974-02-07', 'dvd':'1997-08-27']
            assert ratings['critics'].rating == 'Certified Fresh'
            assert ratings['critics'].score == 89
            assert ratings['audience'].rating == 'Upright'
            assert ratings['audience'].score == 89
            assert synopsis == ''
            assert posters.size() == 4
            assert abridgedCast.size() == 5
            assert abridgedCast[0].name == 'Cleavon Little'
            assert abridgedCast[0].id == 162693977
            assert abridgedCast[0].characters == ['Bart']
            assert links.size() == 6
        }
    }
}
```

Use Movie methods in the closure

Lessons learned (NoSQL[19])

1. NoSQL databases like MongoDB, Neo4J, and Redis are becoming quite common for specific use cases.
2. Most NoSQL databases make a Java-based API available, which can be called directly from Groovy.
3. Often a Groovy library will be available that wraps the Java API and simplifies it. Here, GMongo is used as an example.

Once the mapping works, finding all vampire movies that have a critic's consensus is as simple as the following script:

```
GMongo mongo = new GMongo()
def db = mongo.getDB('movies')
db.vampireMovies.find([critics_consensus : ~/.*/]).each { movie ->
    println Movie.fromJSON(movie)
}
```

[19] NoSQL version of Worst SQL Joke Ever Told: DBA walks into a NoSQL bar; can't find a table, so he leaves.

It's hard to be much simpler than that. Working with MongoDB[20] is just as easy as using a traditional relational database.[21]

8.6 Summary

Virtually every significant application requires persistent data. The vast majority of those are based on relational databases. In the Java world, relational persistence uses either JDBC or an object-relational mapping tool like Hibernate or JPA. This chapter reviewed both approaches and examined how Groovy can simplify them.

The Groovy `Sql` class removes most of the clutter that accompanies raw JDBC. Any code that uses JDBC directly can be significantly simplified using the `Sql` class.

Many modern applications use JPA for persistence, especially with Hibernate as the underlying API and the Spring framework to handle singletons and transactions. Just configuring such an application is a nontrivial task. On the other hand, the Grails framework handles all of it elegantly and with a minimum of effort.

Finally, many so-called NoSQL databases have a Java API. Some, like MongoDB, include a Groovy wrapper that makes working with the underlying databases simple.

---

[20] A detailed treatment of MongoDB is contained in the book *MongoDB in Action* (Manning, 2011) by Kyle Banker: www.manning.com/banker/.

[21] For some reason, none of the *Twilight* movies were returned from the "vampire" query. I thought about fixing that, and ultimately decided it wasn't a bug, but a feature.

9 RESTful web services

This chapter covers

- The REST architectural style
- Implementing REST in Java using JAX-RS
- Using a Groovy client to access RESTful services
- Hypermedia

RESTful web services dominate API design these days, because they provide a convenient mechanism for connecting client and server applications in a highly decoupled manner. Mobile applications especially use RESTful services, but a good RESTful design mimics the characteristics that made the web so successful in the first place.

After discussing REST in general, I'll talk about the server side, then about the client side, and finally the issue of hypermedia. Figures 9.1, 9.2, and 9.3 show the different technologies in this chapter.

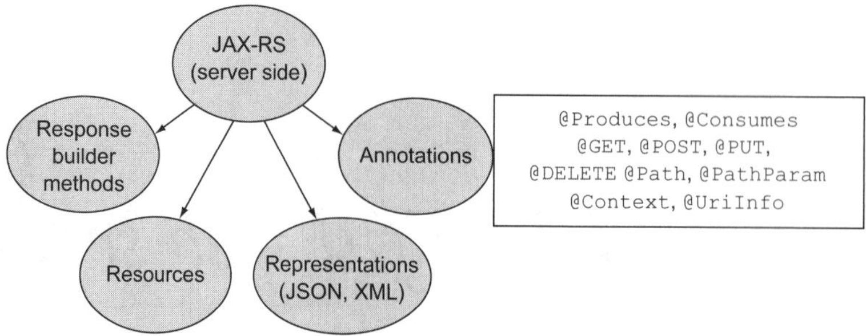

Figure 9.1 Server-side JAX-RS technologies in this chapter. JAX-RS 2.0 is annotation-based but includes builders for the responses. URIs are mapped to methods in resources, which are assigned using annotations. Resources are returned as representations using content negotiation from client headers.

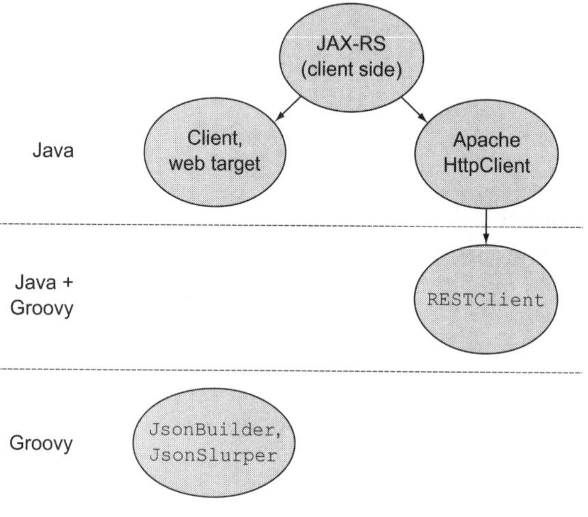

Figure 9.2 Client-side REST technologies in this chapter. Unlike JAX-RS 1.x, version 2.0 includes client classes. Apache also has a common client, which is wrapped by Groovy in the HttpBuilder project. Finally, you can use standard Groovy classes to parse requests and build responses manually.

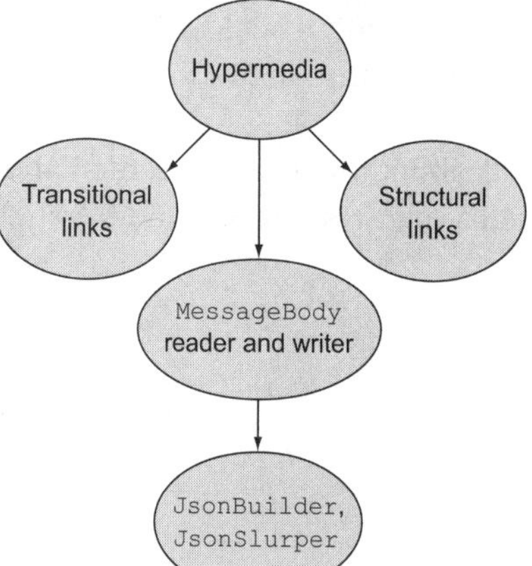

Figure 9.3 Hypermedia approaches in this chapter. Hypermedia in JAX-RS is done through transitional links in the HTTP headers, structural links in the message body, or customized responses using builders and slurpers.

9.1 The REST architecture

The term Representational State Transfer (REST) comes from the 2000 PhD thesis[1] by Roy Fielding, a person with one of the all-time great resumes.[2]

In his thesis, Fielding defines the REST architecture in terms of addressable resources and their interactions. When restricted to HTTP requests made over the web (not a requirement of the architecture, but its most common use today), RESTful web services are based on the following principles:

- *Addressable resource*—Items are accessible to clients through URIs.
- *Uniform interface*—Resources are accessed and modified using the standard HTTP verbs GET, POST, PUT, and DELETE.[3]
- *Content negotiation*—The client can request different representations of resources, usually by specifying the desired MIME type in the `Accept` header of a request.
- *Stateless services*—Interactions with resources are done through self-contained requests.

Web services based on these ideas are intended to be highly scalable and extensible, because they follow the mechanisms that make the web itself highly scalable and extensible.

Part of the scalability of a RESTful web service comes from the terms *safe* and *idempotent*:

- *Safe*—Does not modify the state of the server
- *Idempotent*—Can be repeated without causing any additional effects

GET requests are both safe and idempotent. PUT and DELETE requests are idempotent but not safe. They can be repeated (for example, if there's a network error) without making any additional changes.[4] POST requests are neither safe nor idempotent.

Another key concept is Hypermedia as the Engine of Application State, which has the truly unfortunate, unpronounceable acronym HATEOAS. Most REST advocates[5] I know simply say "hypermedia" instead.

---

1 "Architectural Styles and the Design of Network-based Software Architectures," available online at www.ics.uci.edu/~fielding/pubs/dissertation/top.htm.

2 Fielding is a cofounder of the Apache Software Foundation; was on the IETF working groups for the URI, HTTP, and HTML specifications; and helped set up some of the original web servers. I place him easily in the Top Ten of CS resumes, along with people like James Duncan Davidson (creator of the first versions of both Tomcat *and* Ant; he basically owned the 90s), Sir Timothy Berners-Lee (create the web → knighthood FTW), and Haskell Curry (whose first name is the definitive functional programming language, and whose last name is a fundamental coding technique; if your *name* is your resume, you win).

3 Some services support HEAD requests as GET requests that return headers with empty responses and OPTIONS requests as an alternate way to specify what types of requests are valid at a particular address. PATCH requests are proposed as a way to do a partial update.

4 Sometimes it's hard to picture DELETE requests as idempotent, but if you delete the same row multiple times, it's still gone.

5 Often known, believe it or not, as RESTafarians.

The principles defined in this section are architectural and are thus independent of implementation language. In the next section I'll address[6] the Java-specific specification intended to implement RESTful services, JAX-RS.

9.2 The Java approach: JAX-RS

The Java EE specification includes the Java API for RESTful Services. Version 1.18 is from JSR 311. The new version, 2.0, is an implementation of JSR 339 and was released in May of 2013.

In this section I'll implement a set of CRUD methods on a simple POJO.[7] The JAX-RS part doesn't depend on this, so I'll discuss that separately. I'll start with the basic infrastructure and then move to REST.

> **What do Java developers actually use for REST?**
>
> In this book I normally start with what Java developers use for a particular problem, then show how Groovy can help the Java implementations, and finally discuss what Groovy offers as an alternative. When I describe what Java developers typically use, I default to what the Java SE or EE specification provides.
>
> That's not the case with REST. In addition to the spec, JAX-RS, Java developers use several third-party alternatives. Among the most popular are Restlet (http://restlet.org/), RestEasy (www.jboss.org/resteasy), and Restfulie (http://restfulie.caelum.com.br/), and there are other alternatives as well.[8] It's hard at this point to know which, if any, is going to be the REST framework of choice for Java developers in a few years.[9]
>
> Therefore, I'm basing this chapter on the JAX-RS specification, even though it's not necessarily the most popular alternative. When the alternative is not blindingly obvious, the spec usually wins.[10]

The application in this section exposes a POGO called `Person` as a JAX-RS 2.0 resource. The application supports GET, POST, PUT, and DELETE operations and (eventually) supports hypermedia links.

The infrastructure for the project includes the POJO, Spock tests, and a DAO implementation based on an H2 database. While the implementations are interesting, they are ancillary to the real goal of discussing RESTful services and how Groovy can simplify their development. Therefore they will not be presented in detail in this chapter. As usual, the complete classes, including Gradle build files and tests, can be found in the book source code repository.

As a brief summary, the `Person` class is shown in the next listing.

---

6 Sorry.

7 Yes, that's a URL-driven database, and yes, that violates hypermedia principles. I promise to get to that later.

8 Spring REST doesn't follow the JAX-RS specification. Apache CXF was designed for JAX-WS, but the latest version has JAX-RS support. Apache Wink is another JAX-RS 1.x implementation.

9 If I had to bet, I'd go with Restlet. Most of the good REST people I know really like it.

10 Except when it doesn't. See, for example, JDO, which is still part of Java EE.

Listing 9.1 A `Person` POGO, used in the RESTful web service

```
class Person {
    Long id
    String first
    String last

    String toString() {
        "$first $last"
    }
}
```

The DAO interface for the `Person` objects includes finder methods, as well as methods to create, update, and delete a `Person`. It's shown in the following listing.

Listing 9.2 The DAO interface with the CRUD methods for `Person`

```
import java.util.List;

public interface PersonDAO {
    List<Person> findAll();
    Person findById(long id);
    List<Person> findByLastName(String name);
    Person create(Person p);
    Person update(Person p);
    boolean delete(long id);
}
```

The implementation of the DAO is done in Groovy using the `groovy.sql.Sql` class, just as in chapter 8 on databases. The only part that differs from that chapter is that the `id` attribute is generated by the database. Here's how to use the `Sql` class to retrieve the generated ID:

```
Person create(Person p) {
    String txt = 'insert into people(id, first, last) values(?, ?, ?)'
    def keys = sql.executeInsert txt, [null, p.first, p.last]
    p.id = keys[0][0]
    return p
}
```

The `executeInsert` method returns the collection of generated values, and in this case the new ID is found as the first element of the first row.

The Spock test for the DAO is similar to those shown in chapter 6 on testing or chapter 8 on databases. The only new part is that the `when/then` block in Spock is repeated to insert and then delete a new `Person`. When Spock sees a repeat of the `when/then` pair, it executes them sequentially. Listing 9.3 shows this test, which inserts a row representing Peter Quincy Taggart,[11] verifies that he's stored properly, and then

[11] Remember him? Commander of the NSEA Protector? "Never give up, never surrender?" That's *Galaxy Quest*, a *Star Trek* parody, but arguably one of the better *Star Trek* movies. Did you know that the designation of the Protector was NTE-3120, and that NTE stood for "Not The Enterprise"? By Grabthar's hammer, that's the kind of research you are obligated to do when you write a Groovy/Java integration book.

deletes the row. Recall that the seriously cool `old` method in Spock evaluates its argument before executing the `when` block, so it can be compared to the rest of the expression evaluated after the `when` block is done.

Listing 9.3 The Spock test method to insert and delete a new `Person`

```
def 'insert and delete a new person'() {
    Person taggart = new Person(first:'Peter Quincy', last:'Taggart')

    when:
    dao.create(taggart)

    then:
    dao.findAll().size() == old(dao.findAll().size()) + 1
    taggart.id

    when:
    dao.delete(taggart.id)

    then:
    dao.findAll().size() == old(dao.findAll().size()) - 1
}
```

Now that the preliminaries are out of the way it's time to look at the features provided by the JAX-RS API.

9.2.1 *JAX-RS resource and tests*

Moving now to the RESTful part of the application, there are several features of the JAX-RS API involved in the implementation. Here I'll use a `PersonResource` class to implement the CRUD methods.

> **COLLECTION AND ITEM RESOURCES** Normally two resources are provided: one for a collection of person instances and one for an individual person. In this case both are combined to keep the sample short.

First, each method that's tied to a particular type of HTTP request uses one of these annotations: `@GET`, `@POST`, `@PUT`, or `@DELETE`. For example, the `findAll` method can be implemented as follows:

```
@GET
public List<Person> findAll() {
    return dao.findAll();
}
```

A GET request returns the HTTP status code 200 for a successful request. The `@Produces` annotation identifies to the client the MIME type of the response. In this case I want to return JSON or XML:

```
@Produces({MediaType.APPLICATION_JSON, MediaType.APPLICATION_XML})
```

The annotation accepts an array of `MediaType` instances, which are used for content negotiation based on the `Accept` header in the incoming request.

If I want to specify the response header, JAX-RS provides a factory class called Response using the builder design pattern. Here's the implementation of the findById method that uses it:

```
@GET @Path("{id}")
@Produces({MediaType.APPLICATION_JSON, MediaType.APPLICATION_XML})
public Response findById(@PathParam("id") long id) {
    return Response.ok(dao.findById(id))
        .build();
}
```

The ok method on the Response class sets the response status code to 200. It takes an object as an argument, which is added to the response. The @PathParam annotation also converts the input ID from a string to a long automatically.

Inserting a new instance is a bit more complicated, because the newly inserted instance needs its own URI. Because in this case the generated URI will contain an ID generated by the database, the resource method is tied to HTTP POST requests, which are neither safe nor idempotent.

> **IMPLEMENTATION DETAIL** The create method returns a URL that includes the primary key from the database table. That detail is not something you want to expose to the client. Some unique identifier is required; here the ID is used for simplicity.

The new URI is added to the response as part of its Location header. The new URI is generated using the UriBuilder class from JAX-RS, based on the incoming URI:

```
UriBuilder builder =
    UriBuilder.fromUri(uriInfo.getRequestUri()).path("{id}");
```

The uriInfo reference in that expression refers to a UriInfo object injected from the application context. This is added as an attribute to the implementation:

```
@Context
private UriInfo uriInfo;
```

In general, the response from any insert method in a REST application is either "no content" or the entity itself. Here in the create method I decided to use the entity, because it includes the generated ID in case the client wants it.

Putting it all together, the create method is as follows:

```
@POST
@Consumes({MediaType.APPLICATION_JSON, MediaType.APPLICATION_XML})
@Produces({MediaType.APPLICATION_JSON, MediaType.APPLICATION_XML})
public Response create(Person person) {
    dao.create(person);
    UriBuilder builder =
        UriBuilder.fromUri(uriInfo.getRequestUri()).path("{id}");
    return Response.created(builder.build(person.getId()))
        .entity(person)
        .build();
}
```

The @POST annotation sets the HTTP status code in the response to 201.

The URL patterns for the resource are summarized as follows:

- The base resource pattern is /people. A GET request at that URL returns all the Person instances. The plural form of Person is used for this reason.
- A POST request at the same URL (/person) creates a new Person, assigns it a URL of its own, and saves it in the database.
- A sub-resource at /people/lastname/{like} uses a URL template (the like parameter) to do an SQL-like query and find all Person instances who have a last name satisfying the clause.
- A sub-resource using the URL template {id} supports a GET request that returns the Person instance with that ID.
- PUT and DELETE requests at the {id} URL update and delete Person instances, respectively.

The following listing shows the complete PersonResource class for managing Person instances.

Listing 9.4 Java resource class for Person POJO

```
@Path("/people")
public class PersonResource {
    @Context
    private UriInfo uriInfo;

    private PersonDAO dao = JdbcPersonDAO.getInstance();

    @GET
    @Produces({MediaType.APPLICATION_JSON, MediaType.APPLICATION_XML})
    public List<Person> findAll() {
        return dao.findAll();
    }

    @GET @Path("lastname/{like}")
    @Produces({MediaType.APPLICATION_JSON, MediaType.APPLICATION_XML})
    public List<Person> findByName(@PathParam("like") String like) {
        return dao.findByLastName(like);
    }

    @GET @Path("{id}")
    @Produces({MediaType.APPLICATION_JSON, MediaType.APPLICATION_XML})
    public Response findById(@PathParam("id") long id) {
        return Response.ok(dao.findById(id))
            .build();
    }

    @POST
    @Consumes({MediaType.APPLICATION_JSON, MediaType.APPLICATION_XML})
    @Produces({MediaType.APPLICATION_JSON, MediaType.APPLICATION_XML})
    public Response create(Person person) {
        dao.create(person);
        UriBuilder builder =
            UriBuilder.fromUri(uriInfo.getRequestUri()).path("{id}");
```

URI template parameter like

Access template parameter

URI template parameter ID

```
        return Response.created(builder.build(person.getId()))
            .entity(person)
            .build();
    }

    @PUT @Path("{id}")
    @Consumes({MediaType.APPLICATION_JSON, MediaType.APPLICATION_XML})
    @Produces({MediaType.APPLICATION_JSON, MediaType.APPLICATION_XML})
    public Person update(Person person) {
        dao.update(person);
        return person;
    }

    @DELETE @Path("{id}")
    @Produces({MediaType.APPLICATION_JSON, MediaType.APPLICATION_XML})
    public Response remove(@PathParam("id") long id) {
        dao.delete(id);
        return Response.noContent().build();
    }
}
```

To verify that everything is working properly, I'll again present a test class using Spock. Testing a RESTful API requires a server where the application can be deployed. The Jersey reference implementation includes a server called Grizzly for that.

The Spock test methods `setupSpec` and `shutdownSpec` are executed once each, before and after the individual tests, respectively. They therefore become the appropriate places to start and stop the server, as shown:

```
@Shared static HttpServer server

void setupSpec() {
    server = GrizzlyHttpServerFactory.createHttpServer(
        'http://localhost:1234/'.toURI(), new MyApplication())
}

void cleanupSpec() {
    server?.stop()
}
```

The `createHttpServer` method starts a server on the specified URI and deploys a RESTful application to it. The `MyApplication` class is very simple:

```
public class MyApplication extends ResourceConfig {
    public MyApplication() {
        super(PersonResource.class, JacksonFeature.class);
    }
}
```

The class `MyApplication` extends a JAX-RS class called `ResourceConfig`, which has a constructor that takes the desired resources and features as arguments. The `JacksonFeature` used here provides the mechanism to convert from `PersonResource` instances to JSON and back.[12]

---

[12] As soon as I mention JSON, I'm talking about representations, not resources. Again, I'll discuss that in section 9.5 on hypermedia.

Note the convenience of the safe-dereference operator, `?.`, used when shutting down the server. That will avoid a null pointer exception when the server fails to start properly.

The first actual test verifies that the server is up and running, using the `isStarted` method on the `HttpServer` class:

```
def 'server is running'() {
    expect: server.started
}
```

Again, the `isStarted` method is invoked using the standard Groovy idiom of accessing a property. There's no reason you couldn't call the method instead, though, if you prefer.

The rest[13] of the test methods require a client to generate the HTTP request using the proper verb. GET requests are trivial with Groovy, because you can take advantage of the `getText` method that the Groovy JDK adds to the `java.net.URL` class. So the request to retrieve all the instances could be written as

```
'http://localhost:1234/people'.toURL().text
```

While that would work, the response would then need to be parsed to get the proper information. Often that isn't a problem, but here I'm using an alternative.

The class `RESTClient` is part of the HttpBuilder (http://groovy.codehaus.org/modules/http-builder/) project. I'll discuss that further in section 9.4 on Groovy clients, but for now let me say it defines Groovy classes that wrap Java classes supplied by Apache's `HttpClient` project. The test therefore contains an attribute of type `RESTClient`, as follows:

```
RESTClient client
    new RESTClient('http://localhost:1234/', ContentType.JSON)
```

The client points to the proper endpoint, and the second argument specifies the content type for the `Accept` header in the request. A GET request using this client returns an object that can be interrogated for header properties as well as data:

```
def 'get request returns all people'() {
    when:
    def response = client.get(path: 'people')

    then:
    response.status == 200
    response.contentType == 'application/json'
    response.data.size() == 5
}
```

Other finder methods are tested similarly. To keep the tests independent, the insert and delete methods are tested together; first a person is inserted, then it's verified, and then it's deleted again. The test uses another feature of Spock: each block (`when/then/expect`, and so on) can be given a string to describe its purpose. It's not exactly behavior-driven development, but it's as close as Spock comes at the moment.

[13] Again, no pun intended.

The insert and delete test looks like the following:

```
def 'insert and delete a person'() {
    given: 'A JSON object with first and last names'
    def json = [first: 'Peter Quincy', last: 'Taggart']

    when: 'post the JSON object'
    def response = client.post(path: 'people',
        contentType: ContentType.JSON, body: json)

    then: 'number of stored objects goes up by one'
    getAll().size() == old(getAll().size()) + 1
    response.data.first == 'Peter Quincy'
    response.data.last == 'Taggart'
    response.status == 201
    response.contentType == 'application/json'
    response.headers.Location ==
        "http://localhost:1234/people/${response.data.id}"

    when: 'delete the new JSON object'
    client.delete(path: response.headers.Location)

    then: 'number of stored objects goes down by one'
    getAll().size() == old(getAll().size()) - 1
}
```

Given a JSON object representing a person, a POST request adds it to the system. The returned object holds the status code (201), the content type (application/json), the returned person object (in the `data` property), and the URI for the new resource in the `Location` header. Deleting the object is done by sending a DELETE request to the new URI and verifying that the total number of stored instances goes down by one.

Updates are done through a PUT request. To ensure that PUT requests are idempotent, the complete object needs to be specified in the body of the request. This is why PUT requests aren't normally used for inserts; the client doesn't know the ID of the newly inserted object, so POST requests are used for that instead.

The complete test is shown in the next listing.

Listing 9.5 A Spock test for the `PersonResource` with a convenient test server

```
class PersonResourceSpec extends Specification {
    @Shared static HttpServer server
    RESTClient client =
        new RESTClient('http://localhost:1234/', ContentType.JSON)

    void setupSpec() {
        server = GrizzlyHttpServerFactory.createHttpServer(
            'http://localhost:1234/'.toURI(), new MyApplication())
    }

    def 'server is running'() {
        expect: server.started
    }

    def 'get request returns all people'() {
        when:
        def response = client.get(path: 'people')
```

Client from HttpBuilder project

JSON representation

Shared server

```
    then:
    response.status == 200
    response.contentType == 'application/json'
    response.data.size() == 5
}

@Unroll
def "people/#id gives #name"() {
    expect:
    def response = client.get(path: "people/$id")
    name == "$response.data.first $response.data.last"
    response.status == 200

    where:
    id |       name                              <-- Spock data table
    1  | 'Jean-Luc Picard'
    2  | 'Johnathan Archer'
    3  | 'James Kirk'
    4  | 'Benjamin Sisko'
    5  | 'Kathryn Janeway'
}

def 'people/lastname/{like} searches for last names like'() {
    when:
    def response = client.get(path: "people/lastname/a")

    then:
    response.data.size() == 3
    response.data*.last ==~ /.*[aA].*/
}

def 'insert and delete a person'() {
    given: 'A JSON object with first and last names'
    def json = [first: 'Peter Quincy', last: 'Taggart']

    when: 'post the JSON object'
    def response = client.post(path: 'people',
        contentType: ContentType.JSON, body: json)

    then: 'number of stored objects goes up by one'
    getAll().size() == old(getAll().size()) + 1
    response.data.first == 'Peter Quincy'
    response.data.last == 'Taggart'
    response.status == 201
    response.contentType == 'application/json'
    response.headers.Location ==                        <-- Location header for inserted resource
        "http://localhost:1234/people/${response.data.id}"

    when: 'delete the new JSON object'
    client.delete(path: response.headers.Location)

    then: 'number of stored objects goes down by one'
    getAll().size() == old(getAll().size()) - 1
}

def 'can update an existing person'() {
    given:
    def kirk = client.get(path: 'people/3')
    def json = [id: 3, first:'James T.', last: 'Kirk']
```

```
        when:
        def response = client.put(path: "people/${kirk.data.id}",
            contentType: ContentType.JSON, body: json)

        then:
        "$response.data.first $response.data.last" == 'James T. Kirk'
    }

    private List getAll() {
        client.get(path: 'people').data
    }

    void cleanupSpec() {
        server?.stop()
    }
}
```

The JAX-RS annotations are easy enough to use. Building a URL-driven API with them isn't difficult. The 2.0 version of the spec also includes a client-side API, but that's not shown here.

> **Lessons learned (JAX-RS)**
>
> 1 JAX-RS 2.0 is part of the Java EE specification and, like most of the recent specs, is annotation-based.
>
> 2 It's very easy to build a hyperlink-driven database using JAX-RS.
>
> 3 Hypermedia mechanisms do exist in JAX-RS, but they're well hidden.

Instead, I want to illustrate the Groovy implementation of the same specifications, mostly to illustrate the code simplifications. After that I'll deal with the issue of hypermedia.

9.3 Implementing JAX-RS with Groovy

Groovy doesn't change JAX-RS in any fundamental way, though as usual it simplifies the implementation classes. JAX-RS is already simplifying the implementation by providing its own kind of DSL, so the Groovy modifications are minimal.

The previous section used Groovy implementations but didn't present them. Here I'll show just enough to illustrate the Groovy features.

To begin, here's the `Person` POGO. Note the `@XmlRootElement` annotation, used to control the serialization of the `Person` for the response. Normally that's used for Java API for XML Binding (JAXB), but the presence of the Jackson JSON parser causes the serialization process to produce JSON objects instead:

```
@XmlRootElement
@EqualsAndHashCode
class Person {
    Long id
    String first
    String last

    String toString() { "$first $last" }
}
```

Getters, setters, and constructors are all generated in the normal manner. The `@EqualsAndHashCode` AST transformation takes care of `equals` and `hashCode` method implementations. The `@ToString` annotation could also have been used, but the desired `toString` method is barely longer than that, so I just wrote it out.

Speaking of AST transformations, the `@Singleton` annotation is applied to the `JdbcPersonDAO` class when implemented in Groovy. That automatically implements and enforces the `singleton` property on the class by making the constructor private, adding a static `instance` variable, and so on. That class implements the same interface as before. Here's the beginning of the class:

```
@Singleton
class JdbcPersonDAO implements PersonDAO {
    static Sql sql = Sql.newInstance(
        url:'jdbc:h2:db', driver:'org.h2.Driver')

    static {
        sql.execute 'drop table if exists people'
        ...
    }
...
}
```

GROOVY AND JAVA INTERFACES Java tools prefer Java interfaces. Most Java/Groovy integration problems vanish if you use Java interfaces with Groovy implementations.

There's one slight syntax variation required by the switch from Java to Groovy. The `@Produces` and `@Consumes` annotations take a list of media types that they support. In the Java implementation this is expressed as an array, using the braces notation:

```
@Produces({MediaType.APPLICATION_JSON, MediaType.APPLICATION_XML})
```

In Groovy, braces indicate closures. Square brackets delimit a list, however, so the Groovy implementation just replaces the braces with brackets.

BRACES VS. BRACKETS Groovy uses curly braces for closures, so the literal notation to define a Java array should use square brackets for a `java.util.ArrayList` instead.

The complete `PersonResource` implementation in Groovy is shown in the next listing.

Listing 9.6 A Groovy implementation of the `PersonResource` class

```
@Path('/people')
class PersonResource {
    @Context
    private UriInfo uriInfo

    PersonDAO dao = JdbcPersonDAO.instance

    @GET
    @Produces([MediaType.APPLICATION_JSON, MediaType.APPLICATION_XML])
```

```
    List<Person> findAll() {
        dao.findAll();
    }

    @GET @Path("lastname/{like}")
    @Produces([MediaType.APPLICATION_JSON, MediaType.APPLICATION_XML])
    List<Person> findByName(@PathParam("like") String like) {
        dao.findByLastName(like);
    }

    @GET @Path("{id}")
    @Produces([MediaType.APPLICATION_JSON, MediaType.APPLICATION_XML])
    Response findById(@PathParam("id") long id) {
        Response.ok(dao.findById(id))
            .build()
    }

    @POST
    @Consumes([MediaType.APPLICATION_JSON, MediaType.APPLICATION_XML])
    @Produces([MediaType.APPLICATION_JSON, MediaType.APPLICATION_XML])
    Response create(Person person) {
        dao.create(person);
        UriBuilder builder =
            UriBuilder.fromUri(uriInfo.requestUri).path("{id}")
        Response.created(builder.build(person.id))
            .entity(person)
            .build()
    }

    @PUT @Path("{id}")
    @Consumes([MediaType.APPLICATION_JSON, MediaType.APPLICATION_XML])
    @Produces([MediaType.APPLICATION_JSON, MediaType.APPLICATION_XML])
    Person update(Person person) {
        dao.update(person)
        person
    }

    @DELETE @Path("{id}")
    Response remove(@PathParam("id") long id) {
        dao.delete(id);
        Response.noContent().build()
    }
}
```

Most discussions of JAX-RS end at this point, with a working, URL-driven database. True REST is more flexible than that, however. A RESTful service is supposed to act like the web, in that it presents a single URL to the client, which accesses it and receives additional links in return. This is known as HATEOAS, or simply hypermedia.

Lessons learned (JAX-RS with Groovy)

1. Groovy doesn't significantly change JAX-RS.
2. The real Groovy simplifications are in the POGO and DAO classes. The resource implementation is essentially the same in both languages.

Hypermedia links are exposed to clients, which consume them. JAX-RS 1.x doesn't include a client-side API. Version 2.0 does, and there's a convenient project in the Groovy ecosystem known as HttpBuilder for performing HTTP requests. Both are the subjects of the next section.

9.4 RESTful Clients

Accessing a RESTful web service involves creating an HTTP request of the proper type and adding any necessary information to the body. One of the biggest changes in JAX-RS when moving from version 1 to version 2 is the addition of a standard client API. The API includes `Client` and `WebTarget` classes, which are used as follows:

```
Client cl = ClientBuilder.newClient()
WebTarget target = cl.target('http://localhost:1234/people/3')
def resp = target.request().get(Response.class)
```

A `Client` instance is created from a `ClientBuilder`, which in turn leads to a `WebTarget`. A GET request uses the `get` method, whose argument is the data type of the returned object. This example is taken from a hypermedia test, shown in the next section.

In Groovy, the Groovy JDK makes GET requests trivial. Groovy adds the `toURL` method to `java.lang.String`, which converts a `String` into an instance of `java.net.URL`. The Groovy JDK also adds the `getText` method to `java.net.URL`. Pulling information from the web can therefore be as simple as

```
String response = 'http://localhost:1234/people/3'.toURL().text
```

Making POST, PUT, and DELETE requests is done in Groovy the same way it's done in Java, which isn't fun. Instead, client access is best done through a library.

One of the most popular HTTP libraries is the open source Apache HTTP Client library (http://hc.apache.org/httpcomponents-client-ga/index.html), which is part of the Apache HttpComponents project.

Rather than show the details of that library I'd rather focus on the corresponding Groovy project, HttpBuilder. The HttpBuilder project (http://groovy.codehaus.org/modules/http-builder/) follows the classic Groovy idiom: wrap a Java library and make it easier to use. While the documentation on the website isn't bad, I recommend looking at the test cases in the source code for guidance on how to use the API.

Like most cool projects, the source code is hosted at GitHub at https://github.com/jgritman/httpbuilder. The API includes a convenient class for REST applications called `RESTClient`, which I used in the tests in this chapter. The corresponding test class, `RESTClientTests`, shows how to access Twitter using all the standard HTTP verbs.

I used the `RESTClient` class in the `PersonResourceSpec` tests. The `RESTClient` class has a constructor that takes two arguments, the base URL and a content type:

```
RESTClient client = new RESTClient(
    'http://localhost:1234/', ContentType.JSON)
```

In this case I'm running the Grizzly test server on port 1234, and for this demo the data is in JSON form. The test for the GET method produces the following:

```
def response = client.get(path: 'people')
response.status == 200
response.contentType == 'application/json'
response.data.size() == 5
```

The `RESTClient` provides a `get` method that takes a `path` parameter. The response comes back with special properties for (most of) the typical headers. Other headers can be retrieved either by requesting the `allHeaders` property or by calling `getHeader("...")` with the required header. Any returned entity in the body of the response is in the `data` property.

See the rest[14] of the `PersonResourceSpec` class for examples of POST, PUT, and DELETE requests.

Lessons learned (REST clients)

1. JAX-RS 2.0 includes classes for building REST clients.[15]
2. The Groovy project HttpBuilder wraps the Apache HttpClient project and makes it easier to use.

Both the `RESTClient` and the JAX-RS 2.0 client are used in the test cases in the hypermedia section, which is as good a segue as any to finally discuss HATEOAS in Java.

9.5 Hypermedia

A series of resource URLs is not a RESTful web service. At best, it's a URL-driven database. Yet applications like that, which claim to be RESTful services, are all over the web.

A true[16] REST application understands that specific resource URLs may evolve, despite attempts to keep them as stable as possible. The idea therefore is to make requests that discover the subsequent URLs to follow. We're so accustomed to having a fixed API that this can be a difficult concept to adopt. Instead of knowing exactly what you're going to get back from any given request, you know how to make the first request and interrogate the result for whatever may come next. This is similar to the way we browse the web, which is no coincidence.

It does place a higher burden on the client and the server, though. The server needs to add some sort of metadata to explain what the subsequent resources are

14 Again, sorry. At some point (and that may already have happened), when I say, "No pun intended," you're simply not going to believe me.

15 The JAX-RS client classes are very easy to use, too, which is unfortunate when you're trying to show how cool Groovy is, but helpful for users. Oh well.

16 The word *true* here is defined as "at least trying to follow the principles in Roy Fielding's thesis."

and how to access them, and the client needs to read those responses and interpret them correctly.

This section will illustrate the ways you can add links to the service responses. I'll start by showing an example from a public API, then demonstrate how to add links to the HTTP response headers or to the response bodies, and finally demonstrate how to customize the output however you want.

9.5.1 A simple example: Rotten Tomatoes

As a simple example, consider the API provided by the movie review website Rotten Tomatoes used in chapter 8 on Groovy with databases. The Rotten Tomatoes API only supports GET requests, so it isn't a full RESTful service.[17]

Using the site's URL-based API to query for movies including the word *trek* looks like this:

```
api.rottentomatoes.com/api/public/v1.0/movies.json?q=trek&apikey=3...
```

Out of the resulting 151 (!) movies,[18] if I select *Star Trek Into Darkness*, I get a JSON object that looks like the following (with a lot of parts elided):

```
{
    "id": "771190753",
    "title": "Star Trek Into Darkness",
    "year": 2013,
    ...,
    "synopsis": "The Star Trek franchise continues ...",
    ...,
    "links": {
       "self": "http://api.rottentomatoes.com/.../771190753.json",
       "cast": "http://api.rottentomatoes.com/.../771190753/cast.json",
       "clips": "http://api.rottentomatoes.com/.../771190753/clips.json",
       "reviews": "http://api.rottentomatoes.com/.../771190753/reviews.json",
       "similar": "http://api.rottentomatoes.com/.../771190753/similar.json"
    }
}
```

The movie object (a resource using a JSON representation) includes an entry called `links`, which itself is a map of keys and values. The keys in the `links` objects all point to additional resources, such as a full cast listing or reviews.

The Rotten Tomatoes service adds links to the individual resources rather than appending them to the response headers. The site uses its own format rather than

[17] RESTful services that only support GET can be called GETful services. If they're stateless, too, doesn't that make them FORGETful services? Thank you, thank you. I'll be here all week. Try the veal, and don't forget to tip your waitresses.

[18] Including one called, I kid you not, *Star Trek versus Batman*. The Enterprise goes back in time to the 1960s and gets taken over by the Joker and Catwoman. Seriously.

some other standard.[19] It also handles content negotiation by embedding the ".json" string in the URL itself.

The client, of course, needs to know all of that, but by including a `links` section in the response the server is identifying exactly what's expected next. The client can simply present those links to the user, or it can try to place them in context, which requires additional understanding.

Generating a good client for a hypermedia-based RESTful service is not a trivial task.

Notice one interesting point: the entire API uses JSON to express the objects. So far in this chapter I've used the term *resource* to represent not only the server-side object exposed to the client, but also how it's expressed. Formally, the term *representation* is used to describe the form of the resource.

REPRESENTATION A representation is an immutable, self-descriptive, stateless snapshot of a resource, which may contain links to other resources.

The most common representations are XML and JSON, with JSON becoming almost ubiquitous.

The Richardson maturity model: a rigged demo

The Richardson Maturity Model (RMM) is based on a 2008 presentation made by Leonard Richardson, who described multiple levels of REST adoption.

RMM has four levels, numbered from zero to three:

- *Level 0: Plain old XML (POX) over HTTP*—HTTP is merely a transport protocol, and the service is essentially remote procedure calls using it. Sounds a lot like SOAP, doesn't it? That's no accident.
- *Level 1: Addressable resources*—Each URI corresponds to a resource on the server side.
- *Level 2: Uniform interface*—The API utilizes only the HTTP verbs GET, PUT, POST, and DELETE (plus maybe OPTIONS and TRACE).
- *Level 3: Hypermedia*—The representation of the response contains links defining additional steps in the process. The server may even define custom MIME types to specify how the additional metadata is included.

Now, honestly, I have no objections to this model. It's fundamental to Roy Fielding's thesis to include all of it; you're not really adopting REST unless you have hypermedia, too.

The word *maturity*, however, carries a lot of emotional baggage. Who wants their implementation to be less mature? It also can't be a coincidence that SOAP is considered maturity level 0. The model is fine, but there's no need to load it down with judgmental overtones that make it feel like a rigged demo.

[19] Attempts at standardizing JSON links include www.subbu.org/blog/2008/10/generalized-linking and www.mnot.net/blog/2011/11/25/linking_in_json.

Transitional links

```
HTTP/1.1 200 OK
Link: <http://localhost:1234/people/2>; rel="prev"
Link: <http://localhost:1234/people/3>; rel="self"
Link: <http://localhost:1234/people/4>; rel="next"
Content-Type: application/json
Date: Thu, 11 Apr 2013 16:08:47 GMT
Content-Length: 257

{"id":3,"mrst":"James","last":"Kirk",
    "prev":{"params":{"rel":"prev"},"href":"http://localhost:1234/people/2"},
    "self":{"params":{"rel":"self"},"href":"http://localhost:1234/people/3"},
    "next":{"params":{"rel":"next"},"href":"http://localhost:1234/people/4"}}
```

Structural links

Figure 9.4 Transitional links appear in the HTTP response headers, while structural links are part of the response objects. In each case the links can be used to access other resources from this one.

Hypermedia[20] in JAX-RS works through links, which come in two types:

- Transitional links in HTTP headers
- Structural links embedded in the response

Figure 9.4 shows both in a single HTTP response.

Version 2.0 of the JAX-RS specification supports transitional links using the `Link` and `LinkBuilder` classes, and structural links using a special JAXB serializer.

To illustrate both, I'll continue with the `Person` example from earlier by adding links to each instance. Each person has three possible links:

- A `self` link, containing the URL for that person
- A `prev` link, pointing to the person with an ID one less than the current person
- A `next` link, pointing to the person with an ID one greater than the current person

This is a rather contrived case, but it has the advantage of simplicity.

First I'll add the links to the HTTP headers and show how to use them. Then I'll use structural links instead, using the JAXB serializer. Finally, I'll take control of the output generation process and customize the output writer using Groovy's `JsonBuilder`.

9.5.2 *Adding transitional links*

To create transitional links, the JAX-RS API starts with the inner class `Response.ResponseBuilder` in the `javax.ws.rs.core` package. `ResponseBuilder` has three relevant methods:

```
public abstract Response.ResponseBuilder link(String uri, String rel)
public abstract Response.ResponseBuilder link(URI uri, String rel)
public abstract Response.ResponseBuilder links(Link... link)
```

---

[20] Believe it or not, neither the words hypermedia nor HATEOAS *appears at all* in the JSR 339 specification. I have no explanation for this.

The first two add a single `Link` header to the HTTP response. The third adds a series of headers to the response. Here's an example from the `PersonResource` class:

```
@GET @Produces(MediaType.APPLICATION_JSON)
Response findAll() {
    def people = dao.findAll();
    Response.ok(people).link(uriInfo.requestUri, 'self').build()
}
```

The `link` method in this case uses the request URI as the first argument and sets the `rel` property to `self`. The corresponding test accesses the link as follows:

```
def 'get request returns all people'() {
    when:
    def response = client.get(path: 'people')

    then:
    response.status == 200
    response.contentType == 'application/json'
    response.headers.Link ==
        '<http://localhost:1234/people>; rel="self"'
}
```

This example returns only a single `Link` header. For multiple links (for example, the three transitional links `prev`, `next`, and `self` for each individual person), the method `getHeaders('Link')` retrieves them all.

In the `PersonResource` the links are set with a private method, shown in the next listing.

Listing 9.7 Setting `prev`, `self`, and `next` link headers for each person

```
private Link[] getLinks(long id) {
    long minId = dao.minId                          Getter methods for
    long maxId = dao.maxId                          min and max IDs
    UriBuilder builder = UriBuilder.fromUri(uriInfo.requestUri)
    Link self = Link.fromUri(builder.build()).rel('self').build()
    String uri = builder.build().toString() - "/$id"      Subtract to
    switch (id) {                                         get base URI
    case minId:
        Link next = Link.fromUri("${uri}/${id + 1}").rel('next').build()
        return [self, next]
    case maxId:
        Link prev = Link.fromUri("${uri}/${id - 1}").rel('prev').build()
        return [prev, self]
    default:
        Link next = Link.fromUri("${uri}/${id + 1}").rel('next').build()
        Link prev = Link.fromUri("${uri}/${id - 1}").rel('prev').build()
        return [prev, self, next]
    }
}
```

So-called "self" links are generated for each person. Next and previous links are generated for those elements between the first and last. The links themselves are simply generated by string manipulation.

Adding the links to the resource is done with the links method:

```
Response findById(@PathParam("id") long id) {
    Person p = dao.findById(id)
    Response.ok(p)
        .links(getLinks(id))
        .build()
}
```

It turns out that converting the Link headers into something useful isn't simple with the RESTClient. In this case the JAX-RS Client class works better. The Client class has a method called getLink, which takes a string argument, in which the string is the relation type. That method returns an instance of the javax.ws.rs.core.Link class, which corresponds to specification RFC 5988, Web Linking, of the IETF.

I'll demonstrate the hypermedia capability by walking through the links one by one in a client. The following listing is a JUnit test case, written in Groovy, that accesses the next links.

Listing 9.8 Walking through the data using link headers

```
@Test
void testNextAndPreviousHeaders() {
    Client cl = ClientBuilder.newClient()
    int id = 1
    WebTarget target = cl.target("http://localhost:1234/people/$id")
    def resp = target.request().get(Response.class)
    def next = resp.getLink('next').uri
    assert next.toString()[-1] == (++id).toString()
    println 'following next links...'
    while (next) {
        println "Accessing $next"
        target = cl.target(next)
        resp = target.request().get(Response.class)
        next = resp.getLink('next')?.uri
        if (next)
            assert next.toString()[-1] == (++id).toString()
    }
    println 'following prev links...'
    def prev = resp.getLink('prev').uri
    assert prev.toString()[-1] == (--id).toString()
    while (prev) {
        println "Accessing $prev"
        target = cl.target(prev)
        resp = target.request().get(Response.class)
        prev = resp.getLink('prev')?.uri
        if (prev)
            assert prev.toString()[-1] == (--id).toString()
    }
    cl.close()
}
```

Annotations: JAX-RS 2.0 client; Use rel to return link and extract URI; Following the link; Last char should be proper ID

The client uses the `getLink` method with the relation type (`next` or `prev`), which returns a `Link` instance. The `getUri` method then returns an instance of `java.net.URI`, which can be followed by the client on the next iteration.[21]

If you would rather put the links in the body of the response, you need a different approach, as described in the next section.

9.5.3 Adding structural links

Structural links in JAX-RS are instances of the `Link` class inside the entity itself. Converting them to XML or JSON then requires a special serializer, which is provided by the API.

Here's the `Person` class, expanded to hold the `self`, `next`, and `prev` links as attributes:

```
@XmlRootElement
@EqualsAndHashCode
class Person {
    Long id
    String first
    String last

    @XmlJavaTypeAdapter(JaxbAdapter)
    Link prev

    @XmlJavaTypeAdapter(JaxbAdapter)
    Link self

    @XmlJavaTypeAdapter(JaxbAdapter)
    Link next
}
```

The `prev`, `self`, and `next` links are instances of the `javax.ws.rs.core.Link` class, as before. `Link.JaxbAdapter` is an inner class that tells JAXB how to serialize the links.

Setting the values of the link references is done in the resource, this time using an interesting Groovy mechanism:

```
Response findById(@PathParam("id") long id) {
    Person p = dao.findById(id)
    getLinks(id).each { link ->
        p."${link.rel}" = link
    }
}
```

The same `getLinks` private method is used as in the headers section, but this time the links are added to the `Person` instance. By calling `link.rel` (which calls the `getRel` method) and injecting the result into a string, the effect is to call `p.self`, `p.next`, or `p.prev`, as the case may be. In each case, that will call the associated setter method and assign the attribute to the link on the right-hand side.

---

[21] I have to mention that this is probably one of the only times in the last decade that I really could have used a `do/while` loop. Ironically, that's just about the only Java construct not supported by Groovy.

A test of the structural links using the `RESTClient` looks like this:

```
def 'structural and transitional links for kirk are correct'() {
    when:
    def response = client.get(path: 'people/3')

    then:
    'James Kirk' == "$response.data.first $response.data.last"
    response.getHeaders('Link').each { println it }
    assert response.data.prev.href == 'http://localhost:1234/people/2'
    assert response.data.self.href == 'http://localhost:1234/people/3'
    assert response.data.next.href == 'http://localhost:1234/people/4'
}
```

The response wraps a `Person` instance, accessed by calling `getData`. Then the individual links are retrieved as the `prev`, `self`, and `next` properties. The result is a `Link` instance whose `getHref` method can be used to verify the links.

There's only one problem, and it's more of a nuisance than anything else. In the Rotten Tomatoes example at the beginning of the hypermedia section, the links were not top-level attributes of the movies. Instead, each movie representation contained a JSON object whose key was `links`, and which contained the list of individual links and relations. Here's the snippet from the Rotten Tomatoes response:

```
"links": {
    "self": "http://api.rottentomatoes.com/.../771190753.json",
    "cast": "http://api.rottentomatoes.com/.../771190753/cast.json",
    "clips": "http://api.rottentomatoes.com/.../771190753/clips.json",
    "reviews": "http://api.rottentomatoes.com/.../771190753/reviews.json",
    "similar": "http://api.rottentomatoes.com/.../771190753/similar.json"
}
```

In the JAX-RS approach using the serializer, the relation is the attribute name. What if I want to make a collection of links as shown in the movie example? For that I need to take control of the serialization process.

9.5.4 Using a JsonBuilder to control the output

To customize output generation, JAX-RS includes an interface called `javax.ws.rs.ext.MessageBodyWriter<T>`. This interface is the contract for converting a Java type into a stream. It contains three methods to be implemented.

The first method is called `isWriteable`, and it returns true for types supported by this writer. For the `Person` class the implementation is simple:

```
boolean isWriteable(Class<?> type, Type genericType,
       Annotation[] annotations, MediaType mediaType) {
    type == Person && mediaType == MediaType.APPLICATION_JSON_TYPE
}
```

The method returns true only for `Person` instances and only if the specified media type is JSON.

The second method is called `getSize`, and it's deprecated in JAX-RS 2.0. Its implementation is supposed to return -1:

```
long getSize(Person t, Class<?> type, Type genericType,
        Annotation[] annotations, MediaType mediaType) {
    return -1;
}
```

The `writeTo` method does all the work. Here I use `groovy.json.JsonBuilder` to generate the output in the form I want, as shown in the following listing.

Listing 9.9 Using a `JsonBuilder` to produce nested links

```
void writeTo(Person t, Class<?> type, Type genericType,
        Annotation[] annotations, MediaType mediaType,
        MultivaluedMap<String, Object> httpHeaders,
        OutputStream entityStream) throws IOException,
    WebApplicationException {
    def builder = new JsonBuilder()                    // Using a Groovy JsonBuilder
    builder {
        id t.id
        first t.first
        last t.last
        links {                                        // Nesting links
            if (t.prev) {
                prev t.prev.toString()
            }
            self t.self.toString()
            if (t.next) {
                next t.next.toString()
            }
        }
    }
    entityStream.write(builder.toString().bytes)       // Conversion to bytes to write to the output stream
}
```

One special quirk is notable here. The method calls `toString` on the individual `Link` instances. As the JavaDocs for `Link` make clear, the `toString` and `valueOf(String)` methods in `Link` are used to convert to and from strings.

The `MessageBodyReader` interface is quite similar. In that case there are only two methods: `isReadable` and `readFrom`. The implementation of `isReadable` is the same as the `isWriteable` method:

```
public boolean isReadable(Class<?> type, Type genericType,
        Annotation[] annotations, MediaType mediaType) {
    type == Person && mediaType == MediaType.APPLICATION_JSON_TYPE
}
```

The `readFrom` method uses a `JsonSlurper` to convert string input into a `Person`, as shown in the next listing.

Listing 9.10 Parsing a `Person` instance from a string

```
public Person readFrom(Class<Person> type, Type genericType,
        Annotation[] annotations, MediaType mediaType,
        MultivaluedMap<String, String> httpHeaders,
```

```
        InputStream entityStream)
            throws IOException, WebApplicationException {

    def json = new JsonSlurper().parseText(entityStream.text)
    Person p = new Person(id:json.id, first:json.first, last:json.last)
    if (json.links) {
        p.prev = Link.valueOf(json.links.prev)
        p.self = Link.valueOf(json.links.self)
        p.next = Link.valueOf(json.links.next)
    }
    return p
}
```

The `readFrom` method uses the `JsonSlurper`'s `parseText` method to convert the input text data into a JSON object and then instantiates a `Person` based on the resulting properties. If links exist in the body, they're converted using the `valueOf` method.

To use the `MessageBodyWriter`, I need to add an `@Provider` annotation to the implementation class and make sure it's loaded in the application. The latter is done by adding the provider to the `MyApplication` class:

```
public class MyApplication extends ResourceConfig {
    public MyApplication() {
        super(PersonResource.class, PersonProvider.class,
              JacksonFeature.class);
    }
}
```

In this case both the `PersonProvider` and the `JacksonFeature` are used. The `Person` provider converts individual `Person` instances to JSON, and the `JacksonFeature` handles collections. A test of the resulting structure looks like this:

```
def 'transitional links for kirk are correct'() {
    when:
    def response = client.get(path: 'people/3')

    then:
    'James Kirk' == "$response.data.first $response.data.last"
    Link.valueOf(response.data.links.prev).uri ==
         'http://localhost:1234/people/2'.toURI()
    Link.valueOf(response.data.links.self).uri ==
         'http://localhost:1234/people/3'.toURI()
    Link.valueOf(response.data.links.next).uri ==
         'http://localhost:1234/people/4'.toURI()
}
```

The response body now has a `links` element, which contains `prev`, `self`, and `next` as child elements.

Lessons learned (hypermedia)

1 JAX-RS mostly ignores hypermedia but does make some methods available for it.
2 Transitional link headers are added by the `link` and `links` methods in `ResponseBuilder`.

> ***(continued)***
>
> 3 Structural links in the body are added through a special JAXB annotation.
> 4 You can manage the parsing and response generation stages yourself by writing a provider class that implements `MessageBodyReader` and/or `MessageBodyWriter`.

Between the transitional links, the structural links with the JAXB serializer, and the Groovy `JsonBuilder`, hopefully you now have enough mechanisms to implement hypermedia links in any way your application requires. The choice of which to use is largely a matter of style, but there are some guidelines:

- Structural links are contained in the response, so the client has to parse the response to get them.
- Transitional links are in the HTTP headers. That gets them out of the response but forces the client to parse the HTTP response headers to retrieve them.
- Custom links can be anything, so they must be clearly documented.

Examples of all three approaches can be found on the web.

9.6 Other Groovy approaches

There are three other approaches in the Groovy ecosystem that I should mention for RESTful web services. Here I'll specifically discuss groovlets, the Ratpack project, and Grails.

9.6.1 Groovlets

Groovlets are discussed in chapter 10 on web applications as well as the simple example in chapter 2, but essentially they're groovy scripts that receive HTTP requests and return HTTP responses. Groovlets contain many implicit variables, including `request`, `response`, `session`, and `params` (to hold input variables).

In a groovlet you can use the `getMethod` method on the request object to determine if the request is a GET, PUT, POST, or DELETE. Then you can build the response accordingly.

The book source code has a project in chapter 10 called `SongService`, which demonstrates how to use a groovlet. The service itself is a groovlet, which is shown in the following listing.

Listing 9.11 A groovlet that processes and produces XML

```
def dao = SongDAO.instance

switch (request.method) {
case 'GET' :
    if (params?.id) {
        def s = dao.getSong(params.id)
        html.song(id:s.id) {          <-- Implicit MarkupBuilder html
```

```
                title s.title
                artist s.artist
                year s.year
            }
        } else {
            def songs = dao.getAllSongs()
            html.songs {
                songs.each { s ->
                    song(id:s.id) {
                        title s.title
                        artist s.artist
                        year s.year
                    }
                }
            }
        }
        break
    case 'POST' :
        def data = new XmlSlurper().parse(request.reader)
        def s = new Song(id:data.@id,title:data.title,
            artist:data.artist,year:data.year)
        def exists = dao.exists(s.id)

        if (!exists) {
            dao.addSong s
            response.addHeader 'Location',
               "http://localhost:8080/GroovySongs/SongService.groovy?id=${s.id}"
               out.print "${s.title} added with id ${s.id}"
        } else {
            out.print "${s.title} already exists"
        }
        break
    case 'DELETE' :
        dao.deleteSong params.id
        out.print "${params.id} deleted"
        break
    default:
        print 'Only GET, POST, and DELETE supported'
}
```

Converting request data to XML

The groovlet uses `request.method` in a `switch` statement to determine the correct implementation. Then it uses a built-in `MarkupBuilder` called `html` to produce XML, and an `XmlSlurper` to convert XML to song instances. Now that groovlets have a built-in `JsonBuilder` as well,[22] JSON could easily be used instead.

This approach is pretty low-level, but it may be useful for quick-and-dirty implementations or if you need such detailed control.

---

[22] That's my great contribution to Groovy—the implicit `json` object in groovlets, which I not only added, but with which I managed to break the build in the process. Sigh. If you're interested, details can be found at http://mng.bz/5Vn6.

9.6.2 Ratpack

The second alternative is to look at the Ratpack project (https://github.com/ratpack/ratpack). Ratpack is a Groovy project that follows the same ideas as the Sinatra[23] project in the Ruby world. Ratpack is called a "micro" framework, in that you write simple Groovy scripts that govern how to handle individual requests.

For example, a simple Ratpack script looks like this:

```
get("/person/:personid") {
    "This is the page for person ${urlparams.personid}"
}

post("/submit") {
    // handle form submission here
}

put("/some-resource") {
    // create the resource
}

delete("/some-resource") {
    // delete the resource
}
```

The project shows a lot of promise, and Sinatra is very popular in the Ruby world, so it's probably worth a look. The project has recently come under the control of Luke Daley, who is a major player in the Groovy world, so I expect significant improvements soon.

9.6.3 Grails and REST

Finally, Grails has REST capabilities as well. For example, in a Grails application you can edit the `URLMappings.groovy` file as follows:

```
static mappings = {
    "/product/$id?"(resource:"product")
}
```

The result is that GET, POST, PUT, and DELETE requests for products will be directed to the `show`, `save`, `update`, and `delete` actions in the `ProductController`, respectively. Grails also automatically parses and generates XML and/or JSON, as desired.

There's also a JAX-RS plugin available for Grails. At the moment it's based on JAX-RS version 1, but the implementation can use either the Jersey reference implementation or Restlets. Of course, once again, nothing is said about hypermedia in either case, though anything you can do in Groovy you can, of course, do in Grails as well.

REST capabilities are a major design goal of Grails 3.0, so by then the situation will no doubt change.

---

[23] Sinatra, Ratpack, get it? If nothing else, it's a great name.

9.7 Summary

The topic of RESTful web services is very hot these days, for good reason. The REST architecture enables developers to build flexible, highly decoupled applications that take advantage of the same features that made the web itself so successful.

In the Java world many libraries are available for implementing the REST architecture. This chapter focused on the JAX-RS 2.0 specification and how Groovy can be used with it. In addition to the basic URL-driven database, hypermedia can be implemented using transitional links in the HTTP headers, structural links in the entity bodies, or even through a Groovy `JsonBuilder`. Hopefully some combination of techniques in this chapter will enable you to build the service you want.

10 Building and testing web applications

This chapter covers

- Groovy servlets and `ServletCategory`
- Groovlets
- Unit and integration testing of web apps
- The Groovy killer app, Grails

While Java on the desktop has its adherents, Java found a true home on the server side. Java's growth and adoption in the early days neatly follow that of the web itself. It's a rare Java developer who hasn't at least worked on a web application.

In this chapter I'm going to look at modern web application development and where Groovy can make the process simpler and easier. Sometimes Groovy just simplifies the code. Other times it provides helpful testing tools, like Gradle and HTTPBuilder. Finally, there's the most famous framework in the Groovy ecosystem, Grails. I'll review them all and try to place them in the overall context of web applications.

Figure 10.1 is a guide to the technologies discussed in this chapter.

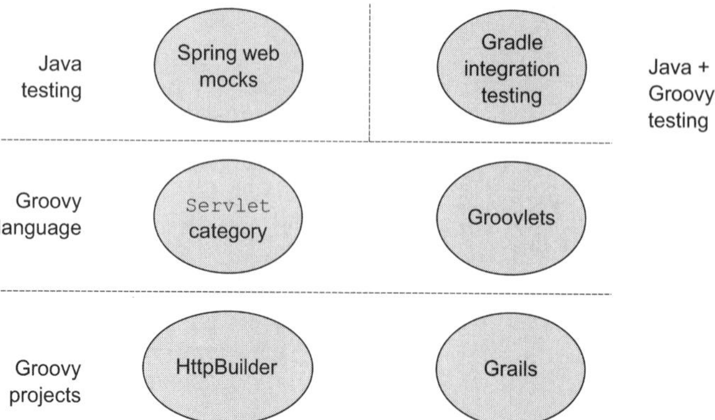

Figure 10.1 Guide to the technologies in this chapter. Spring provides mock objects for testing that are also used in Grails. Using plugins and some configuration, Gradle builds can do integration testing of web applications. The `ServletCategory` class makes session, request, and other objects easier to use. Groovlets are a quick way to build simple applications. Finally, the HTTPBuilder project provides a programmatic web client, and Grails applications use Groovy DSLs and elegant metaprogramming to combine Spring and Hibernate in a standard convention-over-configuration framework.

10.1 Groovy servlets and ServletCategory

Groovy doesn't add a lot to basic servlet development, but the standard library does provide a category class that illustrates what Groovy's metaprogramming can do. The following listing shows a trivial servlet, `HelloGroovyServlet.groovy`, part of a web application implemented in Groovy.

Listing 10.1 A simple servlet implemented in Groovy

```
class HelloGroovyServlet extends HttpServlet {
    void doGet(HttpServletRequest req, HttpServletResponse resp)
        throws ServletException, IOException {
        resp.writer.print 'Hello from a Groovy Servlet!'
    }
}
```

Other than the normal Groovy simplifications (omitting the word `public`, lack of semicolons, use of `writer` rather than `getWriter()`, and the optional parentheses on `print`), this isn't much different from a Java implementation. Use Groovy if you prefer the slightly shorter code, but really the choice of language is a matter of style.

What Groovy does provide is a category class to simplify the code even further. Category classes are an example of Groovy's metaprogramming capabilities. They show how to add methods to existing classes in a specified block of code, unlike using the metaclass object to add them everywhere in your program. If you ever wanted to understand categories, `ServletCategory` is a great, extremely simple, useful example.

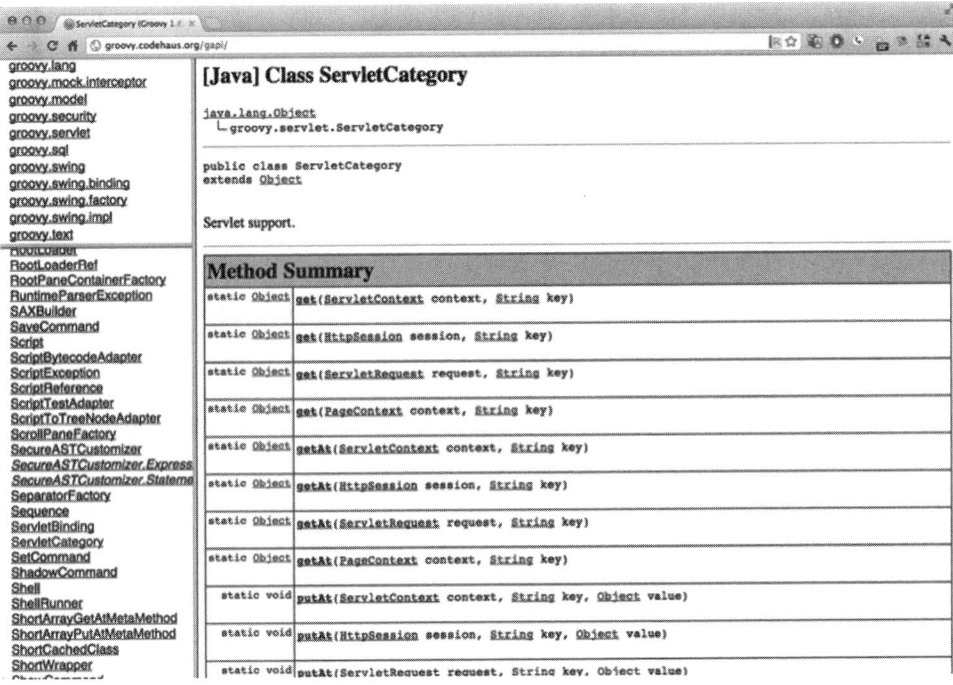

Figure 10.2 The GroovyDocs for `ServletCategory`. Each method is static and is added to the class listed in the first argument.

> **CATEGORIES** Use a Groovy category to add methods to existing classes when you only need those methods under specific circumstances. Category methods are only available in a `use` block.

Figure 10.2 shows a sample of the GroovyDocs for the `groovy.servlet.ServletCategory` class.

A Groovy category consists of static methods having one or more arguments. The first argument to the method is the class that receives the method. In `ServletCategory` there are only four methods, with lots of overloads (see table 10.1).

Table 10.1 The `ServletCategory` methods for different scopes

Method Name	First Argument
`get(arg, String key)`	`ServletContext`, `HttpSession`, `ServletRequest`, `PageContext`
`getAt(arg, String key)`	Same as above
`putAt(arg, String key, Object value)`	Same as above
`set(arg, String key, Object value)`	Same as above

See a pattern? The job of this category is to make it easy to add attributes at page scope (`PageContext`), request scope (`ServletRequest`), session scope (`HttpSession`), and application scope (`ServletContext`). Remember that in Groovy all operators correspond to methods. In this case, the `get` and `set` methods correspond to the dot operator, and the `getAt` and `putAt` methods implement the array subscript operator. Before I show an example, take a look at a portion of the actual implementation class, `groovy.servlet.ServletCategory`, in the following listing, implemented in Java.

Listing 10.2 Methods for `HttpSession` from `groovy.servlet.ServletCategory`

```
public class ServletCategory {

    public static Object get(HttpSession session, String key) {
        return session.getAttribute(key);
    }
    ...
    public static Object getAt(HttpSession session, String key) {
        return session.getAttribute(key);
    }
    ...
    public static void set(HttpSession session,
        String key, Object value) {
        session.setAttribute(key, value);
    }
    ...
    public static void putAt(HttpSession session,
        String key, Object value) {
        session.setAttribute(key, value);
    }
}
```

The first interesting thing to note is that this class is written in Java (!), even though it's being used in Groovy. When overloading operators, Groovy doesn't care which language you use to implement the methods, only that you use the operators that delegate to the methods in Groovy. In this case, I don't even plan to use the methods directly. Instead, I'm using the dot operator and/or the array subscript notation to invoke them implicitly.

The other important detail here is that all the methods are delegating to either the `getAttribute` or `setAttribute` method. The effect is that either the dot operator or the subscript operator can be used to add attributes to the page, request, session, or application scope.

> **SERVLETCATEGORY** Whether you use `ServletCategory` or not, its combination of metaprogramming and operator overloading make it an excellent example of how Groovy helps Java.

Categories in Groovy 2.0

Groovy 2.0 introduced an alternative syntax for defining categories. In the `ServletCategory` discussed in this section, the category class contains static methods whose first argument is the class being modified. In the new notation you can use annotations and instance methods instead.

As an example, consider formatting numbers as currency. The `java.text.NumberFormat` class has a method called `getCurrencyInstance`, which has both a no-arg method that formats for the current locale and an overloaded version that takes a `java.util.Locale` argument. The classic way to add an `asCurrency` method to `Number` that employs the currency formatter is

```
import java.text.NumberFormat

class CurrencyCategory {
    static String asCurrency(Number amount) {
        NumberFormat.currencyInstance.format(amount)
    }

    static String asCurrency(Number amount, Locale loc) {
        NumberFormat.getCurrencyInstance(loc).format(amount)
    }
}

use(CurrencyCategory) {
    def amount = 1234567.89012
    println amount.asCurrency()
    println amount.asCurrency(Locale.GERMANY)
    println amount.asCurrency(new Locale('hin','IN'))
}
```

The new way to implement a category uses the `@Category` annotation, which takes the class to be modified as an argument. Then instance methods are used inside the category, and the `this` reference refers to the object where the category is invoked. The analogous implementation for the currency category is

```
import java.text.NumberFormat

@Category(Number)
class AnnotationCurrencyCategory {
    String asCurrency() {
        NumberFormat.currencyInstance.format(this)
    }

    String asCurrency(Locale loc) {
        NumberFormat.getCurrencyInstance(loc).format(this)
    }
}

Number.mixin AnnotationCurrencyCategory
def amount = 1234567.89012
println amount.asCurrency()
println amount.asCurrency(Locale.GERMANY)
println amount.asCurrency(new Locale('hin','IN'))
```

(continued)

Note also the use of the `mixin` method to add the category to the `Number` class.

Presumably, if the `ServletCategory` was being implemented now, it would use the annotation approach. The result is the same either way, of course.[1]

An example will make this clear. The next listing shows a class called `HelloNameServlet`, implemented in Groovy, which receives a `name` parameter and replies with the standard welcome.

Listing 10.3 The `HelloNameServlet` class, which uses the `ServletCategory`

```
import groovy.servlet.ServletCategory;

import javax.servlet.ServletException
import javax.servlet.http.HttpServlet
import javax.servlet.http.HttpServletRequest
import javax.servlet.http.HttpServletResponse

class HelloNameServlet extends HttpServlet {
    void doGet(HttpServletRequest request, HttpServletResponse response)
        throws ServletException, IOException {
        def session = request.session                  // Get session from request
        use (ServletCategory) {                        // Make category methods available
            request.name = 'Hello, ' +
                (request.getParameter('name') ?: 'World')   // Delegate to get/set and
            session['count'] = (session.count ?: 0) + 1     // getAt/putAt methods
        }
        request.getRequestDispatcher('hello.jsp')
            .forward(request,response)
    }
}
```

This class works with attributes in both the request and the session. After getting the session from the request (which is standard "property access means get method" style, not the category), the use block defines the region where the category is active. Inside the `use` block, a `name` attribute is added to the `request` using the dot notation, whose value is either supplied by the user in the form of a parameter, or consists of the default value `World`. Next, a `count` attribute is placed in the session; its value is either incremented from its existing value or set to `1` if it doesn't already exist.

The test class, `HelloNameServletTest`, is shown in the next listing. It uses the Spring API mock objects to test the `doGet` method both with and without a supplied name.

Listing 10.4 The `HelloNameServletTest` class, which uses Spring's mock objects

```
import static org.junit.Assert.*;

import org.junit.Test;
import org.springframework.mock.web.MockHttpServletRequest;
```

[1] The book source code includes the two ways of doing the currency category as well as a test case.

```
import org.springframework.mock.web.MockHttpServletResponse;
import org.springframework.mock.web.MockHttpSession;

class HelloNameServletTest {
    HelloNameServlet servlet = new HelloNameServlet()

    @Test
    void testDoGetWithNoName() {
        MockHttpServletRequest request = new MockHttpServletRequest()
        MockHttpServletResponse response = new MockHttpServletResponse()
        MockHttpSession session = new MockHttpSession()
        request.session = session
        servlet.doGet(request, response)
        assert 'hello.jsp' == response.forwardedUrl
        assert request.getAttribute("name") == 'Hello, World'
        assert session.getAttribute("count") == 1
    }

    @Test
    void testDoGetWithName() {
        MockHttpServletRequest request = new MockHttpServletRequest()
        MockHttpServletResponse response = new MockHttpServletResponse()
        MockHttpSession session = new MockHttpSession()
        request.session = session
        request.setParameter('name','Dolly')
        servlet.doGet(request, response)
        assert 'hello.jsp' == response.forwardedUrl
        assert request.getAttribute("name") == 'Hello, Dolly'
        assert session.getAttribute("count") == 1
    }
}
```

The `ServletCategory` isn't needed in the tests, because I'm already using mock objects rather than the Servlet API classes. Note that the tests check both the `request` and `session` attributes and the forwarded URL from the `doGet` method. The `ServletCategory` class is a simple example of how to use Groovy's metaprogramming capabilities to simplify an API.

As a simple alternative to normal servlet development, Groovy provides groovlets.

10.2 Easy server-side development with groovlets

Groovlets are groovy scripts that are executed in response to HTTP requests. A built-in library class called `groovy.servlet.GroovyServlet` executes them. Like all Groovy scripts, they're associated with a binding that holds many pre-instantiated variables.

To use a groovlet, first configure the `GroovyServlet` to receive mapped requests. A typical way of doing so is to add the following XML to the standard web application deployment descriptor, web.xml:

```
<servlet>
    <servlet-name>Groovy</servlet-name>
    <servlet-class>groovy.servlet.GroovyServlet</servlet-class>
</servlet>
<servlet-mapping>
    <servlet-name>Groovy</servlet-name>
```

```
    <url-pattern>*.groovy</url-pattern>
</servlet-mapping>
```

The GroovyServlet class is part of the standard Groovy library. Here it's mapped to the URL pattern `*.groovy`, which means that any URL that ends in that pattern will be directed to this servlet. For example, the URL http://localhost/.../hello.groovy would match a script named `hello.groovy` in the root of the web application. Keep in mind that this is literally the source file, not the compiled class.

GROOVLETS Groovlets are deployed as source code, not compiled.

When invoked, the GroovyServlet class finds the script whose name ends the URL, pre-instantiates a series of variables, creates an instance of the GroovyScriptEngine class, and executes the script. The actual script code can be placed in any accessible directory from the web application root, or in any subdirectory of /WEB-INF/groovy.

The key to the simplicity of groovlets is this already-configured infrastructure. With this in place a developer has a lot less work to do.

10.2.1 A "Hello, World!" groovlet

Because every technology needs a "Hello, World!" application, here's a groovlet to greet the user. Assume that the GroovyServlet has already been configured, and add a file called `hello.groovy` in the root of a web application. In a standard Maven structure that would be src/main/webapp/hello.groovy. The contents of the groovlet are

```
name = params.name ?: 'World'
println "Hello, $name!"
```

It's a simple groovlet, but it should still be tested. Integration-testing of web applications is discussed later in this chapter, but the syntax in the next listing uses the same mechanism for transmitting a GET request (use the Groovy JDK to convert a string to a URL and then call URL's `getText` method) that was used in several earlier chapters.

Listing 10.5 `HelloGroovletTest`, an integration test for the `hello` groovlet

```
class HelloGroovletTest {
    int port = 8163

    @Test
    void testHelloGroovletWithNoName() {
        String response =
            "http://localhost:$port/HelloGroovlet/hello.groovy"
            .toURL().text
        assert 'Hello, World!' == response.trim()
    }

    @Test
    void testHelloGroovletWithName() {
        String response =
            "http://localhost:$port/HelloGroovlet/hello.groovy?name=Dolly"
            .toURL().text
```

```
        assert 'Hello, Dolly!' == response.trim()
    }
}
```

There's nothing particularly surprising or unusual about this test, which is simple because the groovlet only responds to GET requests.

Unit tests are also doable, based on the fact that the `GroovyServlet` is executing the groovlet as a script with predefined variables. For example, the next listing shows a unit test for the groovlet that uses an instance of the `GroovyShell` class and the `Binding` class in a manner similar to that described in chapter 6 on testing.

Listing 10.6 A unit test for the groovlet using `GroovyShell` and `Binding`

```
class HelloGroovletUnitTest {
    String groovlet = 'src/main/webapp/hello.groovy'
    GroovyShell shell
    Binding binding = new Binding()
    StringWriter content = new StringWriter()

    @Before
    void setUp() {
        binding.params = [:]                          // Setting the params map
        binding.out = new PrintWriter(content)        // Capturing the output stream
        shell = new GroovyShell(binding)
    }

    @Test
    void testGroovletWithNoName() {
        shell.evaluate(new File("$groovlet"))
        assert 'Hello, World!' == content.toString().trim()
    }

    @Test
    void testGroovletWithName() {
        binding.params = [name:'Dolly']
        shell.evaluate(new File("$groovlet"))
        assert 'Hello, Dolly!' == content.toString().trim()
    }
}
```

The interesting parts of this test are first that the groovlet expects a map of input parameters, so the test has to provide one, and that I need a way to capture the output stream from the groovlet, which is done through the `out` variable of the binding.

Recall from chapter 6 that Groovy also provides a subclass of `GroovyTestCase`, called `GroovyShellTestCase`, which is designed to test scripts like this. The following listing shows the same unit test using `GroovyShellTestCase`. Note that it's noticeably simpler.

Listing 10.7 Using `GroovyShellTestCase` to simplify unit-testing groovlets

```
class HelloGroovletShellTest extends GroovyShellTestCase {
    String groovlet = 'src/main/webapp/hello.groovy'
    StringWriter content = new StringWriter()
    def capturedOut = new PrintWriter(content)
```

```
    @Test
    void testGroovletWithNoName() {
        withBinding([out: capturedOut, params:[:]]) {
            shell.evaluate(new File("$groovlet"))
        }
        assert 'Hello, World!' == content.toString().trim()
    }

    @Test
    void testGroovletWithName() {
        withBinding([out: capturedOut, params:[name:'Dolly']]) {
            shell.evaluate(new File("$groovlet"))
        }
        assert 'Hello, Dolly!' == content.toString().trim()
    }
}
```

Pass binding variables through the method

The `GroovyShellTestCase` class instantiates a `GroovyShell` internally and allows you to pass a map of binding parameters through the `withBinding` method.

10.2.2 Implicit variables in groovlets

The previous example shows that groovlets expect that all the request parameters are bundled into a map called `params`. Groovlets operate in an environment containing many implicit variables. Table 10.2 shows the complete list.

Table 10.2 Implicit variables available in groovlets

Variable	Represents	Notes
`request`	`ServletRequest`	
`response`	`ServletResponse`	
`session`	`getSession(false)`	May be null
`context`	`ServletContext`	
`application`	`ServletContext` (same as `context`)	
`params`		Map of request parameters
`headers`		Map of request/response headers
`out`	`response.getWriter()`	
`sout`	`response.getOutputStream()`	
`html`	`new MarkupBuilder(out)`	

The previous example used only the `params` variable. Now I'll discuss a slightly more elaborate example, which was used in the Groovy Baseball application first presented in chapter 2. The following listing shows the complete source.

Listing 10.8 The `GameService` groovlet from the Groovy Baseball application

```
import beans.GameResult;
import beans.Stadium;
import service.GetGameData;

response.contentType = 'text/xml'        <-- Setting a response header
def month = params.month
def day = params.day                      Access request parameters
def year = params.year

m = month.toInteger() < 10 ? '0' + month : month
d = day.toInteger() < 10 ? '0' + day : day
y = year

results = new GetGameData(month:m,day:d,year:y).games

html.games {                              <-- Writing out XML data
    results.each { g ->
        game(
            outcome:"$g.away $g.aScore, $g.home $g.hScore",
            lat:g.stadium.latitude,
            lng:g.stadium.longitude
        )
    }
}
```

The goal of the `GameService` groovlet is to get the date provided by the user interface, invoke the `getGames` method in the `GetGameData` service, and provide the results to the user in XML form. The groovlet sets the `contentType` header in the response to XML, retrieves the input parameters representing the requested date, normalizes them to the proper form if necessary, calls the game service, and uses the built-in markup builder to write out the game results as a block of XML.

Using the markup builder to write out XML is helpful here. One of the problems faced by current web applications is that JavaScript code used in the user interface can't parse the Java or Groovy objects produced by the server side. An intermediate format is needed that both sides can interpret and generate. There are only two realistic options for that: XML and JavaScript Object Notation (JSON). The recent trend has been to use JSON objects as much as possible, but the markup builder inside groovlets makes it easy to produce XML instead. The amount of XML generated by this application is minimal, so it's not a problem to parse-in the user interface.

> **PRODUCING XML** Use the `html` markup builder in groovlets to write out XML when needed, not to produce a web page in HTML.

This demonstration is simple, but that's the point. Groovlets are a convenient way to receive input data, access back-end services, and produce responses or forward the user to a new destination. Because they have a built-in way to convert objects into XML (and it wouldn't be hard to add a `JsonBuilder` to convert to JSON instead[2]), they're ideal as a front-end for RESTful web services.

Lessons learned (groovlets)

1. Groovlets are Groovy scripts executed by an embedded servlet.
2. Groovlets contain implicit objects for request parameters, the HTTP session, and more.
3. Groovlets use builders to generate formatted output.

Before demonstrating the Grails framework, let me now discuss the issue of testing web applications, both in isolation as unit tests and automated integration tests using Gradle.

10.3 Unit- and integration-testing web components

Chapter 6 discussed techniques for unit-testing Java and Groovy classes and demonstrated how Groovy's mock capabilities provide a standard library of mocks and stubs to support unit tests. It's easy to test individual classes and to run those tests automatically as part of a build process.

Testing is so important that most modern web frameworks consider testability a major design goal, so they try to make the individual components easy to test. For example, one of the major differences between the original Struts framework and the more modern Struts 2, Spring MVC, JSF, or any of a number of others is how their parts are designed with testing in mind. Despite this, testing of web components is far less pervasive than you might expect.

Still, unit-testing and integration-testing web applications is as important as testing anything else in the system, and doing so automatically is critical. Integration-testing a web application by making a tester manually enter data in forms and click links is an extremely expensive and error-prone mechanism. There has to be a better way, and fortunately Groovy helps a lot in that area.

To lay the foundation, however, I'll begin with a library of mock classes that comes from one of the biggest Java libraries of them all, the Spring framework.

10.3.1 Unit-testing servlets with Spring

The Spring framework is one of the most popular open source libraries in the Java world. Chapter 7 on Groovy and Spring discusses it in some detail, but I want to use it here for two reasons: (1) Spring provides a great collection of mock objects for unit-testing web applications, and (2) Spring is one of the underlying technologies for Grails, so knowing more about how Spring works helps you use Grails more effectively.

To illustrate the challenge and highlight the dependencies that need to be mocked during testing, let me start with a simple servlet class, written in Java, called `HelloServlet`:

---

[2] In fact, I helped do exactly that. That's open source for you; if you get an idea, go do it.

```
public class HelloServlet extends HttpServlet {
    protected void doGet(HttpServletRequest req, HttpServletResponse resp)
        throws ServletException, IOException {
        resp.getWriter().print("Hello, Servlet!");
    }
}
```

Servlets are all created by inheritance, normally by extending `javax.servlet.http.HttpServlet`. `HttpServlet` is an abstract class with no abstract methods. It receives HTTP requests and delegates them to a `do` method corresponding to each HTTP verb, like `doGet`, `doPost`, `doPut`, `doTrace`, or `doOptions`. Each of these methods takes two arguments, one of type `HttpServletRequest` and one of type `HttpServletResponse`.

The `HelloServlet` class overrides the `doGet` method to respond to HTTP GET requests. It uses the `resp` argument (an instance of `HttpServletResponse`) to get the associated output writer, which is used to print to the output stream.

Even in a class this simple, it's apparent that unit testing is going to be a challenge. As a reminder of what unit testing is all about, let me say this:

> **UNIT-TESTING WEB COMPONENTS** The goal of unit-testing web applications is to run tests outside of a container. This requires mock objects for all the container-provided classes and services.

In this case I need objects representing the two arguments of type `HttpServletRequest` and `HttpServletResponse`. In most cases I'll also need objects representing `HttpSession`, `ServletContext`, and possibly more.

This is where the set of mock classes from the Spring framework helps. The Spring API includes a package called `org.springframework.mock.web` that, as described in the API, contains "a comprehensive set of Servlet API 2.5[3] mock objects, targeted at usage with Spring's web MVC framework." Fortunately they can be used with any web application, whether it's based on Spring MVC or not.

The next listing shows a JUnit test for the `doGet` method of my "Hello, World!" servlet.

Listing 10.9 `HelloServletJavaTest`: a servlet test class using mock objects

```
import static org.junit.Assert.*;

import org.junit.Test;
import org.springframework.mock.web.MockHttpServletRequest;
import org.springframework.mock.web.MockHttpServletResponse;

public class HelloServletJavaTest {
    @Test
    public void testDoGet() {
        HelloServlet servlet = new HelloServlet();
        MockHttpServletRequest req = new MockHttpServletRequest();
        MockHttpServletResponse resp = new MockHttpServletResponse();
```

[3] The mock objects work for Servlet 3.0 as well, with some minor exceptions listed in the JavaDocs.

```
        try {
            servlet.doGet(req, resp);
            assertEquals("Hello, Servlet!",
                resp.getContentAsString().trim());
        } catch (Exception e) {
            e.printStackTrace();
        }
    }
}
```

The `try/catch` blocks do their best to bury the essence in ceremony, but the intent is clear. The method instantiates the servlet and mock objects representing the servlet request and servlet response classes, and then it invokes the `doGet` method on the servlet with the mocks as arguments. The good part is that the `MockHttpServletResponse` class has a method called `getContentAsString`, which captures the data written to the output writer in the servlet so it can be compared to the expected answer.

Note that the mock classes are being used not as Spring beans in the traditional sense (as they are in chapter 7 on Spring), but simply as an available API.

Unit-testing servlets is that simple, as illustrated in figure 10.3. Instantiate the servlet, provide it with whatever mock objects it needs, invoke the proper `do` method, and check the results. This example showed `getContentAsString`; additional tests in this chapter will illustrate two other convenient methods: `getForwardedUrl` and `getRedirectedUrl`. With these classes and methods available, no deployment to a servlet container is required.

```
doGet(HttpServletRequest, HttpServletResponse) {
  ...
  response.getWriter().print(...);
}
```


Figure 10.3 Servlet tests using Spring mocks. The Spring API provides mock classes for the request, response, and session, and captures outputs, forwards, and redirected URLs.

So far, however, I haven't used Groovy at all. What does Groovy provide to make servlet development and testing easier? I'll answer that in the next section.

Unit testing isn't always enough, though. I'd like to prove that my application classes work in practice as well, so I want to do an integration test, too. That means I need a servlet container, some way to deploy my web application, and a way to trigger requests types other than simple GETs. That's the subject of the next section.

10.3.2 Integration testing with Gradle

Gradle is a build tool implemented in Groovy, which was discussed extensively in chapter 5 on build processes. Gradle uses Groovy builder syntax to specify repositories, library dependencies, and build tasks. Executing a build using one of the normal plugins (like the Groovy plugin used throughout this book) downloads any needed dependencies, compiles and tests the code, and prepares a final report of the results.

One of the advantages of working with Gradle is its large variety of available plugins. In this chapter I'm working with web applications, and Gradle understands their structure as well as regular Java or Groovy applications. All you need to do is include the war plugin, and everything works. Even better, Gradle also includes a jetty plugin, which is designed for testing web applications.

Simply add the following line to a Gradle build:

```
apply plugin:'war'
```

The project will then use the default Maven structure of a web application. That means the web directory src/main/webapp will hold any view layer files, like HTML, CSS, and JavaScript. That directory will also contain the WEB-INF subdirectory, which contains the web deployment descriptor, web.xml. The source structure can be mapped any way you want, but for this section I'll stick with the default Maven approach.

Consider a web application that holds `HelloServlet` from the previous section. The project layout is shown in figure 10.4.

At this stage, the Gradle build file is very simple, as shown in the following listing.

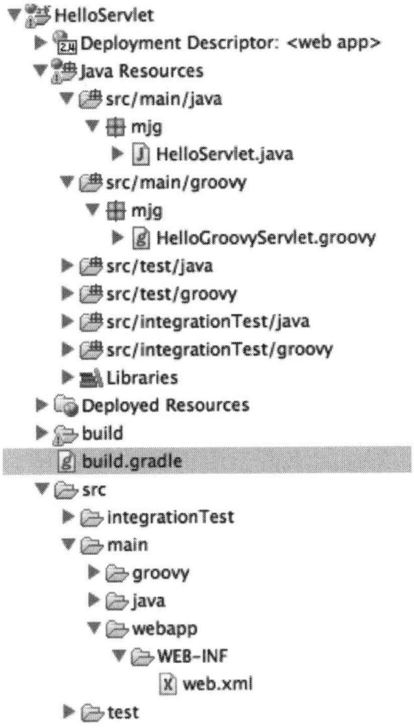

Figure 10.4 Web project layout. The integrationTest directories are discussed later in this chapter. The project has the standard Maven structure for a web application.

Listing 10.10 Gradle build file for web application, using the `war` plugin

```
apply plugin:'groovy'
apply plugin:'war'                          <-- Gradle war plugin

repositories {
    mavenCentral()
}

def springVersion = '3.2.2.RELEASE'

dependencies {
    groovy "org.codehaus.groovy:groovy-all:2.1.5"
    providedCompile 'javax.servlet:servlet-api:2.5'          | Use but do
    providedCompile 'javax.servlet.jsp:jsp-api:2.2'          | not deploy

    testCompile "junit:junit:4.10"
    testCompile "org.springframework:spring-core:$springVersion"
    testCompile "org.springframework:spring-test:$springVersion"
}
```

The listing includes the war plugin. As usual, dependencies come from Maven central. The dependent libraries include JUnit and the Spring API libraries used for unit-testing. The interesting feature is the providedCompile dependency. That tells Gradle that the servlet and JSP APIs are required during compilation but not at deployment, because the container will provide them.

The war plugin really shines when it's combined with the jetty plugin. Jetty is a lightweight, open source servlet container hosted by the Eclipse foundation.[4] This makes it convenient for testing web applications, and Gradle includes a jetty plugin with the standard distribution.

10.3.3 Automating Jetty in the Gradle build

To use Jetty in Gradle, you need to add the plugin dependency, but you also need to configure some settings:

```
apply plugin:'jetty'

httpPort = 8080
stopPort = 9451
stopKey = 'foo'
```

The httpPort variable is the port that Jetty will use for HTTP requests. Using 8080 is typical, because it's the default port for both Tomcat and Jetty, but it's certainly not required. The Jetty container will listen for shutdown requests on the stopPort, and the plugin will send the stopKey to Jetty when it's time to shut down.

Adding the plugin and properties to the Gradle build enables three new tasks:

1. jettyRun, which starts the server and deploys the application
2. jettyRunWar, which creates a WAR file before deployment
3. jettyStop, which stops the server

That's helpful, but I want to automate the process of deploying my application so that I can run an integration test without human intervention. To make that happen, I need the jettyRun and jettyRunWar tasks to run in "daemon" mode, which means that after starting, control will be returned to the build so it can continue with other tasks.

Therefore, I add the following line to the build:

```
[jettyRun, jettyRunWar]*.daemon = true
```

Remember that the spread-dot operator (*.) in Groovy here means to set the daemon property on each element of the collection. Without the star, the dot operator would try to set the property on the collection itself, which wouldn't work.

The test itself can then be defined as a private method in the build file and called from inside a Gradle task, as follows:

---

[4] See www.eclipse.org/jetty/ for details.

```
task intTest(type: Test, dependsOn: jettyRun) << {
    callServlets()
    jettyStop.execute()
}

private void callServlet() {
    String response = "http://localhost:$httpPort/HelloServlet/hello"
        .toURL().text.trim()
    assert response == 'Hello, Servlet!'
}
```

The `intTest` task is defined using the left-shift operator (`<<`), which is an alias for adding a `doLast` closure. In other words, this defines the task but doesn't execute it. Because the task depends on the `jettyRun` task, `jettyRun` will be called first if this task is invoked. The task calls the private `callServlet` method, which converts a `String` to a URL, accesses the site, and compares the response to the expected value. Once the method completes, the `intTest` task tells Jetty to shut down, and I'm finished.

I can invoke the `intTest` task directly from the command line, but I'd rather make it part of my normal build process. To do that, I notice that in the directed acyclic graph (DAG, see chapter 5) formed by the Gradle build file, the next task after the test task is completed is called `check`.

That sounded way more complicated than it actually was. All I needed to do was run Gradle with the `-m` flag to keep it from actually executing, which gives the following output:

```
prompt> gradle -m build
:compileJava SKIPPED
:processResources SKIPPED
:classes SKIPPED
:war SKIPPED
:assemble SKIPPED
:compileTestJava SKIPPED
:processTestResources SKIPPED
:testClasses SKIPPED
:test SKIPPED
:check SKIPPED
:build SKIPPED

BUILD SUCCESSFUL
```

As you can see, the `check` task occurs right after the `test` task completes, and the `intTest` task doesn't execute at all unless I call for it. To put my task into the process, I set it as a dependency of the `check` task:

```
check.dependsOn intTest
```

Now if I run the same build task again, the integration test runs at the proper time:

```
prompt> gradle -m build
:compileJava SKIPPED
:processResources SKIPPED
:classes SKIPPED
:war SKIPPED
```

```
:assemble SKIPPED
:jettyRun SKIPPED
:compileTestJava SKIPPED
:processTestResources SKIPPED
:testClasses SKIPPED
:intTest SKIPPED
:test SKIPPED
:check SKIPPED
:build SKIPPED

BUILD SUCCESSFUL
```

Note that the `jettyRun` task is also triggered before the tests. Now everything works the way I want.

From one perspective, this is quite a feat of engineering. The class structure in Gradle makes it easy to define new tasks, I can make sure my task runs at the proper time, and I can even embed the test as Groovy code right in my build file.

The problem, of course, is that I can embed the test as Groovy code right in my build file. That works in this instance, but doing business logic (even testing) in a build file can't be a good long-term solution. Test cases aren't part of a build; a build calls them. Inside the build, they're hard to maintain and not easily reusable.

10.3.4 Using an integration-test source tree

A good way to separate the testing infrastructure from the actual tests is to create a special source tree for it. That provides a convenient location for the tests, which will run automatically at the proper point in the build.

Gradle projects have a `sourceSets` property, which can be used to map source directories if they don't fit the default Maven pattern. An example of this was given in chapter 5. Here I want to add an additional testing directory. For both the Java and Groovy plugins, simply defining a source set name generates the proper tasks.

In the current build I add a source set called `integrationTest`:

```
sourceSets {
    integrationTest
}
```

This causes Gradle to generate tasks called `compileIntegrationTestJava`, `compileIntegrationTestGroovy`, `processIntegrationTestResources`, and `integrationTestClasses`. The directory tree now includes src/integrationTest/java, src/integrationTest/groovy, and src/integrationTest/resources.

For this source set I would like the compile and runtime dependencies to match their counterparts in the regular test directory:

```
dependencies {
    // ... Various libraries ...
    integrationTestCompile configurations.testCompile
    integrationTestRuntime configurations.testRuntime
}
```

As before, I'll use the intTest task, but now I need to configure it to have the proper classpath and test directories. Here's the new version of the task:

```
task intTest(type: Test, dependsOn: jettyRun) {
    testClassesDir = sourceSets.integrationTest.output.classesDir
    classpath = sourceSets.integrationTest.runtimeClasspath
    jettyStop.execute()
}
```

The testClassesDir property points to the compiled test sources. The classpath is set to the runtime classpath of the source set, which is simply the runtime classpath of the regular tests. I can now place integration tests into the src/integrationTest directory tree, and they'll be executed at the proper time.

One final issue remains before presenting the integration tests. It's easy to create an HTTP GET request: you convert the string URL to an instance of java.net.URL and then access its text property, as shown previously. It's not as simple to create POST, PUT, and DELETE requests, however. These are discussed in some detail in chapter 8, but for now I'll use a third-party open source library.

The HTTPBuilder library (http://groovy.codehaus.org/modules/http-builder/) is a Groovy wrapper around Apache's HttpClient library. It uses Groovy to make it easy to execute HTTP requests and process the responses. To use it, I added the following dependency to my Gradle build file:

```
testCompile 'org.codehaus.groovy.modules.http-builder:http-builder:0.6'
```

With this addition, the following listing now shows a variety of integration tests. The test class includes tests both with the HTTPBuilder client and without.

Listing 10.11 ServletIntegrationTests.groovy: accessing deployed servlets

```
class ServletIntegrationTests {
    def httpPort = 8080

    @Test
    void testHelloServlet() {                                  <-- GET request
        String response =
            "http://localhost:$httpPort/HelloServletWithHttpBuilder/hello"
            .toURL().text.trim()
        assert response == 'Hello, Servlet!'
    }
                                                              GET request with
    @Test                                                     HTTPBuilder
    void testHelloServletGetWithHttpBuilder() {               <--
        def http = new HTTPBuilder("http://localhost:$httpPort/")
        def resp = http.get(path:'HelloServletWithHttpBuilder/hellogs',
            contentType: ContentType.TEXT) { resp, reader ->
            reader.text.trim()
        }
        assert resp == 'Hello from a Groovy Servlet!'
    }
```

```
    @Test
    void testHelloServletPostWithName() {
        def http = new HTTPBuilder("http://localhost:$httpPort/")
        def resp = http.post(path:'HelloServletWithHttpBuilder/hellogs',
            requestContentType: ContentType.TEXT,
            query:[name:'Dolly']) { resp, reader ->
            reader.text.trim()
        }
        assert resp == 'Hello, Dolly!'
    }
}
```

POST request with HTTPBuilder

The listing demonstrates three different types of tests. The first shows a simple GET request without any library dependencies. The second uses the HTTPBuilder[5] library to execute a GET request, and the last does the same with a POST request. The detailed syntax comes from the library documentation.

With this infrastructure in place, both unit and integration tests can be added to a standard project tree, and both can be executed with an embedded Jetty server using a plugin in the Gradle build.

GRADLE INTEGRATION TESTS Using Gradle's `web` and `jetty` plugins with an integration source tree, web applications can be tested in "live" mode during a normal build.

The Geb web testing framework

Geb (www.gebish.org) (pronounced "jeb," with a soft g) is a Groovy testing tool based on Spock that allows tests to be written using a page-centric approach to web applications. Website interactions can be scripted in terms of page objects, rather than simple screen scraping. It uses a jQuery-like syntax along with Groovy semantics to do browser automation, using the WebDriver library under the hood.

The Geb project shows a lot of promise and has a growing number of adherents. It's certainly worth considering as a functional testing tool, along with alternatives like Canoo WebTest (http://webtest.canoo.com) and the Selenium[6] (http://seleniumhq.org) JavaScript library. An entire chapter could be written covering those tools alone, but this book is arguably already long enough.

Because this an active area of development, I recommend the testing presentations at Slide Share by Paul King (for example, www.slideshare.net/paulk_asert/make-tests-groovy), one of the coauthors of *Groovy in Action* (Manning, 2007) and an outstanding developer, as a helpful reference.[7]

---

5 HTTPBuilder includes a class called `RESTClient`, which is used extensively in the discussion of REST in chapter 9.

6 By the way, do you know why it's called Selenium? When it was developed, there was a much-loathed product called Mercury Test Runner. As it happens, the element Selenium (Se) is the cure for Mercury (Hg) poisoning.

7 I'll just say it here: everything Paul King says is right. Start with that assumption and you'll be fine.

Groovy has other classes that support server-side configuration, like `ServletBinding`, which extends the regular script `Binding` class.

> **Lessons learned (testing)**
>
> 1. Spring provides a library of mock objects for unit-testing web applications. The same library is built into Grails.
> 2. The web and Jetty plugins in Gradle make it easy to build and deploy web applications. With some work, Gradle can do automatic integration testing.

Larger applications require more structure to be easily maintainable. The Java world is full of web frameworks, from Struts (both versions 1 and 2) to Tapestry to Wicket to JSF to Spring MVC and more. In the Groovy world, one particular framework is dominant, to the point of attracting developers to Groovy just so they can use this framework. That's the definition of a killer app: an application so cool people will learn a new language just to use it. That framework, as most readers well know, is called Grails.

This is a book about using Java and Groovy together, so I won't present a standard tutorial on how to get started with Grails. There are plenty of references for that available.[8] Instead, I'll show a simple, but hopefully nontrivial, application, discuss some of the architectural choices made when creating Grails, and show how existing Java classes can be incorporated into a Grails application.

10.4 Grails: the Groovy "killer app"

It's hard to overstate the impact on the Java world made by the Ruby on Rails (RoR) comet that streaked across the Java sky back in 2005. Java web development at the time consisted of a series of layers composed of a wide mix of technologies, each with its own configuration files and dependencies. Just starting a new web application was a challenge.

Ruby on Rails, with its strong emphasis on the DRY (Don't Repeat Yourself) principle and Convention over Configuration, demonstrated how much simpler life could be. While a lot of Java web developers embraced the RoR approach, not everyone was in a position to simply abandon the Java world. The big question was, how do we bring the rapid development principles from the RoR world into Java enterprise development?

I'll address that in a moment, but first I want to discuss every web application ever created,[9] from the 30,000-foot level. Figure 10.5 shows the standard architecture.

The user interface in the standard model is a browser, also known as a lightweight client, as opposed to a heavyweight (desktop) Java client. The browser presents views

---

[8] See especially the excellent *Grails in Action*, by Peter Ledbrook and Glen Smith (Manning, 2009).

[9] True for most non-web applications as well. These layers are pretty universal.

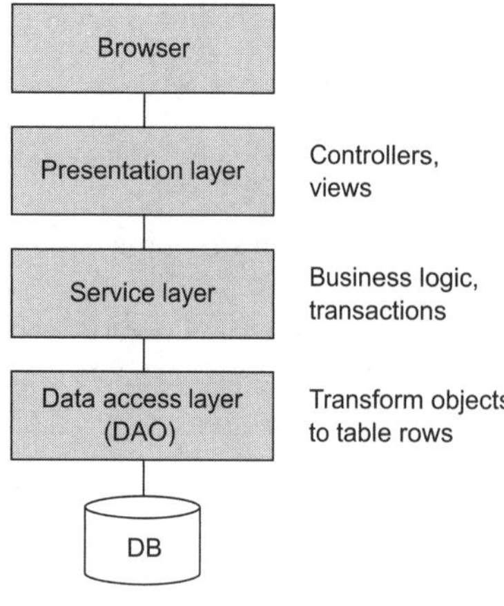

Figure 10.5 The layered design of every Java web application ever made. Presentation layer classes, including controllers, go through transactional services to access persistent data.

to the user, who occasionally submits information back to the server side. The information goes through controllers, which are classes that decide where to go, what business logic to invoke, and what view to use when the request has been processed.

A key principle of Java web application development is to keep the controllers thin, meaning minimal in the amount of actual processing that they do. Instead, the business logic is delegated to service classes. The services are needed also as transactional boundaries, because data access is handled through a set of classes in a data access layer. The data access classes follow the Data Access Object (DAO) design pattern, which encapsulates[10] a data source and transforms entities into database tables and back.

While I'm on the subject, I need to show you one more figure that's inevitable in the web application world. It's the standard Model-View-Controller (MVC) architecture, illustrated in figure 10.6.

The basic idea behind MVC is separation of concerns. Views display model objects, collect data from users, and submit it to controllers. Controllers create and configure model objects and forward them to the views. While the controllers and views are tightly coupled, the model objects are not tied to either. If anything in the system is

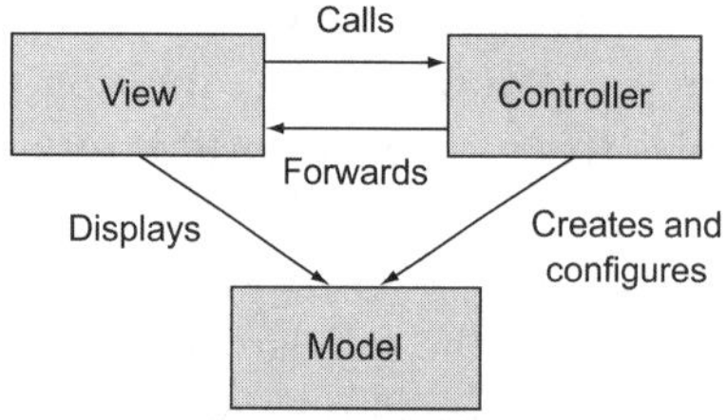

Figure 10.6 The Model-View-Controller (MVC) architecture, little changed since the days of Smalltalk. Views display model objects, which are created and configured by controllers.

[10] Encapsulates. Sigh. Can't we just say "wraps"? Why does every term from OOP have to be so overly complicated? Why can't we just "make" or "create" something, rather than "instantiate" it? And I get the whole "many forms" idea, but who thought the term "polymorphism" was exactly what we needed? Who talks like that (other than me, after all these years)?

reusable, it's the model classes. By the way, noticeably absent from this architecture are the services from the previous figure, but the approach is an oversimplification anyway, so I choose not to worry about it.

Grails is typical of the MVC-based, layered architecture just described, with some interesting variations that are discussed in this section. Grails is notable for several reasons:

- Grails is *built on top of existing, mature technologies.* Grails combines a series of Groovy domain-specific languages (DSLs) on top of Spring and Hibernate.
- Grails is a *complete stack framework* (in much the same way as RoR) that combines open source solutions from the view layer to the persistence layer and everything in between.
- Grails has an *interactive scripting* capability that makes it easy to rapidly prototype applications.
- The design of Grails is based on a *plugin system* that makes it very easy to extend.[11]
- Grails applications *deploy on existing Java-based infrastructure.*

Grails relies on the Spring framework for its internal infrastructure, so anything Spring can do, Grails can do, either directly or through a plugin. Persistence is managed through the Hibernate Object-Relational Mapping layer, which is powerful enough but can also be replaced for the modern family of NoSQL databases.

To show how Grails fits into the standard architecture, I'll walk through the components of an example.

10.4.1 The quest for the holy Grails

Grails can be used to design arbitrarily complex web applications, but one of its sweet spots is to provide a web interface on a set of database tables. I'll come back to that after showing the components, because it's both a blessing and a curse.

> **GRAILS** The goal of this section is to demonstrate a portion of a small but nontrivial Grails application. Chapter 8 examines GORM in more detail. Chapter 9 on REST briefly talks about REST in Grails. Finally, chapter 7 on Spring talks about the underlying infrastructure.

Consider a web application with four domain classes: `Quest`, `Task`, `Knight`, and `Castle`.

> **DOMAIN CLASSES** In Grails, instances of domain classes map to database table rows.

The Grails approach to convention over configuration means that there's a specific directory for everything, as illustrated in figure 10.7. Domain classes have their own directory, as do controllers, services, and views. This makes it easy to understand a Grails application you haven't written, because they all store their elements in the same place.

---

[11] At latest count, there are over 800 plugins available for Grails (of widely varying quality).

Grails domain classes are normally written in Groovy, though that's not required. In the application shown in the next listing, a quest has a name and is associated with many tasks and knights.

Listing 10.12 The `Quest` domain class

```
class Quest {
    String name
    String toString() { name }

    static hasMany = [knights:Knight, tasks:Task]
    static constraints = {
        name blank:false
    }
}
```

The `Quest` has a `name` property and an override of `toString` to return it. The keyword `hasMany` is part of GORM, the Grails Object-Relational Mapping DSL, which programmatically configures Hibernate. Other ORM tools are available, but Hibernate is the default. The `hasMany` keyword implies a foreign key relationship between both the `Knight` and `Task` tables and the `Quest` table.

Domain classes also have constraints, which are enforced by Grails when creating new instances. For the `Quest`, the `name` field cannot be empty.

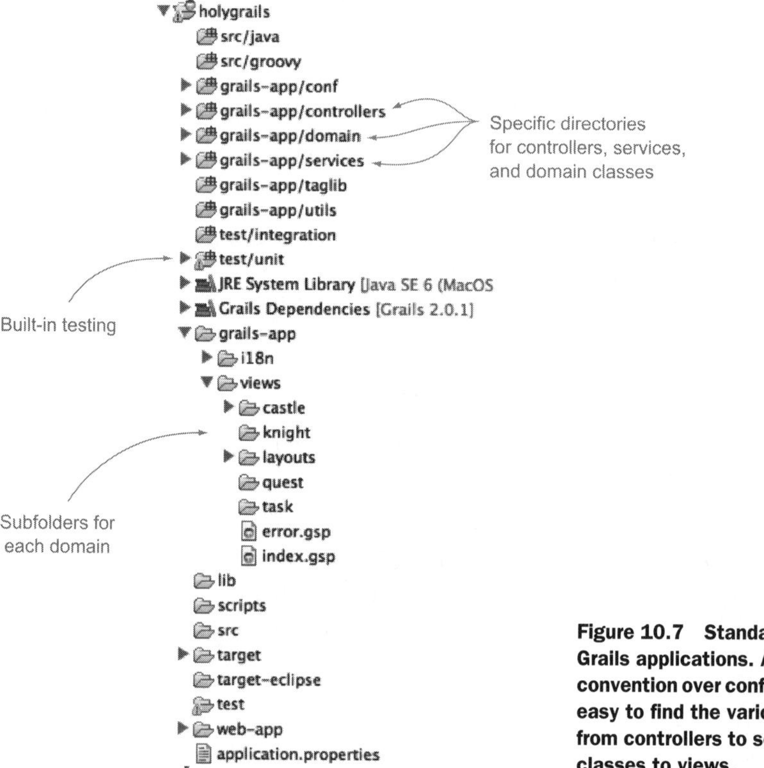

Figure 10.7 Standard layout for all Grails applications. Adherence to convention over configuration makes it easy to find the various components, from controllers to services to domain classes to views.

The Task class is shown in the next listing. Tasks have a name, a priority, a start and end date, and a completion marker.

Listing 10.13 Tasks belong to a Quest

```
class Task {
    String name
    int priority = 3
    Date startDate = new Date()
    Date endDate = new Date()
    boolean completed

    String toString() { name }

    static belongsTo = [quest:Quest]

    static constraints = {
        name blank:false
        priority range:1..5
        startDate()
        endDate validator: { value, task ->
            value >= task.startDate
        }
        completed()
    }
}
```

The constraints closure states that Tasks must have a name, a priority that falls between 1 and 5, and an end date that's greater than or equal to the start date. The other notable part of this class is the belongsTo keyword, which implies a cascade delete relationship between quests and tasks. If a Quest is deleted, all its associated Tasks are removed from the database as well.

Knights are associated with both Quests and Castles, but not through a cascade delete. In fact, a Knight can be between Quests and not belong to a Castle, so both references are listed as nullable in the next listing.

Listing 10.14 The Knight class, which is associated with a Quest and a Castle

```
class Knight {
    String title = 'Sir'
    String name
    Quest quest
    Castle castle

    String toString() { "$title $name" }

    static constraints = {
        title inList: ['Sir','King','Lord','Squire']
        name blank: false
        quest nullable: true
        castle nullable: true
    }
}
```

The last domain class is `Castle`, which has a name, a city, a state, and a computed latitude/longitude pair, as shown in the following listing.

Listing 10.15 The `Castle`, which stores location information

```
class Castle {
    String name
    String city
    String state
    double latitude
    double longitude

    String toString() { "$name Castle" }

    static hasMany = [knights:Knight]

    static constraints = {
        name blank: false
        city blank: false
        state blank: false
        latitude min: -90d, max: 90d
        longitude()
    }
}
```

The `hasMany` variable in `Castle` indicates that the `Knight` table will have a foreign key to the `Castle` table.

In a trivial Grails demonstration, all the associated controllers would be scaffolded. In Grails, that means they have a single property, called `scaffold`, as shown:

```
class QuestController {
    static scaffold = Quest
}
```

The `scaffold` term tells Grails to dynamically (that is, at runtime) generate views to `list`, `show`, `edit`, `update`, and `delete` a quest. The code for each of those actions is produced at runtime, so it's not visible here. Eventually, however, I need to customize the controllers and views, so I need to generate the static versions.

A portion of the `Castle` controller is shown in the next listing.

Listing 10.16 The static `Castle` controller class

```
class CastleController {
...
    def list(Integer max) {
        params.max = Math.min(max ?: 10, 100)
        [castleInstanceList: Castle.list(params),
         castleInstanceTotal: Castle.count()]
    }
...}
```

The `list` action checks to see if the `params` map already contains a key called `max`. If so it's converted to an integer and reset to the minimum of the provided value and 100. If the parameter doesn't exist, then 10 is used as the `max`. Starting in Grails 2.0, request parameters can be used as arguments to controller actions, and type conversions will be done automatically.

> **CONTROLLERS** Grails controllers contain methods called *actions* that map to URLs. They either forward to other resources, render outputs directly, or redirect to other URLs.

More important for the architecture discussion, however, is the map provided as the return value of the action. The map contains two keys, `castleInstanceList` and `castleInstanceTotal`. The former is associated with a list of 10 castles (or whatever the `max` parameter evaluates to), and the latter gives their total number. That's fine, but it's how those values are computed that's truly interesting. Grails adds both a `list` method and a `count` method as static methods on the domain classes.

> **NO DAO CLASSES** Instead of Data Access Objects, Grails uses Groovy metaprogramming to add static methods to the domain classes. This follows the Active Record[12] approach, which is unusual in Java frameworks but very popular in Ruby.

According to the standard architecture, a controller is supposed to access DAO classes through a service layer. In the static scaffolding there's no service layer. That's fine if the application really is little more than a web-driven database, but in general applications need more than that.

> **SERVICES** Business logic in Grails should be placed in services, which are transactional, Spring-managed beans that can be automatically injected into other artifacts.

This application does contain a service. It's the `Geocoder`, familiar from the Groovy Baseball application. In the next listing it operates on `Castles`.

Listing 10.17 The `Geocoder`, yet again, which works on `Castles` this time

```
class GeocoderService {

    String base = 'http://maps.googleapis.com/maps/api/geocode/xml?'

    def fillInLatLng(Castle castle) {
        String encodedAddress =
            [castle.city, castle.state].collect {
                URLEncoder.encode(it, 'UTF-8')
            }.join(',+')
        String qs =
            [address: encodedAddress, sensor: false].collect { k,v ->
                "$k=$v"
            }.join('&')
```

[12] From Martin Fowler's *Patterns of Enterprise Application Architecture* (Addison-Wesley Professional, 2002). See http://en.wikipedia.org/wiki/Active_record for a brief summary.

```
        def root = new XmlSlurper().parse("$base$qs")
        castle.latitude = root.result[0].geometry.location.lat.toDouble()
        castle.longitude = root.result[0].geometry.location.lng.toDouble()
    }
}
```

That much code certainly has to be tested.[13] Grails has had testing capabilities from the beginning, which were originally based on JUnit subclasses. Since version 2.0, Grails test cases use annotations (specifically, the `@TestFor` annotation) to control so-called *mixin* classes. The `@TestFor` annotation applied to a controller or service test automatically instantiates the test and assigns it to an attribute.

For example, the next listing shows the test for the `GeocoderService` class.

Listing 10.18 The unit test for the `GeocoderService`

```
@TestFor(GeocoderService)
class GeocoderServiceTests {

    void testGoogleHeadquarters() {
        Castle google = new Castle(name: 'Google',
            city: 'Mountain View', state: 'CA')

        service.fillInLatLng(google)                    <-- Automatically instantiated by @TestFor

        assertEquals(37.4, google.latitude, 0.1)        | Using JUnit assertEquals for
        assertEquals(-122.1, google.longitude, 0.1)     | doubles with a precision
    }
}
```

TEST CASES Grails generates a unit-test class for each artifact (domain class, controller, or service) that it produces. The default implementations fail on purpose to encourage you to implement them properly.

In a Grails application, services use Spring's dependency injection. Here the `Geocoder` service is injected into `CastleController` to update the latitude and longitude before an instance is saved in a database. Injecting a service is done by declaring an attribute with the same name as the service with a lowercase first letter.[14] To illustrate, the following code is another section of the `CastleController` implementation.

Listing 10.19 Dependency injection of a service into a controller

```
class CastleController {
    def geocoderService                                  <-- Injecting the dependency by declaring a variable with the proper name

    def save() {
        def castleInstance = new Castle(params)
        geocoderService.fillInLatLng(castleInstance)     <-- Using the injected service
```

[13] In pure test-driven development (TDD), the test would be written first. Then you watch it fail, implement the service, and watch the test eventually pass.

[14] In Spring parlance, this is "autowiring by name."

```
        if (!castleInstance.save(flush: true)) {
        ...
    }
```

Services are injected by name (the term is *autowiring* in Spring) into the controller, so declaring a variable of the same name as the service using a lowercase first letter tells Grails to provide an instance of the service at that point. The service is used inside the `save` method to update the `Castle` before saving it.

> **GRAILS SERVICES** Use Grails applications with the standard, layered architecture. Let controllers delegate to services, and let the transactional services work with the databases.

As noted earlier in this section, Grails has a rich set of available plugins. One that's useful in this application is the Google Visualization plugin, which provides a custom library of GSP tags that generate JavaScript for Google Maps applications.

As with everything else, Grails manages plugin installations in a standard way. The file `BuildConfig.groovy` in the grails-app/conf folder has a section on plugins. Adding the proper statement to that file causes Grails to automatically download and install the plugin on its next application start.

Here's the relevant section of the `BuildConfig.groovy` file:

```
plugins {
    runtime ":hibernate:$grailsVersion"
    runtime ":jquery:1.8.3"
    runtime ":resources:1.1.6"

    compile ":google-visualization:0.6.2"
    build ":tomcat:$grailsVersion"
}
```

The documentation for the Google Visualization plugin says that to use it, add the tag `<gvisualization:apiImport />` to the `<head>` section of the GSP where you want the map to appear. Then the plugin provides a `<gvisualization:map />` tag to produce the map itself. The `map` tag uses `columns` and `data` attributes for the information for the map points, which I need to specify.

The Quest application provides a nice demonstration of the process involved. Suppose I want the map to appear on the list.gsp page associated with the castles. Grails maps the URL http://<host>:<port>/holygrails/castle/list to the list action in the `CastleController` class. The last expression in that action is a map (a Groovy one rather than a Google one), so Grails automatically adds the entries to the HTTP request and forwards to the list.gsp page.

The goal, therefore, is to add the information needed by the map to the proper controller action. As usual, the data should come from a service, and I already have the `GeocoderService` available. The next listing shows the additional methods.

Listing 10.20 Methods added to the GeocoderService to support the mapping plugin

```
class GeocoderService {

    // ... fillInLatLng from before ...

    def columns =
        [['number','Lat'],['number','Lon'],['string','Name']]

    def getMarkers() {
        Castle.list().collect { c ->
            [c.latitude, c.longitude, c.toString()]
        }
    }
}
```

Column names and types required by Google Maps

Transforms the Castles into a list of triples

The list action in the CastleController is already returning a list of castles and the total count, which are used to display them in a table. I might as well use the same action to return the columns and data for the map.

The revised list action in CastleController looks like this:

```
def list() {
    params.max = Math.min(params.max ? params.int('max') : 10, 100)
    [castleInstanceList: Castle.list(params),
     castleInstanceTotal: Castle.count(),
     mapColumns:geocoderService.columns, mapData:geocoderService.markers]
}
```

The following listing shows the additions made to the view, list.gsp, in order to display a map of castles.

Listing 10.21 Modifications to list.gsp to display a Google Map of castles

```
<%@ page import="mjg.Castle" %>
<!doctype html>
<html>
    <head>
        ...
        <gvisualization:apiImport />
    </head>
    <body>
        ...
        <gvisualization:map elementId="map" showTip="${true}"
            columns="${mapColumns}" data="${mapData}"/>
        <div id="map" style="width: 400px; height: 300px"></div>
    ...
</html>
```

Additions for Google Visualization plugin

<div> to hold the Google Map

The result is shown in figure 10.8, which displays the castles on a Google Map. The plugin generates the JavaScript required by the Google Maps API.

Grails is a large, powerful framework with lots of features, and the features it lacks are provided with plugins. If you spend any time with Groovy, it's worth a look whenever you have to build web applications.

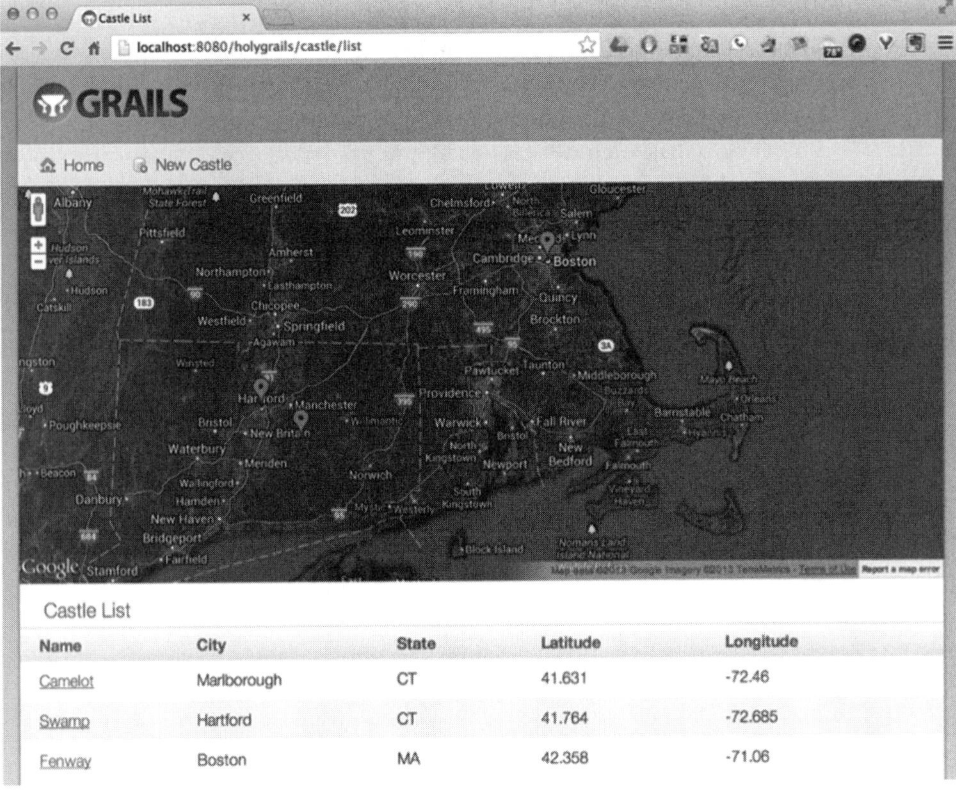

Figure 10.8 Displaying the castles on a Google Map. The `Castle` domain classes have their latitude and longitude coordinates set by the `GeocoderService`. The Google Visualization plugin generates the proper JavaScript to add them to a Google Map.

> **Lessons learned (Grails)**
>
> 1. Grails is a convention-over-configuration framework for producing web applications.
> 2. Grails domain classes are managed by Hibernate and mapped to database tables.
> 3. Grails services are Spring-managed beans that are autowired by name into other artifacts. They use Spring's transaction management by default.
> 4. The plugin design of the Grails architecture makes it easy to add additional capabilities.

Grails uses Spring and Hibernate under the hood, so it mixes Groovy-based domain-specific languages on top of major Java libraries.

10.5 Summary

This chapter examined ways Groovy helps with testing and building web applications. Unit tests are similar to their Java counterparts, but the Gradle build framework provides a great way to do integration testing of deployed applications.

The Groovy JDK includes classes like `ServletCategory`, which simplify the implementation of web components. Groovy also has a built-in web scripting engine called groovlets, which makes it easy to work with requests, responses, sessions, and input parameters in a web application.

Finally, this chapter includes a brief discussion of Grails, possibly the biggest Java/Groovy integration success story of them all.

appendix A Installing Groovy

Installing Groovy is easy. This appendix shows you how to do it, with a review of the various options involved.

A.1 Installing a JDK

Groovy generates Java bytecodes that are interpreted by a Java virtual machine. This means you have to have Java installed in order to install Groovy. You need a full Java Development Kit (JDK), rather than a Java Runtime Environment (JRE). You only need the Standard Edition (SE) of Java, rather than the Enterprise[1] Edition.

The official JDK for Java SE is available from Oracle at http://mng.bz/83Ct. At the time of this writing, the current version is Java SE 7u25 (Java 7, update 25), but Groovy works on any version of Java 1.5 and above.

Be sure to set an environment variable called `JAVA_HOME` to point to the installation directory. You also probably want to add the bin folder under `JAVA_HOME` to your path.

On Windows that will look like this:

```
C:\> set JAVA_HOME="C:\Program Files\Java\jdk1.7.0"
C:\> set PATH=%JAVA_HOME%\bin;%PATH%
```

Those commands will set the `JAVA_HOME` and `PATH` properties in the local shell. To set them everywhere, right-click My Computer, select Properties, click Advanced, and then click Environment Variables. Add them as System variables, and start a new shell.[2]

---

1 Just as an aside, when did the word *business* get deprecated in favor of the word *enterprise*? Is it a *Star Trek* thing? Does being an Enterprise Architect mean you design starships for a living? Are Enterprise Java Beans used when making coffee on a starship?

2 The specifics of the process will be slightly different on different Windows versions, but the concepts are the same. Set the variables as System environment variables, and start a new shell because Windows won't update an existing one.

On Macs or Unix flavors, the same settings are

```
$ export JAVA_HOME=/Library/Java/…
$ export PATH=$PATH:$JAVA_HOME/bin
```

There are too many variations on these statements to count, depending on directory structure and version numbers, but the principles are always the same: install Java, set the `JAVA_HOME` variable to point to it, and add its bin subdirectory to your path.

A.2 Installing Groovy

Assuming you've installed Java, installing Groovy is easy. Again, there are several options, but the basic process comes down to downloading and unzipping the distribution, setting a `GROOVY_HOME` environment variable, and adding its bin subdirectory to your path.

If you're not a fan of automated installers or you don't have root privileges on your machine, you can download a zipped, binary distribution of Groovy directly. The current version can always be found at http://groovy.codehaus.org/Download. You can get either the binary release or the source release (or both). Either way, unzip the download into a directory of your choice.

On Windows, following the same pattern as the Java installation, it's

```
C:\> set GROOVY_HOME=C:\Groovy\groovy-2.1.6
C:\> set PATH=%GROOVY_HOME%\bin;%PATH%
```

On a Mac or Unix, the same process is

```
$ export GROOVY_HOME=...
$ export PATH=$PATH:$GROOVY_HOME/bin
```

If you don't mind installers, a good one is available for Windows. An EXE installer is available on the same download page, which will install Groovy to a directory of your choice, set the `GROOVY_HOME` variable for you, and add the bin folder underneath it to your path. It also offers to install some optional libraries for you, which are useful and do not interfere with your regular installation in any way. I've been using the Windows installer at client sites for years and have never had a problem with it. It will, by the way, notify you if you don't have a `JAVA_HOME` environment variable set.

If you're on a Mac or other Unix box, you have other convenient alternatives available. First, there's a MacPorts (www.macports.org) option. Run

```
$ sudo port install groovy
```

That will download and install the latest version. If you prefer HomeBrew (http://mxcl.github.io/homebrew), the relevant command is

```
$ brew install groovy
```

That, too, will download the latest version, install it, and create soft links to the executable scripts in your path.

The other major alternative is to use GVM, the Groovy enVironment Manager (http://gvmtool.net). This is the best option if you plan to switch versions at any time. GVM is installed using `curl`, with this command:

```
$ curl -s get.gvmtool.net | bash
```

GVM assumes you are using a bash shell, but the same process works for most Unix flavors. It also works on Windows if you install Cygwin. See the web page for details.

The great advantage of GVM is that it makes switching versions almost trivially easy. If you have GVM installed, you can find out which versions of Groovy are available by typing

```
$ gvm list groovy
```

You can install the latest one like this:

```
$ gvm install groovy
```

If you supply a version number to the `install` command, you can select which version of Groovy to install. You can switch from one version of Groovy to another using

```
$ gvm use groovy [version]
```

If the version you request isn't installed, GVM will download and install it for you. In my own work, I don't switch Groovy versions that often, but I switch Grails versions frequently and the same tool works for Groovy, Grails, Griffon, and a few other software distributions. GVM installs software under a .gvm folder in your home directory, so you should set the `GROOVY_HOME` variable to point there. For example, on my Mac, I have

```
$ export GROOVY_HOME=/Users/kousen/.gvm/groovy/current
```

That's useful because switching versions through GVM updates the current link. I don't have to explicitly add that folder to my path, though, because the tool adds soft links to a bin folder already in my path.

A.3 Testing your installation

The easiest way to see if your Groovy installation is working is to try out the Groovy shell or the Groovy console. If you type

```
$ groovysh
```

you should get a response like this:

```
Groovy Shell (2.1.5, JVM: 1.7.0_11)
Type 'help' or '\h' for help.
------------------------------------
groovy:000> println 'Hello, World!'
Hello, World!
===> null
groovy:000>
```

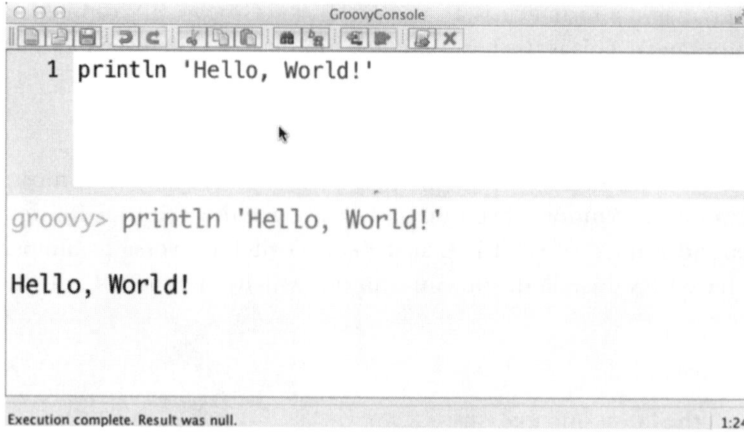

Figure A.1 The Groovy console, which comes with the Groovy distribution. Remember to go under the View menu and select Auto Clear Output On Run to make the tool far more practical.

The Groovy shell is essentially the REPL[3] for Groovy (or even Java). Note that the response here is `null` because the `println` command has a `void` return type.

The Groovy console is a bit more useful. Start it with this command:

```
$ groovyConsole
```

On Windows, that spawns a separate process. On Macs and Unix flavors, the `groovyConsole` command locks up that particular shell, so you might want to run it in the background by appending an ampersand (`&`). The result looks like figure A.1.

The Groovy console appends its results to the output window, which can be problematic. Worse, if you type a line that throws an exception,[4] the result window stops scrolling, even if you later fix the error. My recommendation, therefore, is to select the last entry under the View menu, entitled Auto Clear Output On Run. That will make the console clear the output every time you execute a script. The Groovy console includes an Abstract Syntax Tree browser, among other things. It's useful even if you normally work with an IDE.

Speaking of IDEs, the next section documents their current level of support.

A.4 IDE support

If you're an Eclipse user, the Groovy Eclipse plugin is state-of-the-art. To add it to an existing Eclipse distribution, use the update string found on the page at http://groovy.codehaus.org/Eclipse+Plugin. The plugin can also be found at the Eclipse Marketplace.

Eclipse has an annoying bug that requires the installation directory to be writable by the user. Groovy Eclipse cannot be installed into a so-called "shared" install, which

---

3 Read-Eval-Print-Loop, discussed further in appendix B.

4 I know you would never do that, but you know what your coworkers are like. They're capable of anything.

often includes the c:\Program Files directory on Windows. Simply move your Eclipse installation somewhere else, and you'll be fine.

If you only want to use Groovy, the Groovy Eclipse plugin is sufficient. If you want to use Grails as well, then you can install the Groovy and Grails Tool Suite, GGTS. GGTS is a set of plugins based on Eclipse and is managed by Pivotal (formerly SpringSource). You can download GGTS from www.springsource.org/downloads/sts-ggts. Be careful: the site lists the STS downloads first and the GGTS downloads below that.

Both STS and GGTS come from the same code base. The difference is the initial set of plugins. GGTS comes with both the Groovy Eclipse plugin and Grails support that provides an entire Grails perspective, various wizards, keyboard shortcuts, and more.

The major IDE alternative is IntelliJ IDEA. The page at www.jetbrains.com/idea/features/groovy_grails.html discusses its Groovy and Grails features. It even has Griffon support, which is pretty unusual at this point. IntelliJ IDEA is the tool of choice of most of the core Groovy, Grails, and Griffon team members, but it's a commercial product and therefore requires a license.[5] If you participate in an open source project or make presentations at your local Java/Groovy/Grails user group, you can get a free license, which is one more reason to participate in the open source world.

The web page at http://groovy.codehaus.org/IDE+Support lists plugins and support for other IDEs, ranging from Emacs to TextMate to UltraEdit. If you can't find the one you're interested in, be sure to ask on the mailing lists. Somebody will know and tell you where to find what you need.

A.5 Installing other projects in the Groovy ecosystem

The GVM tool currently will install and manage Groovy, Grails, Griffon, and Gradle distributions, among other projects.[6] That's the easiest way to proceed if you're on a Mac or Unix distribution. Again, on Macs both HomeBrew and MacPorts have options for the same set of projects. On Windows, Groovy has the installer mentioned earlier in this chapter.

Grails is always a ZIP file that you download and unzip. Then you set an environment variable (`GRAILS_HOME` in this case) and add the bin subdirectory to your path. Griffon and Gradle work much the same way.

Note that all of these projects have their own source code repositories on GitHub. You can always clone the distribution and build it yourself, though that tends to get involved. See the respective project pages for details. One of the best things about GitHub is that you can browse the source code without downloading anything. It's a good idea to get familiar with the test cases contained in the various projects, because they're the executable documentation for each. Web pages can go out of date, but

---

5 There's a community edition that didn't used to offer Grails support, but that may be changing. Be sure to check the website for current capabilities.

6 The current list of candidates is Groovy, Grails, Griffon, Gradle, Lazybones, Vertx, and Groovyserv.

continuous integration servers execute test cases all the time. When they break everybody knows about it, and they get fixed right away.

The only other project discussed extensively in this book is Spock. Spock is a library rather than a framework and is usually installed as part of a Gradle (or Maven) build. Its source code is on GitHub, too.

appendix B Groovy by feature

Some people learn by example. Some people learn by feature. In this book I'm trying to satisfy both. If you're a Java developer with only passing familiarity with Groovy, hopefully either this appendix or chapter 2, "Groovy by example," will bring you up to speed on the Groovy language.

This appendix walks through most of the major features of Groovy and provides short snippets of code illustrating them. While this chapter does not claim to be an exhaustive reference like *Groovy in Action* (Manning, 2007; called *GinA* in the rest of this appendix), it has a couple of features that favor it over the more comprehensive treatment: (1) it's considerably shorter, and (2) it has the words "Don't Panic!" written in nice, friendly letters in the appendix (in this sentence, actually).[1] More seriously, in this appendix I review the major features of the Groovy programming language that are used throughout the book.

Because this isn't going to be a comprehensive treatment, I've chosen aspects of Groovy to review based on two criteria: (1) how often they're used in practice and (2) how much they offer an advantage over corresponding features in Java (assuming the corresponding feature in Java even exists). After getting the basics of Groovy out of the way (like how to run Groovy programs and basic data types like numbers and strings), I'll move on to issues like collections, I/O, XML, and more. Some topics, like SQL, are covered in other chapters, but you'll find the essentials here.

---

[1] For those born too late, that was a *Hitchhiker's Guide to the Galaxy* reference. I could go on to say that this chapter "contains much that is apocryphal, or at least wildly inaccurate," but that probably wouldn't be good for sales.

B.1 Scripts and the traditional example

Assuming you already have Groovy installed,[2] I'll start with the traditional "Hello, World!" program, as shown here:

```
println 'Hello, Groovy!'
```

That's the whole program. In Java, you need a `main` method inside a class, and inside the `main` method you call `System.out.println` to write to the console. Java developers are used to it, but there are roughly 8 to 10 different object-oriented concepts involved, depending on how you count them.[3] In Groovy, the whole program is a single line.

To demonstrate, consider one of the two execution environments that come with Groovy, the `groovysh` command, which starts the Groovy shell. The Groovy shell is a REPL[4] that allows you to execute Groovy code a line at a time. All of the lines in the following listing produce the same result.

Listing B.1 Running "Hello, World!" in the Groovy shell

```
$ groovysh
Groovy Shell (2.1.5, JVM: 1.7.0_11)
Type 'help' or '\h' for help.
-------------------------------------------
groovy:000> System.out.println("Hello, World!");      // Java syntax
Hello, World!
===> null
groovy:000> System.out.println("Hello, World!")       // Semicolons are optional
Hello, World!
===> null
groovy:000> println("Hello, World!")                  // Default Groovy method
Hello, World!
===> null
groovy:000> println "Hello, World!"                   // Optional parentheses
Hello, World!
===> null
groovy:000> println 'Hello, World!'                   // Single-quoted string
Hello, World!
===> null
groovy:000>
```

In each case the `println` method prints to the console and returns `null`. When there's no ambiguity, the parentheses can be omitted. Semicolons work as in Java, but they're optional.

---

2 See appendix A for details.

3 A rough count includes classes, methods, strings, arrays, public access, static methods and attributes, void return types, overloaded methods like `println`, and more. It's no accident that Bruce Eckel's *Thinking in Java* (Prentice-Hall, 2002) takes over 100 pages just to get to his first "Hello, World" program.

4 Read-Eval-Print Loop; see http://en.wikipedia.org/wiki/REPL for details.

This is an example of a Groovy *script*. A script is a code listing that doesn't explicitly include a class definition. In Java, everything has to be inside a class. Groovy is able to work with both scripts and classes.

A Groovy script is a form of *syntactic sugar*.[5] A class is, in fact, involved. If I compile this script and then run the `javap` command on it, I get the following response:

```
> groovyc hello_world.groovy
> javap hello_world
Compiled from "hello_world.groovy"
public class hello_world extends groovy.lang.Script{
    public static transient boolean __$stMC;
    public static long __timeStamp;
    public static long __timeStamp__239_neverHappen1309544582162;
    public hello_world();
    public hello_world(groovy.lang.Binding);
    public static void main(java.lang.String[]);
    public java.lang.Object run();
...
```

There are about 30 more lines of output from the `javap` command, mostly involving superclass methods. The interesting part is that the `groovy` command generates a class called `hello_world`, along with a pair of constructors and a `main` method. The class is generated at compile time and extends a class from the Groovy library called `groovy.lang.Script`. In effect, scripts in Groovy become classes in Java, where the code in the script ultimately (after a few layers of indirection) is executed by the `main` method. I don't want to give the impression that Groovy is generating Java, however. Groovy code is compiled directly into bytecodes for the JVM.

> **COMPILED GROOVY** Groovy is compiled, not interpreted. It's not a code generator; the compiler generates Java bytecodes directly.

Because the bytecodes run on the JVM, you can execute Groovy scripts using the `java` command as long as you include the necessary JAR file in your classpath:

```
> java -cp .;%GROOVY_HOME%\embeddable\groovy-all-2.1.5.jar hello_world
Hello, World!
```

> **EXECUTING GROOVY** At runtime, Groovy is just another JAR file. As long as the groovy-all JAR file is in the classpath, Java is perfectly happy to execute compiled Groovy code.

The `groovy` command is used to execute Groovy programs. It can be used with either the compiled code (similar to the `java` command) or Groovy source. If you use the source, the `groovy` command first compiles the code and then executes it.

---

[5] Syntactic sugar is syntax that simplifies writing code but doesn't change anything under the hood. There may be some evidence that an overuse of syntactic sugar leads to syntactic diabetes.

B.2 Variables, numbers, and strings

Groovy is an optionally typed language. Groovy uses classes to define data types, just as Java does, but Groovy variables can either have a static type or use the `def` keyword.

For example, I'm perfectly free to declare variables of type `int`, `String`, or `Employee`, using the standard Java syntax:

```
int x
String name
Employee fred
```

If I don't know the type of the variable, or I don't care, Groovy provides the keyword `def`:

```
def arg
```

> **Typed vs. untyped variables**
>
> When should you use `def` as opposed to the actual type? There's no strict answer, but recently I had a (very mild) Twitter debate about this issue with Dierk Koenig (lead author of *GinA*), Andres Almiray (lead author of *Griffon in Action* and head of the Griffon project), and Dave Klein (lead author of *Grails: A Quick-Start Guide*). Dierk had the best recommendation I've ever heard on the subject. He said, "If I think of a type, I type it (pun intended)."
>
> My own experience is that as I get more experienced with Groovy, I tend to use `def` less and less. I agree with Dierk's recommendation, with the added advice that now when I declare a type, I pause for a moment to see if any actual type occurs to me. If so, I use it.
>
> In some cases `def` is preferred, most notably when using mock objects in testing. That subject is discussed in chapter 6.

Moving on to data types themselves, Java makes a distinction between primitives and classes. In Groovy there are no primitives. Numbers in Groovy are first-class objects, with their own set of methods.

B.2.1 Numbers

Because in Groovy numbers are objects, I can determine their data types. For integer literals, the data type depends on the value, as shown in this script:

```
x = 1
assert x.class == java.lang.Integer
x = 10000000000000000
assert x.class == java.lang.Long
x = 100000000000000000000000
assert x.class == java.math.BigInteger
```

There are a few points to be made about this script. First, the variable `x` doesn't have a declaration at all. This is only legal in a script, where the variable becomes part of the script's binding and can be set and accessed from outside. Details of this procedure are shown in chapter 3 on integration with Java. Suffice it to say here that this is legal in a script, but not in a class. If it makes you feel more comfortable, you're free to add the word `def` in front of x.

> **SCRIPT VARIABLES** If a variable in a script is not declared, it becomes part of the script's binding.

As mentioned earlier, the script lacks semicolons. Semicolons as statement separators are optional in Groovy and can be omitted if there's no ambiguity. Again, you're free to add them in without a problem.

> **SEMICOLONS** In Groovy, semicolons work but are optional.

Next, Groovy uses the method called `assert` extensively. The word `assert` can be written without parentheses, as done here, or you can surround an expression with them. The resulting expression must evaluate to a Boolean, but that's a much looser requirement than in Java. In Java, the only available Booleans are `true` and `false`. In Groovy, non-null references are true, as are nonzero numbers, non-empty collections, non-empty strings, and the Boolean value `true`.

That bears repeating and goes by the term *The Groovy Truth.*

> **THE GROOVY TRUTH** In Groovy, non-null references, non-empty collections, non-empty strings, nonzero numbers, and the Boolean value `true` are all true.

Finally, the default data type for floating-point values in Java is `double`, but in Groovy it's `java.math.BigDecimal`. The `double` type in Java has approximately 17 decimal places of precision, but if you want to get depressed about its accuracy, try this tiny sample:

```
println 2.0d - 1.1d
```

The `d` appended to the literals makes them doubles. You would expect the answer here to be 0.9, but in fact it's 0.8999999999999999. That's not much of a difference, but I've only done a single subtraction and I'm already off. That's not good. That's why any serious numerical calculations in Java require `java.math.BigDecimal`, but that means you can't use the standard operators (`+`, `-`, `*`, `/`) anymore and have to use method calls instead.

Groovy handles that issue without a problem. Here's the analogous Groovy script:

```
println 2.0 - 1.1
```

The answer in this case is 0.9, as expected. Because the calculations are done with `BigDecimal`, the answer is correct. Groovy also has operator overloading, so the plus operator can be used with the `BigDecimal` values. To summarize:

> **LITERALS** Numbers without a decimal point are of type `Integer`, `Long`, or `java.math.BigInteger`, depending on size. Numbers with a decimal point are of type `java.math.BigDecimal`.

Because numbers are objects, they have methods as well. Listing B.2 shows a script putting some numbers through their paces. Several of the expressions use closures, which are the subject of section B.4. The simplest definition is to consider them a block of code that's executed as though it's an anonymous method call.

Listing B.2 numbers.groovy, showing method calls on numeric literals

```
assert 2**3 == 8
assert 2**-2 == 0.25 // i.e., 1/(2*2) = 1/4

def x = ""
3.times { x += "Hello" }
assert x == "HelloHelloHello"

def total = 0
1.upto(3) { total += it }
assert total == 1 + 2 + 3

def countDown = []
5.downto 1, { countDown << "$it ..." }
assert countDown == ['5 ...', '4 ...', '3 ...', '2 ...', '1 ...']
```

Groovy has an exponentiation operator, unlike Java. Numbers have methods like `times`, `upto`, and `downto`. The `times` operation takes a single argument of type `Closure`. When the last argument to a method is a closure, you can put it after the parentheses. Because the method has no other arguments, you can leave out the parentheses altogether.

> **CLOSURE ARGUMENTS** If the last argument to a method is a closure, it can be placed after the parentheses.

The `upto` and `downto` methods take two arguments, so the parentheses are shown in the former and a comma is used in the latter to indicate that both the number and the closure are arguments to the method. The `countDown` variable is a list, which will be discussed in section B.3. The left-shift operator has been overloaded to append to the collection, and its argument here is a parameterized string. Groovy has two types of strings, discussed in the next section.

B.2.2 *Strings and Groovy strings*

In Java, single quotes delimit characters (a primitive) and double quotes surround instances of `java.lang.String`. In Groovy, both single and double quotes are used for strings, but there's a difference. Double-quoted strings are used for parameter replacement. They're not instances of `java.lang.String`, but rather instances of `groovy.lang.GString`.

Here are a couple of examples to show how they're used:

```
def s = 'this is a string'
assert s.class == java.lang.String

def gs = "this might be a GString"
assert gs.class == java.lang.String
assert !(gs instanceof GString)
```

```
gs = "If I put in a placeholder, this really is a GString: ${1+1}"
assert gs instanceof GString
```

Single-quoted strings are always instances of `java.lang.String`. Double-quoted strings may or may not be Groovy strings, depending on whether parameter replacement is done or not.

Groovy also has multiline strings, with either single or double quotes. The difference again is whether or not parameter replacement is done:

```
def picard = '''
    (to the tune of Let It Snow)
    Oh the vacuum outside is endless
    Unforgiving, cold, and friendless
    But still we must boldly go
    Make it so, make it so, make it so!
'''

def quote = """
    There are ${Integer.toBinaryString(2)} kinds of people in the world:
    Those who know binary, and those who don't
"""
assert quote == '''
    There are 10 kinds of people in the world:
    Those who know binary, and those who don't
'''
```

There's one final kind of string, used for regular expressions. Java has had regular-expression capabilities since version 1.4, but most developers either aren't aware of them or avoid them.[6] One particularly annoying part of regular expressions in Java is that the backslash character, \, is used as an escape character, but if you want to use it in a regular expression, you have to backslash the backslash. This leads to annoying expressions where you have to double-backslash the backslashes, making the resulting expressions almost unreadable.

Groovy provides what's called the *slashy* syntax. If you surround an expression with forward slashes, it's assumed to be a regular expression, and you don't have to double-backslash anymore.

> **STRINGS** Groovy uses single quotes for regular strings, double quotes for parameterized strings, and forward slashes for regular expressions.

Here's an example that checks strings to see if they are palindromes: that is, if they are the same forward and backward. To check for palindromes you first need to remove any punctuation and ignore case before reversing the string:

```
def palindromes = '''
    Able was I ere I saw Elba
    Madam, in Eden, I'm Adam
```

[6] Perl programmers love regular expressions. Ruby developers are fond of them, but reasonable about it. Java developers take one look at the JavaDocs for the `java.util.regex.Pattern` class and recoil in horror.

```
    Sex at noon taxes
    Flee to me, remote elf!
    Doc, note: I dissent. A fast never prevents a fatness. I diet on cod.
'''
palindromes.eachLine {
    String str = it.trim().replaceAll(/\W/,'').toLowerCase()
    assert str.reverse() == str
}
```

Once again, a little Groovy code packs a lot of power. The method `eachLine` has been added to the `String` class to break multiline strings at line breaks. It takes a closure as an argument. In this case, no dummy variables were used in the closure, so each string is assigned to the default variable called `it`.

> **THE IT VARIABLE** In a closure, if no dummy name is specified the term `it` is used by default.

The `trim` method is applied to the line to remove any leading and trailing spaces. Then the `replaceAll` method is used to replace all non-word characters with an empty string. Finally, the string is converted to lowercase.

The assert test uses another method added by Groovy to `String`, called `reverse`. Java has a `reverse` method in `StringBuffer`, but not `String`. Groovy adds the `reverse` method to `String` for convenience.

Groovy adds lots of methods to the Java standard libraries. Collectively these are known as the *Groovy JDK* and are one of the best features of Groovy. The Groovy documentation includes GroovyDocs for both the Groovy standard library and the Groovy JDK.

> **THE GROOVY JDK** Through its metaprogramming capabilities, Groovy adds many convenient methods to the standard Java libraries. These additional methods are known as the Groovy JDK.

In summary, Groovy uses numbers and objects and has both regular and parameterized strings with additional methods. Another area where Groovy greatly simplifies Java is collections.

B.3 Plain Old Groovy Objects

Java classes with getters and setters for the attributes are often known as POJOs, or Plain Old Java Objects. In Groovy, the same classes are Plain Old Groovy Objects, or POGOs.[7] POGOs have additional characteristics that are discussed in this section.

Consider the following `Person` class in Groovy:

---

7 Python occasionally uses the term POPOs, which sounds vaguely disgusting. If you really want to annoy a Ruby developer, refer to POROs. Ruby people hate anything that sounds like Java.

```
class Person {
    String firstName
    String lastName

    String toString() { "$firstName $lastName" }
}
```

POGOs don't require access modifiers, because in Groovy attributes are private by default and methods are public by default. The class is public by default, as well. Any property without an access modifier automatically gets a public getter and setter method. If you want to add `public` or `private` you can, and either on an attribute will prevent the generation of the associated getter and setter.

> **GROOVY PROPERTIES** In Groovy, property access is done through dynamically generated getter and setter methods.

Here's a script using the `Person` class:

```
Person mrIncredible = new Person()
mrIncredible.firstName = 'Robert'
mrIncredible.setLastName('Parr')
assert 'Robert Parr' ==
    "${mrIncredible.firstName} ${mrIncredible.getLastName()}"

Person elastigirl = new Person(firstName: 'Helen', lastName: 'Parr')
assert 'Helen Parr' == elastigirl.toString()
```

The script shows that you also get a default, *map-based* constructor, so called because it uses the same `property:value` syntax used by Groovy maps.

This idiom is so common in Groovy that getter and setter methods anywhere in the standard library are typically accessed with the property notation. For example, `Calendar.instance` is used to invoke the `getInstance` method on the `Calendar` class.

Moving now to collections of instances, I'll start with ranges, then move to lists, and finally look at maps.

B.4 Collections

Since J2SE 1.2, the Java standard library has included the collections framework. The framework defines interfaces for lists, sets, and maps, and provides a small but useful set of implementation classes for each interface, as well as a set of polymorphic utility methods in the class `java.util.Collections`.

Groovy can use all of these collections but adds a lot:

- Native syntax for lists and maps
- A `Range` class
- Many additional convenience methods

I'll present examples of each in this section.

B.4.1 Ranges

Ranges are collections in Groovy consisting of two values separated by a pair of dots. Ranges are normally used as parts of other expressions, like loops, but they can be used by themselves.

The class `groovy.lang.Range` has methods for accessing the boundaries of a range, as well as checking whether it contains a particular element. Here's a simple example:

```
Range bothEnds = 5..8
assert bothEnds.contains(5)
assert bothEnds.contains(8)
assert bothEnds.from == 5
assert bothEnds.to == 8
assert bothEnds == [5, 6, 7, 8]
```

Using two dots includes the boundaries. To exclude the upper boundary, use a less-than sign:

```
Range noUpper = 5..<8
assert noUpper.contains(5)
assert !noUpper.contains(8)
assert noUpper.from == 5
assert noUpper.to == 7
assert noUpper == [5, 6, 7]
```

A range of numbers iterates over the contained integers. Other library classes can be used in ranges. Strings go letter by letter:

```
assert 1..5 == [1,2,3,4,5]
assert 'A'..'E' == ["A","B","C","D","E"]
```

Dates iterate over the contained days, as shown in the next listing.

Listing B.3 Using dates in a range with Java's `Calendar` class

```
def cal = Calendar.instance                        <-- Invokes getInstance()
cal.set 2013, Calendar.FEBRUARY, 27
def now = cal.time                                 <-- Retrieve the
cal.set 2013, Calendar.MARCH, 1                        assigned Date
def then = cal.time                                <--

def days = []
(now..then).each { day ->                          <-- Iterate over the range
    days << day.format('MMM dd, yyyy')
}
assert days == ['Feb 27, 2013', 'Feb 28, 2013', 'Mar 01, 2013']
```

For all its gifts, even Groovy can't tame Java's awkward `java.util.Date` and `java.util.Calendar` classes, but it can make the code for using them a bit simpler. `Calendar` is an abstract class with the factory method `getInstance`, so in Groovy I call it by accessing the `instance` property. The Groovy JDK adds the `format` method to `Date`, so it isn't necessary to separately instantiate `SimpleDateFormat`.

In the listing, after setting the year, month, and day, the `Date` instance is retrieved by invoking `getTime`.[8] In this case, that's equivalent to accessing the `time` property. The dates are used as the boundaries of a range by the `each` method, which appends each one to a list.

In fact, any class can be made into a range if it includes three features:

- A `next()` method, for forward iteration
- A `previous()` method, for backward iteration
- An implementation of the `java.util.Comparable` interface, for ordering

Here the range is used as the basis of a loop, where the dates are appended to a list.

B.4.2 Lists

Lists in Groovy are the same as lists in Java, except that the syntax is easier and there are some additional methods available. Create a list in Groovy by including values between square brackets:

```
def teams = ['Red Sox', 'Yankees']
assert teams.class == java.util.ArrayList
```

The default list is of type `java.util.ArrayList`. If you prefer to use a `LinkedList`, instantiate it in the normal way.

Groovy has operator overloading. The Groovy JDK shows that the plus, minus, and left-shift operators have been defined to work with lists:

```
teams << 'Orioles'
assert teams == ['Red Sox', 'Yankees', 'Orioles']
teams << ['Rays', 'Blue Jays']
assert teams ==
    ['Red Sox', 'Yankees', 'Orioles', ['Rays', 'Blue Jays']]
assert teams.flatten() ==
    ['Red Sox', 'Yankees', 'Orioles', 'Rays', 'Blue Jays']
assert teams + 'Angels' - 'Orioles' ==
    ['Red Sox', 'Yankees', ['Rays', 'Blue Jays'], 'Angels']
```

Accessing elements of a list can be done with array-like syntax. Again, this is done by overriding a method—in this case, the `getAt` method:

```
assert teams[0] == 'Red Sox'
assert teams[1] == 'Yankees'
assert teams[-1] == ['Rays','Blue Jays']
```

As shown in figure B.1, access to elements from the left end starts at index 0. Access from the right end starts at index –1. You can use a range in the square brackets, too:

```
def cities = ['New York', 'Boston', 'Cleveland','Seattle']
assert ['Boston', 'Cleveland'] == cities[1..2]
```

---

[8] Yes, you read that correctly. You *get* the *date* by calling … `getTime`. Hey, I didn't write it.

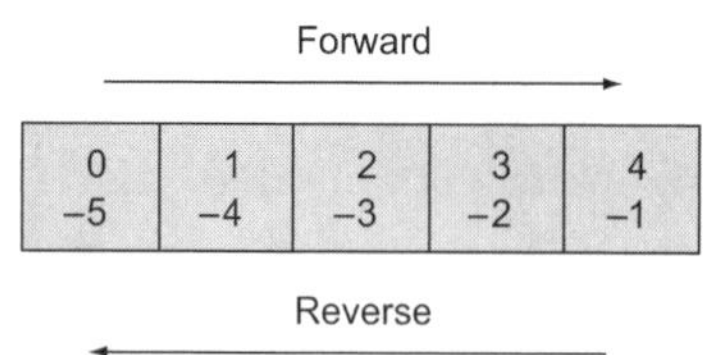

Figure B.1 Access any linear collection using an index from either end. The first element is at index 0. The last element is at index –1. You can also use subranges, as in mylist[-4..-2].

> **ARRAY-LIKE ACCESS** Linear collections support element access through an index from either end, or even using a range.

Groovy adds methods like `pop`, `intersect`, and `reverse` to collections. See the GroovyDocs for details.

There are two ways to apply a function to each element. The *spread-dot* operator (`.*`) makes it easy to access a property or apply a method to each element:

```
assert cities*.size() == [8, 6, 9, 7]
```

The `collect` method takes a closure as an argument and applies it to each element of the collection, returning a list with the results. This is similar to the spread-dot operator, but can do more general operations:

```
def abbrev = cities.collect { city -> city[0..2].toLowerCase() }
assert abbrev == ['new', 'bos', 'cle', 'sea']
```

The word `city` here used before the arrow is like a dummy argument for a method call. The closure extracts the first three letters of each element of the list and then converts them to lowercase.

One particularly interesting feature of collections is that they support type coercion using the `as` operator. What does that mean? It's not terribly difficult to convert a Java list into a set, because there's a constructor for that purpose. Converting a list into an array, however, involves some awkward, counterintuitive code. Here's Groovy's take on the process:

```
def names = teams as String[]
assert names.class == String[]

def set = teams as Set
assert set.class == java.util.HashSet
```

That was easy.[9] A set in Groovy is just like a set in Java, meaning it doesn't contain duplicates and doesn't guarantee order.

> **THE AS OPERATOR** Groovy uses the keyword `as` for many purposes. One of them is type coercion, which converts an instance of one class into an instance of another.

[9] I know I say that a lot, but with Groovy I think it a lot, too.

One of the nicest features of Groovy collections is that they're searchable. Groovy adds both `find` and `findAll` methods to collections. The `find` method takes a closure and returns the first element that satisfies the closure:

```
assert 'New Hampshire' ==
    ['New Hampshire','New Jersey','New York'].find { it =~ /New/ }
```

The `findAll` method returns all the elements that satisfy the closure. This example returns all the cities that have the letter *e* in their name:

```
def withE = cities.findAll { city -> city =~ /e/ }
assert withE == ['Seattle', 'New York', 'Cleveland']
```

Groovy also supplies the methods `any` and `every`, which also take closures:

```
assert cities.any { it.size() < 7 }
assert cities.every { it.size() < 10 }
```

The first expression states that there's at least one city whose name is less than 7 characters. The second expression says that all of the city names are 10 characters or less.

Table B.1 summarizes the searchable methods.

Table B.1 Searchable methods added to Groovy collections

Method	Description
`any`	Returns true if any element satisfies closure
`every`	Returns true if all elements satisfy closure
`find`	Returns first element satisfying closure
`findAll`	Returns list of all elements satisfying closure

Finally, the `join` method concatenates all the elements of the list into a single string, using the supplied separator:

```
assert cities.join(',') == "Boston,Seattle,New York,Cleveland"
```

The combination of native syntax and added convenience methods makes Groovy lists much easier to work with than their Java counterparts. As it turns out, maps are improved the same way.

B.4.3 Maps

Groovy maps are like Java maps, but again with a native syntax and additional helper methods. Groovy uses the same square-bracket syntax for maps as for lists, but each entry in the map uses a colon to separate the key from its corresponding value.

You can populate a map right away by adding the elements when you declare the map itself:

```
def trivialMap = [x:1, y:2, z:3]
assert 1 == trivialMap['x']
assert trivialMap instanceof java.util.HashMap
```

This defines a map with three entries. When adding elements to the map, the keys are assumed to be strings, so you don't need to put quotes around them. The values can be anything.

> **MAP KEYS** When adding to a map, the keys are assumed to be of type `string`, so no quotes are necessary.

You can add to a map using either Java or Groovy syntax:

```
def ALEast10 = [:]
ALEast.put('Boston','Red Sox')
assert 'Red Sox' == ALEast.get('Boston')
assert ALEast == [Boston:'Red Sox']
ALEast['New York'] = 'Yankees'
```

Accessing values can be done with either the array-like syntax shown, or using a dot. If the key has spaces in it, wrap the key in quotes:

```
assert 'Red Sox' == ALEast.Boston
assert 'Yankees' == ALEast.'New York'
```

I've been using `def` to define the map reference, but Groovy understands Java generics:

```
Map<String,String> ALCentral = [Cleveland:'Indians',
   Chicago:'White Sox',Detroit:'Tigers']
assert 3 == ALCentral.size()
assert ALCentral.Cleveland == 'Indians'
```

Maps have a `size` method that returns the number of entries. Actually, the `size` method is universal.

> **SIZE** In Groovy, the `size` method works for arrays, lists, maps, strings, and more.

Maps have an overloaded `plus` operation that combines the entries from two maps:

```
def both = ALEast + ALCentral
assert 5 == both.size()
```

Like Java maps, you can extract the set of keys from a map using the `keySet` method:

```
assert ALEast.keySet() == ['Boston','New York'] as Set
```

Maps also have a rather controversial method that lets you add a new element with a default in case the element doesn't exist:

```
assert 'Blue Jays' == ALEast.get('Toronto','Blue Jays')
assert 'Blue Jays' == ALEast['Toronto']
```

Here I'm trying to retrieve a value using a key that isn't in the map (`Toronto`). If the key exists, its value is returned. If not, it's added to the map, with the second argument

---

[10] For non-baseball people, ALEast is short for the Eastern division of the American League.

to the get method being its new value. This is convenient, but it means that if you accidentally misspell a key when trying to retrieve it you don't get an error; instead, you wind up adding it. That's not true when using the single-argument version of get.

Finally, when you iterate over a map using a closure, the number of dummy arguments determines how the map is accessed. Using two arguments means that the map is accessed as keys and values:

```
String keys1 = ''
List<Integer> values1 = []
both.each { key,val ->
    keys1 += '|' + key
    values1 << val
}
```

The each iterator has two dummy variables, so the first represents the key and the second the value. This closure appends the keys to a string, separated by vertical bars. The values are added to a list.

Alternatively, using a single argument assigns each entry to the specified argument, or it if none:

```
String keys2 = ''
List<Integer> values2 = []
both.each { entry ->
    keys2 += '|' + entry.key
    values2 << entry.value
}
```

Because a single dummy argument was used in the closure, I need to access its key and value properties (equivalent to invoking the getKey and getValue methods, as usual) to do the same operation as in the previous example.

Both mechanisms produce the same results:

```
assert keys1 == keys2
assert values1 == values2
```

Throughout this section I've used closures in examples without defining what they are. That's the subject of the next section.

B.5 Closures

Like many developers, I started out in the procedural world. I started my career as a research scientist, studying unsteady aerodynamics and acoustics. Most of that involved numerically solving partial differential equations.

That meant that unless I wanted to write all my own libraries, I had to adopt Fortran as my professional language of choice.[11] My first assignment in my first job was to take a 3000-line program my boss had written in Fortran IV[12] and add functionality to

---

[11] The fact that I seriously considered writing those libraries in a different language anyway was yet another sign I was in the wrong profession.

[12] Shudder. Holy arithmetic-if statements, Batman. The nightmares have stopped, but it took a while.

it. The best part was that the original program had only two subroutines in it: one that was about 25 lines long, and the other 2975. Needless to say, I learned refactoring long before I knew the actual term.

I rapidly learned what at the time were considered good development practices, meaning that I wrote structured programs that used existing libraries as much as possible. It was only in the mid-90s, when I first learned Java, that I was introduced to object-oriented programming.

That's when I first encountered what influential blogger Steve Yegge has since referred to as the subjugation of verbs in the kingdom of the nouns.[13] In most OO languages, methods (verbs) can only exist as part of nouns (classes). Java certainly works that way. Even static methods that don't require objects still have to be defined inside classes somewhere.

The first language I learned that changed all that was JavaScript, which is an object-based language rather than object-oriented. In JavaScript, even the classes are functions. Then, because the methods in the classes are also functions, you wind up with functions operating inside of functions, possibly passing around references to still other functions, and suddenly everything gets confusing and difficult. Closures in JavaScript are confusing not because functions are difficult, but because a closure includes the environment in which it executes. A closure may have references to variables declared outside of it, and in JavaScript it's easy to get lost determining the values.

I had no idea how simple closures could be until I encountered Groovy.[14] In Groovy, it's easy enough to treat a closure as a block of code, but it's always clear where the nonlocal variables are evaluated because there's no confusion about the current object.

> **CLOSURES** In practice, a closure is a block of code along with its execution environment.

In Groovy, the term *closure* is used broadly to refer to blocks of code, even if they don't contain explicit references to external variables. Closures feel like methods and can be invoked that way. Consider this trivial example, which returns whatever it's sent:

```
def echo = { it }
assert 'Hello' == echo('Hello')
assert 'Hello' == echo.call('Hello')
```

The `echo` reference is assigned to the block of code (a closure) delimited by curly braces. The closure contains a variable whose default name is `it`, whose value is supplied when the closure is invoked. If you think of the variable like a method parameter, you've got the basic idea.

The closure can be invoked in one of two ways: either by using the reference as though it's a method call, or by explicitly invoking the `call` method on it. Because the

---

[13] "Execution in the Kingdom of Nouns," at http://mng.bz/E4MB

[14] Others can say the same about Ruby or other JVM languages. This is my history, though.

last value computed by a closure is returned automatically, both ways return the argument to the closure, which is why it was called `echo` in the first place.

CLOSURE RETURN VALUES The last evaluated expression in a closure is returned automatically.

If a closure takes more than one argument, or if you don't want to use the default name, use an arrow to separate the dummy argument names from the body of the closure. Here's a simple sum, once with the default and once with a named argument:

```
def total = 0
(1..10).each { num -> total += num }
assert (1..10).sum() == total

total = 0
(1..10).each { total += it }
assert (1..10).sum() == total
```

Closures are used throughout this book and fill an entire chapter in *GinA*. This little amount of information is enough to make a lot of progress.

Returning to the basic constructs of the language, I'll now show how Groovy differs from Java when using loops and conditional tests.

B.6 Loops and conditionals

In this section, I'll discuss two features that appear in any programming language: looping through a set of values and making decisions.

B.6.1 Loops

When Groovy was first created, and for some time afterward, it didn't support the standard Java `for` loop:

```
for (int i = 0; i < 5; i++) { ... }
```

In version 1.6, however, the core committers decided that it was more important to support Java constructs than to try to keep the language free of that somewhat awkward syntax that Java inherited from its predecessors. Many demonstrations of Groovy start with a Java class, rename it with a `.groovy` extension, and show that it still compiles successfully with the Groovy compiler. The result is far from idiomatic Groovy, but it does illustrate a valid point: Groovy is the closest to Java of the new family of JVM languages.

JAVA LOOPS Groovy supports the standard Java `for` loop and `for-each` loop, as well as the `while` loop. It does not, however, support the `do-while` construct.

The `for-each` loop in Java was introduced in Java SE 1.5 and works for any linear collection, including both arrays and lists:

```
for (String s : strings) { ... }
```

The `for-each` loop is helpful, because it means you don't always need to get an iterator to loop over the elements of a list. The price you pay is that there's no explicit index. Inside the loop, you know what element you're currently on, but not where it appears in the list. If you need to know the index, you can either keep track of the index yourself or go back to the traditional `for` loop.

Groovy supplies a variation on the `for-each` loop that avoids the colon syntax, called a `for-in` loop:

```
def words = "I'm a Groovy coder".tokenize()
def capitalized = ''
for (word in words) {
    capitalized += word.capitalize() + ' '
}
assert capitalized == "I'm A Groovy Coder "
```

Note that unlike the `for-each` loop, the value variable is not declared to have a type: not even `def`.

Still, none of those loops are the most common way of iterating in Groovy. Rather than write an explicit loop, as in the previous examples, Groovy prefers a more direct implementation of the Iterator design pattern. Groovy adds the `each` method, which takes a closure as an argument, to collections. The `each` method then applies the closure to each element of the collection:

```
(0..5).each { println it }
```

Again, because the closure is the last argument of the method, it can be placed after the parentheses. Because there are no other arguments to the `each` method, the parentheses can be eliminated entirely.

EACH The `each` method is the most common looping construct in Groovy.

The Iterator design pattern recommends separating the way you walk through the elements of a collection from what you plan to do with those elements. The `each` method does the iterating internally. The user determines what to do with the elements by supplying a closure, as shown. Here the closure prints its argument. The `each` method supplies each value in the range, one by one, to the closure, so the result is to print the numbers from zero to five.

Like the `for-in` loop, inside the closure you have access to each element, but not to the index. If you want the index, though, there's an additional method available called `eachWithIndex`:

```
def strings = ['how','are','you']
def results = []
strings.eachWithIndex { s,i -> results << "$i:$s" }
assert results == ['0:how', '1:are', '2:you']
```

The closure supplied to the `eachWithIndex` method takes two dummy arguments. The first is the value from the collection, and the second is the index.

I should mention that although all these loops work correctly, there can be differences in how much time each of them takes. If you're dealing with a collection of a few dozen elements or less, the differences will probably not be noticeable. If the number of iterations is going to be in the tens of thousands or more, you probably should profile the resulting code.

B.6.2 Conditionals

Java has two types of conditional statements: the `if` statement and its related constructs, like `if-else` and `switch` statements. Both are supported by Groovy. The `if` statement works pretty much the same way it does in Java. The `switch` statement, however, has been taken from Java's crippled form and restored to its former glory.

Groovy's version of the `if` statement is similar to Java's, with the difference being the so-called Groovy Truth. In Java, the argument to an `if` statement must be a Boolean expression, or the statement won't compile. In Groovy, lots of things evaluate to true other than Boolean expressions.

For example, nonzero numbers are true:

```
if (1) {
    assert true
} else {
    assert false
}
```

The result is `true`. This expression wouldn't work in Java. There you would have to compare the argument to another value, resulting in a Boolean expression.

> **Return to C?**
>
> The Groovy Truth is a case where Java restricted something C supported (non-Boolean expressions in decision statements), but Groovy brought it back. That can certainly lead to bugs that Java would avoid.
>
> From a philosophical point of view, why do it? By restricting what was allowed, Java made certain types of bugs much less likely. Groovy, by restoring those features, increases the possibility of those bugs again. Is the gain worth it?
>
> My opinion is that this is a side effect of the increased emphasis on testing that has swept through the development community. If you're going to have to write tests to prove your code is correct anyway, why not take advantage of the greater power? Sure, you've introduced the possibility of getting some bugs past the compiler, but just because it compiles doesn't mean it's right. The tests prove correctness, so why not use shorter, more powerful code when you can?

Returning to decision statements, Java also supports a ternary operator, and Groovy does the same:

```
String result = 5 > 3 ? 'x' : 'y'
assert result == 'x'
```

The ternary expression reads, is five greater than three? If so, assign the result to x, otherwise use y. It's like an if statement, but shorter.

There's a reduced form of the ternary operator that highlights both Groovy's helpfulness and its sense of humor: the Elvis operator.

B.6.3 Elvis

Consider the following use case. You're planning to use an input value, but it's optional. If the client supplies it, you'll use it. If not, you plan to use a default instead.

I'll use a variable called name as an example:

```
String displayName = name ? name : 'default'
```

This means if name is not null, use it for displayName. Otherwise, use a default. I'm using a standard ternary operator to check whether name is null or not. The way this is written has some repetition in it. After all, I want to use name if it's available, so why do I have to repeat myself?

That's where the Elvis operator comes in. Here's the revised code:

```
String displayName = name ?: 'default'
```

The Elvis operator is the combination of a question mark and a colon formed by leaving out the value in between them in the ternary operator. The idea is that if the variable in front of the question mark is not null, use it. The ?: operator is called Elvis because if you turn your head to the side, the result looks vaguely like the King:

```
def greet(name) { "${name ?: 'Elvis'} has left the building" }
assert greet(null) == 'Elvis has left the building'
assert greet('Priscilla') == 'Priscilla has left the building'
```

The greet method takes a parameter called name and uses the Elvis operator to determine what to return. This way it still has a reasonable value, even if the input argument is null.[15]

B.6.4 Safe de-reference

There's one final conditional operator that Groovy provides that saves many lines of coding. It's called the safe de-reference operator, written as ?..

The idea is to avoid having to constantly check for nulls. For example, suppose you have classes called Employee, Department, and Location. If each employee instance has a department, and each department has a location, then if you want the location for an employee, you would write something like this (in Java):

```
Location loc = employee.getDepartment().getLocation()
```

But what happens if the employee reference is null? Or what happens if the employee hasn't been assigned a department, so the getDepartment method returns null? Those possibilities mean the code expands to

[15] Thank you, thank you very much.

```
if (employee == null) {
    loc = null;
} else {
    Department dept = employee.getDepartment();
    if (dept == null) {
        loc = null;
    } else {
        loc = dept.getLocation();
    }
}
```

That's quite an expansion just to check for nulls. Here's the Groovy version:

```
Location loc = employee?.department?.location
```

The safe de-reference operator returns `null` if the reference is null. Otherwise it proceeds to access the property. It's a small thing, but the savings in lines of code is nontrivial.

Continuing on the theme of simplifying code over the Java version, consider input/output streams. Groovy introduces several methods in the Groovy JDK that help Groovy simplify Java code when dealing with files and directories.

B.7 File I/O

File I/O in Groovy isn't fundamentally different from the Java approach. Groovy adds several convenience methods and handles issues like closing your files for you. A few short examples should suffice to give you a sense of what's possible.

First, Groovy adds a `getText` method to `File`, which means that by asking for the text property you can retrieve all the data out of a file at once in the form of a string:

```
String data = new File('data.txt').text
```

Accessing the `text` property invokes the `getText` method, as usual, and returns all the text in the file. Alternatively, you can retrieve all the lines in the file and store them in a list using the `readLines` method:

```
List<String> lines = new File("data.txt").readLines()*.trim()
```

The `trim` method is used in this example with the spread-dot operator to remove leading and trailing spaces on each line. If your data is formatted in a specific way, the `splitEachLine` method takes a delimiter and returns a list of the elements. For example, if you have a data file that contains the following lines

```
1,2,3
a,b,c
```

then the data can be retrieved and parsed at the same time:

```
List dataLines = []
new File("data.txt").splitEachLine(',') {
    dataLines << it
}
assert dataLines == [['1','2','3'],['a','b','c']]
```

Writing to a file is just as easy:

```
File f = new File("$base/output.dat")
f.write('Hello, Groovy!')
assert f.text == 'Hello, Groovy!'
```

In Java, it's critical to close a file if you've written to it, because otherwise it may not flush the buffer and your data may never make into the file. Groovy does that for you automatically.

Groovy also makes it easy to append to a file:

```
File temp = new File("temp.txt")
temp.write 'Groovy Kind of Love'
assert temp.readLines().size() == 1
temp.append "\nGroovin', on a Sunday afternoon..."
temp << "\nFeelin' Groovy"
assert temp.readLines().size() == 3
temp.delete()
```

The `append` method does what it sounds like, and the left-shift operator has been overridden to do the same.

Several methods are available that iterate over files, like `eachFile`, `eachDir`, and even `eachFileRecurse`. They each take closures that can filter what you want.

Finally, I have to show you an example that illustrates how much simpler Groovy I/O streams are than Java streams. Consider writing a trivial application that does the following:

1. Prompts the user to enter numbers on a line, separated by spaces
2. Reads the line
3. Adds up the numbers
4. Prints the result

Nothing to it, right? The next listing shows the Java version.

Listing B.4 `SumNumbers.java`, an application to read a line of numbers and add them

```
package io;

import java.io.BufferedReader;
import java.io.IOException;
import java.io.InputStreamReader;

public class SumNumbers {                                    <-- Must be in a class
    public static void main(String[] args) {
        System.out.println("Please enter numbers to sum");
        BufferedReader br =                                  <-- Has readLine method
           new BufferedReader(new InputStreamReader(System.in));
        String line = "";
        try {
            line = br.readLine();                            <-- try/catch for checked exception
        } catch (IOException e) {
            e.printStackTrace();
        }
```

```
        String[] inputs = line.split(" ");
        double total = 0.0;
        for (String s : inputs) {
            total += Double.parseDouble(s);          <-- Convert strings to doubles
        }
        System.out.println("The sum is " + total);
    }
}
```

That's nearly 30 lines to do something extremely simple. All Java code has to be in a class with a `main` method. The input stream `System.in` is available, but I want to read a full line of data, so I wrap the stream in an `InputStreamReader` and wrap that in a `BufferedReader`, all so I can call `readLine`. That may throw an I/O exception, so I need a `try/catch` block for it. Finally, the incoming data is in string form, so I need to parse it before adding up the numbers and printing the results.

Here's the corresponding Groovy version:

```
println 'Please enter some numbers'
System.in.withReader { br ->
    println br.readLine().tokenize()*.toBigDecimal().sum()
}
```

That's the whole program. The `withReader` method creates a `Reader` implementation that has a `readLine` method and automatically closes it when the closure completes. Several similar methods are available for both input and output, including `withReader`, `withInputStream`, `withPrintWriter`, and `withWriterAppend`.

That was fun, but here's another version that has more capabilities. In this case, the code has a loop that sums each line and prints its result until no input is given:

```
println 'Sum numbers with looping'
System.in.eachLine { line ->
    if (!line) System.exit(0)
    println line.split(' ')*.toBigDecimal().sum()
}
```

The `eachLine` method repeats the closure until the line variable is empty.

Groovy's contribution to file I/O is to add convenience methods that simplify the Java API and ensure that streams or files are closed correctly. It provides a clean façade on the Java I/O package.

Groovy makes input/output streams much simpler to deal with than in Java, so if I have a Java system and I need to work with files, I try to add a Groovy module for that purpose. That's a savings, but nothing compared to the savings that result from using Groovy over Java when dealing with XML, as shown in the next section.

B.8 XML

I've saved the best for last. XML is where the ease-of-use gap between Groovy and Java is the largest. Working with XML in Java is a pain at best, while parsing and generating XML in Groovy is almost trivial. If I ever have to deal with XML in a Java system, I always add a Groovy module for that purpose. This section is intended to show why.

B.8.1 Parsing and slurping XML

Some time ago, I was teaching a training course on XML and Java. One of the exercises started by presenting an XML file similar to this one:

```
<books>
    <book isbn="9781935182443">
        <title>Groovy in Action (2nd edition)</title>
        <author>Dierk Koenig</author>
        <author>Guillaume Laforge</author>
        <author>Paul King</author>
        <author>Jon Skeet</author>
        <author>Hamlet D'Arcy</author>
    </book>
    <book isbn="9781935182948">
        <title>Making Java Groovy</title>
        <author>Ken Kousen</author>
    </book>
    <book isbn="1933988932">
        <title>Grails in Action</title>
        <author>Glen Smith</author>
        <author>Peter Ledbrook</author>
    </book>
</books>
```

The goal of the exercise was to parse this file and print out the title of the second book. Because this file is small, you might as well use a DOM parser to read it. To do that in Java you need a factory, which then yields the parser, and then you can invoke a `parse` method to build the DOM tree. Then, to extract the data, there are three options:

- Walk the tree by getting child elements and iterating over them.
- Use the `getElementById` method to find the right node, and then get the first text child and retrieve its value.
- Use the `getElementsByTagName` method, iterate over the resulting `NodeList` to find the right node, and then retrieve the value of the first text child.

The first approach runs into problems with whitespace. This document has carriage returns and tabs in it, and because no DTD or schema is provided, the parser doesn't know which whitespace elements are significant. Traversing the DOM is complicated by the fact that methods like `getFirstChild` will return whitespace nodes as well as elements. It can be done, but you'll need to check the node type of each element to make sure you are working with an element rather than a text node.

The second approach only works if the elements have an attribute of type `ID`, and that's not the case here.

You're left with the `getElementsByTagName` method, which results in the following code:

```
import java.io.IOException;

import javax.xml.parsers.DocumentBuilder;
import javax.xml.parsers.DocumentBuilderFactory;
import javax.xml.parsers.ParserConfigurationException;
```

```
import org.w3c.dom.Document;
import org.w3c.dom.Element;
import org.w3c.dom.NodeList;
import org.xml.sax.SAXException;

public class ProcessBooks {
    public static void main(String[] args) {
        DocumentBuilderFactory factory =
            DocumentBuilderFactory.newInstance();
        Document doc = null;
        try {
            DocumentBuilder builder = factory.newDocumentBuilder();
            doc = builder.parse("books.xml");
        } catch (ParserConfigurationException e) {
            e.printStackTrace();
        } catch (SAXException e) {
            e.printStackTrace();
        } catch (IOException e) {
            e.printStackTrace();
        }
        NodeList titles = doc.getElementsByTagName("title");
        Element titleNode = (Element) titles.item(1);
        String title = titleNode.getFirstChild().getNodeValue();
        System.out.println("The second title is " + title);
    }
}
```

Parsing the document can throw all sorts of exceptions, as shown. Assuming nothing goes wrong, after parsing, the code retrieves all the `title` elements. After getting the proper element out of the `NodeList` and casting it to type `Element`, you then have to remember that the character data in the element is in the first text child of the element rather than the element itself.

Here's the Groovy solution:

```
root = new XmlSlurper().parse('books.xml')
assert root.book[1].title == 'Making Java Groovy'
```

Wow. Groovy includes the `XmlSlurper` class, which is in the `groovy.util` package (no import required). `XmlSlurper` has a `parse` method that builds the DOM tree and returns the root element. Then it's a question of walking the tree, using the dot notation for child elements. Elements that appear multiple times form a collection that can be accessed with an index in the normal way. The contrast in both size and complexity between the Groovy version and the Java version is clear.

The next listing demonstrates working with the XML file.

Listing B.5 Slurping XML

```
String fileName = 'books.xml'
def books = new XmlSlurper().parse(fileName)

assert books.book.size() == 4
assert books.book[0].title == "Groovy in Action"
```

```
assert books.book.find {
    it.@isbn == "9781935182948"
}.title == "Making Java Groovy"

def prices = []
books.book.price.each {
    prices << it.toDouble()
}
assert prices == [39.99, 35.99, 35.99, 27.50]
assert prices.sum() == 139.47
```

Groovy uses two different classes for working with XML. The previous example used an `XmlSlurper`. Groovy also includes an `XmlParser`. The `XmlParser` creates a tree of `Node` instances, so if you need to approach the file from a node point of view, use the parser. The result is that you'll need to invoke a `text` method on each node to retrieve the text data, but otherwise the two approaches are virtually the same.

Parsing XML is therefore quite easy. What about generating XML? That's the subject of the next subsection.

B.8.2 Generating XML

So far, most of the Groovy capabilities presented are similar to what Java can do, just simpler or easier. In this section I'll show a Groovy builder, which uses Groovy's metaprogramming to go beyond what Java can do.

To generate XML, Groovy provides a class called `groovy.xml.MarkupBuilder`. You use a `MarkupBuilder` by invoking methods that don't exist, and the builder interprets them by generating XML elements and attributes.

That sounds strange, but is simple in practice. The next listing shows an example.

Listing B.6 Generating XML using a `MarkupBuilder`

```
def builder = new groovy.xml.MarkupBuilder()
def department = builder.department {
    deptName "Construction"
    employee(id:1) {
         empName "Fred"
    }
    employee(id:2) {
         empName "Barney"
    }
}
```

After instantiating the `MarkupBuidler` I invoke the `department` method on it, omitting the optional parentheses. There's no `department` method on `MarkupBuilder`, so what does Groovy do?

If this was Java, I would fail with something like a `MissingMethodException`. Every class in Groovy has an associated `meta` class, however, and the `meta` class has a method called `methodMissing`. The `meta` class is the key to Groovy's code generation capabilities. When the `methodMissing` method in `MarkupBuilder` is called, the implementation ultimately is to generate an XML element with the method name as the element name.

The braces that follow are interpreted to mean a child element is next. The name of the child element will be `deptName`, and its character data will be the supplied string. The next element is an `employee`, and the map-like syntax for the `id` implies an attribute on the employee element is needed, and so on.

The result of executing this script is

```
<department>
  <deptName>Construction</deptName>
  <employee id='1'>
    <empName>Fred</empName>
  </employee>
  <employee id='2'>
    <empName>Barney</empName>
  </employee>
</department>
```

The `MarkupBuilder` generates the XML. It's hard to imagine a simpler way to solve that problem.

I want to illustrate one final aspect of XML processing with Groovy, which involves validating a document.

B.8.3 Validation

XML documents are validated in one of two ways: through either a Document Type Definition (DTD) or an XML schema. The DTD system is older, simpler, and much less useful, but the Java parsers have been able to validate against them almost from the beginning. Schema validation came much later but is far more important, especially when dealing with, for example, web services.

Validating XML with Groovy is an interesting demonstration both of what Groovy provides, and what to do if Groovy doesn't provide anything.

First, consider validation against a DTD. Here's a DTD for the library XML shown earlier:

```
<!ELEMENT library (book+)>
<!ELEMENT book (title,author+,price)>
<!ATTLIST book
    isbn CDATA #REQUIRED>
<!ELEMENT title (#PCDATA)>
<!ELEMENT author (#PCDATA)>
<!ELEMENT price (#PCDATA)>
```

The idea is that a `library` element contains one or more `book`s. A `book` element contains a `title`, one or more `author` elements, and a `price`, in that order. The `book` element has an attribute called `isbn`, which is a simple string but is required. The `title`, `author`, and `price` elements all consist of simple strings.

To tie the XML file to the DTD, I add the following line before the root element:

```
<!DOCTYPE library SYSTEM "library.dtd">
```

Validating the XML file against the DTD is then almost trivial. The `XmlSlurper` class has an overloaded constructor that takes two arguments, both of which are Booleans. The first is to trigger validation, and the second is namespace awareness. Namespaces aren't relevant when discussing a DTD, but it doesn't hurt to turn on both properties:

```
def root = new XmlSlurper(true, true).parse(fileName)
```

That's all that's needed to do the validation. If the XML data doesn't satisfy the DTD, errors will be reported by the parsing process.

Validation against an XML schema has always been more of a challenge. Schemas understand namespaces and namespace prefixes, and there are many things you can do in a schema that you can't do in a DTD.

Consider the next listing, which shows a schema for the library.

Listing B.7 An XML schema for the library XML

```
<?xml version="1.0" encoding="UTF-8"?>
<schema
    xmlns="http://www.w3.org/2001/XMLSchema"
    targetNamespace="http://www.kousenit.com/books"
    xmlns:tns="http://www.kousenit.com/books"
    elementFormDefault="qualified">

    <element name="library" type="tns:LibraryType" />
    <complexType name="LibraryType">
        <sequence>
            <element ref="tns:book" maxOccurs="unbounded" />
        </sequence>
    </complexType>
    <element name="book">
        <complexType>
            <sequence>
                <element name="title" type="string" />
                <element name="author" type="string"
                    maxOccurs="unbounded" />
                <element name="price" type="tns:PriceType" />
            </sequence>
            <attribute name="isbn" type="tns:ISBNtype" />
        </complexType>
    </element>
    <simpleType name="PriceType">
        <restriction base="decimal">
            <fractionDigits value="2" />
        </restriction>
    </simpleType>
    <simpleType name="ISBNtype">
        <restriction base="string">
            <pattern value="\d{10}|\d{13}" />
        </restriction>
    </simpleType>
</schema>
```

This is the same as the DTD, except that it says that `price` elements have two decimal places, and `isbn` attributes are composed of either 10 or 13 decimal digits. Tying the XML document to this schema can be done by modifying the root element as follows:

```
<library
    xmlns:xsi="http://www.w3.org/2001/XMLSchema-instance"
    xmlns="http://www.kousenit.com/books"
    xsi:schemaLocation="
        http://www.kousenit.com/books
        books.xsd">
```

The rest of the `library` is the same as before. Here's the code used to validate the XML document against the schema:

```
String file = "books.xml"
String xsd = "books.xsd"
SchemaFactory factory = SchemaFactory.newInstance(
    XMLConstants.W3C_XML_SCHEMA_NS_URI)
Schema schema = factory.newSchema(new File(xsd))
Validator validator = schema.newValidator()
validator.validate(new StreamSource(new FileReader(file)))
```

This looks relatively simple, but here's the interesting part: the mechanism used is Java. If I was to write this code in Java, it would look almost identical. Unlike the `XmlSlurper` used for DTD validation, Groovy doesn't add anything special to do schema validation. So you fall back on the Java approach and write it in Groovy. Because Groovy didn't add anything, these lines could be written in either language, depending on your needs. Still, Groovy normally does help, as most of the code in this appendix shows.

Whenever the issue of XML comes up these days, someone always asks about JSON support. I'll address that issue in the next section.

B.9 JSON support

The trend in the industry has been away from XML and toward JavaScript Object Notation, known as JSON. If your client is written in JavaScript, JSON is a natural, because JSON objects are native to the language. Java doesn't include a JSON parser, but several good libraries are available.

As of Groovy 1.8, Groovy includes a `groovy.json` package, which includes a JSON slurper and a JSON builder.

B.9.1 Slurping JSON

The `groovy.json` package includes a class called `JsonSlurper`. This class is not quite as versatile as the `XmlSlurper` class because it has fewer methods. It contains a `parse` method that takes a `Reader` as an argument, as well as a `parseText` method that takes a `String`.

A JSON object looks like a map inside curly braces. Parsing it results in a map in Groovy:

```
import groovy.json.JsonSlurper;

def slurper = new JsonSlurper()
def result = slurper.parseText('{"first":"Herman","last":"Munster"}')
assert result.first == 'Herman'
assert result.last == 'Munster'
```

Instantiate the slurper and call its `parseText` method, and the result is a map that can be accessed in the usual way, as shown. Lists work as well:

```
result = slurper.parseText(
    '{"first":"Herman","last":"Munster","kids":["Eddie","Marilyn"]}')
assert result.kids == ['Eddie','Marilyn']
```

The two children wind up in an instance of `ArrayList`. You can also add numbers and even contained objects:

```
result = slurper.parseText(
'{"first":"Herman","last":"Munster","address":{"street":"1313 Mockingbird
     Lane","city":"New York","state":"NY"},"wife":"Lily",
     "age":34,"kids":["Eddie","Marilyn"]}')

result.with {
    assert wife == 'Lily'
    assert age == 34
    assert address.street == '1313 Mockingbird Lane'
    assert address.city == 'New York'
    assert address.state == 'NY'
}
```

The `age` becomes an integer. The `address` object is also parsed into a map, whose properties are also available in the standard way. Here, by the way, I used the `with` method, which prepends whatever value it's invoked on to the contained expressions. `wife` is short for `result.wife`, and so on.

If parsing is easy, building is also a simple operation, much like using `MarkupBuilder`.

B.9.2 Building JSON

I discussed builders earlier, and I use them throughout the book. In various chapters I use `MarkupBuilder` (shown in this chapter), `SwingBuilder`, and `AntBuilder`. Here I'll illustrate the builder for generating JSON, called `JsonBuilder`.

The `JsonBuilder` class can be used with lists, maps, or methods. For example, here's a trivial list:

```
import groovy.json.JsonBuilder;

def builder = new JsonBuilder()
def result = builder 1,2,3
assert result == [1, 2, 3]
```

This builder takes a list of numbers as an argument and builds a JSON object containing them. Here's an example of using a map:

```
result = builder {
    first 'Fred'
    last 'Flintstone'
}
assert builder.toString() == '{"first":"Fred","last":"Flintstone"}'
```

The result is a standard JSON object (contained in braces), whose properties are the strings provided in the builder.

In the builder syntax you can use parentheses to build a contained object, so let's continue on with the example:

```
result = builder.people {
    person {
        first 'Herman'
        last 'Munster'
        address(street:'1313 Mockingbird Lane',
            city:'New York',state:'NY')
        wife 'Lily'
        age 34
        kids 'Eddie','Marilyn'
    }
}
assert builder.toString() ==
    '{"people":{"person":{"first":"Herman","last":"Munster",' +
    '"address":{"street":"1313 Mockingbird Lane",' +
    '"city":"New York","state":"NY"},"wife":"Lily","age":34,' +
    '"kids":["Eddie","Marilyn"]}}}'
```

The generated JSON can get difficult to read, so the class adds a `toPrettyString()` method:

```
println builder.toPrettyString()
```

This results in nicely formatted output, as shown:

```
{
    "people": {
        "person": {
            "first": "Herman",
            "last": "Munster",
            "address": {
                "street": "1313 Mockingbird Lane",
                "city": "New York",
                "state": "NY"
            },
            "wife": "Lily",
            "age": 34,
            "kids": [
                "Eddie",
```

```
                    "Marilyn"
                ]
            }
        }
    }
```

JSON data is therefore almost as easy to manage as XML, both when creating it and when managing it.

index

Symbols

A

B

H

I

J

K

L

M

N

O

T

U

V

W

X

Y

RELATED MANNING TITLES

Groovy in Action, Second Edition
by Dierk König, Guillaume Laforge, Paul King, Cédric Champeau, Hamlet D'Arcy, Erik Pragt, and Jon Skeet

ISBN: 978-1-935182-44-3
700 pages, $49.99
November 2013

Grails in Action, Second Edition
by Glen Smith and Peter Ledbrook

ISBN: 978-1-617290-96-1
525 pages, $49.99
December 2013

Gradle in Action
by Benjamin Muschko

ISBN: 978-1-617291-30-2
390 pages, $44.99
November 2013

Griffon in Action
by Andres Almiray, Danno Ferrin, and James Shingler

ISBN: 978-1-935182-23-8
384 pages, $44.99
June 2012

For ordering information go to www.manning.com